British TV Streaming Guide

US Edition: Autumn 2022

Your guide to streaming 2400+ British TV shows in the US

See more of our British TV books & news at:

IHeartBritishTV.com

Shop.IHeartBritain.com

Cover: In recognition of HRH Queen Elizabeth II's lifetime of service to her country and its people

We've included a feature on documentaries and tributes to Queen Elizabeth II on page 190.

Published by IHeartBritishTV.com

Sacramento, California

ISBN: 978-1-956058-02-4

Welcome - and thank you for buying or borrowing this guide! We're a small business, and we genuinely appreciate your support.

We put hundreds of hours into researching, writing, updating, and laying out this book, and as far as we know, it's the only one of its kind in the world. That doesn't mean it's perfect.

For a long time, we resisted the idea of putting out a printed streaming guide, simply because it's impossible to put out a guide that will be 100% accurate by the time it goes through printing and shipping.

Though we've done our best to work with our contacts at streaming networks to get the most up-to-date information on new and departing shows, even the streaming services themselves don't always have a lot of advance notice - and occasionally, there are last-minute changes. That said, most services change no more than 3-5% of their offerings in any given month. This guide should still be mostly accurate for months to come, and we leave spaces here and there where you make updates.

There are a couple other quirks you should be aware of as you dig in:

- Few services offer a simple list of all their British programming. That means many of these lists were gathered through sheer force. It's possible we've missed a few.
- For Acorn TV and BritBox, we listed ALL programming - including movies. On other platforms, we stuck to television.
- Our primary focus was on British programming. We've included a handful of shows from Australia, New Zealand, Canada, and Europe, but those are just happy little extras. This guide is far from comprehensive on those.

- We've underlined show names that are new additions (including new seasons) since the last guide.
- We've bundled all "Free with Ads" services in one section, since there's no added cost to having/using all of them at once and there are a lot of duplicates.

This is our seventh time publishing this guide, and we hope you like it. It's constantly evolving based on what we hear from readers like you. We welcome your feedback at areyoufree@iheartbritishtv.com.

New Show Highlights

While we've gone through and underlined shows and seasons which are new to the guide, we know it's long - so we thought we'd take a moment up front to mention some of the biggest and most popular releases of the last several months. We realise not everyone lives and breathes British TV 24/7 (but no judgment if you do).

- **Acorn TV**: *Harry Wild, Hidden Assets, Signora Volpe, Butterfly Breath,* and *Ten Percent* - along with new seasons of *Hidden, London Kills, Doc Martin* (October 17th), and *The Other One.*
- **BritBox**: *Why Didn't They Ask Evans?, The Barking Murders, The Responder,Sherwood, Suspect,* and *Screw* - along with new episodes of *Death in Paradise, Grace, McDonald & Dodds, Silent Witness,* and *Kate & Koji.*
- **PBS Masterpiece**: *Annika, Before We Die, Hotel Portofino, Magpie Murders* (October 16th), and *Ridley Road* - along with new episodes of *All Creatures Great & Small, Cobra, Endeavour, Grantchester, Guilt, Miss Scarlet & the Duke* (October 16th), and *Van der Valk.*
- **Netflix**: *You Don't Know Me, The Sandman, Hard Cell* - along with new seasons of *Call the Midwife, Great British Baking Show, Peaky Blinders*, and *Derry Girls* (October 7th).
- **Hulu**: New seasons of *The Split* and *What We Do in the Shadows*
- **Sundance Now**: *This is Going to Hurt, The Ipcress Files, The Light in the Hall, Murder in the Valleys, The Replacement,* and *Showtrial - along with new episodes of The Split.*
- **AMC+**: A new season of *Gangs of London* arrives November 17th (plus everything on Sundance Now is included in AMC+)
- **Starz**: *The Serpent Queen* and *Becoming Elizabeth*
- **HBO Max**: *The Staircase, House of the Dragon*, and *The Time Traveler's Wife* - along with new seasons of *Gentleman Jack* and *His Dark Materials* (date TBD, but expected in autumn).
- **Peacock**: *Last Light* and *Trigger Point* - along with a new season of *The Capture*

We hope we're adding something valuable to the British TV community, and we really do appreciate your support! If you're so inclined, we'd be forever grateful if you share photos, links, or recommendations to your British TV-loving friends and social media communities.

Happy Watching!
Stefanie & David
IHeartBritishTV.com

TABLE OF CONTENTS

ACORN TV

Website: http://acorn.tv

Description: Acorn TV describes itself as "world-class TV from Britain and Beyond". British programming dominates, but they also include shows from Australia, Ireland, Canada, New Zealand, Scandinavia, and mainland Europe.

Available On: Roku, Amazon Fire TV, Apple TV, Apple iPhone & iPad, Android TV, Android phones and tablets, Google Chromecast, computer (via web browser). You can also subscribe via Amazon Prime Video.

Cost: $6.99/month, $69.99/year

Now Streaming
Mysteries & Crime Dramas

19-2 - *Canada* - 2014 to 2017 - This Canadian police drama follows two unwilling partners: Officers Nick Barron and Ben Chartier. Together, they patrol downtown Montreal's 19th precinct in cruiser number 2. Though they have wildly different backgrounds and outlooks on life, they eventually learn to work together and trust one another.

Acceptable Risk - 2017 to present – When Sarah's husband is murdered, she realises how little she knows about his past.

The Agatha Christie Hour - 1982 - This series is a collection of one-hour dramas based on Agatha Christie's short stories. Each of the adaptations feature talented casts with British actors like John Nettles (*Midsomer Murders*), Amanda Redman (*The Good Karma Hospital*), and Stephanie Cole (*Doc Martin*).

Agatha Christie's Partners in Crime - 2015 - David Walliams (*Little Britain*) and Jessica Raine (*Call the Midwife*) star in this updated adaptation of Agatha Christie's Tommy and Tuppence Beresford stories. Together, they solve mysteries and search for enemy spies in Cold War Britain.

Agatha Christie's The Witness for the Prosecution - 2016 - In 1920s London, a handsome townhouse is the setting for the brutal murder of Emily French, a glamorous young socialite. Toby Jones (*Detectorists*) and Kim Cattrall (*Sex and the City*) are among the members of this feature film's all-star cast.

Agatha Raisin - 2016 to present - Based on the M.C. Beaton novels, Agatha Raisin leaves her high-flying London PR life for a peaceful existence in The Cotswolds - or so she thinks. In no time at all, she finds herself mixed up in murders and playing the amateur sleuth.

Alibi - 2003 - Michael Kitchen (*Foyle's War*), Sophie Okonedo (*Hotel Rwanda*), and Phyllis Logan (*Downton Abbey*) star in this thriller about a man discovered with the dead body of his business partner. When a nearby witness helps him dispose of the body, the situation spirals out of control and she wonders what she's gotten herself into. This series is presented in three episodes.

Amber - 2014 - In the suburbs of Dublin, Ben and Sarah are a separated couple trying to do their best to raise their shared kids. Unfortunately, 14-year-old Amber disappears, setting off a two-year search full of guilt, fear, and grief. Each episode in this unique series takes a look at the search from a different perspective.

A Model Daughter: The Killing of Caroline Byrne - *Australia* - 2009 - In 1995, model Caroline Byrne's body was recovered from a popular suicide spot in Sydney, Australia. Did she jump? Did someone push her? Though her boyfriend claimed she had been depressed, not everyone agreed. It was only through her father's unfailing determination that she finally got justice.

And Then There Were None - 2015 - Based on the Agatha Christie novel, this miniseries sees 10 strangers invited to an island, only to be killed off one by one.

Bäckström - *Sweden* - 2020 to present - This Swedish crime drama follows detective Evert Bäckström, a stand-out detective with a record of solving nearly every case he takes on. **Season 2 premiered September 19th.**

Balthazar - *France* - 2018 to present - This French crime drama revolves around Raphael Balthazar, a brilliant forensic pathologist who's haunted by the memory of his murdered wife. Highly unconventional in his approach, he frequently helps police commander Hélène Bach solve some of Paris' most baffling murder cases. **Season 4 premiered April 25th.**

The Beast Must Die - 2021 - Cush Jumbo (*Deadwater Fell*) stars as Frances, a woman who takes matters into her own hands after police drop the investigation into the hit-and-run accident that killed her young son.

Blinded: Those Who Kill - 2021 - This Danish drama follows criminal profiler Louise Bergstein (Natalie Madueño, *Bedrag*) as she dives into the psychology of suspects in murder cases. When she embarks on a new case, she quickly uncovers a pattern to the unsolved murders of three young men – but she may have a blindspot where this particular case is concerned. The series is a spin-off of *Darkness: Those Who Kill*, and there are eight episodes in the first season.

Blood - 2018 to 2020 - *Ireland* - Adrian Dunbar (*Line of Duty*) stars as a respected doctor and new widower in a small Irish town. Though everyone else believes his wife's death was an accident, his daughter has her doubts. Carolina Main (*Unforgotten*) stars alongside Dunbar as his daughter, Cat.

Bloodlands - 2020 - Produced by Jed Mercurio (*Line of Duty*), this series begins when an expensive car is pulled out of the water with a suicide note but no body. James Nesbitt (*Cold Feet*) stars as Northern Ireland police detective Tom Brannick, who instantly sees a connection to a cold case.

Bloodlines - 2010 - It seems there will always be a few relatively smart people who think they're capable of committing the perfect murder – and this true crime movie tells the story of one of them. In November 1999, Dr. Colin Bouwer (Mark Mitchinson, *Mystery Road*), head of Psychiatry at Otago Hospital, decided to slowly kill his wife with insulin. It was only through the observant young consulting physician Andrew Bowers (Craig Hall, *A Place To Call Home*) that he was caught.

The Brokenwood Mysteries - 2014 to present - DI Mike Shepherd arrives in the seemingly peaceful New Zealand town of Brokenwood with a classic car, loads of country music, and a string of ex-wives. There, he quickly finds that all is not as it seems, and both secrets and animosities run deep in the local community. He's assisted in his crime-fighting efforts by the highly capable, by-the-books assistant DC Kristin Sims. **Season 8 premiered on July 1.**

The Broker's Man - 1997 to 1998 - An ex-cop now puts his detective skills to work for insurance companies. Kevin Whately (*Lewis*) stars.

Candice Renoir - *France* - 2013 to present - Candice Renoir (Cécile Bois) is a French policewoman and single mother of four. After putting her career on hold for a decade, she's returning to work in a port town in the South of France. Now, she'll face the challenging task of solving crime while balancing the need to care for her family. **Season 4 premiered April 11th. Dates for further seasons have not been announced.**

The Chelsea Detective - 2022 - Adrian Scarborough (*Gavin & Stacey, Miranda*) stars as Detective Inspector Max Arnold, a recently-separated officer who lives on a battered houseboat while holding out hope that he'll soon be welcome back in the flat he once shared with his wife.

The Circuit - *Australia* - 2007 to 2010 - This drama follows a magistrate and an entourage of court officers and lawyers on a regular five-day 2000 kilometer round-trip to dispense justice to the remote communities of north Western Australia. It's a hard job for anyone, but for newly-hired Aboriginal lawyer Drew Ellis (Aaron Pedersen, *Mystery Road*) who had a white upbringing and has a white wife, it's a rude awakening as he gets a close-up view of the inequalities in the system.

Code of a Killer - 2015 - This criminal drama tells the story of the first time DNA fingerprinting was used to help solve a murder case. David Threlfall (*Shameless*) stars as DCS David Baker, who heads up the investigation. John Simm (*Life on Mars*) plays Dr. Alec Jeffreys, the scientist who invents the process for fingerprinting DNA.

The Commander - 2003 to 2008 - Amanda Burton (*Silent Witness*) stars in this thriller about the murder investigations of Commander Clare Blake, highest-ranking female officer at New Scotland Yard. The series was written by *Prime Suspect* creator Lynda La Plante.

Conviction: The Case of Stephen Lawrence - 2021 - In 1993, black student Stephen Lawrence was murdered in London during a racially motivated attack. This three-part true crime dramatisation stars Steve Coogan (*Philomena*) as detective Clive Driscoll, the man who worked with the family to build an investigation that would secure a conviction more than 18 years later.

The Cry - *Australia* – 2018 – Jenna Coleman stars in this miniseries about a young couple dealing with the abduction of their baby.

Cuffs – 2015 - In quirky coastal Brighton, police officers are over-stretched and under-resourced, but they do the best they can with what they've got.

Dalgliesh - 2021 - This Acorn TV original is based on the successful Inspector Dalgliesh novels by Phyllis Dorothy James, Baroness James of Holland Park – otherwise known as P.D. James. Bertie Carvel stars as the clever, poetry-loving widower with a knack for solving crimes.

Darby & Joan - *Australia* - 2022 - Former police officer Jack Darby (Bryan Brown, *Bloom*) travels in a battered Landcruiser with only his dog for company. English nurse Joan (Greta Scacchi, *War & Peace*) is doing much the same, but in a comfortable new motor home. Both of them are on the road looking for something, but when their nomadic lives collide, they'll be drawn into a series of unexpected mysteries. **Premiered August 8th.**

Darkness: Those Who Kill - *Denmark* - 2019 - This Danish crime drama follows two investigators looking into a series of murders in hopes of rescuing the next victim in time. When a young woman disappears from the streets of Copenhagen, only Detective Jan Michelsen (Kenneth M. Christensen, *The Legacy*) believes she could still be alive. Joining forces with an expert profiler (played by Natalie Madueño, *Follow the Money*), they discover the disappearance is linked with another kidnapping and murder 10 years prior.

Dead Lucky - *Australia* - 2018 – When a dangerous armed robber resurfaces in Sydney, two very different detectives are forced to work together to catch him. **Premiered May 30th.**

Dead Still - *Ireland* - 2020 - Set in 1880s Ireland, this period mystery takes place in the world of post-mortem photography. Michael Smiley (*Luther*) stars as Brock Blennerhasset, a memorial photographer who's drawn into a series of murders seemingly linked to his work.

Deadwater Fell - 2019 - David Tennant stars in this dark miniseries about a Scottish family that's murdered one night, tearing apart their otherwise peaceful village and bringing secrets to the surface.

The Drowning - 2021 - Jodie (Jill Halfpenny) has spent eight years rebuilding her life after the death of her son, but when she sees a teenage boy who looks just like him, she's convinced she's found her missing son. In that moment, she'll set off on a path that takes her to the edge of all reason.

East West 101 - *Australia* - 2007 to 2011 - Malik and Crowley are a study in opposites as they investigate major crimes.

Fallen Angel - 2007 - Charles Dance (*Foyle's War*) and Emilia Fox (*Silent Witness*) star in this miniseries based on the acclaimed "Requiem for an Angel" crime trilogy by Andrew Taylor. The series begins by revealing a murderer, then rewinding back through her life to examine what made her that way. It begins in modern London, where we meet a woman whose granddaughter has been abducted by a woman known only as "Angel". It's only then that we're taken back to see Angel's childhood in the idyllic English countryside.

The Field of Blood - 2011 to 2013 - Set in early 1980s Glasgow, a young woman skillfully solves murders on a police force full of men. Unfortunately, her dedication to the truth also puts her in danger. The series stars BAFTA winner Jayd Johnson (*River City*) as Paddy Meehan, working alongside Peter Capaldi (*Doctor Who*) and David Morrissey (*The Missing*).

Foyle's War - 2002 to 2015 - DCS Foyle fights a war against crime in southern England as WWII goes on around him. Michael Kitchen (*The Life of Rock with Brian Pern*) and Honeysuckle Weeks (*The Five*) star.

George Gently - 2007 to 2017 - Loosely based on the Inspector Gently novels by Alan Hunter, this 1960s-based series follows Martin Shaw as Inspector George Gently, along with Lee Ingleby as DS John Bacchus. Together, they scour North East England's criminal underworld.

The Gulf - *New Zealand* - 2019 - This series follows Detective Jess Savage (Kate Elliott, *Wentworth*) as she investigates crimes in Waiheke Island. After losing her memory in the same car crash that killed her husband, she sets her sights on finding the killer and bringing him or her to justice. Unfortunately, her memory issues and increasing reliance on morphine make the investigation difficult, and she begins to become paranoid that someone is out to get her because of something she knows.

Hamish Macbeth - 1995 to 1997 - Hamish Macbeth (Robert Carlyle, *The Full Monty*) is a talented but unambitious Highlands constable who doesn't always follow the rules. The series was filmed in the lovely Highland village of Plockton on the shores of Loch Carron, and it's a great watch for those who enjoy good scenery.

Harry - *New Zealand* - 2013 - Detective Harry Anglesea returns to work just four weeks after his wife's suicide, and it may be too soon.

Harry Wild - *Ireland* - 2022 - Jane Seymour (*The Kominsky Method*) stars in this series

about a recently retired English professor with a knack for investigation and a tendency to interfere in her police detective son's cases. **Premiered April 4th, renewed for season 2.**

Hidden (2018) - 2018 to present - In Wales, DI Cadi John (Sian Reese-Williams, *Requiem*) explores the human side of horrific crimes. **Season 3 premiered on June 20th.**

Hidden Assets - *Ireland* - 2022 - Set in County Clare, Ireland and the Belgian diamond capital of Antwerp, this series follows the action after a routine raid uncovers a link between a wealthy Irish family, a stash of rough diamonds, and a number of bombings in Belgium. The series stars Angeline Ball (*Keeping Faith*) as DS Emer Berry, along with Simone Kirby (*His Dark Materials*) and Peter Coonan (*Cold Courage*). **Premiered on April 18th.**

Hinterland - 2013 to 2016 - This Welsh-noir police procedural follows DCI Tom Mathias and his team as they solve grisly crimes around the coastal town of Aberystwyth.

In Deep - 2001 to 2003 - Nick Berry (*Heartbeat*) and Stephen Tompkinson (*DCI Banks, Trollied*) star in this 2001 series about undercover detectives and the unique challenges they face while leading double lives.

Jack Irish - *Australia* - 2012 to 2018 - Guy Pearce (*Memento*) stars as Jack Irish, a talented PI and ex-lawyer with a checkered past. Marta Dusseldorp (*A Place to Call Home*) also appears as his occasional girlfriend and talented journalist helper.

Jack Taylor - *Ireland* - 2010 to 2016 - Resistant to rules, ex-cop Jack Taylor becomes a private investigator after losing his job with the Guard. Iain Glen (*Game of Thrones*) stars in this series set against the city of Galway. It's based on a series of novels written by Ken Bruen.

Jericho of Scotland Yard - 2005 - This period mystery gives us DI Michael Jericho, a WWII veteran who investigates murders while also seeking to figure out the circumstances surrounding his father's death.

Keeping Faith - 2017 to present - A Welsh lawyer cuts her maternity leave short when her husband goes missing. As she tries to solve the crime before she's arrested for it, she finds herself knee-deep in the criminal underworld of her small town. Eve Myles

(*Torchwood*) stars, though some might argue her yellow anorak deserves a mention, too.

Kidnap & Ransom - 2011 to 2012 - Trevor Eve (*Waking the Dead*) stars as Dominic King, a skilled hostage negotiator about to embark on some of the most difficult cases in his career. In Season 1, he'll negotiate for the release of a businesswoman who's been snatched in South Africa. In Series 2, we'll see him dealing with a tour bus that's been taken hostage in India.

Killer Net - 1998 - A psychology student becomes obsessed with a computer game about murder, but it gets scary when it suddenly seems to be connected to real murders. Tam Williams (*Spectre*) and Paul Bettany (*The Avengers* films) star in this dark miniseries.

Lawless - *New Zealand* - 1999 - This TV movie sees undercover cop John Lawless wrongly accused of murder. To prove his innocence, he'll have to get help from friends on both sides of the law.

The Level - 2016 to 2017 - A detective is the missing witness in the murder of a drug trafficker. The police want her, and the killer wants her dead.

Line of Duty – 2012 to present - This suspenseful British police series is set in the fictional "anti-corruption unit" AC-12, where the police police the police. Yes, we know that sounds a bit odd. Lennie James, Vicky McClure, Martin Compston, and Adrian Dunbar all feature. **Acorn TV has seasons 1-5.**

Liverpool 1 - 1998 to 1999 - This gritty, Liverpool-based police drama dives into the city's underworld. We follow the vice squad at Bridewell as they fight drug dealers, paeodophiles, pimps, and porn peddlers in this rough-around-the-edges port city. Samantha Womack stars as DC Isobel de Pauli.

Loch Ness - 2017 to present - Highlands Detective Annie Redford faces her first murder case when a human heart is found.

London Kills - 2019 - This Acorn TV Original follows a team of London's top detectives as they investigate homicides. Hugo Speer (*The Full Monty*) stars as DI David Bradford, the lead investigator whose talents seem to solve every case but the disappearance of his wife. Sharon Small (*The Inspector Lynley Mysteries*) and Bailey Patrick (*Bodyguard*) also star. **All**

episodes of season 3 premiered on June 6th.

Lovejoy - 1986 to 1994 - Ian McShane (*Deadwood*) stars as Lovejoy, the slightly shady antiques dealer and part-time detective. *Downton Abbey* fans will be delighted to see a young Phyllis Logan (aka Mrs. Hughes) in this early role.

The Madame Blanc Mysteries - 2022 - This series follows Jean White, a respected antiques dealer in Chesire who's left bereft after her husband tragically dies on the way home from their favourite antiquing spot in the South of France. Things turn dark(er) when she learns their money is gone, their shop has been re-mortgaged, and nearly everything they own is gone. **Renewed for season 2 and an upcoming Christmas special (no dates yet).**

Manhunt - 2018 to present - Martin Clunes (*Doc Martin*) stars in this series based on the real investigation into the death of French student Amélie Delagrange. Clunes plays DCI Colin Sutton, the man who led the task force that ultimately brought her killer to justice.

Mayday - 2013 - When the May Queen disappears just before May Day celebrations, a small town is thrown into chaos.

Midsomer Murders - 1998 to present - In Midsomer County, the landscapes are beautiful, the villagers all have secrets, and murder is rampant. This British mystery classic features John Nettles as DCI Tom Barnaby through the first 13 seasons, with Neil Dudgeon as DCI John Barnaby for the later seasons.

Midsomer Murders: 20th Anniversary Special - 2019 - John Nettles presents this look back at Midsomer Murders on its 20th anniversary. The hour-long special features appearances by Neil Dudgeon, Nick Hendrix, Daniel Casey, Jason Hughes, Jane Wymark, and more.

Midsomer Murders: Neil Dudgeon's Top 10 - This special collection doesn't include any new episodes of Midsomer Murders, but it does feature commentary and behind-the-scenes stories from Neil Dudgeon.

Mind Games - 2001 - Fiona Shaw (*Killing Eve*) stars in this television movie about a nun turned criminal profiler who's called in to investigate the deaths of two middle-aged women. She quickly realises that these aren't just home robberies gone wrong - they're the work of a serial killer.

Miss Fisher's Murder Mysteries - *Australia* -2012 to 2015 - In 1920s Melbourne, Miss Phryne Fisher works as a skilled private detective. Essie Davis and Nathan Page star.

Miss Fisher & The Crypt of Tears - *Australia* - 2020 to present - This movie is a continuation of the original Miss Fisher's Murder Mysteries stories, and it premiered in early 2020. In this one, Essie Davis returns to the role of Phryne in 1929 Jerusalem. There, she rescues a young Bedouin girl and finds herself on a globe-trotting adventure with her favourite handsome detective, Jack Robinson (Nathan Page).

Missing (2006) - 2006 - Joanne Froggatt (*Downton Abbey*) stars as a young runaway who scams men to survive. When one of them turns up dead, she becomes the main suspect in a string of murders.

Missing (2009) - 2009 to 2010 - Pauline Quirke (*Birds of a Feather*) stars as DS Mary Jane "MJ" Croft, head of a busy missing persons unit in Dover. In each case, she and her team will confront situations that make friends and family wonder how well they really know their loved ones.

Mr. and Mrs. Murder - *Australia* - 2013 - A married couple runs a crime scene cleaning business while also helping to solve the murders they clean up.

Ms. Fisher's Modern Murder Mysteries - *Australia* - 2019 to present - In this spin-off to the original *Miss Fisher's Murder Mysteries* series, Phryne Fisher's long-lost niece follows in her aunt's footsteps as a 1960s lady detective with her own handsome officer. Geraldine Hakewill stars as Peregrine Fisher, and Joel Jackson plays Detective James Steed.

Murder Investigation Team - 2003 to 2005 - A London-based team of elite investigators handles exceptionally challenging murders.

Murderland - 2009 - This miniseries looks at a murder from the perspectives of the daughter, the detective, and the murder victim.

Murdoch Mysteries - *Canada* - 2008 to present - Set in the 1890s, Murdoch uses early forensics to solve murders. Yannick Bisson stars as Detective William Murdoch,

Helene Joy plays Dr. Julia Ogden, and Thomas Craig and Jonny Harris fill the roles of Inspector Thomas Brackenreid and Constable George Crabtree, respectively. **Season 15 is now available in full.**

Murdoch Mysteries: The Movies - *Canada* - 2004 to 2005 - Before it was a hit television series, there were three Murdoch Mysteries movies. Also set in 1890s Canada, the movies feature Peter Outerbridge as Detective William Murdoch (as opposed to Yannick Bisson) and Keeley Hawes (*The Durrells, Bodyguard*) as Dr. Julia Ogden.

Murphy's Law - 2001 to 2007 - James Nesbitt (*Cold Feet*) stars as Tommy Murphy, a charming but tough Northern Irish cop with a tragic past.

My Life is Murder - *Australia* - 2019 to present - Lucy Lawless (*Xena: Warrior Princess*) stars as retired Melbourne cop Alexa Crowe. Alexa is a mystery, but we know she's tough, smart, hurting from a past trauma, and great at baking bread. She's also slowly warming up to the cat who's invited itself to live with her. In each episode, she gets a bit of extra help from her protégé Madison (Ebony Vagulans). **Season 3 premieres October 10th with two episodes weekly and a total of 10.**

The Mystery of a Hansom Cab - 2012 - Set in 1880s Melbourne, this period drama is based on the bestselling novel by Fergus Hume. It follows the murder of a man connected to a wealthy benefactor, along with an accused man unable to provide an alibi.

Mystery Road - *Australia* - 2018 to present - Detective Jay Swan investigates crimes in the Australian Outback.

Mystery Road: Origin - *Australia* - 2022 - This *Mystery Road* prequel stars Mark Coles Smith (Halifax: Retribution) as a young Jay Swan. Set in 1999, the period mystery sees the young constable leaving the city to work in the small town where his estranged father lives. **Premieres September 26th.**

No Offence - 2015 to 2018 - This gritty Manchester-based police drama showcases the work of some talented serious crimes investigators under the straight-talking DI Viv Deering.

The Oldenheim 12 - *The Netherlands* - 2017 - A traditional Dutch village is shaken to its core when multiple residents suddenly go missing without a trace.

One Lane Bridge - *New Zealand* - 2020 - While working a murder investigation, a young Maori detective accidentally awakens a spiritual gift that may harm the case.

Outlier - *Norway* - 2020 - This mystery begins when a teenager on her way home from a party finds a mobile phone ringing. The phone belongs to a missing girl, Sofie, whose body was later discovered at a camping resort a few hours away. Criminology student Maja Angell (Hanne Mathisen Haga) hears about this puzzling case in her hometown and leaves university to head north to deliver a message to the police. She believes the man who's been arrested is not the true killer, and her efforts to prove it will push her towards some of her most dangerous and repressed childhood memories.

The Paradise - *Finland* - 2020 - In a tiny corner of Malaga lies the Finnish community of Fuengirola. It's a peaceful place – until two murders destroy the tranquility. To help with the investigation, 60-year-old veteran detective Hikka Mäntymäki (Riitta Havukainen) travels in from Oulu, Finland. Unfortunately, the case will continue to claim new victims as Hikka and the local police scramble to untangle the case.

Pie in the Sky - 1994 to 1997 - When DI Crabbe leaves the police force to open a restaurant, they continue to pull him back in for part-time crime-solving. Richard Griffiths (Vernon Dursley in *Harry Potter*) stars, but you'll also spot guest appearances from actors like Phyllis Logan (*Downton Abbey*), Jim Carter (*Downton Abbey*), Jane Wymark (*Midsomer Murders*), Keeley Hawes (*Bodyguard*), Ian McNeice (*Doc Martin*), Michael Kitchen (*Foyle's War*), Derren Litten (*Benidorm*), Abigail Thaw (*Endeavour*), Nicola Walker (*Unforgotten*), and Joan Sims (*As Time Goes By*).

The Poison Tree - 2012 - Matthew Goode (*A Discovery of Witches*) stars in this psychological thriller about a man who returns home after being released from prison. Though his devoted wife (MyAnna Buring, *Ripper Street*) has always maintained his innocence, he comes to realise she may be hiding more than her fair share of dark secrets.

Prisoners' Wives - 2012 - Gemma thinks she has a perfect life until her husband is arrested for murder.

Proof - *Ireland* - 2004 to 2005 - When an investigative reporter finds a connection between a local thief's murder and a corrupt accountant's death, he soon finds himself neck-deep in the middle of a scandal involving human trafficking, politics, and the world of high finance. Finbar Lynch (*Breathless*) and Orla Brady (*The South Westerlies*) star.

Queens of Mystery - 2019 - Young Matilda Stone is just beginning her career in law enforcement and she has not one, not two, but three crime-writing aunts. Her quirky aunts raised her after the disappearance of her mother, and they always manage to worm their way into her cases. This series was created by *Doc Martin* writer Julian Unthank, and features appearances by Olivia Vinall (Season 1), Florence Hall (Season 2), Julia Graham (*Bletchley Circle*), Siobhan Redmond (*Taggart*), and Sarah Woodward (*Gems*).

Rebecka Martinsson - *Sweden* - 2017 to present - This crime drama follows a young Stockholm lawyer as her life is turned upside down by the violent murder of a childhood friend. She quits her job and returns to her hometown to investigate a world that's not what it seems.

Recipes for Love & Murder - *South Africa* - September 2022 - Maria Doyle Kennedy will star in this upcoming South African cozy mystery series based on the novel by Sally Andrew. She plays a recipe advice columnist for a small-town paper, and she'll investigate the murder of one of her correspondents. Tony Kgoroge will co-star as the local chief detective. **Premiered September 5th.**

Republic of Doyle - Canada - 2010 to 2014 - This delightful crime dramedy follows a father and son investigative agency in lovely Newfoundland. Allan Hawco stars as the rough-around-the-edges PI Jake Doyle, while Sean McGinley (Bleak House) plays his father and partner Malachy Doyle.

Resort to Murder - 1995 - After a woman is murdered on the West Pier in Brighton, her son dives into the local underworld to find her killer. This intricately plotted thriller stars Ben Chaplin (*The Thin Red Line*), Steven Waddington (*Jamestown*), Kelly Hunter (*The Hole*), and Peter Firth (*Cheat*). **Premiered May 23rd.**

Signora Volpe - 2022 - Emilia Fox (*Silent Witness*) stars in this series about a disillusioned British spy turned detective living in the heart of Italy. Trouble seems to follow wherever she goes, but her career as a spy has certainly left her with the right skills for it. **Premiered May 2nd.**

The Silence - *Australia* - 2006 - *Rake* star Richard Roxburgh stars as Detective Richard Treloar, an officer under investigation for a fatal shooting. He's been re-assigned to a desk job at the Police Museum, and his new position draws him into an old mystery. While working on a photographic exhibition, he becomes obsessed with an archival image of a beautiful murder victim. Searching through more images, he looks for her face – seeing her first in the background of images, then in the company of criminals, and later, as the victim of an unsolved crime.

The Silence – 2010 - While struggling to integrate into the hearing world, a young girl with a new cochlear implant witnesses the murder of a police officer. Douglas Henshall (*Shetland*) is among the stars of this miniseries.

Single-Handed - 2007 to 2010 - *Ireland* - Jack Driscoll is transferred back to his hometown to take over the Garda Sergeant role his father left.

Small Claims - *Australia* - 2004 to 2006 - Starring Rebecca Gibney (*Under The Vines*) and Claudia Karvan (*Love My Way*), this series follows a couple of Australian mums who become unlikely suburban sleuths. The series is made up of three TV movies.

The Sommerdahl Murders - *Denmark* - 2020 - In the beautiful Danish coastal town of Helsingør, Detective Chief Inspector Dan Sommerdahl (Peter Mygind, *Flame and Citron*) is the undisputed hero at North Sjælland Police. When the body of a young woman washes up on a beach, Dan and his best friend and colleague, Detective Flemming Torp (André Babikian, *The Protectors*), quickly determine this wasn't an accident, and they are in hot pursuit to find the murderer and the baby the female victim had just given birth to. **Season 3 premiered July 4th.**

The Sounds - 2020 - A happily married Canadian couple moves to New Zealand to escape the husband's domineering family, but when he disappears soon after relocating, long-buried secrets come to light.

The Stalker's Apprentice - 1998 - This film follows a man who sees a woman on the train and decides she will be his. That same man also works as a book editor, and in the course of his job he comes across an interesting manuscript that, unbeknownst to him, was written by convicted serial killer Helmut Kranze (James Bolam, *Cold Feet*). The book's influence soon leads him to take action on his obsession. Peter Davison (*Gentleman Jack*) also appears as DI Maurice Burt.

Still Life: A Three Pines Mystery - *Canada* - 2013 - In this television movie, Chief Inspector Armand Gamache (Nathaniel Parker) arrives in Three Pines to investigate a strange death in the sleepy village of Three Pines.

The Strange Calls - 2012 - This oddball comedy/mystery series follows a disgraced Australian cop, Toby Banks, after he's transferred to the seemingly idyllic coastal town of Coolum Beach. There, his job is to answer night calls from locals – calls that reveal bizarre truths about something sinister lurking beneath the town's cozy surface.

Supply and Demand - 1997 to 1998 - This crime drama features an elite team of detectives charged with investigating large-scale smugglers and importers.

Suspects - 2014 to 2016 - Three Greater London detectives investigate serious crimes in this heavily improvised series.

Thorne - 2010 - This collection of two Thorne movies inclu des *Scaredy Cat* and *Sleepyhead*. In *Sleepyhead*, DI Thorne (David Morrissey, *Men Behaving Badly*) is in a race against time to find a serial killer who enjoys making unusual attacks on young women. *Scaredy Cat* sees Thorne is working with a new team to tackle a tough double murder case, but it's not long before he's hunting down two different serial killers.

Trial & Retribution - 1997 to 2009 - DS Walker and his team follow criminals from their crime to the courts.

The Truth Will Out - 2018 to present - Detective Peter Wendel sets out to create an elite task force to help solve cold cases, but when he finally gets his chance, the only available officers seem to be some of Sweden's worst. Meanwhile, he's dealing with the possibility that a noted serial killer may not have killed all his victims - leaving another murderer, or even many murderers, running free. **Season 2 premiered May 16th.**

Vexed – 2010 to 2012 - A young male and female detective team frustrate each other with their different attitudes and complicated personal lives.

Whitstable Pearl - 2021 - Based on Julie Wassmer's *Whitstable Pearl* mystery novels, this Kent-based series follows restaurant owner Pearl Nolan as she follows her long-deferred dream of investigative work. Unfortunately, her first case begins when a friend's body is found in mysterious circumstances. Kerry Godlimann (*After Life*) stars as Pearl, with Frances Barber (*Silk*) playing her mother, Dolly. Howard Charles (*The Musketeers*) plays DCI Mike McGuire, the friendly officer who will, of course, bristle occasionally at her meddling. **Renewed for season 2, date TBD.**

Winter - 2015 - *Australia* - Eve Winter, a Sydney homicide detective, solves some of the most difficult cases while dealing with bureaucracy and the challenges of being a woman in her field. Rebecca Gibney (*Packed to the Rafters*) stars.

Wire in the Blood - 2002 to 2009 - An eccentric psychologist helps the police solve murders by getting inside the minds of the killers. Robson Green (*Grantchester*) stars.

Wisting - 2019 - This Norwegian drama follows homicide detective William Wisting as he investigates the possibility of an American serial killer living in Norway.

The Witnesses - *Germany* - 2020 - When a 10-year-old girl is kidnapped from a crowded museum in Berlin, the family and police await a ransom demand that never comes. No one claims responsibility, and there's nothing to go on except the memories of eye witnesses. The child's prominent father asks researcher Dr. Jasmin Braun (Alexandra Maria Lara) to step in and evaluate the memories of eight key witnesses in hopes of reconstructing the crime and returning the girl home safely.

Dramas

800 Words - *New Zealand* - 2015 to 2018 - After the death of his wife, a man relocates his family from Sydney to a small coastal community in New Zealand.

Ackley Bridge - 2017 to present - Two struggling schools merge to form one, and it creates big problems for the headmistress.

Aftertaste - *Australia* - 2021- After burning his bridges and ruining his last chance, chef Easton West (Erik Thomson, *800 Words*), he finds himself back in his hometown with the dysfunctional family he left 30 years earlier. Understandably, they're not too keen on him. Only his 19-year-old pastry chef niece, Diana, will have anything much to do with him. As he works to rebuild his life, he takes Diana under his wing. But can she stand working with him?

A Nightingale Falling - 2014 - Set in Ireland during the War of Independence (1919 – 1921), this period film follows two sisters whose lives are forever altered by their interactions with a wounded soldier. Tara Breathnach (Jack Taylor) and Muireann Bird (Deep Shock) star. **Premieres October 24th.**

Anne - 2022 - Based on the real story of the Hillsborough Disaster, this series follows Anne Williams (Maxine Peake, *The Village*) as she attempts to get answers about her 15-year-old son's "accidental" death verdict. Over the course of 24 years, she dug relentlessly to find witnesses, get medical advice, and get justice for the 96 people who lost their lives in the fatal human crush incident at the 1989 FA Cup semi-final. **Premiered August 22nd.**

A Place to Call Home - *Australia* - 2013 to 2018 - A mysterious woman begins a new life in Australia after World War II.

The Attaché - *France/Israel* - 2019 - Eli Ben David (Buba Shel-Medina) based this series on his own experiences of living in Paris as an Israeli Jewish man of Moroccan descent. He plays a successful musician who relocated to the city for his wife's new job as the attaché to the Israeli embassy in Paris, highlighting the troubles he experiences with his marriage, masculinity, and fatherhood.

A Suitable Boy - 2020 - This Andrew Davies (*House of Cards*) adaptation of Vikram Seth's novel of the same name follows the story of a young woman coming of age in 1951 North India. The series filmed in India featuring Bollywood celebrities Ishaan Khatter and Tabu (*Life of Pi*) alongside rising star Tanya Maniktala in the role of Lata.

A Woman of Substance - 1985 - Deborah Kerr, Jenny Seagrove, and Liam Neeson star in this Emmy-nominated miniseries about Emma Harte's rise from a poor Yorkshire servant to a wealthy tycoon. The nine-part series is based on Barbara Taylor Bradford's novel of the same name. **Premiered May 2nd.**

B&B - 1992 - After getting fired from his architectural job, single dad Steve Shepherd (Keven Whately, *Inspector Morse*) opens his home to guests to help pay the bills. Not long after he loses his job, his former boss, Horace Gilbert (Ian McNeice, *Doc Martin*) learns that his former employee's home lies right in the middle of their intended development site for vacation homes.

Bang - 2017 to present - In this bilingual Welsh crime drama, a man comes into possession of a gun and his life is forever changed.

The Beautiful Lie - *Australia* - 2015 - This acclaimed Australian drama re-imagines Tolstoy's *Anna Karenina* as a tale of middle-class modern life, following happy and unhappy families as they move through love, scandal, and more over three generations.

Belonging - 2003 - Brenda Blethyn (*Vera*) and Kevin Whately (*Lewis*) star as a married couple who've been happily married for decades and now live with a number of extended family members. Jess (Blethyn) has given up her job to care for the older family members, and it's all going rather well until her husband disappears.

The Blue Rose - New Zealand - 2013 - This investigative drama sees a group of law firm employees joining together to figure out what happened in the mysterious death of a co-worker.

Bodily Harm - 2002 - Timothy Spall (*Blandings*) stars as a suburban man whose life is changed forever after he loses his job, finds out his father is dying, and catches his wife cheating.

The Boy with the Topknot - 2017 - This film tells the story of Sathnam, young Indian raised in Britain, as he tries to adjust to his multicultural life.

Brief Encounters - 2016 - When a group of women start selling lingerie and other marital aids through at-home parties in the early 1980s, their lives are transformed.

Butterfly Breath (aka Pili Pala) - 2019 - This four-part Welsh-English drama takes a look at what happens when a bad medical decision sets off a chain of events that quickly spins out of control. Sara Morris (Sian Reese-Davies, *Hidden*) goes against the advice of colleagues when she takes on her friend as a patient. The series explores issues of loyalty and betrayal, as well as the challenges of infertility and termination. Those sensitive to these topics may wish to skip over this one. **Premiered July 25th.**

Capital - 2015 - Toby Jones and Rachael Stirling (both of *Detectorists*) star in this drama about residents on a fictional street who receive strange postcards that read: "We want what you have." As the mystery unfolds, their interweaving stories will also play out.

Care - 2018 - Sheridan Smith (*Gavin & Stacey*) stars as a single mother struggling to raise her two children after a family tragedy. After her husband's departure, she's fully reliant on the childcare her mother Mary (Alison Steadman, also from *Gavin & Stacey*) provides. That all changes when Mary suffers a devastating stroke and develops dementia.

The Case - 2011 - This legal drama tells the story of a man put on trial for the murder of his terminally ill partner after he helped her commit suicide.

Clean Break - 2015 - When a car dealer realises he's in trouble and about to lose everything, he sets out to fix his problems while also exacting revenge on those who have hurt him.

Close to the Enemy - 2016 - After WW2, a German engineer is taken to Britain in hopes of gaining his cooperation. Jim Sturgess (*Across the Universe*) and Charlotte Riley (*Press*) star.

Cold Call - 2019 - When a single mum gets caught up in a cold call phone scam, her entire life is turned upside down.

Coming Home - 1998 - This two-part miniseries is an adaptation of Rosamunde Pilcher's *Coming Home*, and it follows Judith Dunbar (Emily Mortimer) as she heads off to boarding school and befriends the carefree Loveday Carey-Lewis (Katie Ryder-Richardson). From there, an entire world of glamorous and wealthy people opens to her – but her immense happiness is soon overshadowed by the spectre of war. **Premiered April 11th.**

The Crimson Petal & the White - 2011 - In late 1800s London, a prostitute finds her position greatly improved after becoming the mistress to a powerful man. Romola Garai (*The Hour*) stars as prostitute Sugar, with Chris O'Dowd (*The IT Crowd*) playing William Rackham, the perfume heir who becomes involved with her.

Crownies - *Australia* - 2011 - This Australian legal drama follows a group of solicitors who've recently completed law school as they go to work as public prosecutors in New South Wales. As twentysomethings in a high-pressure job, they'll have to balance their active personal lives with a challenging and stressful position. **Premiered June 13th.**

Danger UXB - 1979 - This vintage series was titled after the shorthand term for "danger, unexploded bomb", and it tells the story of the men who worked in bomb disposal during WWII. Each hour-long episode follows these brave young men as they carried out one of the most difficult and terrifying jobs in the war effort.

Delicious - 2016 to present - Two women in Cornwall try to get on somewhat peacefully after circumstances in their lives change dramatically.

Dominion Creek - *Ireland* - 2015 to present - Three Irish brothers dream of striking it rich in the Klondike Gold Rush.

East of Everything - *Australia* - 2008 to 2009 - When an Australian woman dies, she dictates in her will that her two estranged sons must reopen the family hostel in Broken Bay.

Family Business - *France* - 2017 - A mother-daughter lawyer pair juggle the ins and outs of running a family law practice, all while balancing and navigating their own issues away from the office.

Finding Alice - 2021 - Keeley Hawes (*Bodyguard, Line of Duty*) stars in this ensemble drama about a woman's emotional journey after the death of her partner. After moving into her dream home with her family, Alice's life is torn apart when she finds her husband dead at the bottom of the stairs. The series also stars Joanna Lumley (*Absolutely Fabulous*), Nigel Havers (*Benidorm, Coronation Street*), Jason Merrells (*Agatha Raisin*) and Gemma Jones (*Gentleman Jack*).

Fingersmith - 2005 – In Victorian England, a young female thief hatches a plan to get close to an heiress and scam her. It doesn't go as planned.

Flame Trees of Thika - 1981 - Hayley Mills (*Wild at Heart*), David Robb (*I, Claudius*), and Holly Aird (*Waking the Dead*) star in this miniseries about a British family who relocate to British East Africa (now Kenya) to set up a coffee plantation.

Four Seasons - 2008 - This four-part Rosamunde Pilcher miniseries offers a sweeping family saga played out over a single year at Endellion, the country home of the Combe family. It follows the women of three different generations after the return of the once-banished Julia (Senta Berger, Unter Verdacht). **Premiered May 30th.**

The Gods of Wheat Street - *Australia* - 2014 - This Australian series gives us a closer look at the lives of the Freeburns, a rough-around-the-edges Aboriginal Australian family with a complicated and chaotic life.

Gold Digger - 2019 - Julia Ormond (*Sabrina*) stars as Julia Day, a wealthy 60-year-old woman who falls in love with a handsome man 26 years her junior. As secrets come to light, no one can be sure what's real and what's merely convenient.

The Good Karma Hospital - 2017 to present - After a relationship sours, a young British-Indian woman decides to move to India to work in an impoverished hospital. Little does she know, she's got a lot to learn. Amanda Redman stars alongside Amrita Acharia.

The Heart Guy (aka Doctor Doctor) - *Australia* - 2016 to present - When a prominent heart surgeon falls from grace, he's forced to go work as a country GP in his former hometown. At his lowest moment, he'll have to face the people and places he's spent his life trying to get away from.

The Helen West Casebook - 2002 - Amanda Burton (Silent Witness) stars as crown prosecutor Helen West, a justice-driven woman who pursues tough cases even as her boss recommends dropping them.

Help - 2021 - Jodie Comer (*Killing Eve*) and Stephen Graham (*Line of Duty*) star in this award-winning film about a young care worker who forges an unlikely bond with an early-onset dementia patient, only to see their friendship tested during the COVID-19 pandemic. The film was written by BAFTA winner Jack Thorne (*Enola Holmes*), and also stars Ian Hart (*The Last Kingdom*) and Lesley Sharp (*Scott & Bailey*).

The Hour - 2011 - This period drama takes us behind the scenes during the launch of a new London news programme during the mid-1950s. Ben Whishaw (*Spectre*), Romola Garai (*Emma*), Dominic West (*The Affair*), and Peter Capaldi (*Doctor Who*) are among the cast members.

I, Claudius - Sir Derek Jacobi (*Last Tango in Halifax*) and Sir Patrick Stewart (*Star Trek*) star in this BBC television adaptation of Robert Graves' 1934 novel of the same name (along with its sequel, *Claudius the God*). The series covers the early history of the Roman Empire, with an elderly Emperor Claudius narrating.

The Indian Doctor - 2010 to 2013 - An Indian doctor and his wife move to a small Welsh mining village during the 1960s. They must adjust to culture shock, and Dr. Sharma must win the trust of the locals.

The Invisibles - 2008 - A couple of retired master burglars tried living in Spain, but after a bout of homesickness, they returned to England with their wives to live in a Devon fishing village. It's not long before a return to familiar shores sees them taking up the same old bad habits.

The Irish R.M. - *Ireland* - 1983 to 1985 - When an Englishman leaves home to become an Irish Resident Magistrate, he quickly learns the normal rules don't apply with his eccentric new neighbours.

Janet King - Australia - 2014 to 2017 - This spinoff from the legal drama *Crownies* follows Senior Crown Prosecutor Janet King as she returns from maternity leave and progresses through her career. Marta Dusseldorp (*A Place to Call Home*) stars.

Jericho - 2016 - This Yorkshire-based 1870s period drama tells the story of a community dominated by the construction of a new viaduct. Jessica Raine (*Call the Midwife*) stars.

Just William - 2010 - This BBC series follows the entertaining adventures of a mischievous 11-year-old boy, William Brown (Daniel Roche, *Outnumbered*), and his friends in 1950s England. The series takes us back to a fun, carefree time when kids could run off for the day and not return home until teatime. The series also includes appearances from Daniel Ryan (*Home Fires*), Caroline Quentin (*Jonathan Creek*), Lily James (*Cinderella*), and Warren Clark (*Poldark*).

Lady Chatterley - 1993 - Sean Bean and Judy Richardson star in this adaptation of the scandalous DH Lawrence novel.

Land Girls - 2009 to 2011 - Land Girls follows four women in the Women's Land Army during WW2.

Law & Order: UK - 2009 to 2014 - This adaptation of the successful American courtroom drama sees the format carried over to the British legal system. It's one-part law (investigative work) and one-part order (the court proceedings).

Like Father Like Son - 2005 - Eleven years ago, Dee Stanton's husband was arrested for brutally murdering four young women. She's moved on from those times, but now, her 15-year-old son Jamie is determined to learn more about his father. When her son is accused of strangling a fellow pupil, she'll come face to face with her worst nightmare. Jemma Redgrave and Robson Green star.

Love, Lies, & Records - 2017 - Ashley Jensen (*Agatha Raisin*) stars as Kate Dickinson, a woman constantly challenged in her efforts to balance a personal life with the stress of the records she oversees.

Love My Way - 2004 to 2007 - This Australian drama follows a thirtysomething woman as she attempts to juggle her desires for a rewarding career, a good relationship, and a healthy family life. Claudia Karvan (*Newton's Law*) stars.

Marvellous - 2014 - Toby Jones (*Detectorists*) stars in this drama about a man with learning disabilities who did better than anyone expected.

The Mayor of Casterbridge - 2003 - Ciarán Hinds (*Above Suspicion*) and James Purefoy (*Rome*) star in this adaptation of Thomas Hardy's novel of the same name. It tells the story of a drunken farmer who auctions off his family, only to realise the horror of what he's done and change his life.

Mr. Palfrey of Westminster - 1984 to 1985 - Mr. Palfrey might seem like a typical, mild-mannered civil servant, but he's actually a charming, highly-trained spy. Alec McCowan stars.

The Nest - 2020 - Sophie Rundle (*Bodyguard*) and Martin Compston (*Line of Duty*) star in this Glasgow-based drama about a couple who would do almost anything to have a child. When they meet a troubled young woman, they make her an irresistible offer.

New Worlds - 2014 - Jamie Dornan (*50 Shades of Grey*) stars in this period drama set in the 1680s. The story takes place in both England and the new American colonies, and it focuses on love and conflict in the uncertain time period. It was produced as a follow-up to *The Devil's Whore* (aka *The Devil's Mistress* in North America).

Newton's Law - *Australia* - 2017 - Josephine Newton (Claudia Karvan, *Love My Way*) is a suburban solicitor whose life has hit a few bumps. When an old friend suggests she join Knox Chambers, she decides to take on a new challenge and return to her barrister's robe.

The Norman Conquests - 1977 - Based on a trilogy of Alan Ayckbourn plays, this miniseries depicts six characters over the same weekend, but in different parts of a house. Dames Penelope Keith and Penelope Wilton are among the cast, and both appeared in stage versions of the plays. The late Richard Briers (*The Good Life*) is also among the stars.

Nothing Trivial - 2011 to 2014 - For one group of New Zealand-based friends, a weekly trivia night is the one constant in their lives. They're all in their thirties and forties and none of them have great luck with love, but they always meet up for the weekly pub quiz and some friendly banter.

Party Tricks - *Australia* - 2014 - This Australian series follows Kate Ballard (Asher Keddie, *X-Men Origins: Wolverine*), a woman facing her first election for State Premier. Victory seems guaranteed until the opposition brings in a shock candidate – David McLeod (Rodger Corser, *The Heart Guy*). McLeod is a popular media figure, but more concerning is the fact that she had a secret affair with him years earlier.

Pitching In - 2019 - Larry Lamb and Melanie Walters (both of *Gavin & Stacey*) reunite in this fun family drama about a North Wales holiday camp owner who contemplates selling up after his Welsh wife dies. Though the series has been criticised for inauthentic North Wales accents, it offers a feel-good viewing experience and scenery from a different part of the UK than we typically see in TV and film. Hayley Mills (*Wild at Heart*) also appears as Iona.

Place of Execution - 2008 - Based on the novel by Scottish novelist Val McDermid, this series follows a journalist making a film about the 1963 disappearance of a young schoolgirl.

Poldark - 1975 to 1977 - Based on the Poldark novels by Winston Graham, this series tells the story of a man who went off to fight a war and came back to find everything changed. Robin Ellis stars as Captain Ross Poldark in this older adaptation.

The Prime of Miss Jean Brodie - 1978 - This classic adaptation of Muriel Spark's novel sees Geraldine McEwan (*Agatha Christie's Marple*) in the iconic role of Jean Brodie. She's an unorthodox teacher who does her best to fill her students with confidence and a love of art. The series is set in 1930s Edinburgh, and even though it's an older miniseries, it's very much worth the watch.

Public Enemies - 2012 - This series tells the story of a young man recently released from prison after serving 10 years, and the parole officer working with him after returning from a professional suspension.

Rake - *Australia* - 2011 to 2018 - Defense lawyer Cleaver Greene makes a career out of hopeless cases, perhaps because his own personal life is troubled enough to help him relate. **Only season 5 remains on Acorn TV.**

Restless – 2012 – This two-part TV movie is based on a bestselling spy novel by William Boyd. It focuses on a young woman who finds out her mother was a spy for British intelligence during WWII, and that she's been on the run ever since.

Réunions - 2020 - This French drama follows two half-brothers who learn about each other's existence after their father dies and they inherit a hotel on the island of Réunion. With their newly-acquired hotel on the verge of bankruptcy, the two brothers and their families make big

sacrifices and move to the beautiful island to help turn things around.

Run - 2013 - Olivia Colman and Lennie James star in this four-part miniseries about four seemingly unconnected people whose lives intersect after a random act of violence.

The Scapegoat - 2012 - Set in 1952, this period drama sees two men with similar faces switching places. The film is based on the novel by Daphne du Maurier, and Matthew Rhys (*The Americans*) stars.

The Scarlet Pimpernel - 1982 - Jane Seymour, Anthony Andrews, and Sir Ian McKellen star in this period drama set during the French Revolution. While many aristocrats are facing the guillotine, quite a few have escaped thanks to the efforts of a young Englishman known as the "Scarlet Pimpernel". The film is based on Baroness Orczy's 1905 novel by the same name.

Seachange - *Australia* - 1998 to 2000 - After her husband is arrested for fraud and has an affair with her sister, Laura Gibson decides to undergo a "seachange" with her children. They move to the coastal village of Pearl Bay and embark on a new kind of life.

Seachange: Paradise Reclaimed - 2019 - This 2019 reboot features original cast members Sigrid Thornton (*The Man from Snowy River*), Kerry Armstrong (*Lantana*) and John Howard (*All Saints*), and takes place 20 years after the final season. After divorce and job loss, Laura Gibson (Thornton) finds herself questioning her place in the world. But when she returns to the beachside paradise of Pearl Bay, she's able to start putting the pieces back together.

The Secret - 2016 - Based on a true story, this miniseries stars James Nesbitt (*Bloodlands*) as killer dentist Colin Howell, a man whose affair leads to deadly consequences.

Secret Daughter - *Australia* - 2016 to 2017 - When a wealthy man goes out looking for the daughter he never knew, a young singer pretends to be her.

The Shell Seekers - 2006 - Based on Rosamunde Pilcher's 1987 novel of the same name, this series tells the story of 60-something Penelope Keeling as she looks back on her life, her children, and a past love. She finds herself with the opportunity to sell a valuable painting done by her father, and the decision has her re-evaluating everything. This 2006 adaptation stars Vanessa Redgrave (*Call the Midwife*). **Premiered May 9th.**

Slings & Arrows - *Canada* - 2003 to 2006 - This Canadian dark comedy is set at a fictitious Shakespeare festival in Canada as they embark on a production of Hamlet. Paul Gross (*Due South*) stars as washed-up actor Geoffrey Tennant, along with Rachel McAdams (*Wedding Crashers, The Notebook*), Luke Kirby (*The Marvelous Ms. Maisel*), Stephen Ouimette (*Mentors*), and Mark McKinney (*Kids in the Hall, Superstore*), who is also the co-creator/co-writer.

The South Westerlies - *Ireland* - 2020 - In this Irish six-part comedy-drama, Orla Brady (*Mistresses*) plays Kate, an environmental consultant for a Norwegian energy firm. She's asked to go undercover among Irish protesters and help eliminate their objections to a wind farm near their small coastal town. Her task's difficulty is compounded by the arrival of a surfer who bears a strong resemblance to her son.

Straight Forward - *Denmark / New Zealand* - 2019 - After attempting to get revenge for her father's death, a Danish conwoman is forced to flee to New Zealand.

Striking Out - *Ireland* - This Acorn Original stars Amy Huberman (*Finding Joy*) as Tara Rafferty, a successful Dublin lawyer who abandons her safe life after discovering that her fiancé is cheating on her. She cancels the wedding, quits her job, and begins a new and unconventional private practice. Neil Morrissey (*Men Behaving Badly*) and Rory Keenan (*War & Peace*) also star.

The Syndicate: All or Nothing - 2013 - Each series of The Syndicate follows a different group of lottery winners as they grapple with personal dramas, newfound wealth, and temptation. Acorn has just one series, but there are two others (and another one recently announced).

Taken Down - *Ireland* - 2018 - When a Nigerian girl is killed in Dublin, Inspector Jen Rooney is drawn into a refugee community where some may know more than they're letting on.

Ten Percent - 2022 - Based on the hit French series, *Dix pour cent* (*Call My Agent* in the US), this UK adaptation follows a talent agency that's forever scrambling to keep their clients happy. **Premiered July 1st.**

Terry Pratchett's The Colour of Magic - 2009 - This series is based on the *Discworld* series of novels by Terry Pratchett, and features Sean Astin as tourist Twoflower alongside Sir David Jason as wizard Rincewind. When a fire breaks out during Twoflower's holiday, the two flee the city together, beginning an interesting magical journey.

Therese Raquin - 1980 - Based on the novel by Emile Zola, this miniseries tells a tale of passion, obsession, and desperate acts. When first published, the novel was described as "putrid" by the newspaper *Le Figaro*, and it's not recommended for young audiences.

The Time of Our Lives - *Australia* - 2013 to 2014 - This drama follows the lives of an extended family in inner-city Melbourne as they build families, pursue careers, and work on their relationships.

Trust - 2000 - Caroline Goodall (*Schindler's List*) stars as Anne, a successful young woman in what seems like a happy marriage. Unfortunately, there's something quite dark on the horizon.

Turning Green - *Ireland* - 2005 - When a teenage boy's mother dies, he's forced to live with his three Irish aunts. He wants nothing more than to return to America, and in pursuit of the funds to do so, he starts a business selling illegal magazines.

Under the Vines - *New Zealand* - 2021 - Australian TV star Rebecca Gibney (*Wanted*) stars as Sydney socialite Daisy Munroe, who heads to her recently deceased stepfather's winery with intent to sell. Before she can do that, she finds out there's a co-owner - a grumpy British lawyer who's come to New Zealand to escape unpleasant problems in his life. Together, they'll have to make the place successful so it can attract a good offer.

Vidago Palace - *Portugal* - 2017 - Set in 1936, this Portuguese romance is set at the Vidago Palace hotel where Europe's elite flee from the Spanish Civil War.

War & Peace - 2007 - Based on the Tolstoy novel, this series follows four aristocratic families during the Napoleonic era. Malcolm McDowell (*A Clockwork Orange*), Brenda Blethyn (*Vera*), Clemence Poesy (*The Tunnel*), and Ken Duken (*Inglourious Basterds*) are among the stars.

The Way Back - 2010 - A group of prisoners escape from a Siberian gulag and trek across four thousand miles to reach freedom in India. Ed Harris, Colin Farrell, and Saoirse Ronan are among the stars.

What to Do When Someone Dies - 2011 - Anna Friel (*Marcella*) plays schoolteacher Ellie Manning, a woman trying to have a baby with her husband Greg (Marc Warren, *Jonathan Strange & Mr. Norrell*). One night, he doesn't return home from work. Ellie is horrified to learn he has been killed in a terrible car accident, and he wasn't alone – there was a woman in the passenger seat. A tormented Ellie begins to question: who is the mystery woman and was Greg having a secret affair?

Wild at Heart - 2006 to 2013 - Stephen Tompkinson (*DCI Banks*, *Ballykissangel*) stars in this series about a British veterinarian who takes his family along to South Africa to release an animal back into the wild. When he sees the area and meets pretty game reserve owner Caroline (Hayley Mills), he ultimately decides to stay.

The Wipers Times - 2013 - Ben Chaplin, Julian Rhind-Tutt, Michael Palin, and Steve Oram star in this dramedy about the publication of a satirical newspaper during WWI. Based on a true story, the film celebrates the resilience of the human spirit in the face of adversity.

Wreckers - 2011 - Benedict Cumberbatch (*Sherlock*), Claire Foy (*The Crown*), and Shaun Evans (*Endeavour*) star in this film about a couple who move to an idyllic town to start a family, only to find new stress on their relationship when husband David's disturbed brother starts sharing old secrets.

Comedies

Ain't Misbehavin' - 1997 - Robson Green (*Grantchester*) and Jerome Flynn star as two bandsmen during 1940s London. Julia Sawalha (*Absolutely Fabulous, Press Gang*) stars as the lovely Dolly Nightingale, Green's character's love interest. *Downton Abbey*'s Jim Carter also appears.

Birds of a Feather - 2014 to 2020 - When two very different sisters see their husbands sent to prison, they move in together to support each other. It originally ran from 1989 through 1998, but the episodes on Acorn TV are from after the revival of the series in 2014.

Decline and Fall - 2017 - After a prank, an Oxford student is wrongly dismissed for indecent exposure, going to work at a sub-par private school in Wales. This series is an adaptation of Evelyn Waugh's novel of the same name.

Detectorists - 2014 to 2017 - Two quirky friends scan the fields of England with metal detectors, hoping for the big find that will finally let them do the gold dance.

Doc Martin - 2004 to present - Martin Clunes (*Men Behaving Badly*) stars in this comedy about a brilliant but grumpy London surgeon who suddenly develops a fear of blood. He leaves his high-flying career and takes a post in a Cornish fishing village where he spent holidays as a child with his Aunt Joan. His bad attitude and lack of social skills makes it a challenge to adapt to his new life. **Season 10 premieres October 17th, with 2 episodes weekly for a total of 8.**

Finding Joy - *Ireland* - 2018 to present - A young Irish woman named Joy struggles in the aftermath of a breakup, but not nearly as much as her dog (who becomes incontinent). At the same time, Joy is promoted to a position that takes her out of her comfort zone.

Golden Years - 2016 - This quirky film sees a couple of pensioners lose their hard-earned retirement funds in a financial crisis, only to turn to robbing banks to replenish the loss.

Henry IX - 2017 to present - King Henry has a mid-life crisis.

How to Murder Your Wife - 2015 - This dark comedy tells the true story of Alfred Benning, the mild-mannered animal welfare inspector who ended up becoming a famous murderer at the age of sixty-five. The unlikely murderer decided life is simply too short to live with a woman you can't stand – so the obvious solution is to hack her into bits.

It Takes a Worried Man - 1981 to 1983 - This retro, early 80s British comedy follows 35-year-old Philip Roath, a lazy, self-centered, and insecure man trying to come to terms with aging and a life that hasn't lived up to his lofty expectations. Constantly bothered by his overdraft, his boss (who wants him to work), his ex-wife (who wants to remind him how inadequate he is), and his analyst, actor and series writer Peter Tilbury manages to find humour in the mundane.

Kingdom - 2007 to 2009 - Stephen Fry (*QI*) stars as a country solicitor in the small town of Market Shipborough. Working with his trusty secretary Gloria and reasonably capable assistant Lyle, it should be a peaceful life. The only problem? He has a crazy sister and he recently lost his half-brother in mysterious circumstances. Hermione Norris (*Cold Feet*) and Celia Imrie (*Bergerac*) also star.

The Labours of Erica - 1989 to 1990 - *Vera* star Brenda Blethyn stars in this delightful retro comedy about a woman who has spent her whole life looking after everyone else. As her 40th birthday approaches, she revisits a list of all the things she wanted to accomplish by 40. In an instant, she gives up much of her current life in pursuit of something different and better.

Ladies of Letters - 2009 to 2010 - Two widows meet under a table at a wedding, then maintain a friendship via letters.

The Larkins - 2021 - This adaptation of H.E. Bates' novel, *The Darling Buds of May*, follows the adventures of the always-scheming Larkin family in the Kent countryside. Set in the 1950s, the series is a mix of village life and family adventures. Bradley Walsh (*Law & Order UK*), Joanna Scanlan (*No Offence*) and Sabrina Bartlett (*Bridgerton*) are among the stars.

Life Isn't All Ha Ha Hee Hee - 2005 - Based on Meera Syal's novel of the same name, this three-episode series tells the stories of three childhood friends who are now in their thirties. The women each find themselves at a crossroads, but their friendships help them through it all.

Love & Marriage - 2013 - Alison Steadman (*Gavin & Stacey*) stars in this series about a woman who's had enough of her own family and moves in with her unconventional sister.

The Man Who Lost His Head - 2007 - Martin Clunes stars in this film about a curator at the British Museum who gets in over his head while returning an ancient Maori carving to New Zealand.

Monday, Monday - 2009 - Fans of *Lucifer* and *Miranda* will love this quirky 2009 series about a woman, Sally (Morven Christie, *Grantchester*), who relocates with her company in hopes of a fresh start after a breakup. Fay Ripley (*Cold Feet*) plays Christine, her wildly incompetent boss, while Tom Ellis (*Miranda*) plays the role of Steven. He's the resident "charming fella", but their first meeting was less than ideal. He's also the boy-toy of the company's COO.

Mount Pleasant - 2011 to 2017 - This dramedy dives into the lives of a tight-knit Manchester family, focusing on their everyday struggles and hurdles. The cast includes Pauline Collins (*Upstairs Downstairs*), Sally Lindsay (*Coronation Street, Scott & Bailey*), and Daniel Ryan (*Black Sea*). Robson Green (*Grantchester*) also appears in a handful of episodes.

The Other One - 2017 to present - After a man drops dead at his birthday party, his family learns he has another, entirely separate family they didn't know about - just 13 miles away. What else can they do but decide to make the best of it? **Season 2 premiered July 18th.**

Parents - 2012 - A businesswoman finds out her husband has lost their life savings on the day she loses her job, and they have to go live with her parents.

The Rebel - 2016 to 2017 - A grumpy retired man rebels against everything, leaving his friends and family to clean up whatever messes he makes. Simon Callow stars in this Brighton-based comedy.

Reggie Perrin - 2009 to 2010 - Martin Clunes stars in this remake of the classic Reginald Perrin stories.

Sando - 2018 to present - *Australia* - Sando is the queen of package furniture deals in Australia.

The Simple Heist - *Sweden* - 2017 - When two older women find themselves cash-strapped and overlooked, they decide to turn to crime.

The Straits - *Australia* - 2012 - This darkly comedic series follows a family of smugglers operating in the Northern Straits. Brian Cox (*Succession*) stars as patriarch Harry, a man busy planning his succession while simultaneously dealing with family power struggles and the constant threat of attack by other gangs. **Premiered April 4th.**

Trivia - *Ireland* - 2011 to 2012 - A highly-dedicated quiz team leader in Ireland knows everything but how to deal with other people. **Premiered July 18th.**

Upper Middle Bogan - *Australia* - 2013 to 2016 - This Australian family comedy follows Bess Denyar, a wealthy doctor who learns she's adopted and actually comes from a family of suburban drag racers. As she explores her new family identity, she finds herself positioned as the "Upper Middle Bogan", a woman forever caught between two tribes. Though her snooty architect husband, private school-educated kids, and adoptive mother disagree, she's determined to unite the two sides of her life.

Very Small Business - 2008 - This series follows two unlikely business partners. One, Don Angel, is a small businessman with a pile of failures behind him. The other, Ray Leonard, is a former noted feature writer returning to the workforce after six years off battling depression. Working together is a series of small but amusing disasters.

Worst Week of My Life - 2004 to 2007 - Ben Miller (*Death in Paradise*) stars with Sarah Alexander (*Coupling*) as the world's most disastrously awkward fiancé and husband.

You, Me, & Them - 2013 to 2015 - Anthony Head and Eve Myles star in this sitcom about an age gap romance.

Documentary & Lifestyle

50 Shades of Green - 2019 - In celebration of Alan Titchmarsh's 70th birthday and 50 years as a gardener, this production visits some of the most spectacular gardens in the UK – including Blenheim Palace and Kew Gardens. Presenters like Mary Berry and Griff Rhys Jones join him on this ambitious tour of the country's flora. **Premiered on June 13th.**

A Berry Royal Christmas - 2019 - Mary Berry teams up with Will and Kate to celebrate the holidays and prepare a special meal for a group of people working and volunteering over Christmas.

Adrian Dunbar's Coastal Ireland - *Ireland* - 2021 - Actor Adrian Dunbar (*Line of Duty*) reconnects with his Irish roots, taking us on a scenic journey around the rugged north and west coasts of Ireland. Along the way, he'll share history, tradition, and some of his own thoughts about the breathtaking coastal landscapes.

A Stitch in Time – 2016 - Amber Butchart takes a look at historical figures through the clothing they wore.

A Tale of Two Sisters - 2018 - This docuseries takes a look at some of history's most iconic women and their relationships with their sisters.

A Taste of Italy - 2021 - Chef Nisha Katona takes us to some of the lesser-known regions of Italy to discover unique dishes that go beyond simple pizza and pasta. Along the way, we'll see plenty of stunning scenery and landscapes.

Alexandria: The Greatest City - 2016 - Historian Bettany Hughes explores the once-grand city of Alexandria, founded by Alexander the Great and home to Cleopatra.

Being Poirot - 2015 - Generally regarded as the best Poirot of all time, David Suchet held the iconic role for roughly a quarter of a century. In this three-part series, he attempts to share some of his experiences and explain why people have loved Poirot for so long.

The Big Bread Experiment - 2012 - This delightfully calm series follows a group of Yorkshire women who are learning to bake bread. And that's it. It's not a competition, nobody's voted out, and there are no attention-seeking celebrity types cracking jokes. It's full of ordinary people learning a skill, with plenty of laughs and mistakes along the way.

Bollywood: The World's Biggest Film Industry - 2018 - This two-part series examines the world's largest film industry, complete with access to stars and active productions.

Bone Detectives - 2007 to 2008 - This docuseries follows a group of women who piece together the stories of bodies found via archaeological discoveries. From battles to disease to tragic accidents, they piece together the untold stories of Britain's past.

Britain's Bloodiest Dynasty - 2014 - Historian Dan Jones tells the story of the Plantagenets, one of Britain's darkest and most brutal dynasties.

Britain's Bloody Crown - 2016 - Dan Jones presents this four-part documentary about the War of the Roses.

Caligula with Mary Beard - 2013 - Cambridge classicist Mary Beard takes a look at the life and times of the scandalous Roman emperor Caligula.

Cat Hospital - 2019 - This reality series takes a look at daily life in Ireland's first veterinary hospital dedicated exclusively to our feline friends. We follow cat expert Clare Meade and the rest of her team at Cork Cat Hospital as they help with everything from grooming and checkups to life or death emergencies.

The Churchills - 2012 - David Starkey looks at the links between Winston Churchill and his ancestor John Churchill, a man who dared to go up against Louis XIV of France.

Civil War - 2002 - Dr. Tristram Hunt takes a look at the conflict that briefly toppled the English monarchy back in the 17th century.

Digging for Britain - 2010 to 2016 - Professor Alice Roberts shares her passion for Britain's history as she takes us to a variety of exciting archaeological sites. From Roman burial sites to Viking treasures to history as recent as World War II, there's a bit of everything in this one.

Discovering Britain - 2018 - In this fun travel series, Maureen Lipman (*Metamorphosis*) and Larry Lamb (*Gavin &*

Stacey) join a number of their fellow British actors as they travel the country exploring its heritage.

Discovering Hamlet - 2016 - This documentary takes a look at Hamlet through the actors and directors who've helped bring the play to life for modern audiences. Filmed in Stratford-upon-Avon, London, Canada, and Italy, it features appearances by British TV favourites like Christopher Plummer, Sir Trevor Nunn, John Nettles, David Tennant, John Simm, and Franco Zeffirelli. **Premiered April 18th.**

Elizabeth I & Her Enemies - 2017 - Presenters Dan Jones (*Britain's Bloody Crown*) and Suzannah Lipscomb (*Hidden Killers*) take a look at those who wanted to bring down the much-respected Queen Elizabeth I.

England's Forgotten Tudor Queen: The Life & Death of Lady Jane Grey - 2018 - Lady Jane Grey ruled for just nine days, but they were important days. Though she was manipulated by powerful men in the palace and lost her life as a result, she was the first woman to sit on the English throne as reigning queen rather than consort. Historian Helen Castor guides us through this important part of Tudor history. **Premieres October 3rd.**

Farm Fixer - 2012 - This reality series sees The Apprentice's Nick Hewer returning to his Northern Irish roots to help struggling farmers improve their businesses. Though the farmers are desperately in need of help, many struggle with the idea of changing their old ways.

Genius of the Ancient World – 2015 - Historian Bettany Hughes travels the world to study the lives and times of great philosophers like Socrates, Confucius, and Buddha. **Premiered August 1st.**

Genius of the Modern World – 2016 - Historian Bettany Hughes looks at the world that helped shape intellectual greats like Friedrich Nietzsche, Sigmund Freud, and Karl Marx. **Premiered September 5th.**

Grand Tours of Scotland - 2010 to 2012 - Armed with a Victorian guidebook, historian Paul Murton sets out to explore his homeland. In the first season, he takes a look at some of the earliest Scottish tourist destinations to see how the rugged country has changed over the years. **Premiered May 2nd.**

Growing Up Gracefully - 2017 - Comedians Hannah and Eliza Reilly star in this humourous series about what it means to be a woman in the 21st century. The reality series follows the sisters as one follows a set of "the old rules" for women, while another follows the new.

Highwaymen, Pirates, & Rogues - 2015 - This three-part docuseries is hosted by Dr. Sam Willis, and it takes a look at some of the rogues and highwaymen of yesteryear - and why they continue to capture our imagination.

Inside the Bank of England - 2019 - In June 2016, the UK voted to leave the EU, sending massive shockwaves through the economy. This two-part series takes a look at the Bank of England's work to keep the country's finances in check during a period of unprecedented uncertainty. **Premiered August 29th.**

Inside the Ritz Hotel - 2019 - It's not often that the Ritz Hotel in London invites cameras behind the scenes, but that's exactly where we're going in this two-part docuseries. Featuring long-time employees like head hall porter Michael de Cozar and resident pianist Ian Gomes, we'll learn what it takes to maintain such high standards and continue to attract celebrities, royals, politicians, and the just plain wealthy. **Premiered August 15th.**

Joanna Lumley in the Land of the Northern Lights - 2008 - *Absolutely Fabulous* star Joanna Lumley takes us on a tour of the Arctic Circle in hopes of catching a glimpse of the Northern Lights.

The Life of Verdi - 1982 - This biographical miniseries tells the story of Giuseppe Verdi, composer of operas like Aida, Rigoletto, and La Traviata.

Martin Clunes: Islands of America - 2019 - Martin Clunes travels the islands of the US, stopping off in Hawaii, Alaska, Washington, California, Louisiana, Puerto Rico, Georgia, North Carolina, Virginia, New York, Massachusetts, and Maine.

Martin Clunes: Islands of Australia - 2016 - Martin Clunes explores some of the lesser-known islands off Australia's coast

Martin Clunes: Islands of the Pacific - 2022 - Martin Clunes returns for another set of tours – and this time, he's in the islands of the Pacific. He explores French Polynesia, Vanuatu, Galapagos, and more. **Premiered June 27th.**

Mary Berry: Love to Cook - 2021 - Over the course of six episodes, British national treasure Mary Berry introduces us to some of the country's most passionate producers of food. Along the way, we'll get to see plenty of her own favourite dishes, too. **Premieres September 26th.**

Mary Berry's Country House Secrets - 2017 - In this four-part series, Mary Berry gets behind-the-scenes access to some of the UK's most spectacular country houses. She ventures beyond the tourist areas to show us the families that occupy the homes and how they live today.

Monty Don's Adriatic Gardens - 2021 - This two-part series sees British gardening expert Monty Don visiting Europe and exploring gardens along the Adriatic coast. His journey begins Venice and continues on through Croatia and Greece. **Premiered July 11th.**

Monty Don's Japanese Gardens - 2018 - Over the course of two episodes, British gardening expert Monty Don explores how Japanese culture and climates have shaped some of the best gardens scattered across their islands. **Premiered July 11th.**

Monty Don's Paradise Gardens - 2018 - Gardening expert Monty Don takes us to the Middle East and beyond in search of some of the world's finest "paradise" gardens.

Murder Maps - 2015 to present - Host Nicholas Day guides us through a number of shocking murder cases, focusing on the clever police work and early forensics that brought killers to justice.

Muse of Fire: A Shakespearean Road Movie - 2013 - This documentary follows a couple of actors who once shied away from Shakespeare – until they became actors. Over four years, they journey around the world trying to get at what makes Shakespeare's work so great. The film includes appearances by Dame Judi Dench, Sir Ian McKellan, Ewan McGregor, Ralph Fiennes, and Jude Law.

My Welsh Sheepdog - 2016 - BBC presenter Kate Humble travels around Wales with her dog Teg to learn more about the rare Welsh sheepdog breed.

Off the Beaten Track - 2018 - BBC presenter Kate Humble is back with her Welsh sheepdog Teg, this time travelling through some of the wildest bits of Wales.

Only Foals & Horses - 2019 - This series follows horse vets Lisa Durham and Philippa Hughes as they care for their four-legged clients in Wales.

Penelope Keith's Hidden Coastal Villages - 2018 - Penelope Keith (*The Good Life*) travels the UK, visiting some of the most beautiful coastal villages.

Poirot: Super Sleuths - 2006 - David Suchet takes us behind the scenes to look at the enduring appeal of Hercule Poirot. The programme features interviews with cast, crew, and a variety of Agatha Christie experts.

Pride & Prejudice: Having a Ball - 2013 - This BBC documentary was created to celebrate the 200th anniversary of Jane Austen's most popular novel. To reveal the hidden world behind the story, hosts Amanda Vickery and Alistair Sooke lead a team of experts in reconstructing a Regency-era ball at Chawton House, the grand estate of Jane Austen's brother.

Prince Charles: Inside the Duchy of Cornwall - 2019 - Back in 1337, the Duchy of Cornwall was established to provide income for heirs to the throne – and roughly 700 years later, it continues to do just that. The land and people associated with the Duchy of Cornwall currently generate more than £21 million in yearly income for the man lucky enough to have inherited it. This two-episode series offers exclusive access to Prince Charles, William, and Camilla to offer insight into this royal money machine.

The Real Manhunter - 2021 - DCI Colin Sutton is a real-life hero who devoted thirty years of his life to keeping England safe. Though he's best known for the arrests and convictions of Levi Bellfield and Delroy Grant, Sutton left behind an impressive record of closing cases. Of the 37 homicide cases he and his teams worked, 35 were solved with convictions. This series allows Sutton to tell us about his career in his own words – talking through the cases, revisiting key locations, and sharing insight about those wonderful breakthrough moments that helped victims get justice.

The Real Prince Philip - 2019 - This documentary celebrates the life of Prince Philip, from his early years in Greece to his many years of service to the UK.

Rome: Empire Without Limit - 2016 - Historian Mary Beard takes a look at how a small city like Rome was able to capture an empire - and why it ultimately fell.

Saving Britain's Worst Zoo - 2019 - When the Tweedy family bought a zoo in West Wales, they never could have imagined the troubles that would follow. With no experience and more than 300 exotic animals to care for, the situation quickly evolved into lawsuits, threats, and massive debts. This series tells the real, behind-the-scenes story.

The Savoy - 2020 - This five-part docuseries takes a look at the history and present reality of Britain's first true luxury hotel. Filmed during the coronavirus shutdown, it gives us a look at what it's like to stay there and what goes on behind the scenes to make it all happen. **Premiered June 20th.**

Scotch! The Story of Whisky – 2015 - This short series takes a look at the history and science of the Scottish whisky industry.

The Secret History of the British Garden - 2015 - Gardening expert Monty Don takes a look at the stories behind four of Britain's most famous gardens, digging deep for the details that tell us how British gardens have changed in the last 400 years.

The Secret Story of Stuff: Materials of the Modern Age - 2018 - Material scientist Zoe Laughlin explains the science behind new materials that will change the way we live. From homes of the future to digital storage made from sand, exciting new materials will pave the way for more efficient, effective, and eco-friendly changes. **Premiered September 19th.**

Shakespeare: The Legacy - 2016 - Host John Nettles presents this hour-long special celebrating the 400th anniversary of Shakespeare's death (April 23rd, 2016). Long considered a man of mystery, the documentary aims to help unlock some of the secrets about Shakespeare's life. **Premiered April 18th.**

The Shelter: Animal SOS - *Ireland* - 2021 - This Irish reality series offers a look at what goes on in the country's oldest and largest animal welfare organisation, the Dublin Society for the Prevention of Cruelty to Animals (DSPCA). Filmed over the course of a year at their 32-acre facility in the Dublin Mountains, it sees them working hard to help everything from cats and dogs to birds and ponies.

She-Wolves: England's Early Queens - 2012 - Presenter Helen Castor explores the lives of seven of England's early queens and how they managed to challenge male power and rule in a time where women had comparatively few rights.

Shock & Awe: The Story of Electricity - 2011 - Professor Jim Al-Khalili teaches us about man's attempts to master and harness nature's most mysterious force. For years, electricity was viewed as a magical power – but today, it's an essential resource that fuels nearly everything we do.

Stealing Van Gogh - 2018 - On December 7th, 2002, two thieves broke into Amsterdam's Van Gogh Museum, stole two paintings, and disappeared into the night. In this true crime documentary, Andrew Graham-Dixon will take a closer look at the theft, the eventual recovery, and how the crime fits into the wider world of art crimes. **Premiered July 25th.**

Swallowed by the Sea: Ancient Egypt's Greatest Lost City - 2014 - Ancient writings tell of a prosperous Egyptian city called Heracleion, but after a point in time, it no longer exists within written records and seems to have vanished from the face of the earth. In 2000, the city's remains were finally discovered – under 10 meters of water off the coast of Egypt. This documentary follows a team of maritime archaeologists as they explore the site. **Premiered September 12th.**

Tales of Irish Castles - 2014 - Actor Simon Delaney hosts this six-part series about the stories and legends associated with some of Ireland's most majestic and interesting castles. Visiting Dublin, Blarney, Limerick, Trim, Carrickfergus, Kilkenny, Birr, and more, this series takes us on a journey around the island where more castles were built than in the rest of the British Isles combined.

VE Day: Minute by Minute - 2020 - Tony Robinson (*Blackadder*) narrates this special commemorating the 75th anniversary of VE Day, guiding us through the events of May 8, 1945. The special also features historians Sam Willis and James Holland.

Victorian Farm - 2008 to 2009 - This BBC Two observational series sees historian Ruth Goodman and archaeologists Alex Langlands and Peter Ginn immersing themselves in the lifestyle of a Victorian farmer. They spend a full calendar year living on the Acton Scott Estate in Shropshire, working the land with antique tools and machinery.

Victoria Wood's A Nice Cup of Tea - 2013 - Comedian Victoria Wood travels the globe to investigate Britain's love of tea.

Wainwright Walks - 2007 - Julia Bradbury stars in this outdoor series following some of guidebook author Alfred Wainwright's best walks.

Wainwright Walks: Coast to Coast - 2009 - This continuation of Julia Bradbury's *Wainwright Walks* series follows her from the Pennines to the North York Moors and over to the breathtaking coastal town of Robin Hood's Bay. This particular walk was Wainwright's last big adventure, and it links three national parks between the Irish Sea and the North Sea.

Walking Through History - 2013 to 2014 - Actor Tony Robinson (*Blackadder*) takes us on a variety of historic walks through the beautiful British countryside. In Season 1, we're treated to walks through the Weald in Kent and East Sussex to discover its rich Tudor heritage, hikes into the dramatic Kintail region of the west Scotland Highland, a 40-mile walk through the glorious Peak District, and a visit to the site of the world's first factory which would lay the foundations for today's skyscrapers. **Season 3 premiered April 4th.**

Walking Tudor England - 2021 - Professor Suzannah Lipscomb sets out to explore the legacy of the Tudor kings and queens, looking at how they shaped Britain's identity more significantly than any before them. She examines how they influenced the formation of the Royal Navy and tore down the monasteries – but also how they reigned over a time full of betrayal, religious persecution, and an abnormally large number of beheadings. **Premiered July 18th.**

Wartime Farm - 2012 - Made by the producers of *Edwardian Farm* and *Victorian Farm*, this series sees Alex Langlands, Peter Ginn, and Ruth Goodman taking on the challenge of running a farm for an entire year – using only those tools and resources that would have been available during WWII.

The Wine Show - 2016 to present - Matthew Goode (*A Discovery of Witches*) and Matthew Rhys (*Perry Mason*) star in this series about some of the world's best, most exotic, and most interesting wines. Travelling the world and chatting with prestigious chefs and experts, they offer an educational but also accessible take on the popular beverage.

The Yorkshire Vet - 2015 to present - This engaging series follows the staff of Skeldale Veterinary Centre as they work with the animals.

Coming Soon to Acorn TV

These Acorn TV Originals haven't been assigned official release dates yet, but they're all coming in the not-too-distant future. Dates below were provided by **Acorn TV** (thanks, Eddie!) and all are subject to change.

Cannes Confidential - 2022 - This France-based mystery focuses on the relationship between an underdog female cop and an ex-conman who's on the run from both the mob and the police. It's a classic odd-couple investigative series with a broader arc focusing on the main character's quest to find out who framed her father for murder.

Mrs. Sidhu Investigates - 2023 - Based on the BBC Radio 4 series of the same name, this mystery stars Meera Kyal (*Yesterday*) as a recently-widowed, crime-solving Indian caterer in Berkshire. Craig Parkinson (*Line of Duty*) plays DCI Burton, a world-weary detective she often assists.

BRITBOX

Website: http://britbox.com

Description: A joint venture between the BBC and ITV, this service focuses exclusively on British programming - including soaps, quiz shows, panel shows, and live events.

Available On: Roku, Fire TV, Apple TV, Apple iPhone & iPad, Chromecast, Android phones and tablets, and computer (via web browser). You can also subscribe via Amazon Prime Video.

Cost: $7.99/month, $79.99/year

Now Streaming
Mysteries & Crime Dramas

15 Days - 2019 - This crime thriller is a mystery told in reverse. It immediately flashes back to 15 days prior to the crime, allowing viewers to watch a family crisis as it festers and develops into something truly terrible. The series is a re-make of the Welsh series *35 Diwrnod*, and even includes some of the same actors.

35 Days - 2014 to 2019 - Each season of this Welsh mystery begins with a murder, then rolls the clock back 35 days to follow the events that led to the murderous conclusion.

A Confession - 2019 - Martin Freeman (*Sherlock*), Siobhan Finneran (*Downton Abbey*), and Imelda Staunton (*Cranford*) star in this drama based on a real-life tragedy. The series dramatises the search for Sian O'Callaghan, a young woman who went missing in Swindon after a taxi ride.

A Touch of Frost - 1992 to 2010 - Rumpled and slovenly DI Jack Frost follows his instincts to find justice for the underdogs. The gritty series is set in the fictional South Midlands town of Denton, and Sir David Jason (*Only Fools and Horses*) stars.

Agatha Christie's Evil Under the Sun - 1982 - On the trail of a millionaire's fake diamond, Poirot finds himself at a resort full of rich and famous people – and a murderer. This film was Peter Ustinov's first outing as the Belgian detective, and you'll also see Dames Maggie Smith and Diana Rigg looking quite a bit younger.

Agatha Christie's Marple - 2004 to 2013 - Geraldine McEwan portrays the iconic sleuth in the first three seasons, with Julia McKenzie taking over after that.

Agatha Christie's Partners in Crime - 1983 to 1984 - Francesca Annis (*Bancroft*) and James Warwick (*Iron Man*) star as the famous crime-fighting duo, Tommy and Tuppence Beresford, as they solve mysteries and search for enemy spies in 1950's Britain. Our two sleuths, Tommy and Tuppence, are now married and well-established as secret agents working under the watchful eye of Scotland Yard.

Agatha Christie's Poirot - 1989 to 2020 - David Suchet portrays the eccentric Belgian Detective Poirot in this long-running series of Agatha Christie mysteries. **Seasons 7 and 8 premiere on July 19th.**

Agatha Christie's Seven Dials Mystery - 1981 - Cheryl Campbell (*Breathless*) stars as Lady Eileen "Bundle" Brent, a young and glamorous aristocrat who insinuates herself into all sorts of unsavoury situations...including murder.

Agatha Christie's Sparkling Cyanide - 2003 - Pauline Collins (*Dickensian*) and Oliver Ford Davies (*A Royal Scandal*) star in this modern-day adaptation of Agatha Christie's classic. It sees an elderly husband and wife working as secret agents brought in to investigate the murder of a football club manager's trophy wife. As more secrets come to light, it becomes a race against time to find the killer before there's another victim.

Agatha Christie's The Mirror Crack'd - 1980 - This star-studded movie features Angela Lansbury (*Murder, She Wrote*) as Miss Marple, investigating a murder that occurs while a movie films in her village (as if we needed more evidence that murders follow Angela Lansbury). The supporting cast includes Rock Hudson, Tony Curtis, Kim Novak, and Elizabeth Taylor.

Agatha Christie's The Murder of Roger Ackroyd (Radio Play) - 1939 - Orson Welles directs and plays Hercule Poirot in this radio dramatisation of the classic Agatha Christie story. When a woman is found dead of an overdose, a rumour links her to Roger Ackroyd, who is then also found dead. Hercule Poirot is left to unravel the mystery.

Agatha Christie's The Secret Adversary - 1983 - In this Tommy and Tuppence mystery, James Warwick (*Agatha Christie's Partners in Crime*) and Francesca Annis (also in *Agatha Christie's Partners in Crime*) star as two friends who decide to become investigators to get a bit of extra money. What seems like a simple idea quickly becomes quite dangerous. This production immediately preceded the related television series.

Agatha Christie's Why Didn't They Ask Evans? - 1981 - When Agatha Christie was alive, she allowed very few television adaptations of her work because she didn't care for the medium. After her death, daughter Rosalind Hicks relaxed the restrictions - and this was the first major production to move forward as a result. While golfing on the coast of Wales, Bobby Jones hits a stranger whose puzzling last words are, "Why didn't they ask Evans?"

Agatha Christie's Why Didn't They Ask Evans? - 2022 - This three-part adaptation is based on Agatha Christie's 1934 novel of the same name. Directed and adapted by Hugh Laurie (*House*), it follows the amiable Bobby Jones (Will Poulter, *Dopesick*) after he discovers a dying man on a golf course. The man uses his final breath to utter, "Why didn't they ask Evans?" – sending Jones and his friend Lady Frances "Frankie" Derwent (Lucy Boynton, *The Politician*) on a crime-solving adventure. **Premiered April 12th.**

An Inspector Calls - 2015 - Set in 1912, this mystery follows Inspector Goole as he investigates the wealthy Birling family in connection with the suicide of a young woman. Each family member has their own set of dark and intriguing secrets.

Bancroft - 2017 to present - DS Elizabeth Bancroft is a brilliant officer, but the questionable tactics she employed in the past are coming back to haunt her.

The Barking Murders - 2022 - Between June 2014 and September 2015, serial killer Stephen Port drugged, raped, and murdered four innocent gay men in his Barking flat. This three-part series by Jeff Pope (*Isolation Stories*) and Neil McKay (*The Moorside*) focuses on the victims' loved ones and the determined investigators who fought to bring the killer to justice. Stephen Merchant (*The Office, The Outlaws*) stars as Stephen Port, while Sheridan Smith (*Gavin & Stacey, Cilla*) is Sarah Sak, mother to one of the victims. **Premiered June 7th.**

The Bay - 2019 to present - Morven Christie (*Grantchester*) plays DS Lisa Armstrong, a family liaison officer who discovers she has a personal connection to a missing persons case.

Bergerac - 1981 to 1991 - John Nettles stars in this classic series about an alcoholic detective in Jersey with his own way of doing things.

Best in Paradise - 2020 - In this exclusive BritBox interview, cast members Kris Marshall (*Sanditon, Love Actually*), Josephine Jobert, Don Warrington (*Holby City*), and Tobi Bakare (*Kingsman, Silent Witness*) share anecdotes and insights about their favourite episodes of *Death in Paradise*.

The Bill - 1984 to 2010 - This long-running police series follows the lives of officers at the fictional Sun Hill Police station.

The Blake Mysteries: Ghost Stories - 2018 - After her husband Lucien's disappearance, Jean Blake (formerly

Beazley) struggles to adapt to life without him. She doesn't get much time to breathe, though, as she's pulled into a murder investigation just eight months after his disappearance.

The Bletchley Circle: San Francisco - 2018 to 2019 - This Bletchley Circle spin-off picks up in 1956 when former colleagues Millie and Jean learn of a set of murders in San Francisco that mimic a murder they saw during the war. They reach out to an American codebreaker they knew during the war, and before too long, they're all solving murders together in the Bay Area.

Blue Murder - 2003 to 2009 - DCI Janine Lewis struggles with the challenge of being a single mom to four kids while leading a team of detectives through homicide investigations. Caroline Quentin (*Jonathan Creek*) stars.

The Body Farm - 2011 to 2012 - This spin-off of *Waking the Dead* follows a team of forensic scientists who've left academia to work in the world of criminal forensics. They team up with a London cold case unit to do research on how people are killed and how criminals try to cover it up.

Boon - 1986 to 1992 - After suffering permanent lung damage rescuing a child from a fire, a fireman retires and begins a new life of odd jobs and later, detective work.

Cadfael - 1994 to 1998 - In 12th century Shrewsbury, a monk solves mysteries. Derek Jacobi (*Last Tango in Halifax*) stars.

Campion - 1989 to 1990 - An aristocrat in the 1930s adopts a fake name and investigates mysteries with help from his servant. Peter Davison (*Doctor Who*) stars as Albert Campion, with Brian Glover (*Rumble*) as his manservant. The series was based on the Albert Campion mystery novels written by Margery Allingham.

The City & The City - 2018 - Inspector Borlú investigates a murder in the twin city, which occupies the same space differently. This unusual series blends mystery with science fiction.

Cold Blood - 2005 to 2008 - A notorious murderer is finally placed in prison, but they can't find his last victim. Now, he's playing a ruthless game with the detective who wants what he knows.

The Coroner - 2015 to 2016 - A solicitor returns to her coastal hometown, becomes coroner, and investigates suspicious deaths.

Cracker - 1993 to 2006 - Though he's obnoxious and anti-social, Fitz is a brilliant criminal psychologist and police consultant.

Crime - 2021 - Dougray Scott (*My Week with Marilyn*) stars as DI Ray Lennox, a man who must put aside his own personal demons to investigate the disappearance of a local schoolgirl. The Edinburgh-based series is based on Irvine Welsh's bestselling novel of the same name.

Dalziel & Pascoe - 1996 to 2007 - Two Yorkshire-based police partners with very different personalities find a way to bond as they solve crimes. This series was based on the Dalziel and Pascoe novels by Reginald Hill, and stars Warren Clarke (*Poldark*) and Colin Buchanan (*The Pale Horse*) in the title roles.

Dark Heart - 2018 - DI Wagstaffe leads an investigation into a series of attacks on accused pedophiles.

DCI Banks – 2010 to 2016 - Stephen Tomkinson (*Ballykissangel, Wild at Heart*) stars as DCI Alan Banks, a skilled but stubborn Yorkshire-based investigator.

Death in Paradise - 2011 to present - A British inspector who's fundamentally incompatible with island life is sent to investigate murders on a tropical island. This long-running series began with Ben Miller (*The Worst Week of My Life*) in the lead role, but the torch was later passed to Kris Marshall (*Love Actually*), Ardal O'Hanlon (*Father Ted*), and Ralf Little (*The Cafe*). **Season 11 premiered May 3rd.**

Death on the Tyne - 2018 - When there's a a serial killer loose on an overnight ferry, a tour hostess and her coach driver must find the killer before the sabotaged ship sinks.

Dial M for Middlesbrough - 2019 - Johnny Vegas (*Benidorm*) and Sian Gibson (*Car Share*) star in this Agatha Christie-inspired whodunnit in which the two must solve a murder after their coach breaks down.

The Doctor Blake Mysteries - 2013 to 2018 - Dr. Lucien Blake left his Australian home in Ballarat as a young man. Now, he finds himself returning to take over not only his dead father's medical practice, but also his on-call role as the town's police surgeon.

Eleventh Hour - 2006 - Sir Patrick Stewart (Star Trek) stars as Professor Ian Hood, a special advisor to the Home Office on threats related to scientific advancements. As he guards against things like deadly cloned viruses, a special branch bodyguard (played by Ashley Jensen of *Agatha Raisin* fame) keeps him safe from those who wish to do him harm. **Premiered July 26th.**

The Fall - 2013 to 2016 - Gillian Anderson (*The X-Files*) and Jamie Dornan (*50 Shades of Grey*) star in this series about a senior investigator who goes head-to-head with a serial killer who's attacking young professional women in Belfast.

Father Brown (Classic) - 1974 - A Catholic priest dips his toe into mysteries in spite of the police warning him off. Kenneth More (*The Forsyte Saga*) stars as Father Brown in this early adaptation of G.K. Chesterson's *Father Brown* stories.

Father Brown - 2013 to present - Based on the mysteries of GK Chesterson, a Catholic priest solves mysteries in his small English village. Mark Williams (*Blandings*) stars as Father Brown in this long-running adaptation.

The Frankenstein Chronicles - 2015 to 2017 - Inspector John Marlott (Sean Bean, Time) makes a horrific discovery, finding a corpse that's actually made up of parts from eight different missing children. The series follows along as he attempts to hunt down the serial killer responsible for the depraved crime. **Premieres October 28th.**

From Darkness - 2015 - In Greater Manchester, Officer Claire is disturbed by four bodies that seem linked to her past cases.

The Gil Mayo Mysteries (aka Mayo) - 2006 - Gil Mayo is an eccentric detective with a life full of complications and awkwardness. His ex-love interest is a colleague, and he's raising a teenage girl on his own. Alistair McGowan (*Leonardo*) stars in this light mystery.

Good Cop - 2012 - When his best friend is killed on duty, a good cop wants revenge. Warren Brown (*Luther*) stars as John Paul Rocksavage.

Grace - 2021 to present - *Endeavour* creator Russell Lewis is behind this new ITV drama starring John Simm (*Life on Mars*). He'll play detective Roy Grace (from Peter James' award-winning novels), a man who fights crime in the coastal city of Brighton, England. Grace is a talented but unorthodox detective who's haunted by the disappearance of his beloved wife Sandy. The series will begin with two feature-length episodes based on the first two stories in the Roy Grace series: *Dead Simple* and *Looking Good Dead*. **Series 2 premiered June 21st.**

Hetty Wainthropp Investigates - 1996 to 1998 - A tough old pensioner becomes a private detective and investigates crimes with the help of her husband and a teenage boy called Geoffrey. Dame Patricia Routledge (*Keeping Up Appearances*) stars in this cozy mystery.

Hound of the Baskervilles - 1982 - Tom Baker steps into the world of Sherlock Holmes in this faithful adaptation of the classic Sherlock Holmes story.

The Ice House - 1997 - The peaceful lives of three women are shattered when a corpse is discovered in the ice house on their property. Daniel Craig (*James Bond* series) stars.

In Plain Sight - 2016 - This series covers serial killer Peter Manuel's crimes in 1950s Lanarkshire, Scotland. Though it's a dramatisation, it's based on a true story.

In the Dark - 2017 - While dealing with an unexpected pregnancy, DI Weeks returns to her hometown to help a childhood friend after an abduction.

The Inspector Lynley Mysteries - 2001 to 2007 - An Oxford-educated detective pairs up with a working-class partner to investigate mysteries.

Inspector Morse - 1987 to 2000 - Grumpy, classical music-loving Inspector Morse investigates crimes around Oxford with his junior partner Sergeant Lewis. This much-loved British mystery series is based on the books of Colin Dexter, and it later spawned two additional television shows (*Inspector Lewis* and *Endeavour*).

Jonathan Creek - 1997 to 2016 - After meeting a pushy investigative journalist, an eccentric magic trick developer finds himself investigating murders.

Karen Pirie - 2022 - Lauren Lyle (*Outlander*) stars in this adaptation of Scottish author Val McDermid's *Karen Pirie* series. The first series begins when teenager Rosie Duff (*Anna Russell-Martin, Casualty*) was found brutally murdered in the Scottish university town of St Andrews back in 1996, it was assumed to be the work of three drunken students who claimed to have found her body. With minimal evidence, however, no charges were brought and the case stalled. 25 years later, a cold case review coincides with a new set of murders – this time, someone's targeting the students who found the body all those years earlier. **Premieres October 25th.**

The Lady Vanishes - 2013 - Based on the 1936 Ethel Lina White novel *The Wheel Spins*, this film follows a young English socialite on a train trip back to England from Croatia. When an English governess disappears, she enlists the aid of fellow passengers Max Hare and his former Oxford professor.

The Last Detective - 2003 to 2007 - Because he's decent, old fashioned and a generally good guy, his fellow detectives and his boss don't like him much. Still, DC Davies proves that his style works by constantly solving the cases no one else wants.

Life of Crime - 2013 - Hayley Atwell (*Agent Carter*) stars as Denise Woods, a bright WPC attempting to solve the murders of three possibly connected victims across three decades. Each episode of the series is filmed in a different decade, and she has a different rank in each.

Life on Mars - 2006 to 2007 - DCI Sam Tyler has a car accident in 2006 and wakes up in the 70s. John Simm (*White Dragon*) stars alongside Philip Glenister (*Living the Dream*) in this much-loved series.

Line of Duty - 2012 to present - This series focuses on a group of officers in the ACU (Anti-Corruption Unit), a team that investigates the wrongdoings of its fellow officers. **BritBox is missing season 5, but you can find it on Acorn TV.**

The Long Call - 2021 - Based on the new books by Ann Cleeves, this series follows Detective Matthew Venn, a troubled gay detective who's recently returned to live in North Devon with his husband Jonathan. Unlike the more brash, confident detectives, Venn is a man scarred by religious extremism, with hefty doses of anger and self-doubt.

Maigret - 1992 to 1993 - Michael Gambon stars as Georges Simenon's iconic French detective in this early-90s adaptation. Each of the 12 episodes is based on a single Maigret novel.

Maigret - 2016 to 2017 - Rowan Atkinson takes on a rare serious role as he fills the role of Maigret in this two series, four episode adaptation. Each of the four episodes are based on a single novel (*Maigret Sets a Trap, Maigret's Dead Man, Maigret at the Crossroads,* and *Inspector Maigret and the Strangled Stripper*).

The Mallorca Files - 2019 - This drama stars Elen Rhys (*Ordinary Lies*) and Julian Looman as a pair of international detectives who solve crimes on the Baleric island of Mallorca. It's a light, action-driven drama with a bit of British and German culture clash between the detectives.

McDonald & Dodds - 2020 - BAFTA-winner Jason Watkins (*The Crown, Trollied*) stars alongside newcomer Tala Gouveia in this fun detective drama that's not quite cozy, but still far from gritty. The series is set in Bath, England and it follows an incredibly mismatched but competent pair as they learn to work together to solve difficult cases. **Season 3 premiered August 16th.**

MI-5 (aka Spooks) - 2002 to 2011 - This dramatic series follows top secret missions of the MI-5, the UK's elite domestic security and counter-intelligence agency. Matthew Macfadyen (*Pride & Prejudice*), Keeley Hawes (*Bodyguard*), Hermione Norris (*Cold Feet*), and Richard Armitage (*North & South*) are among the stars.

Midsomer Murders - 1998 to present - In Midsomer County, the landscapes are beautiful, the villagers all have secrets, and murder is rampant. This British mystery classic features John Nettles as DCI Tom Barnaby through the first 13 seasons, with Neil Dudgeon as DCI John Barnaby for the later seasons. **BritBox only has Series 21.**

Midsomer Murders: 20th Anniversary Documentary - 2019 - John Nettles presents this look back at Midsomer Murders on its 20th anniversary. The hour-long special features appearances by Neil Dudgeon, Nick Hendrix, Daniel Casey, Jason Hughes, Jane Wymark, and more.

Midsomer Murders Favourites - 1998 to 2018 - This collection rounds up the favourite episodes of several Midsomer Murders cast members - Neil Dudgeon, John Nettles, Annette Badland, and Nick Hendrix. Each episode includes commentary from the actor in question.

Miss Marple - 1984 to 1992 - In the small village of St. Mary Mead, Miss Marple helps her community by solving murders. In this collection of Christie tales, Joan Hickson takes the title role.

The Moonstone (1972) - In this Hugh Leonard adaptation, a man goes on a quest to find a stolen but cursed stone that's said to bring ill fortune to all who possess it. This series is based on the Wilkie Collins novel of the same name.

The Moonstone (2016) - This updated adaptation of the Wilkie Collins novel stars Joshua Silver as Franklin Blake alongside Terenia Edwards (*On Chesil Beach*) as Rachel Verinder.

The Mrs. Bradley Mysteries - 1998 - Diana Rigg (*The Avengers*) stars as Mrs. Bradley, a sort of edgy Miss Marple who solves mysteries with the assistance of her devoted chauffeur George Moody (Neil Dudgeon, *Midsomer Murders*).

Murder in Provence - 2022 - Roger Allam (*Endeavour, The Thick of It*), Nancy Carroll (*The Crown, Father Brown*) and Keala Settle (*The Greatest Showman*) star in this upcoming adaptation of M.L. Longworth's *A Provençal Mystery* novels. The series follows Antoine Verlaque (Allam), an investigating judge in Aix-en Provence, and his romantic partner Marine Bonnet (Carroll) as they investigate and solve murders and mysteries in their idyllic homeland.

Murder in Suburbia - 2004 to 2005 - Caroline Catz (*Doc Martin*) and Lisa Faulkner (*Spooks*) star in this playful crime drama about two women with a knack for uncovering the truth about challenging homicide cases in suburban Middleford. Catz plays the diligent and meticulous DI Kate Ashurst, while Faulkner plays the street smart and chaotic DS Emma Scribbins. **Premiered July 5th.**

Murder on the Blackpool Express - 2017 - When a coach driver and tour guide see their passengers start dying off, they realise there's a killer in their midst.

Murder, They Hope - 2022 - After a number of murder-plagued outings, tour guides Gemma and Terry decide to give up coach tours and become private investigators. They bring few skills or qualifications to the work, but plenty of heart. This is the follow-up to *Murder on the Blackpool Express, Death on the Tyne*, and *Dial M for Middlesbrough*.

The Museum (aka Yr Amgueddfa) - 2021 - This Welsh thriller follows Della Howells (Nia Roberts, *The Crown*), a married historian who's finally secured the top position at the Museum of Wales. Unfortunately, her charmed life begins a downward spiral when she has an affair with a mysterious young stranger. Before too long, she finds herself close to Cardiff's criminal underworld.

New Blood - 2016 - Two young investigators are brought together by cases that initially appear unrelated.

New Tricks - 2003 to 2015 - This long-running series stars Amanda Redman as a disgraced detective chosen to head up a group of retired detectives recruited to investigate unsolved cases. Along with the challenges of tracking down old evidence and witnesses, they'll also have to come to terms with the fact that the "old ways" aren't always welcome in modern policing.

The Pembrokeshire Murders - 2021 - The true crime cold case drama follows the investigation into the most notorious serial killer in Welsh history. In 2006, newly-promoted DS Steve Wilkins decided to re-open an unsolved double murder from the 1980s. Using the latest forensic techniques, he and his team were able to connect the murders to a string of burglaries.

Prime Suspect - 1991 to 2006 - Helen Mirren stars as Detective Jane Tennison, battling crime as well as sexism on the job.

Quirke - 2014 - Gabe Byrne plays a pathologist in 1950s Dublin.

Rebus - 2000 to 2004 - Based on the novels of Scottish author Ian Rankin, Inspector Rebus is an old-fashioned detective in every sense of the word. He smokes, drinks, and doesn't have a lot of luck with his personal life.

Redemption - 2022 - This series DI Colette Cunningham (Paul Malcomson, *The Hunger Games*), a talented, plain-speaking Liverpool detective whose life changes when she gets an unexpected call from Dublin. A body has been found, and Colette is listed as the next of kin. She immediately heads to Ireland to identify her daughter Kate - a young woman who's been missing for 20 years. Sad and puzzled, Colette joins the Garda to stay in Ireland and unravel the mystery of her daughter's life and death. **Premiered June 14th.**

The Responder - 2022 - Martin Freeman (*Sherlock*) stars in this gritty drama about an officer on the front lines of the night shift in Liverpool. Inspired by the real-life experiences of former officer and writer Tony Schumacher, it offers a rarely seen glimpse inside the ways police battle crime, violence, and addiction on the streets of one of England's northern cities. **Premiered May 24th.**

Reyka - 2021 - Kim Engelbrecht (*Dominion*) and Iain Glen (*Jack Taylor*) star in this South African thriller about a criminal profiler who investigates serial killers while dealing with the impact of her own traumatic past.

River - 2015 - Stellan Skarsgård, Nicola Walker, and Lesley Manville star in this series about a brilliant police officer haunted by guilt.

Rosemary & Thyme - 2003 to 2008 - Former policewoman Laura and a horticulture professor Rosemary are brought together by a love of gardening, but murder seems to follow them. Felicity Kendal (*The Good Life*) and Pam Ferris (*Call the Midwife*) star in this quaint series.

The Ruth Rendell Mysteries: Next Chapters (aka Ruth Rendell Mysteries) - 1994 to 2000 - This collection includes a variety of suspenseful tales adapted from the novels of author Ruth Rendell.

Sally Lockhart Mysteries - 2006 to 2007 - Two of the four Sally Lockhart novels were adapted into these two television movies starring Billie Piper.

Scott & Bailey - 2011 to 2016 - Two very different female police detectives enjoy a close friendship and productive partnership.

Shakespeare & Hathaway - 2018 to present - In beautiful Stratford-Upon-Avon, an unlikely pair of private investigators solves crimes together.

Sherlock Holmes - 1984 to 1994 - Jeremy Brett and David Burke star in this set of Sherlock Holmes adventures.

Sherwood - 2022 - Inspired by real-life murders in Nottinghamshire back in 2004, this series dives into the world of miners, covert police, and union activists. Cast members include David Morrissey (*Men Behaving Badly*), Lesley Manville (*Mum*), Robert Glenister (*Hustle*), Kevin Doyle (*Downton Abbey*), Philip Jackson (*Agatha Christie's Poirot*), and Joanne Froggatt (*Downton Abbey*). **Premieres October 4th.**

Shetland - 2013 to present - In the remote island community of Shetland, DI Jimmy Perez and his team investigate threats to the peace of their village. This series is based on the Shetland novels by Ann Cleeves. **Season 7 premiered September 13th.**

Silent Witness - 1996 to present - A team of pathologists investigates crimes based on evidence gleaned from autopsies. **Seasons 24 and 25 premiered on July 12th.**

Sister Boniface Mysteries - 2022 - This new light mystery from the creators of *Father Brown* follows a wine-making, crime-solving, Cotswold-dwelling nun. Lorna Watson reprises her role as Sister Boniface, having appeared once before in an early episode of *Father Brown*. Boniface is a forensics maverick in 1960s England, helping the police solve crimes with knowledge that surpasses what they're currently using in their own labs. They may not always understand her, but they know she's usually right.

Stonemouth - 2015 - A man returns to his small Scottish hometown in hopes of finding out the truth about his friend's murder.

Suspect - 2022 - James Nesbitt (*Bloodlands*) plays detective Danny Naylor, a man whose life changes after a routine trip to the morgue for an ID check. Instead of another anonymous corpse, the body turns out to be that of his estranged daughter Christina (Imogen King). Initial findings point to suicide, leading Naylor on a journey to find out what was going on in her life and how it could have ended so tragically.

The Suspicions of Mr. Whicher: Beyond the Pale - 2014 - Whicher is hired to investigate threats made to the son of an important government employee, leading him to some of the most dangerous parts of Victorian London. Paddy Considine (*Informer*) stars.

The Suspicions of Mr. Whicher: The Murder at Road Hill House - 2011 - Based on Kate Summerscale's best-selling novel, this series sees DI Whicher pursuing the murderer of a three-year-old boy. Paddy Considine (*Informer*) stars.

The Suspicions of Mr. Whicher: The Murder in Angel Lane - 2013 - Whicher investigates the death of a young girl, pitting him against some of London's wealthiest and most powerful individuals. Paddy Considine (*Informer*) stars.

The Suspicions of Mr. Whicher: The Ties That Bind - 2014 - This entry sees Whicher taking on what appears to be a simple infidelity case, but it soon turns much darker. Paddy Considine (*Informer*) stars.

Taggart - 1983 to 2010 - This long-running crime series revolves around a group of detectives in Scotland. Initially set in the Maryhill CID of Strathclyde Police, many later storylines were set and shot in other parts of Greater Glasgow and other areas of Scotland.

Thorne: Scaredy Cat - 2010 - Thorne is working with a new team to tackle a tough double murder case, but it's not long before he's hunting down two different serial killers.

Thorne: Sleepyhead - 2010 - DI Thorne (David Morrissey, *Men Behaving Badly*) is in a race against time to find a serial killer who enjoys making unusual attacks on young women.

The Tower - 2021 - DS Sarah Collins (Gemma Whelan, *Gentleman Jack*) investigates the deaths of a beat cop and a teenager who fell from a London tower block. Left alive on the roof is Lizzie Adams, a young officer who's found holding a small child who'd been kidnapped. Unfortunately, Lizzie disappears soon after the incident. The series is based on author Kate London's Metropolitan books.

Traces - 2019 to present - New chemistry graduate Emma Hodges begins work at The Scottish Institute of Forensic Science and Anatomy, but when she joins an online course to build professional skills, she notices the case is eerily familiar. It's the case of how her mother's body was found eighteen years earlier.

Unforgiven - 2009 - Peter Davison (*The Last Detective*) and Suranne Jones (*Scott & Bailey*) star in this series about a woman released from prison after serving 15 years for the murder of two police officers. Having spent half her life in jail, Ruth must build a new life for herself in spite of the damage she's done.

Vera - 2011 to present - DCI Vera Stanhope investigates murders in the Northumberland countryside. Brenda Blethyn (*Chance in a Million*) stars in this long-running crime drama based on Ann Cleeves' *Vera* novels. This series is split between Acorn TV and BritBox, with BritBox having all but season 7.

Vera Postmortem - 2018 - This BritBox exclusive includes interviews with Brenda Blethyn (Vera herself) and author Ann Cleeves. They discuss what it's like making the series, along with some of their favourite moments.

The Vice - 1999 to 2003 - Set in the vice unit of the Metropolitan Police, this hard-hitting series takes a look at London's gritty underworld of prostitution, pornography, and murder. Moving seamlessly between the swankiest Park Lane hotels to the back streets of King's Cross, it's interesting not just for the crimes, but for the unique portrayal of social and class contrasts. **Premiered July 15th.**

Waking the Dead - 2000 to 2011 - Using new forensic technology, DS Boyd and his team open unsolved cases.

Wallander - 2008 to 2016 - This English-language, Sweden-based mystery series is an adaptation of Henning Mankell's novels about Kurt Wallander, a highly empathetic detective.

What Remains - 2013 - When a young couple moves into an apartment, they find a dead body and it kicks off an investigation into a young woman's disappearance two years prior.

Wild Bill - 2019 - Rob Lowe stars as Chief Constable Bill Hixon in this comedy-drama about a widowed American police chief who moves to Lincolnshire with his teenage daughter after he's sacked for assaulting a boy who shared inappropriate images of his daughter online.

Without Motive - 2000 to 2001 - A detective attempts to solve a series of murders that seemingly lack motive.

Wycliffe - 1993 to 1998 - Based on W.J. Burley's novels, this Cornwall-based series features DS Charles Wycliffe, a man who investigates murders with a unique level of determination and accuracy.

Zen - 2011 - A handsome detective works to bring integrity and justice to Roman streets.

Dramas

About a Boy - 2002 - Hugh Grant (*Love Actually*) stars as Will in this classic dramedy about a wealthy, child-free Londoner who invents an imaginary son to help him meet women. Through one of his liaisons, he meets Marcus, a troubled 12-year-old kid who ultimately helps Will grow up. **Premiered August 1st.**

A Christmas Carol - 1977 - Michael Hordern (*The Wind in the Willows*) stars as Ebenezer Scrooge in this adaptation of Dickens' classic Christmas story of greed and redemption.

A Ghost Story for Christmas Collection - 1971 to present - The British tradition of telling ghost stories at Christmas is said to date back to pre-Christian winter solstice celebrations, but it was renewed by authors like Charles Dickens and M.R. James during Victorian times.

A Mother's Son - 2012 - When a teenage girl is murdered, a mother of two (Hermione Norris, *Cold Feet*) begins to suspect that her son Jamie may have played a role in the death. Newly remarried and living in the Suffolk market town of Eastlee, she realises her son lied to her about his activities on the night of the murder. Paul McGann (*Doctor Who*) plays Jamie's birth father, while Martin Clunes (*Doc Martin*) plays his new stepfather. **Premiered July 29th.**

A Royal Scandal - 1996 - Richard E. Grant (*Gosford Park*), Susan Lynch (*From Hell*), Michael Kitchen (*Foyle's War*), and Frances Barber (*Silk*) are among the cast members of this drama about the troubled marriage of King George and Caroline of Brunswick.

Against the Law - 2017 - When Peter Wildeblood and Edward McNally fell in love in 1952, it was still a crime in Britain. This film takes a look at the devastating consequences for each of the two men.

Age Before Beauty - 2018 - This contemporary drama is set in a struggling family-owned beauty salon in Manchester.

An Adventure in Space & Time - 2013 - This television movie is a dramatisation of how Doctor Who was brought to our televisions back in 1963.

Anna of the Five Towns - 1985 - Adapted from Arnold Bennett's 1902 novel of the same title, this series follows a young and strictly-controlled Methodist woman living in Staffordshire around the turn of the century. It follows her struggles for freedom and independence against a dictatorial father and the influence of the church.

Aristocrats - 1999 - This miniseries follows the lives of four aristocratic sisters through 1700s England.

Armadillo - 2001 - When loss adjuster Lorimer Black goes out on a routine appointment, he finds a hanged man. This three-part miniseries is based on William Boyd's 1998 novel of the same name.

A Tale of Two Cities (1980) - This eight-part adaptation of the Dickens classic sees Paul Shelley (*Doctors*) in the roles of Sydney Carton and Charles Darnay, along with Sally Osborne (*King's Royal*) as Lucie Manette. Set against the backdrop of the French Revolution, it follows French Dr. Manette as he is released from an 18-year imprisonment in the Bastille and goes to meet his daughter Lucie in London.

Ballykissangel - *Ireland* - 1996 to 2001 - A young English priest adjusts to the pace of life in a small Irish village. Stephen Tompkinson (*DCI Banks*) stars as Father Peter Clifford.

Banished - 2015 - When British convicts are sent to Australia to pay for their crimes, they and the soldiers who guard them have to adapt to the new world.

The Baron - 1966 to 1967 - American Steve Forrest (*S.W.A.T.*) plays John Mannering, an antiques dealer who also dabbles in undercover work for the British Diplomatic Intelligence. It was the first ITC Entertainment programme made in full colour but without marionettes, and it was based on the Baron series by Anthony Morton.

Bedlam – 2011 to 2012 – When a haunted former asylum is turned into a high-end apartment building, it has unexpected consequences for the building's new tenants.

Blake's 7 - 1978 to 1981 - Set in the far future, this classic British sci-fi series follows Roj Blake (Gareth Thomas) and his band of rebels as they fight against the totalitarian Terran Federation. The series was created by Terry Nation, the same man who created the Daleks of *Doctor Who* fame.

Bleak House (1985) - This eight-part miniseries starred Dame Diana Rigg (*Detectorists*) in the role of Lady Dedlock and Denholm Elliott (*Raiders of the Lost Ark*) as John Jarndyce. It was based on the Dickens novel of the same name that centers around the *Jarndyce and Jarndyce* legal case regarding a number of conflicting wills (with numerous subplots).

Bleak House (2005) - This classic BBC adaptation is based on the Dickens novel of the same name. The miniseries features an all-star cast that includes Gillian Anderson (*The Fall*), Timothy West (*Great Canal Journeys*), Carey Mulligan (*Collateral*), Alun Armstrong (*New Tricks*), Sheila Hancock (*Edie*), Catherine Tate (*Doctor Who*), and Hugo Speer (*The Full Monty*).

Bleak Old Shop of Stuff - 2011 - This Dickens parody stars Robert Webb (*Peep Show*) and Katherine Parkinson (*The IT Crowd*) alongside numerous celebrity guest appearances from actors like David Mitchell (*Peep Show*), Stephen Fry (*Kingdom*), Sarah Hadland (*Miranda*), and Phyllida Law (*Kingdom*). The story follows Jedrington Secret-Past (Webb) and his family as evil lawyer Maxifax Skulkingworm (Fry) terrorises them just before Christmas.

The Blue Boy – 1994 – Emma Thompson and Adrian Dunbar star in this film about a couple who head off to a hotel in rural Scotland to work on their relationship. While there, they learn of a young boy who drowned in the nearby loch, and Marie (Thompson) begins seeing his image in the water.

Bramwell - 1995 to 1998 - Set in 1895, Eleanor Bramwell works first under a doctor's supervision and then opens her own infirmary.

Brideshead Revisited - 1981 - Jeremy Irons and Anthony Andrews star in this adaptation of Evelyn Waugh's novel by the same name. *The Telegraph* awarded it the top position in its list of greatest TV adaptations of all time. *Remastered.*

Broken - 2017 - Sean Bean stars as Father Michael, a flawed but good-hearted Catholic priest in Northern England.

The Buccaneers - 1995 - This series follows four American women who secure wealthy British husbands, only to find it's not all it's cracked up to be.

Casualty - 1986 to present - This *Holby City* spinoff takes place in the A&E (Accidents and Emergency) department of the fictional Holby City Hospital.

Casualty 1900s: London Hospital - 2006 to 2009 - This medical period drama was inspired by the *Holby City* spinoff *Casualty*, but is otherwise unrelated. It takes place in the receiving room of the London Hospital in London's East End, and each case is based on the writings and memoirs of real doctors and nurses from the time period.

Catherine Cookson's The Cinder Path - 1994 - This three-part series follows a prosperous middle-class famer's son, Charlie MacFell, as he navigates a variety of challenges while attempting to keep a dark secret hidden. Lloyd Owen (*Monarch of the Glen*) stars alongside Catherine Zeta-Jones (*The Darling Buds of May*).

Catherine Cookson's The Dwelling Place - 1994 - Tracy Whitwell (*The Accidental Medium*) stars as 16-year-old Cissie Brodie, a young woman forced to care for her younger siblings after the death of her parents and the repossession of the family home.

Catherine Cookson's The Gambling Man - 1995 - Robson Green (*Grantchester*) stars in this three-part miniseries about Rory Connor, a Tyneside rent collector with a taste for high-stakes poker. Some suspect the source novel to have been autobiographical, given that Catherine Cookson's own father was a bigamist and gambler.

Catherine Cookson's The Girl - 1996 - In mid-19th century England, young Hannah Boyle is left with the family of Matthew Thornton, the man who supposedly fathered her. She's treated terribly and ultimately pushed out into an unhappy marriage with the village butcher. *Shakespeare & Hathaway* fans will spot Mark Benton in the role of Fred Loam.

Catherine Cookson's The Glass Virgin - 1995 - This three-part serial stars Emily Mortimer (*The Newsroom*) and Brendan Coyle (*Downton Abbey*). Mortimer plays Annabella Grange, a wealthy young woman who runs away from home after discovering a terrible secret. Coyle plays Mendoza, the young Irish traveller she joins on a lengthy roam around the

Northumberland countryside. One reviewer said the series "might have been sponsored by the Northumbrian tourist board" in reference to the number of sunny shots of the local scenery.

Catherine Cookson's The Man Who Cried - 1993 - Ciarán Hinds (*Above Suspicion*) stars as Abel Mason, a man trapped in a bad marriage with a woman who belittles him and beats their son. When his true love is killed by her husband after his evil wife sends him a letter exposing the affair, Abel grabs his son and leaves.

Catherine Cookson's The Moth - 1987 - In 1913 Northumbria, a young shipyard worker arrives home one day to find his father has died. At the funeral, he meets his father's estranged brother and starts fresh with his newly-discovered family. It's all going rather well until his cousin turns up pregnant and everyone thinks he's the father. Jack Davenport (*Coupling*) stars.

Catherine Cookson's The Rag Nymph - 1997 - *Foyle's War* fans will enjoy seeing a young Honeysuckle Weeks acting alongside her sister Perdita in this three-part miniseries. Young Millie is separated from her prostitute mother as she flees from the police in 19th century Newcastle. From there, she meets rag lady Aggie who helps protect her from a local pimp who wants to add her to his business.

Catherine Cookson's The Tide of Life - 1996 - This three-part miniseries follows housekeeper Emily Kennedy as she learns about life and love through relationships with three different men. Gillian Kearney (*The Forsyte Saga*) stars.

Catherine Cookson's The Wingless Bird - 1997 - Claire Skinner (*Outnumbered*) stars as Agnes Conway in this WWI-era period drama. The twentysomething finds herself managing not only her father's shops, but also the seemingly endless problems of her family. The real question is whether she'll be able to navigate those troubles and carve out a bit of happiness for herself.

The Cazalets - 2001 - This six-part miniseries follows the life of a wealthy Sussex family between the chaotic years of 1937 to 1947. It's based on *The Cazalet Chronicles* by Elizabeth Jane Howard.

The Champions - 1968 to 1969 - After a plane crash in the Himalayas, three secret agents are rescued by members of an advanced civilisation living secretly in the mountains. In the course of the rescue, they grant the three agents a set of supernatural abilities. Now, they use those special talents in service of a mysterious international agency called Nemesis.

Charles II: The Power and the Passion - 2003 - Rufus Sewell (*The Pale Horse*) stars in this four-part drama about the life of Charles II.

Christopher and His Kind - 2011 - This BBC television film tells the story of novelist Christopher Isherwood's youthful experiences as a young gay man living in Berlin in the 1930s. Matt Smith (*Doctor Who*) and Toby Jones (*Detectorists*) star.

Churchill: The Darkest Hour - 2013 - This docu-drama takes a look at Winston Churchill's experiences during World War I.

Coalition - 2015 - This tense political TV movie follows David Cameron, Nick Clegg, and Gordon Brown in the aftermath of the 2010 UK general election.

Cold Feet - 1998 to 2003 - This long-running dramedy follows the lives of six thirtysomething friends living in Manchester, England as they do their best to get their lives sorted.

Cold Feet: The New Years - 2016 to 2020 - Nearly 15 years after the original series ended, it returned for another set of episodes focusing on the Manchester-based friends, now in their 50s. Though 2020 marked the last set of episodes for this run, there's been talk of an additional series when the group is facing the next big phase of life.

The Constant Gardener - 2005 - In a remote part of Kenya, activist Tessa Quayle (Rachel Weisz, *Black Widow*) is found murdered. While the British High Commission in Nairobi assumes her widower will leave the matter to them, they couldn't be more wrong. Eager to get to the truth, Justin Quayle (Ralph Fiennes, *Schindler's List*) sets off on a journey across three continents, risking his own life to find out how his wife's ended. **Premiered August 1st.**

The Cook, the Thief, His Wife, & Her Lover - 1989 - When mobster Albert Spica (Michael Gambon, *Maigret*) takes over an upscale French restaurant in London, he dines there nightly and scares off many of the patrons with his unpleasant behaviour. His wife, Georgina (Helen Mirren, *Prime*

Suspect), is disgusted, and soon begins an affair with one of the guests, Michael (Alan Howard, *Victim*). Spica soon finds out, and doesn't take it well. **Premiered August 1st.**

Coronation Street - 1960 to present - Running since 1960, and there are more than 9400 episodes of this daytime drama classic. The show is set in the fictional area of Wetherfield, where residents walk cobbled streets among terraced houses and the ever-present Rovers Return pub. No service currently offers all 9000+ episodes, but BritBox maintains a running set of the most recent episodes.

Cranford - 2007 to 2009 - *Cranford* tells the story of women in a small, fictional market town at the dawn of the Industrial Revolution. Dame Judi Dench (*As Time Goes By*) stars in this modern adaptation of Elizabeth Gaskell's novellas.

Crime Story - 1992 to 1993 - This series features dramatic reenactments of some of Britain's most heinous and notorious crimes. Among them are the tale of Erwin van Haarlem, the story of Graham Young, and a case in which a young man's body was found by divers in a Lancashire quarry.

Daleks' Invasion Earth 2150 A.D. - 1966 - This theatrical adaptation of "The Dalek Invasion of Earth" sees Peter Cushing reprising his role as Dr. Who, an inventor who created the Tardis to travel through time.

Dandelion Dead - 1994 - Michael Kitchen (*Foyle's War*) stars in this true crime period drama about Herbert Rowse Armstrong, a Hay-on-Wye solicitor who was convicted and hanged for the murder of his wife and attempted murder of fellow solicitor, Oswald Martin.

Daniel Deronda (@002) - This four-part adaptation of George Eliot's final novel focuses on a Victorian man torn between the love of two women. Hugh Dancy (*The Jane Austen Book Club*) stars as Daniel.

David Copperfield (1986) - Simon Callow makes an appearance in this adaptation of the classic Dickens novel.

David Copperfield (1999) - Daniel Radcliffe (*Harry Potter*) stars as young David in this adaptation of the Dickens novel.

Desperate Romantics – 2009 - In 1851 London, a group of artists lead colorful lives amidst the chaos of the Industrial Revolution.

Dickensian - 2015 to 2016 - This ambitious miniseries is set in the world of Charles Dickens's novels, bringing together a variety of characters in 19th century London.

Dirk Gently - 2010 to 2012 - An unusual detective looks to the universe for holistic solutions to mysteries. Stephen Mangan (*Bliss*) stars in this adaptation of the popular Douglas Adams novels.

Doctor Foster – 2015 to 2017 - Dr. Gemma Foster (Suranne Jones, *Scott & Bailey*) seems to have it all – a beautiful home, a happy marriage, a family, and a great career. Unfortunately, that all falls apart when she begins to suspect her husband Simon (Bertie Carvel, *Dalgliesh*) of having an affair. **Premiered April 26th.**

Doctors - 2000 to present - This long-running BBC One hit follows the lives (and love lives) of staff members and patients at a busy British medical practice. It's a popular daytime series in the UK, mixing medicine, humour, and personal drama to create a show that's kept people coming back for over 20 years now.

Doctor Who (Classic) - 1963 to 1989 - *Doctor Who* originally ran for 26 seasons between 1963 and 1989. Though some episodes of the British sci-fi classic no longer exist, those that are available are included on BritBox.

Doctor Who Specials - 1991 to 2013 - This collection features some of the less common *Classic Doctor Who* specials, including the un-aired pilot and reunion episode.

Doctor Who: The Doctors Revisited - 2013 - This series introduces the first seven doctors from Doctor Who. It includes classic footage and interviews from cast and crew members.

Doctor Zhivago - 2002 - Kiera Knightley (*Pride and Prejudice*) and Hans Matheson (*The Tudors*) star in this miniseries adaptation of Boris Pasternak's classic 1957 novel.

Dombey and Son (1983) - This Charles Dickens adaptation reminds us that money can't protect you from the heartbreak of life. Julian Glover (*Game of Thrones*) stars as Paul Dombey Sr.

Downton Abbey - 2010 to 2015 - This popular period drama follows the lives of the Crawley family and their servants during the early 1900s. *See also: Downton Abbey Extras*

Drovers' Gold - 1997 - In 1843 Wales, an English drover refuses to give a widow a fair price for her cattle, so she sends her son to take the herd to market in London.

Dr. Who and the Daleks - 1965 - This feature length adaptation of "The Daleks" stars Peter Cushing as Dr. Who, a man who invented a device to travel across time and space with his granddaughters.

The Duchess of Duke Street - 1976 - Gemma Jones (*Bridget Jones's Diary*) starred in this series about a woman who worked her way up from servant to cook to owner of an upper-class hotel on Duke Street in London. The story is loosely based on the real life of Rosa Lewis, who ran the Cavendish Hotel. Keep an eye out for an appearance from Julian Fellowes (*Downton Abbey*).

Dunkirk - 2004 - Benedict Cumberbatch (*Sherlock*) stars in this docudrama about the Dunkirk evacuation during World War II. The series uses a mixture of eyewitness accounts, archive footage, and newly-dramatised sequences to bring the story to life.

EastEnders - 1985 to present - Known for its diversity and modern storylines, EastEnders is set in the fictional London borough of Walford around a Victorian square that includes a pub (The Queen Vic), a market, a launderette, and a cafe. As with a number of British soaps, BritBox typically keeps a running set of the most recent episodes.

Elizabeth R - 1971 - Brenda Jackson (*Women in Love*) stars as Elizabeth I in this series about the "Virgin Queen". She won two Emmys for the performance.

Emma (1972) - Doran Godwin and John Carson star in this six-part adaptation of Jane Austen's classic novel. Set in the fictional country village of Highbury, it follows would-be matchmaker Emma as she meddles in the affairs of those around her.

Emma (2009) - Romola Garai (*The Hour*) stars as Emma Woodhouse in this four-part adaptation of Jane Austen's classic novel. Jonny Lee Miller (*Elementary*) plays her dear friend Mr. Knightley.

Emmerdale - 1972 to present - Originally known as *Emmerdale Farm*, this series was originally set in a village called Beckindale. In the 90s, the show rebranded and began to focus on the entire village of Emmerdale. Now, storylines are bigger, sexier, and more dramatic than ever.

Fanny by Gaslight - 1981 - This four-part miniseries is an adaptation of Michael Sadleir's novel of the same name. It follows Fanny Hooper, a young woman who's fallen on hard times as an orphan in Victorian London. This adaptation sees Chloe Salaman in the role of Fanny.

Father and Son - 2009 - Michael O'Connor may have been one of the toughest gangsters around, but he thinks he's left that behind when he moves to Ireland to start over. When his son Séan is accused of a murder he didn't commit, Michael must return to Manchester and face his past.

Fields of Gold - 2002 - Benedict Cumberbatch (*Sherlock*) and Anna Friel (*Marcella*) star in this two-part thriller about genetically modified food.

Five by Five - 2017 - Idris Elba (*Luther*) stars in this series of five intertwining short films about random encounters in London.

Florence Nightingale - 2008 - This hour-long film tells the story of Florence Nightingale's defining moments after the Crimean War, and how those moment would shape the impact she would come to have on medicine.

Frankie - 2013 - Eve Myles (*Keeping Faith*) stars as the head nurse on a traveling nursing team.

Gideon's Daughter - 2006 - Emily Blunt (*The Devil Wears Prada*), Tom Hardy (*The Dark Night Rises*), and Bill Nighy (*Love Actually*) star in this film about a public relations guru who rethinks his life as his daughter goes off to study at the University of Edinburgh and he goes through a series of personal changes. The series is set in the late 90s against the backdrop of Princess Diana's death and the development of the Millennium Dome.

Great Expectations (1981) - Joan Hickson (*Miss Marple*) stars as Miss Havisham alongside Gerry Sundquist (*The Last Days of Pompeii*) as Pip in this 1981 adaptation of the Dickens classic. Set in Kent and London, it follows the coming of age of an orphan nicknamed Pip.

Great Expectations (1999) - Ioan Gruffudd (*Harrow*) stars as Pip in this dark and unsentimental retelling of Dickens' classic novel.

Great Expectations (2011) - This star-studded adaptation of the Dickens classic sees Gillian Anderson (*The Fall*) playing Miss Havisham, Douglas Booth (*Worried About the Boy*) as Pip, Vanessa Kirby (*The Crown*) as Estella, and David Suchet (*Poirot*) as Jaggers. Though many criticised the fact that Anderson was just 43 when playing Miss Havisham, reception was generally positive.

Hard Times - 1994 - Thomas Gradgrind is a wealthy merchant who's raised his children to be rational, self-interest, and above imaginative pursuits. Over the course of the film, we see those methods tested. The film is based on the Dickens novel of the same name. *Hard Times* was the shortest of all the Dickens novels, and the only one not to include scenes in London.

Heading Home - 1991 - Gary Oldman (*Bram Stoker's Dracula*) and Joely Richardson (*Nip/Tuck*) star in this film about a young woman who moves to London to start a new life after WWII. She soon finds herself torn between two men and tangled up with both the literary scene and a more criminal element.

Heartbeat - 1992 to 2010 - This Yorkshire-based period crime drama ran for 18 seasons and 372 episodes, focusing on the lives of characters in a small village. Initially, it focused on a central couple, PC Nick Rowan and Dr. Kate Rowan, but as time went on, it branched out to include storylines all over the village. The series is based on the "Constable" novels written by Peter N. Walker under the pseudonym Nicholas Rhea.

Hearts of Gold - 2003 - Doctor Andrew John has always found his girlfriend to be lacking in spirit, but when he meets vibrant miner's daughter Bethan Powell, he falls madly in love in spite of their different social classes.

The Heist at Hatton Garden - 2019 - This series is based on the true story of a spectacular diamond heist carried out in London by a group of elderly criminals. The all-star cast includes Timothy Spall (*Blandings*), Alex Norton (*Taggart*), David Hayman (*The Paradise*), and Kenneth Cranham (*The White Princess*).

Him - 2016 - Fionn Whitehead (*Dunkirk*) stars as a character known only as HIM. Set in suburban London, the series follows as he struggles to adjust to telekinetic powers inherited from his grandfather.

Homefront - 2012 to 2014 - This six-episode miniseries follows the lives of four army wives in the UK while their husbands are serving in Afghanistan.

Honour - 2020 - Keeley Hawes (*Bodyguard*) stars as DCI Caroline Goode, the real-life investigator who vowed to get justice for a young woman whose Muslim extremist family murdered her for daring to love the wrong man.

Hope Street - 2021 - This soap opera is set in the fictional Northern Ireland town of Port Devine, following the arrival of the town's first ever Muslim police officer, English Detective Constable Leila Hussain.

The House of Cards Trilogy - 1990 to 1995 - This sitcom is Andrew Davies' adaptation of Michael Dobbs' novels about greed, ambition, and British politics. It follows Frances Urquhart, an evil but charismatic man who will stop at nothing in the pursuit of power. An American adaptation was later made under the same name.

The House of Eliott - 1991 - Stella Gonet (*Breeders*) and Louise Lombard (*CSI: Crime Scene Investigation*) star in this series about two sisters who start a dressmaking business in 1920s London.

Intruder - 2021 - Affluent married couple Rebecca and Sam see their idyllic lives destroyed after teenagers Tommy and Syed break into their luxurious coastal home – but all is not as it seems. Elaine Cassidy (*No Offence*) plays Rebecca, with Tom Meeten (The Ghoul) starring as her husband. Pauline Quirke (*Birds of a Feather*) plays Bailey, the Family Liaison Officer who gets involved in the ensuing investigation.

The Ipcress File - 1965 - British spy Harry Palmer (Michael Caine, *The Dark Knight*) navigates his way through criminals, secret agents, and bureaucracy to find out the truth about the kidnapping and brainwashing of top scientists. While attempting to bring in a suspect, he discovers a mysterious tape labelled "IPCRESS" that might just help him unravel the mystery. **Premiered August 1st.**

Isolation Stories - 2020 - Filmed remotely during the COVID-19 pandemic of 2020, this limited dramatic series taps into the feelings different people experience during lockdown.

Jane Eyre (1983) - This adaptation of Brontë's classic stars Timothy Dalton and Zelah Clarke as Jane and Mr. Rochester.

Jane Eyre (2006) - Ruth Wilson (*Luther*) stars as Jane Eyre in this mildly steamy adaptation of Charlotte Brontë's classic novel.

Jekyll & Hyde - 1990 - Michael Caine (*The Dark Knight*) stars as Dr. Henry Jekyll (and Mr. Edward Hyde) in this chilling feature-length adaptation of the classic Victorian horror story.

The Jury - 2002 to 2011 - When the killing of a 15-year-old boy rocks the nation, 12 jurors find themselves under intense pressure to make the right decision. The second season is entirely unconnected to the first, and sees a set of jurors called up to handle the controversial retrial of a convicted murderer.

K9 & Company: A Girl's Best Friend - 1981 - This single-episode television pilot was intended as a spin-off of Doctor Who, featuring series regular Sarah Jane Smith (Elisabeth Sladen) and K9, a dog robot voiced by John Leeson. It sees Sarah Jane searching for her missing aunt in a quiet Gloucestershire village.

Kat & Alfie: Redwater - 2017 - 32 years after giving her son up for adoption, Kat moves to the town of Redwater in an attempt to find him.

Kavanagh QC - 1995 to 2001 - John Thaw (*Inspector Morse*) stars as James Kavanagh QC, a barrister with a working-class background and a strong sense of right and wrong. It was one of Thaw's final roles before he died of cancer at 60. Pay close attention to the guest stars in this one, as it's loaded with actors who went on to well-known roles, including Lesley Manville (*Mum*), Larry Lamb (*Gavin & Stacey*), Barry Jackson (*Midsomer Murders*), Phyllis Logan (*Downton Abbey*), Bill Night (*Love Actually*), and Julian Fellowes (*Downton Abbey*).

Killed By My Debt - 2018 - This programme tells the story of Jerome, a young man whose small debt and poor prospects led him to kill himself. Chance Perdomo (*Chilling Adventures of Sabrina*) stars.

Lady Windermere's Fan - 1985 - Based on Oscar Wilde's play of the same name, this comedy follows Lady Windermere, a woman who suspects her husband of being unfaithful. Though he denies it when confronted, he still invites the other woman to his wife's birthday ball, where things quickly get a bit ridiculous.

Lark Rise to Candleford - 2008 to 2011 - Set in the late 19th century in the small Oxfordshire hamlet of Lark Rise and the nearby market town of Candleford, this period drama follows a young woman who moves towns to work in a post office. The series is based on Flora Thompson's semi-autobiographical novels about living in the English countryside.

Life in Squares - 2015 - This series dramatizes the lives of those in the Bloomsbury group, a set of influential artists, writers, and intellectuals in England.

Little Boy Blue - 2017 - This ITV series is a dramatisation of the real-life murder of 11-year-old Rhys Jones during a wave of gang violence in Liverpool in 2007.

Little Dorrit (2008) - Claire Foy (*The Crown*) and Matthew Macfayden (*Ripper Street*) star in this adaptation of Dickens' story of struggle in 1820s London. Andrew Davies (*Pride & Prejudice*) wrote the screenplay for this adaptation.

Little Women - 1970 - Poorly received by critics, this low-budget adaptation of the Louisa May Alcott classic features inauthentic American accents and a cast of actresses noticeably older than their ages in the novel. Patrick Troughton (*Doctor Who*) played the role of Mr. March.

London Road - 2015 - Olivia Colman (*Broadchurch*) and Tom Hardy (*Peaky Blinders*) star in this film adaptation of the musical of the same name (which is based on a series of interviews about the Suffolk Strangler).

Lorna Doone - 2000 - When a man falls in love with a woman from the same clan that killed his father, he's horrified. This adaptation is based on the 1869 Richard Doddridge Blackmore novel of the same name, and it includes appearances from Anton Lesser (*Endeavour*), Richard Coyle (*Coupling*), Honeysuckle Weeks (*Foyle's War*), Martin Clunes (*Doc Martin*), James McAvoy (*Shameless*), Michael Kitchen (*Foyle's War*), and Joanne Froggatt (*Downton Abbey*).

Love in a Cold Climate - 2001 - Between 1929 and 1940, three young women search for love.

Lucan - 2013 - In 1974, the aristocratic Lucan family's nanny was found bludgeoned to death, with Lord Lucan believed to be the prime suspect. Soon after, he vanished without a trace, leading the world to wonder what sort of dark things were going on behind the family's public image. Rory Kinnear (*The Imitation Game*) stars in this two-part true crime dramatisation.

Macbeth (2018) - This unique feature-length adaptation of *Macbeth* bridges the gap between theatre and film to offer a look at Shakespeare's timeless tale with a blend of medieval and modern aesthetics. **Premiered April 8th.**

Madame Bovary (1975) - Francesca Annis (*Home Fires*) stars as Emma Bovary in this classic adaptation of Flaubert's novel about the frustrated, unfaithful wife of a French country doctor. Tom Conti (*Parents*) plays Charles Bovary.

Madame Bovary (2000) - In Flaubert's classic, a woman marries a doctor in hopes of escaping a boring provincial life. It doesn't work. This adaptation features Frances O'Connor (*Mansfield Park*) as Emma Bovary, with Hugh Bonneville (*Downton Abbey*) in the role of Charles Bovary.

Mansfield Park (1983) - Sylvestra Le Touzel stars as Fanny Price in this miniseries adaptation of Jane Austen's third novel. It's about a young woman sent to live with wealthier relatives, who later falls in love with her sensitive cousin.

Martin Chuzzlewit (1994) - When a wealthy old man nears death, everyone comes out of the woodwork to try to get their piece of his riches. This miniseries is based on the Dickens novel of the same name.

Middlemarch (1994) - Robert Hardy, Rufus Sewell, Pam Ferris, Patrick Malahide, and Dame Judi Dench all appear in this adaptation of the classic George Eliot novel. It sees Dorothea Brooke marrying a much older man in an attempt to grow intellectually, only to find he has no interest in involving her in his intellectual pursuits. After his death, she meets his much younger cousin, a man who is interested in her despite the fact that she's oblivious to his intentions.

Midwinter of the Spirit – 2015 – This creepy drama follows a country vicar as she trains to be an exorcist for the Church of England. Before she's able to get much experience, she finds herself faced with powerful supernatural threats.

Miss Austen Regrets - 2008 - This feature-length drama is based on Jane Austen's life and collected letters. Olivia Williams (*An Education*) plays Jane Austen.

Mo - 2010 - Julie Walters (*Dinnerladies*) stars in this biopic about the life of Mo Mowlam, a controversial Labour Party politician in Northern Ireland.

The Moorside - 2017 - This two-part television drama is based on the 2008 disappearance of 9-year-old Shannon Matthews in Dewsbury, West Yorkshire. The cast includes Sheridan Smith (*Gavin & Stacey*), Gemma Whelan (*Game of Thrones*), Sian Brooke (*Doctor Foster*), and Sibhan Finneran (*Downton Abbey*).

Mother's Day - 2018 - Based on a true story, this film follows two mothers, one English and one Irish, as they pave the way for peace in the aftermath of an IRA attack in Warrington, England.

Moving On – 2009 to 2016 - This anthology series gives us stories of people preparing to move on to something new in their lives.

Mrs. Brown - 1997 - Dame Judi Dench stars in this film about Queen Victoria and her unusual friendship with servant John Brown (Billy Connolly). Her portrayal of the scandalous relationship earned an Academy Award nomination.

Murdered by My Boyfriend - 2014 - This dramatisation of a true story tells of a young woman who falls in love with the wrong man. It was commissioned to help educate young viewers about the dangers of relationship abuse.

Murdered by My Father - 2016 - This one-off drama tells the story of a young British Asian Muslim girl who was killed by her father for loving the wrong man.

Murdered for Being Different - 2017 - Based on the real 2007 murder of Sophie Lancaster, this film sees two young goths attacked for being different.

My Boy Jack - 2007 - Daniel Radcliffe (*Harry Potter*), Carey Mulligan (*Pride and Prejudice*), and Kim Cattrall (*Sex and the City*) star in this WWI drama about Rudyard Kipling and his son John. The name of the film is taken from Kipling's poem, "My Boy Jack".

My Family and Other Animals - 2005 - Fans of *The Durrells in Corfu* will enjoy this television film based on Gerald Durrell's autobiographical book about his family's stay on Corfu. The source material was part of the trilogy that ultimately turned into the television series, and this take on it includes Eugene Simon (*Game of Thrones*), Imelda Staunton (*Flesh & Blood*), Matthew Goode (*A Discovery of Witches*), and Russell Tovey (*Flesh & Blood*) among the cast.

North & South - 2004 - Based on the 1855 Victorian novel of the same name by Elizabeth Gaskell, this series follows Margaret Hale, a young woman from southern England who's forced to move north after her father leaves the clergy. The series is a study in class and gender issues of the time, and we see Margaret torn between sympathy for the northern mill workers and increasing attraction to wealthy John Thornton.

Northanger Abbey (1987) - Katharine Schlesinger (*Doctor Who*) stars in this adaptation of Jane Austen's classic parody of Gothic fiction. She plays seventeen-year-old tomboy Catherine Morland, a young woman with a wild imagination and love of Gothic novels. Robert Hardy (*All Creatures Great & Small*) and Peter Firth (*Spooks*) are also among the cast members.

NW - 2016 - Based on Zadie Smith's award-winning novel, this series follows two friends from a northwest London housing estate as they reunite during a challenging time.

Oliver Twist (1985) - This is the 1985 BBC adaptation of the classic Dickens tale with Ben Rodska as Oliver Twist. Keep an eye out for Frank Middlemaas (*As Time Goes By*) and Miriam Margolyes (*Miss Fisher's Murder Mysteries*) as Mr. Brownlow and Mrs. Bumble.

Oliver Twist (2007) - Morven Christie (*Grantchester*), Tom Hardy (*Peaky Blinders*), and Sarah Lancashire (*Happy Valley*) all appear in this star-studded adaptation of the Dickens classic.

One Night - 2012 - In one night, the lives of four people are linked by a single event.

Ordinary Lies - 2015 to 2016 - Each series of this show is set in a perfectly ordinary location, but the people have dark secrets. Series 1 takes place at a car dealership in Warrington, while Series 2 is set in a sporting goods company.

The Other Boleyn Girl - 2003 - Based on Philippa Gregory's novel of the same name,

this film follows Mary Boleyn, sister to Anne and George Boleyn. She's recently gotten married to William Carey, but because Henry VIII favours her, she's also his mistress. Natascha McElhone (*Californication*) stars as Mary Boleyn, with Jodhi May (*A Quiet Passion*) as Anne.

Our Friends in the North - 1996 - This series follows a group of four friends from Newcastle as their lives unfold over a period of 31 years. Daniel Craig (*Quantum of Solace*) and Christopher Eccleston (*Doctor Who*) are among the stars.

Our Girl - 2013 to present - This series follows a young woman from East London as she embarks on her career as an army medic. Lacey Turner (*EastEnders*) stars as Molly Dawes, with Michelle Keegan (*Brassic*) entering later as Georgie Lane.

Our Mutual Friend - 1998 - This adaptation of Dickens's last completed novel contrasts money and poverty in Victorian London. The adaptation features a number of familiar faces, including Paul McGann (*Luther*), Anna Friel (*Marcella*), Pam Ferris (*Rosemary & Thyme*), Peter Vaughan (*Game of Thrones*), and Keeley Hawes (*The Durrells*).

The Paradise - 2012 - In this period drama, a young and ambitious woman heads to the city to make her way working in a department store.

The Passing Bells - 2014 - This British-Polish drama tells the story of two teens, one British and one German, who sign up to fight in WWI.

Persuasion (2007) - Sally Hawkins (*Tipping the Velvet*) and Rupert Penry-Jones (*Whitechapel*) star in this film adaptation of Jane Austen's 1817 novel. Eight years before the story begins, Anne (Hawkins) rejected Wentworth's (Penry-Jones) proposal of marriage. Now, he's made his fortune and he's looking for a wife, so long as it's not Anne.

The Pickwick Papers - 1985 - Nigel Stock and Clive Swift star in this adaptation of Dickens' great comic masterpiece.

Pride and Prejudice (1980) - Elizabeth Garvie and David Rintoul star in this five-part television adaptation of Austen's classic. *Grantchester* fans may also notice Tessa Peake-Jones (Mrs. Maguire) in the role of Mary Bennet. The series follows Mrs. Bennet's efforts to secure good husbands for her five daughters.

Pride & Prejudice (1995) - Jennifer Ehle and Colin Firth star in this much-loved adaptation of Jane Austen's classic novel that starts with "a single man in possession of a good fortune". *Digitally remastered.*

Pride & Prejudice (2005) - This feature-length adaptation of Jane Austen's popular novel is known for being more modernised and less faithful than the much-loved 1995 adaptation. It follows the Bennet sisters as they attempt to find husbands, with a particular focus on sister Elizabeth and the newly-arrived wealthy bachelor Mr. Darcy. Keira Knightley and Matthew Macfadyen star. **Premiered August 1st.**

Reg - 2016 - Tim Roth (*Reservoir Dogs*) stars as Reg Keys in this political drama about a bereaved military father who took on Tony Blair in the 2005 elections.

Robin of Sherwood - 1984 to 1986 - Though nearly 40 years old, this British TV classic is a bit of a cult classic. It offers a retelling of the Robin Hood legend with a mix of history, pagan mythology, and modern artistic license. In it, a mystical forest being appoints men to serve as the outlaw defender of the poor and oppressed. **Premieres October 1.**

The Royal - 2003 to 2011 - This *Heartbeat* spinoff is set in the 1960s and focuses on an NHS hospital serving the seaside Yorkshire town of Elsinby.

Royal Celebration - 1993 - Keira Knightley (*Pride & Prejudice*) and Minnie Driver (*Good Will Hunting*) star in this drama about the wedding of Prince Charles and Lady Diana.

The Royal Today - 2008 - This follow-up to *The Royal* takes place in the same Yorkshire hospital, but 40 years later.

The Sandbaggers - 1978 to 1980 - This spy drama follows the men and woman on the front lines of the Cold War. Based in Leeds and produced by Yorkshire Television, it starred Roy Marsden (Adam Dalgliesh in the P.D. James adaptations), Director of Operations in Britain's Secret Intelligence Service.

Screw - 2022 - This prison drama follows a group of officers working in the C-Wing of Long Marsh men's prison. Gritty and dramatic, it follows not only the happenings in the prison, but also the personal drama and secrets each employee brings with them. **Premiered September 1st.**

The Secret of Crickley Hall – 2012 – Suranne Jones and Tom Ellis star in this supernatural miniseries about a family that relocates to a grand old estate up north after the disappearance of their young son.

Sense and Sensibility (1981) - This seven-part adaptation of Jane Austen's 1811 novel follows the newly widowed and destitute Mrs. Dashwood as she attempts to survive and marry off her three daughters. This adaptation is unique in that it omits the character of Margaret Dashwood.

Sense and Sensibility (2008) - This Andrew Davies adaptation of Austen's 1811 novel featured Mark Gatiss (*Sherlock*) as John Dashwood, a young man whose nasty wife Fanny (Claire Skinner, *Outnumbered*) convinces him to reduce the amount of money he provides to his widowed stepmother and half siblings. Newly widowed and destitute with three unmarried daughters, Mary Dashwood (Janet McTeer, *Tumbleweeds*) downsizes and attempts to find good husbands for her daughters.

Servants - 2003 - Written and created by Lucy Gannon, this series followed the lives of a group of servants in an 1850s English country house.

Sharpe - 1993 to 2010 - Sean Bean (*Game of Thrones*) stars in this 19th century period drama set during the Napoleonic Wars in Spain. It's based on the *Sharpe* novels by Bernard Cornwell.

Silk - 2011 to 2014 - This fast-paced legal drama looks at the lives of the highly-educated professionals working on the front lines of criminal law. Maxine Peake stars as Martha Costello, a defense barrister with a history of defending the poor and downtrodden. She wants nothing more than to become a member of the Queen's Counsel, but she's not the only one after the position. **Premiered June 17th.**

Single Father - 2010 - David Tennant stars in this drama about a regular guy trying to raise his family after the death of his wife.

The Six Wives of Henry VIII - 1971 - This collection of television plays focuses on the wives of Henry VIII, with each play telling the story of one woman. Second Doctor Patrick Troughton (*Doctor Who*) is among the stars.

The Small Hand: A Ghost Story – 2019 – After a visit with a client, an antiquarian book dealer takes a wrong turn and finds himself at a decaying Edwardian manor house. Curious, he decides to investigate – but as he approaches, he feels the cold sensation of a child taking his hand (though no child is actually there).

Small Island - 2009 - Based on the 2004 novel of the same title by Andrea Levy, this film sees Naomie Harris (*28 Days Later*) and Ruth Wilson (*Mrs. Wilson*) playing two women who struggle to achieve their dreams in World War II London. Benedict Cumberbatch (*Sherlock*) and David Oyelowo (*Spooks/MI-5*) also appear.

Sticks and Stones - 2019 - After a sales pitch goes terribly wrong, Thomas Benson begins to feel his colleagues have turned against him. Desperate to fix things, he resorts to extreme measures to get back on top. Ben Miller (*Death in Paradise*) is among the stars of this thriller.

The Street - 2006 to 2009 - Each episode takes a look at what's going on with a different family who lives on the same street.

The Syndicate: Double or Nothing - 2021 - After a six-year absence, Kay Mellor's hit show has returned for a fourth standalone series. Each series features a different cast and setting (aside from Lorraine Bruce as Denise Simpson, who returns in each series). In each case, a group of people who've been playing the lottery together (a "syndicate") end up winning. After the initial happiness, the consequences of the win are often darker than expected.

The Tenant of Wildfell Hall - 1996 - In a remote Yorkshire village, a widow and her son move into the creepy, crumbling Wildfell Hall. Based on the classic story by Anne Brontë.

Tess of the D'Urbervilles (2008) - In this miniseries based on the Thomas Hardy work, Gemma Arterton (*Lost in Austen*) stars as Tess Durbeyfield, the poor country girl with connections to nobility.

That Day We Sang - 2014 - Based on the Victoria Wood musical of the same name, this television adaptation starring Imelda Staunton (*A Confession*) is based in 1969 with flashbacks to 1929. It tells the story of a middle-aged couple that finds love when they meet on a television programme about a choir they were once in.

The Thief, His Wife, and the Canoe - 2022 - Eddie Marsan (*Sherlock Holmes*) and

Monica Dolan (*W1A*) star in this adaptation of the real-life story of John Darwin, a former teacher and prison officer who faked his death to fraudulently collect life insurance. His wife played the part of grieving widow while he hid out in an apartment next door. **Premiered August 23rd.**

Three Girls - 2017 - Authorities ignore the trafficking of young girls by British Pakistani men.

Time - 2021 - This Jimmy McGovern-penned drama stars Sean Bean (*Game of Thrones*) and Stephen Graham (*Line of Duty*) in a powerful depiction of prison life. Bean plays Mark Cobden, a husband and father who is responsible for the death of an innocent man. Though his guilt leads him to welcome the prison sentence, he's not as hardened as his fellow inmates, and he struggles to survive in the understaffed facility. Graham plays the dedicated prison officer who does his best to protect those under this care.

Tina & Bobby - 2017 - This miniseries follows the relationship of Tina Dean and her West Ham United footballer husband, Bobby Moore.

Tipping the Velvet - 2002 - This period drama tells the story of a love affair between two music hall women in the 1890s. Rachael Stirling (*Detectorists*) and Keeley Hawes (*Bodyguard*) star. The series is based on Sarah Waters' best-selling 1998 debut novel of the same name.

Trauma - 2018 - This thriller shows how two fathers' lives collide when one man's son dies at the hands of the other.

The Turn of the Screw - 1999 - This TV movie adaptation of *The Turn of the Screw* stars Colin Firth and Johdi May. Pam Ferris (*Rosemary & Thyme*) also appears as Mrs. Grose.

Tutankhamun - 2016 - This adventure miniseries is based on Howard Carter's discovery of King Tut's tomb.

Upstairs Downstairs (Classic) - 1971 to 1977 - This drama follows the aristocratic Bellamy family and the servants who live downstairs. The series is set between the years of 1903 and 1930, showing the gradual decline of the aristocratic class in Britain.

Upstairs Downstairs - 2010 to 2012 - This series picks up the Upstairs Downstairs saga shortly after the period covered by the original series. Covering 1936 to 1939, it tells the story of the new owners of 165 Eaton Place, ending with the outbreak of World War II. Ed Stoppard (*Home Fires*) and Keeley Hawes (*Bodyguard*) play new owners Sir Hallam Holland and Lady Agnes Holland.

Vanity Fair (1987) - This adaptation of Thackeray's Napoleonic War-era tale starred Eve Matheson, Rebecca Saire, James Saxon, and Simon Dormandy in the lead roles.

Vanity Fair (1998) - This BBC adaptation of Thackeray's novel featured a screenplay by Andrew Davies (*Pride & Prejudice*), with Natasha Little in the role of Becky Sharp.

The Victim - 2019 - This four-part Scottish miniseries tells the story of Anna Dean (Kelly MacDonald, *Boardwalk Empire*), a mother whose young son was murdered more than a decade prior. She's been accused of sharing information about the man she believes to be guilty, damaging his reputation and causing him to be attacked. The series focuses on the trial and a mother's unrelenting search for the truth.

White Heat - 2012 - Claire Foy (*The Crown*) stars in this epic drama about the lives of seven students who meet in a London flatshare during the 1960s. Some have compared it to a more female-friendly version of *Our Friends in the North*. Each of the six episodes take place in a different year: 1965, 1967, 1973, 1979, 1982, and 1990.

The Woman in White - 1981 - Based on the Wilkie Collins novel of the same name, this series sees two Victorian sisters caught up in a mystery that involves a mysterious doppelganger dressed all in white.

Women in Love - 2011 - Rosamund Pike and Rachael Stirling star in this adaptation of DH Lawrence's classic novel. It was originally written as a sequel to *The Rainbow*.

Wuthering Heights (1978) - Widely considered to be one of the most faithful adaptations of Emily Brontë's 1847 novel, this five-part miniseries stars Ken Hutchison (*The Bill*) as Heathcliff, with Kay Adshead (*Family Affairs*) filling the role of Cathy.

The Shakespeare Collection

This collection was added to BritBox in early 2020.

A Midsummer Night's Dream (1981)

A Midsummer Night's Dream (2016)

A Winter's Tale (1981)

All's Well That Ends Well (1981)

Antony and Cleopatra (1981)

As You Like It (1978)

The Comedy of Errors (1983)

Cymbeline (1982)

Hamlet, Prince of Denmark (1980)

Henry IV: Parts 1 and 2 (1979)

Henry V (1979)

Henry VI: Parts 1-3 (1983)

Henry VIII (1979)

Julius Caesar (1979)

King Lear (1982)

The Life and Death of King John (1984)

Love's Labour's Lost (1985)

Macbeth (1983)

Measure for Measure (1979)

The Merchant of Venice (1980)

The Merry Wives of Windsor (1982)

Much Ado About Nothing (1984)

Othello (1981)

Pericles, Prince of Tyre (1984)

Richard II (1979)

Romeo and Juliet (1978)

The Taming of the Shrew (1980)

The Tempest (1980)

Timon of Athens (1981)

Titus Andronicus (1985)

The Tragedy of Coriolanus (1984)

The Tragedy of Richard III (1983)

Troilus and Cressida (1981)

Twelfth Night (1980)

The Two Gentlemen of Verona (1983)

Play for Today Collection

This classic anthology series ran from 1970 to 1984, and brings a collection of adaptations of plays and novels. It includes a number of performances from British acting greats, including Helen Mirren, Nigel Hawthorne, and Alison Steadman.

Abigail's Party

A Cotswold Death

All Good Men

A Photograph

Back of Beyond

Bar Mitzvah Boy

The Black Stuff

Coming Out

Country

The Elephants' Graveyard

The Executioner

The Fishing Party

Funny Farm

The Hallelujah Handshake

Hard Labour

Home Sweet Home

Jessie

Just Another Saturday

Just A Boy's Game

King

Kisses at 50

Leeds United!

Nuts in May

The Other Woman

Penda's Fen

Rainy Day Women

The Slab Boys

Soft Targets

Still Waters

Who's Who

Comedies

'Allo 'Allo - 1982 to 1992 - This classic British comedy follows René, a cafe owner in Nouvion with German soldiers in residence, even as he does his best to aid the Resistance. He's hiding two British airmen and a radio transmitter upstairs, and he's hidden a priceless painting (Fallen Madonna with the Big Boobies) in a large sausage. At the same time, he's having affairs with two sexy waitresses – right under the nose of his nagging wife.

300 Years of French and Saunders - 2017 - This special brings much-loved comedy team Jennifer Saunders and Dawn French back together for another set of hilarious sketches.

8 Out of 10 Cats - 2005 to present - This quirky panel show comes up with unusual questions and then polls the general public to get their take on the issues.

8 Out of 10 Cats Does Countdown - 2012 to present - This show is a mash-up of *8 Out of 10 Cats* and the more intellectually-challenging *Countdown*. Initially created as a special, it proved quite popular and it's now been running since 2012.

A Bit of Fry & Laurie - 1987 to 1989 - This sketch show is an important piece of British comedy history, and it was responsible for turning Stephen Fry (*Kingdom*) and Hugh Laurie (*House*) into household names.

A Child's Christmases in Wales - 2009 - Michael Sheen narrates this nostalgic comedy about a series of Christmases in the life of a South Wales family during the 1980s.

Absolutely Fabulous - 1992 to 2012 - In this groundbreaking classic, two wild women do everything but act their age. The series was based on a sketch comedy called "Modern Mother and Daughter" by Dawn French (*Vicar of Dibley*) and Jennifer Saunders (Edina Monsoon in *Absolutely Fabulous*). Joanna Lumley stars alongside Saunders as Patsy Stone, and Julia Sawalha plays Edina's daughter Saffron.

Alan Davies: As Yet Untitled - 2014 to 2015 - Alan Davies (*Jonathan Creek*) hosts this discussion show featuring a mix of famous and soon-to-be famous faces. Topics of discussion include everything from the US military to giant rabbits to Bob Mortimer's unusually high backside.

Alfresco - 1983 to 1984 - This early-80s variety show is packed with now-famous actors like Emma Thompson, Robbie Coltrane, Hugh Laurie, and Stephen Fry.

All Creatures Great and Small (Classic) - 1978 to 1980 - Set in the lovely Yorkshire Dales, this classic comedy is based on the books of James Herriot (pen name to James Alfred Wight). It follows the adventures of a country veterinarian in 1930s England.

Are You Being Served? - 1972 to 1985 - At the Grace Brothers Department Store, fine fashions are served with a healthy side of mischief.

Are You Being Served? - 2016 - In this one-off reboot of the original series, a young Mr. Grace is determined to bring the store into the 1980s...in 1988. It was poorly reviewed, and no further episodes were made.

Are You Being Served? Again! - 1982 to 1993 - When the Grace Brothers store is closed, the staff takes over managing a manor house in the countryside.

As Time Goes By - 1992 to 2002 - Separated by a lost letter during the war, lovers Lionel and Jean are reunited by chance many years later. Dame Judi Dench stars opposite Geoffrey Palmer in this charming light comedy.

At Last the 1948 Show - 1967 - A must for *Monty Python* fans, this quirky 1967 comedy sketch series features future MP collaborators John Cleese and Graham Chapman.

BBC's Lost Sitcoms - 2016 - This collection features re-enactments of three lost sitcom episodes from iconic BBC sitcoms: *Steptoe & Son*, *Hancock's Half Hour*, and *Till Death Us Do Part*.

Bean: The Movie - 1997 - Rowan Atkinson (*Maigret*) stars in this British comedy classic about an eccentric who works for the British National Gallery in London. All he does is sleep, but instead of firing him, the board sends him to Los Angeles as an "art scholar" to speak at the unveiling of Whistler's Mother. Predictably, the trip does not go as planned. **Premiered August 1st.**

Benidorm - 2007 to 2018 - In this delightfully tacky comedy, a parade of British holidaymakers try to get their money's worth at an all-inclusive resort in Benidorm. If you enjoy spotting well-known British actors in guest roles, this is a great one to check out. It includes guest appearances from Mark Heap (*Friday Night Dinner*), Nigel Havers (*Coronation Street*), Una Stubbs (*Sherlock*), Wendy Richard (*Are You Being Served?*), and Kate O'Mara (*Doctor Who*), among others.

Billionaire Boy - 2016 - When Joe's father Len invents a new sort of toilet roll, they become overnight billionaires. Now, Joe can have anything money can buy - but he soon learns it can't buy everything.

Blackadder - 1983 to 1989 - Rowan Atkinson stars as antihero Edmund Blackadder, accompanied by Sir Tony Robinson as his sidekick Baldrick. Each series of this quirky comedy is set in a different period within British history, and Edmund carries different titles throughout. The "essence" of each character remains largely the same in each series, though.

Blandings - 2013 to 2014 - A nobleman struggles to keep his stately home and strange family in line so he can spend more time with his beloved pig. The series was based on P.G. Wodehouse's *Blandings Castle* stories, and it's one of a relatively small number of scripted programmes filmed on location in Northern Ireland (mostly at Crom Castle in County Fermanagh).

Bliss - 2018 - Stephen Mangan plays a man living an exhausting double life in this family sitcom.

Boy Meets Girl - 2015 to 2016 - This romantic comedy combines a transgender romance with age gap love, pairing a 40-something transgender woman with a 26-year-old man.

Rowan Atkinson Presents: Canned Laughter - 1979 - This short comedy tells the story of a dinner date gone terribly wrong. It's often considered an early inspiration for Atkinson's Mr. Bean character.

The Cafe - 2011 to 2013 - This light, easygoing comedy follows three generations of women who run a seaside cafe in Weston-super-Mare. Though it never made a huge splash, it's packed with talent – including a couple of actors who've gone on to some very well-known roles. The series was written by Michelle Terry and Ralf Little (aka DI Neville Parker on *Death in Paradise*) – and the two also played starring roles.

Chef! - 1993 to 1996 - Lenny Henry (*Broadchurch*) stars as a touchy chef with incredible culinary skills...and little in the way of interpersonal abilities. Though he works hard to keep standards high, his staff cuts corners whenever possible, his wife is bored, and his customers still have the gall to ask for salt.

Clash of the Santas - 2008 - This follow-up to Northern Lights sees Robson Green (*Grantchester*) and Mark Benton (*Shakespeare & Hathaway*) reprising their roles as bickering friends Colin and Howie. In this outing, they're off to the World Santa Championships in Lithuania.

The Cleaner - 2021 - Greg Davies (*The Inbetweeners*) stars in this British adaptation of a hit German comedy, *Crime Scene Cleaner* (*Der Tatortreiniger*). In it, Davies plays Wicky, a crime scene cleaner who helps restore homes and properties to their original state after horrible crimes have occurred. Along the way, he comes into contact with people who own the properties, those who knew the victims - and sometimes the criminals themselves.

Click and Collect - 2018 - Stephen Merchant (*Hello Ladies*) stars as Andrew, a man on a desperate Christmas mission to purchase the elusive Sparklehoof the Unicorn Princess for his daughter.

Craig Ferguson: I'm Here to Help - 2013 - Scottish comedian Craig Ferguson talks fatherhood, Helen of Troy and shark penises. **Premiered April 1st.**

Cruise of the Gods - 2002 - Steve Coogan, David Walliams, and Rob Brydon star in this feature-length comedy about a group of 1980s sci-fi programme actors reuniting to attend a cruise arranged by the show's fan club.

Dad's Army - 1968 to 1977 - One of the most-loved British sitcoms of all time, *Dad's Army* follows the challenges facing a Home Guard platoon during World War II. Under constant threat of invasion by Nazi Germany, the Home Guard was made up of men not able to join the regular army (often older men who wanted to take a more active role in the war effort). Because so many were older, it was often referred to as "Dad's Army".

Damned - 2016 to 2018 - Alan Davies (*Jonathan Creek*) and Jo Brand (*Getting On*) star in this series about workers dealing with endless bureaucracy in a social services department.

The Darling Buds of May - 1991 to 1993 - Based on the 1958 H.E. Bates novel of the same name, this series is set in rural 1950s Kent and follows the Larkin family as they go about their daily lives. This early 90s dramedy was a breakout role for Welsh actress Catherine Zeta-Jones.

Do Not Adjust Your Set - 1967 to 1969 - This innovative British comedy classic was an early evening sketch show featuring a number of actors who would go on to become massively famous. It was written by Michael Palin (*Ripping Yarns*), Terry Jones (*The Meaning of Life*), and Eric Idle (*At Last the 1948 Show*), and it includes some great performances by David Jason (*A Touch of Frost*) and Denise Coffey (*Sir Henry at Rawlinson End*).

Don't Forget the Driver - 2019 - Toby Jones (*Detectorists*) takes on another comedy role in this series about a depressed single dad who works as a coach driver. His mundane existence is shaken up when he takes a group across the English Channel and finds a migrant stowed away in his wheel arch. Jones co-wrote the series with Tim Crouch.

Eddie Izzard: Definite Article - 1996 - This stand-up special was recorded at the Shaftesbury Theatre in London when Eddie was in the middle of her sell-out 12 week run. It includes topics such as Pavlov's dogs, European languages and trivia. **Premiered April 1st.**

Eddie Izzard: Glorious - 1997 - This 1997 performance included topics like the siege of Troy, Noah's Ark, the British royals and baby Jesus. **Premiered April 1st.**

Edge of Heaven - 2014 - In the seaside town of Margate, a close-knit but quirky family runs a 1980s-themed guest house.

Extras - 2005 to 2007 - Ricky Gervais (*The Office*) stars as an actor reduced to working as an extra, forever making himself look bad as he attempts to get ahead. Though he's yet to land a speaking part, his close brushes with fame convince him success is just around the corner. **Premiered August 5th.**

Fawlty Towers - 1975 to 1979 - John Cleese and Prunella Scales star in this classic British comedy about a very poorly managed hotel. Though it only lasted 12 episodes, it's considered one of the great British comedy classics.

Gavin & Stacey - 2007 to 2019 - After months of chatting, Gavin and Stacey leave their homes in Essex and Wales to meet for the first time in London. This much-loved comedy classic features a number of British acting favourites including Larry Lamb, Ruth Jones, Alison Steadman, Rob Brydon, and James Corden.

Gine Yashere: Skinny B*tch - 2008 - Comedian Gina Yashere discusses men, her mom, colonic irrigation, and luggage. **Premiered April 1st.**

Good Neighbors (aka The Good Life) - 1975 to 1978 - *The Good Life* sees Tom Good (Richard Briers) turning 40 and deciding to quit his job designing cereal box toys in favour of "living off the land" at the suburban home he shares with his wife Barbara (Felicity Kendal). Next door, snooty neighbour Margo Leadbetter (Penelope Keith) is rather displeased with the development – while her husband (Paul Eddington) just thinks poor Tom has lost his mind.

The Hitchhiker's Guide to the Galaxy - 1981 - Arthur Dent is one of the last surviving members of the human race. Still in his dressing gown, he's dragged through an intergalactic portal and sent on an adventure through the universe. The series is based on Douglas Adams' novel of the same name, and he also wrote the TV adaptation.

Hold the Sunset - 2018 to 2019 - Two mature neighbors are anxious to start a new life together, but they're interrupted when Edith's adult son arrives on her doorstep. Alison Steadman (*Gavin & Stacey*) and John Cleese (*Fawlty Towers*) star, and Jason Watkins (*The Crown*) plays Edith's adult son Roger.

Insert Name Here - 2017 to 2018 - This comedy panel show focuses on people with one thing in common. They all have the same name. Sue Perkins hosts, and Josh Widdecombe and Richard Osman act as team captains.

Inside No. 9 - 2014 to present. - Dark humor, crime, drama, and horror are showcased in this anthology series. Every

BRITBOX

episode incorporates the number nine in some way, so keep an eye out as you watch. **Season 7 premiered September 6th.**

The Job Lot - 2013 to 2016 - In a Midlands job centre, it's hard to tell if anyone actually works. Sarah Hadland (*Miranda*) stars.

John Bishop: Live: Supersonic - 2015 - Comedian John Bishop performs a special one-off performance at the Royal Albert Hall in London. **Premiered April 1st.**

The Jonathan Ross Show - This comedy chat show has been a British staple for years, and now, BritBox is bringing it to American audiences. This hour-long series sees host Jonathan Ross heading up a show of live music, humour, and celebrity interviews. **Premieres October 13th.**

Kate & Koji - 2020 - Brenda Blethyn (*Vera*) stars as struggling café owner Kate. Jimmy Akingbola (*Rev*) is an African asylum seeker who's also a qualified doctor - but since he's waiting to be granted asylum, he can't work. Neither of them like each other all that much, but they find an arrangement that works. In season 2, Okorie Chukwu replaced Akingbola as Koji. **Season 2 premiered May 10th.**

Keeping Up Appearances - 1990 to 2002 - Dame Patricia Routledge stars as Hyacinth Bucket, a woman in perpetual denial of her working-class roots.

Last of the Summer Wine - 1973 to 2010 - The world's longest-running sitcom features grandpas gone wild in rural Yorkshire.

The League of Gentlemen - 1999 to 2002 - In the fictional Northern England town of Royston Vasey, strange characters exist with interweaving storylines.

Live at the Apollo - 2004 to present - Each episode sees a stand-up legend act as compere and perform to the audience, before introducing two of the best stand-ups currently on the comedy circuit. **Premiered April 1st.**

Live from the BBC - 2016 to 2018 - Filmed live at the BBC's Radio Theatre, this stand-up series presents some of the most distinctive current voices from the world of comedy. **Premiered April 1st.**

Living the Dream - 2017 to present - When a Yorkshire family buys an RV park in Florida and moves to pursue the American dream, they end up with culture shock.

Mapp and Lucia (1985) - 1985 to 1986 - Based on E.F. Benson's novels, this series is set in the fictional coastal Sussex town of Tilling-on-Sea during the 1920s and 30s. Prunella Scales (*Fawlty Towers*) and Geraldine McEwan (*Marple*) star.

Mapp and Lucia (2014) - 2014 - Steve Pemberton (*Inside No. 9*) wrote this later adaptation of E.F. Benson's novels, with Miranda Richardson (*Blackadder*) and Anna Chancellor (*Spooks*, aka *MI-5*) starring. Like the first adaptation, this one was also filmed largely in Rye, East Sussex.

Miranda – 2009 to 2013 - Miranda Hart stars as a lovably awkward woman who runs a joke shop with her best friend and seems to specialize in getting herself into pickles.

Mock the Week - 2005 to present - This satirical celebrity panel show is hosted by Dara Ó Briain and sees two teams of comedians tackling news and world events, often with improvised funny answers.

Monty Python's Meaning of Life - 1983 - This skit/musical film attempts to shed light on the significance of existence and some of the unanswered questions we all face. It's also the last Monty Python feature film to star all six members before Graham Chapman's death in 1989. **Premiered August 1st.**

Moone Boy - *Ireland* - 2012 to 2014 - A young boy copes with life in a small Irish town, thanks to his imaginary friend. Chris O'Dowd (*The IT Crowd*) stars in the series and co-wrote it.

Mr. Stink - 2012 - This hour-long television adaptation is based on David Walliams' novel of the same name. It follows 12-year-old Chloe Crumb as she befriends an unusual homeless man named Mr. Stink.

Mr. Bean - 1992 to 1995 - Bumbling Mr. Bean rarely speaks and has some very peculiar ways of doing things, but it usually works out for him. Rowan Atkinson (*Maigret*) stars as the iconic British character.

Mr. Bean's Holiday - 2007 - When Mr. Bean wins a trip to the South of France, he sets off on a dream holiday that quickly turns into a comedy of errors and unforeseen incidents. **Premiered August 1st.**

Mrs. Brown's Boys - 2011 to 2020 - Brendan O'Carroll stars as Agnes Brown (in drag), powerful Irish matriarch. She's loud, nosy, and fiercely proud of her brood.

Mum - 2016 to 2019 - After her husband dies, a woman tries to rebuild her life amidst all manner of problems from family and friends.

The New Statesman - 1987 to 1994 - This Yorkshire Television classic was written by Laurence Marks and Maurice Gran (*Birds of a Feather, Goodnight Sweetheart, Love Hurts*) and stars Rik Mayall (*The Young Ones*) as Alan B'stard, a Conservative MP who gets elected purely because there are no opposing candidates. He has an unquenchable thirst for power, and he'll stop at nothing to get to the top.

Northern Lights - 2006 to 2007 - Robson Green and Mark Benton are Colin and Howie, best friends with a deep affection for one another...and an intense rivalry. The two work at the same transport depot, they're married to sisters, and they live on the same street.

Not Safe for Work - 2015 - When budget cuts move Katherine's civil servant job to Northampton, she reluctantly goes along with the relocation.

Not the Nine O'Clock News - 1995 - This vintage sketch news comedy features Mel Smith (*Alas Smith and Jones*) and Rowan Atkinson (*Mr. Bean*).

The Office - 2001 to 2003 - Before there was Michael Scott in the US, there was David Brent in Slough, England. Written by Ricky Gervais (*After Life*) and Stephen Merchant (*Hello Ladies*), this mockumentary-style programme takes place in the office of the fictional Wernham Hogg paper company.

One Foot in the Grave - 1990 to 1992 - Victor Meldrew (Richard Wilson, *Merlin*) may be a pensioner, but he still has plenty to say about what goes on in the world. The series follows his misadventures - mostly of his own creation - as he attempts to keep himself busy in retirement. It was created and written by David Renwick, also known for *Jonathan Creek*.

Only Fools and Horses - 1981 to 2003 - This classic comedy follows a couple of dodgy brothers always out for the big score.

Open All Hours - 1973 to 1985 - Penny-pinching Arkwright (Ronnie Barker, *Porridge*) runs a corner shop, spending much of his time separating customers from their money and keeping his wayward nephew Granville (David Jason, *A Touch of Frost*) in line. He also finds plenty of time to pursue the lovely nurse Gladys (Lynda Barron, *Fat Friends*). This British comedy classic is a must-watch for any serious British TV fan.

Pointless - 2009 to present - This quiz series challenges its contestants to score as few points as possible by guessing unpopular but correct answers to general knowledge questions.

Porridge (1974) - 1974 to 1977 - This prison comedy features a man trying to do his time honestly and stay out of trouble. Ronnie Barker (*Open All Hours*) stars as habitual criminal Fletch, and Richard Beckinsale (*The Lovers*) stars as Lennie Godber, the new cellmate he decides to mentor.

Porridge (2016) - 2016 to 2017 - This modern reboot sees Fletch's grandson Nigel Fletcher navigating his way through Wakeley Prison.

Psychoville - 2009 to 2011 - This award-winning comedy is a mash-up of everything from horror to thriller to mystery to black comedy, and it sees Reece Shearsmith and Steve Pemberton (both of *Inside No. 9*) playing a number of characters. In the series, five different characters around England have received threatening letters stating, "I know what you did..."

Puppy Love - 2014 - This heartwarming sitcom sees two women doing their best to handle cute dogs and challenging families. Joanna Scanlan (*No Offence*) and Vicki Pepperdine (*Getting On*) star.

QI - Stephen Fry and Sandi Toksvig star in this entertaining quiz show where contestants are more amply rewarded for interesting answers.

Red Dwarf - 1988 to 2020 - In the far future, the last human lives aboard a spaceship with a highly evolved cat-man. *Remastered.*

Rev. - 2010 to 2014 - This smart sitcom follows the adventures of an Anglican vicar, his wife, and his run-down inner-city parish. Olivia Colman (*Broadchurch*) and Tom Hollander (*Baptiste*) star.

Ripping Yarns - 1976 to 1979 - Monty Python comedians Michael Palin and Terry Jones star in this anthology series that both parodied and celebrated pre-WWII schoolboy literature. Early episodes were directed by Terry Hughes, a BAFTA-winner who would later go on to direct *The Golden Girls* and *3rd Rock from the Sun*.

Rising Damp - 1974 to 1978 - Rupert Rigby runs the most dilapidated, seediest boarding house in all of England. This classic Britcom follows him and his unfortunate tenants – university administrator Ruth Jones, med student Alan, and town and country planning student Phillip.

Russell Brand: Messiah Complex - 2013 - Recorded live at the world famous Hammersmith Apollo, comedian and actor Russell Brand delivers a set questioning the value of traditional heroes. **Premiered April 1st.**

Scarborough - 2019 - In the coastal town of Scarborough, North Yorkshire, a group of locals live, work, and love, punctuated by frequent trips to the pub for karaoke. The series was written by *Benidorm* writer Darren Litten, but it was not commissioned for a second series.

Stand Up for Live Comedy - 2020 - When people were stuck at home due to the pandemic, the BBC came to the rescue, bringing the comedy circuit's best to TV. Each episode comes from a different city including Bristol, Belfast, Birmingham, Glasgow, Margate and London. **Premiered April 1st.**

The Stand Up Sketch Show - 2019 - This unique series takes stand-up comedy routines and turns them into sketches. **Premiered April 1st.**

Steve Coogan's Stand Up Down Under - 2009 - Featuring exclusive behind-the-scenes footage from his 2013 tour of Australia and New Zealand, this documentary gives us a look at what it's like to be a touring performer. **Premiered April 1st.**

Still Open All Hours - 2013 to 2019 - This series is a follow-up to the immensely popular Brit-com classic *Open All Hours*. Written by Roy Clarke (*Keeping Up Appearances*), the series sees Sir David Jason returning as shopkeeper Granville, now the proprietor of the South Yorkshire shop once owned by his uncle. Granville runs the shop with his son Leroy, the result of a romantic encounter decades earlier. Though his son has plenty of romantic

success, Leroy's efforts to woo his old flame Mavis are forever thwarted by her sister Madge. **Premiered May 27th.**

There She Goes - 2018 to present - David Tennant (*Doctor Who*) stars in this dramedy about a family dealing with the challenges of their daughter's chromosomal disorder. The series was based on the real-life experiences of writer and creator Shaun Pye. Miley Locke plays the young Rosie Yates.

The Thick of It - 2005 to 2012 - This political satire follows government officials who lie, cheat, and generally do whatever it takes to keep their jobs.

The Thin Blue Line - 1995 to 1996 - Rowan Atkinson (*Mr. Bean*) stars as Inspector Fowler, an arrogant but ethical uniformed cop who's constantly being shown up by the plain-clothes detectives. This comedy is set in the fictional English town of Gasforth.

Toast of London - 2013 to 2015 - This BAFTA-winning comedy sees Matt Berry (The IT Crowd) in the role of Steven Toast, an actor with more than his fair share of personal issues. Though he's a RADA-trained actor, his life is not working out as he might have hoped. His old-school agent is as much hindrance and help, and his strange flatmate always manages to complicate his life. All he wants is for the world to finally recognise and reward his acting talent. **Premieres October 13th.**

To the Manor Born - 1979 to 1980, 2007 - After her husband dies, Audrey fforbes-Hamilton (Penelope Keith, *The Good Life*) finds out they're broke. Forced to sell the family home, Grantleigh Manor, she takes up residence in the lodge on the property so she can keep an eye on the new owner. That new owner happens to be Richard DeVere, a handsome nouveau riche supermarket owner who proves difficult to hate forever.

Twenty Twelve - 2011 to 2012 - Hugh Bonneville, Olivia Colman, and Jessica Hynes are among the stars of this mockumentary-style series about the team responsible for planning the 2012 London Olympics. Together, they'll deal with everything from horse dung to traffic light timing.

Up the Women - 2013 to 2015 - Set in 1910, this comedy takes place among the women of the Banbury Intricate Craft Circle as they participate in the women's suffrage movement. To support their efforts, they form a league called Banbury Intricate Craft Circle Politely Requests Women's Suffrage (BICCPRWS).

Upstart Crow - 2016 to 2018 - This sitcom gives us William Shakespeare, before he was famous.

The Vicar of Dibley - 1994 to 2015 - When the 100-year-old Vicar of Dibley is replaced by a woman, some villagers are less than pleased. Dawn French (*The Trouble With Maggie Cole*) stars.

W1A - 2014 to 2017 - Hugh Bonneville returns as Ian Fletcher, the hilariously inept former head of the Olympic Deliverance Commission (in *Twenty Twelve*). This time around, he's taking up the position of Head of Values at the BBC. Now, he's handling things like salary scandals, age discrimination accusations, and suggestions of anti-Cornish bias. **Premiered June 10th.**

Waiting for God - 1990 to 1992 - Two grumpy pensioners fall in love while biding their time in a retirement home.

Whites (aka Chef's Whites) - 2010 - Alan Davies (*Jonathan Creek*) stars as a chef in a posh country hotel.

Would I Lie to You? - This comedy panel show sees contestants bluffing about their deepest and darkest secrets whilst the other team attempts to figure out what's true.

Year of the Rabbit - 2019 - Matt Berry (*The IT Crowd*) stars in this period comedy about an eclectic group of Victorian detectives who fight crime whilst mingling with street gangs, spiritualists, politicians, Bulgarian princes, and even the Elephant Man. **Premiered on July 1st.**

Yes, Minister - 1980 to 1984 - James is a Cabinet Minister who thinks he's finally in a position to get things done.

Yes, Prime Minister - 1986 to 1988 - This follow-up to *Yes, Minister* continues with the same cast but a new address on Downing Street.

Young Hyacinth - 2016 - *Keeping Up Appearances* writer Roy Clarke returned to create this prequel to the original series. Kerry Howard (*Him & Her*) stars as young Hyacinth Bucket (then Walton) in this 1950s-based period comedy.

Documentary & Lifestyle

24 Hours in Police Custody - 2014 to 2019 - This dramatic docu-series follows police detectives around the clock as they work to build cases against suspects in custody before running out of time.

7 Up & Me - 2019 - This special takes a look at how "The Up Series" has impacted popular culture over the years it's been produced.

A History of Ancient Britain - 2011 to 2012 - Scottish archaeologist Neil Oliver looks back at thousands of years of ancient history to tell the story of how Britain came to be.

A Queen is Crowned - 1953 - This feature-length documentary is narrated by Sir Laurence Olivier and offers a Technicolor look at Queen Elizabeth II's 1953 coronation.

A Tribute to Her Majesty The Queen - 2022 - Featuring interviews with her children and others who've known her, this tribute takes a look back at a long life dedicated to service of crown and country.

A Very British Murder with Lucy Worsley - 2013 - Historian Lucy Worsley takes a look at the British fascination with murder and mystery, along with some of the famous murders of 19th century Britain.

Africa & Britain: A Forgotten History - 2016 - Historian David Olusoga takes a look at the enduring and occasionally difficult relationship between Great Britain and Africa.

Agatha Christie: 100 Years of Poirot & Miss Marple - 2020 - 100 years after her earliest publications, experts and actors weigh in on Agatha Christie's legacy.

Agatha Christie: Speaking Her Own Words - 2016 - This audio series offers samples from Agatha Christie's personal tapes as she dictated her autobiography. Her grandson, Mathew Pritchard, offers the introduction.

Age of Elizabeth - 2022 - This hour-long documentary takes a look back on Queen Elizabeth II's lifetime of public service.

All Aboard! - 2015 to 2016 - This series takes us on several slow, uninterrupted journeys around Britain. Whether moving by bus, canal boat, or sled, there are no interruptions for talking, just the scenery of the journey with a few facts imposed over parts of the landscape.

Ancient Rome: The Rise and Fall of an Empire - 2006 - This dramatised documentary gives us greater insight into how the Roman Empire was built and destroyed by excessive greed, lust, and ambition.

Antiques Roadshow - 1979 to present - Filmed at a variety of stately homes around the country, this series allows members of the public to bring in cherished items for expert appraisal. **Series 41 premiered April 22nd.**

The Aristocrats - 2011 to 2012 - This series takes a look at four of the families that make up modern-day British high society. These are the individuals who, through no skill, talent, or hard work of their own, have been fortunate enough to inherit titles, incredible opportunities, and grand estates.

Around the World in 80 Faiths - 2009 - Pete Owen Jones takes us on a journey around the world, taking a look at how people worship in six continents.

Autumnwatch - 2021 - This edition of the popular nature series takes us to the Cairngorms in Scotland to see how autumn is unfolding out in the wild.

The BBC at War - 2015 - Presenter Jonathan Dimbleby shows us how the BBC helped out in the fight against Hitler and fascism, and how it's helped to shape the British government over time.

The Beatles & India - 2021 - Ajoy Bose, author of Across the Universe: The Beatles in India, worked with producer Reynold D'Silva (Audrey, The Ninth Gate), and co-director Pete Compton (It was Fifty Years Ago Today!) to create this audio-visual presentation that dives deep into the world of The Beatles. It features unseen recordings and photos, rare archival footage, eye-witness accounts as well as walk-throughs of many of the stunning locations in India the band visited.

Beechgrove Garden - 1978 to present - This popular Scottish gardening series offers practical advice on making the most of your garden – even in some of Scotland's most challenging conditions.

Britain's Biggest Adventures with Bear Grylls - 2015 - Bear Grylls combines history and adrenaline as he visits North Wales, the Yorkshire Dales, and the Scottish Highlands in search of Britain's biggest adventures.

Britain's Secret Treasures - 2012 to 2013 - Presenter Michael Buerk and historian Bettany Hughes take a look at 50 of the greatest treasures ever discovered by members of the public in the UK.

Britain's Tudor Treasure - 2015 - Historian Lucy Worsley celebrates the 500th anniversary of one of the finest surviving Tudor structures, Hampton Court.

Cameraman to the Queen - 2015 - For nearly 20 years, Peter Wilkinson has enjoyed a high level of royal access as he captured both state events and personal moments. This short documentary is a tribute to the effort, discretion, and loyalty involved in his work.

Caroline Quentin's National Parks - 2013 - Caroline Quentin takes us on trips to three of Great Britain's most beautiful national parks - the New Forest, Local Lomond, and Snowdonia.

Carols from King's 2022 - 2022 - Each year, the King's College Chapel Choir performs a carol service from the medieval chapel of King's College. It begins with "Once in Royal David's City" and always includes a newly-commissioned carol for each year. **Premiered April 16th.**

Charles & Diana: Wedding of the Century - 2011 - This documentary takes a look back at the wedding of Prince Charles and Lady Diana Spencer, examining its impact on both participants and viewers.

Charles: The Monarch & the Man - 2022 - Presented by Jonathan Dimbleby, this documentary offers a look back at the new monarch's long and very public life prior to Queen Elizabeth II's death.

Civilisation - 1969 - Art historian Sir Kenneth Clark offers his thoughts on the ideas and values that have influenced the evolution of western civilisation over the years. Though the series is more than 50 years old, many continue to count the series among the greatest documentaries in existence.

Classic Doctor Who Comic Con Panel - 2017 - Colin Baker, Peter Davison, and Sophie Aldred come together to discuss fan questions during Comic Con 2017.

Coast - 2005 to present - This series mixes history, nature, and great scenery as they travel around the coastline of the UK and surrounding areas.

Code Blue: Murder - 2019 - Detectives from the South Wales Police Major Crime team investigate murders and seek justice for those who are grieving.

Countryfile - 2021 - This factual series documents modern country life around the UK.

David Suchet on the Orient Express - 2010 - The quintessential Poirot, David Suchet, sets off on a journey to find out why the Orient Express is so famous around the world.

Days of Majesty - 1993 - This feature-length film celebrates the first 40 years of Queen Elizabeth's reign.

Dead Good Job - 2012 - This series takes a look at the different ways Brits choose to say their final goodbyes to friends and loved ones.

Diana: The Interview that Shook the World - 2020 - In 1995, Diana sat down for a gossip-filled interview with Martin Bashir, spilling all the private details of her marriage with Prince Charles. Twenty-five years later, this documentary takes a look back at what the interview revealed about society, royal life, and her psychological troubles.

Downton Abbey Extras - 2020 - This web series goes behind the scenes with the cast of *Downton Abbey*, sharing stories of their days on set together.

The Edible Garden - 2020 - *Gardeners' World* presenter Alys Fowler shows us how cooking your own fruit and veg can be both rewarding and cost-effective, even in relatively small garden spaces.

Elizabeth: Passions & Pastimes - 2022 - This film celebrates the interests Queen Elizabeth pursued away from her professional duties.

Escape to the Country - 2002 to present - Each episode follows a different set of homebuyers looking to leave crowded areas and find new homes in the British countryside.

Fashioning a Monarch - 2022 - This tribute sees presenter Fiona Bruce examining how Queen Elizabeth's style reflected her commitment to duty and country.

Funny is Funny: A Conversation with Normal Lear - 2018 - Emmy award-winning television pioneer Norman Lear sits down to reflect on his lengthy career.

Gardeners' World - 1968 to present - This long-running gardening series offers ideas, expert advice, and lovely scenery.

Gentlemen, The Queen - 1953 - This vintage film provides an up-close look at the early years of Queen Elizabeth II's life, including King George VI's coronation, her first broadcast, the war years, and her engagement.

Good Morning Britain - 2020 - Each day, Susanna Reid and Pierce Morgan share the latest in news, pop culture, sports, and weather. **GMB programming related to the death and funeral of Queen Elizabeth II has been added.**

Grand Designs - 1999 to present - Kevin McCloud follows people as they attempt to build their dream homes. As the long and complicated projects wear on, the early optimism and enthusiasm is often replaced by relationship and budgetary problems.

The Great British Countryside - 2012 - Hugh Dennis (*Outnumbered*) and Julia Bradbury (*Countryfile*) take us on adventures in four very different but equally stunning British landscapes. The series visits Cornwall and Devon, Yorkshire, the South Downs, and the Scottish Highlands.

The Great Chelsea Garden Challenge - 2015 - Six amateurs compete for a change to design and build a garden for display on Man Avenue at the 2015 RHS Chelsea Flower Show.

Great Escape: The Untold Story - 2001 - During World War II, 76 men attempted escape from the Stalag Luft III prisoner of war camp in Germany. Of those men, 3 made it home, 73 were captured, and 50 were shot on Hitler's instruction. This documentary tells their story.

Hairy Bikers' Bakeation - 2012 - Hairy Bikers Si and Dave take a 5000-mile road trip around Europe, sampling the best baked goods on the continent.

Hairy Bikers' Christmas Party - 2011 - Hairy Bikers Dave Myers and Si King show us how to make the perfect festive finger foods for a Christmas party with friends.

Hairy Bikers' Everyday Gourmets - 2013 - The Hairy Bikers show us how to prepare impressive feasts on very average budgets.

Her Majesty The Queen's Platinum Jubilee Celebration - 2022 - An all-star cast helps celebrate Queen Elizabeth II's 70 years of service.

Hidden: World's Best Monster Mystery - Loch Ness - 2001 - For centuries, there's been rumour of a monster hiding in the murky depths of Scotland's Loch Ness. This programme takes a look at those who claim to have seen it, and those who spend their lives looking for it.

Home Away from Home - 2014 - This series sees families swapping homes for a change of pace. On each swap, homeowners leave packets of information and activities for the new inhabitants of their homes.

Inside Claridge's - 2012 - Over the course of three episodes, we go behind the scenes at one of Britain's poshest hotels, looking at what it takes to deliver five-star service with an emphasis on tradition.

The Instant Gardener - 2015 - Danny Clark, garden designer extraordinaire, renovates the gardens of deserving members of the public.

In the Footsteps of Killers - 2021 - Slammed by some reviewers as tasteless, this controversial series pairs actress Emilia Fox and criminologist David Wilson to go over old ground and re-interview grieving families about unsolved murder cases.

Kirstie's Vintage Home - 2012 - Kirstie Allsopp helps viewers learn to add stylish vintage touches to their homes. This show blends DIY, upcycling, and bit of mid-century inspiration.

Last Night of the Proms - 2021 - For those not familiar with the BBC Proms, it's an eight-week series of classical concerts held annually in London. The "Last Night of the Proms" is quite different from the other nights, taking place on the second Saturday in September with widespread broadcast. The concert usually features some lighter classics and then a second half consisting of patriotic British pieces (like Henry Wood's "Fantasia on British Sea Songs" and Thomas Arne's "Rule, Britannia!"). **The 2022 event was cancelled out of respect for**

Queen Elizabeth II in the immediate aftermath of her death.

Lennon's Last Weekend - 2020 - Recognising the 40th anniversary of John Lennon's passing, this documentary shares the last in-person interview with John Lennon. In it, he spoke about topics including solo albums and The Beatles breakup. Interviewer Andy Peebles travels to New York City to revisit some of the iconic locations of Lennon's life and final days there.

Licence to Thrill: Paul Hollywood Meets Aston Martin - 2015 - Though better known for his baking skills, this series sees Paul Hollywood exploring the world of Aston Martin cars. In addition to meeting with the latest company boss, he also trains up to race.

Life in a Cottage Garden - 2011 to 2013 - *Gardeners' World* veteran Carol Klein takes us through a year of life in her garden at Glebe Cottage in Devon. It's a lovely walk through all four seasons and their unique challenges in southern England.

The Lights Before Christmas - 2019 to present - Each season offers roughly 90 minutes of unhurried footage of some of Britain's best Christmas lights.

Looking for Victoria - 2003 - Prunella Scales (*Fawlty Towers*) takes a look back at Queen Victoria, the monarch she's been portraying in a one-woman show for roughly 20 years.

Marco's Great British Feast - 2008 - Chef Marco Pierre White travels around Britain sourcing some of the best and most unique local ingredients (including gull eggs).

The Monarchy - 1992 - This early 90s series takes a closer look at the British monarchy - the allure, their purpose, and how much they cost the British taxpayer.

Murder Case - 2019 to 2020 - This docuseries offers unparalleled access to the work of the Glasgow-based Major Investigations Team (MIT) as they tackle some of Scotland's most complex investigations. From crime scene to arrest and charging of the suspect, it offers a real-life look at how detectives work together to pursue justice and keep Scotland safe. **Premiered July 8th.**

Murder, Mystery, and My Family - 2018 to present - This true crime series pairs the relatives of convicted killers with talented criminal barristers, allowing for a new examination of evidence using modern forensic techniques. **Season 5 premieres September 23rd.**

Murder, Mystery, & My Family: Case Closed - 2019 to present - This follow-up series returns to the families featured in *Murder, Mystery, & My Family* to see what's happened since the original episodes aired. **Seasons 3-4 premiere September 23rd.**

My Family Secrets Revealed - 2018 - This innovative factual series uses family trees, DNA, and historic records to discover long-hidden family stories and secrets. Always entertaining, episodes uncover stories of scandal, heroic acts, and forbidden love.

The Mystery of Mary Magdalene - 2013 - Melvyn Bragg takes a closer look at the questions surrounding Mary Magdalene, a highly controversial biblical figure.

Nigellissima - 2012 - Nigella Lawson shows viewers how to bring a bit of Italy into their kitchens, even without access to specialty Italian grocery stores.

Our Cops in the North - 2019 - Meet the detectives, emergency response officers, and command centres of the Northumbrian Police Force as they struggle to maintain the peace and catch the guilty in their little corner of the world.

Paul O'Grady: For the Love of Dogs - 2012 - Comedian Paul O'Grady explores the bond between man and dog, Much of the series takes place at the Battersea Dogs & Cats Home.

Picturing Elizabeth: Her Life in Images - 2022 - Over the course of her reign, Queen Elizabeth became the most visually represented person in history. From newspapers and souvenirs to stamps and currency, her face has been everywhere.

Prime Minister's Questions - 2013 to present - In the House of Commons, MPs put their questions to Prime Minister Boris Johnson.

Question Time - 2019 to 2020 - This debate show sees politicians and media figures answering questions from the general public.

Rachel Khoo's Kitchen Notebook: London - 2014 - London-born chef Rachel Khoo goes back to London to explore the food scene and offer tips on how to create great British meals at home.

Rachel's Coastal Cooking - 2015 - Chef Rachel Allen hits the road to track down local food around the Irish coast.

Reel Britannia - 2022 - This four-part docuseries tells the story of modern British cinema and how it has reflected societal changes over time. **Premiered August 7th.**

The RHS Chelsea Flower Show - 2021 - This series offers a peek at what's happening at one of the world's greatest horticultural events, the RHS Chelsea Flower Show.

RPU: Road Policing Unit - 2016 - This docuseries follows traffic cops around Britain as they perform typical daily duties around the UK.

Secrets from the Sky - 2014 - Using drones, historian Bettany Hughes takes a look at Britain's historic sites from the air.

Seven Wonders of the Commonwealth - 2014 - Several presenters travel the globe to see the people and the natural wonders of nations in the Commonwealth.

Shakespeare in Italy - 2012 - Shakespeare placed a number of his most famous plays in cities around Italy. This series sees Francesco da Mosto and a variety of special guests (including Emma Thompson) travelling around the country and visiting Shakespearean locations like Padua, Verona, and Venice.

The Shard: Hotel in the Clouds - 2014 - The Shard is a London hotel that promises the ultimate in luxury. This documentary takes a look behind the scenes.

Springwatch - 2005 to present - Along with *Autumnwatch* and *Winterwatch*, this series follows British flora and fauna through the changing of the seasons each year. *Springwatch* 2022 premiered June 1st.

The Story of Luxury - 2011 - This two-part docuseries takes a look at the things we've valued over the years, with a particular emphasis on luxury in the Classical and Medieval time periods.

Suffragettes - 2018 - Lucy Worsley presents this documentary about a group of working-class women working towards the right to vote.

Swingin' Christmas - 2010 - Michael Parkinson hosts this festive, musical Christmas special. The programme features special guest Seth MacFarlane and music led by conductor John Wilson.

This Farming Life - 2016 to 2019 - This dramatic docuseries gives us an often unromantic look at the highs and lows of modern farm life in Britain.

This is Joan Collins - 2022 - This feature-length documentary takes a look at the long and interesting life of London-born Joan Collins. From the beginning of her career during the Golden Age of Hollywood to later years in *Dynasty*, her life has been full of excitement, glamour, and handsome men. The documentary is narrated by Joan herself, and it uses a mix of interviews, archival footage, and even home videos to tell her story.

Unfinished Portrait: The Life of Agatha Christie - 1990 - Based on the notoriously private Christie's personal correspondence, this biographical programme takes a look at why a proper English lady might spend so much time imagining grisly murders.

The Up Series - 1964 to 2020 - This series is the world's longest-running documentary, following a group of Brits as they pass through life's stages. It began with 14 individuals back in 1964, and they do follow-up interviews every seven years.

Vincent Van Gogh: Painted with Words - 2010 - Benedict Cumberbatch (*Sherlock*) takes on the role of the iconic Dutch post-impressionist. The dialogue is sourced from Van Gogh's own words.

Virgin Atlantic: Up in the Air - 2015 - Virgin Atlantic may be hip (as airlines go), but that hasn't translated to a stable financial situation. This programme follows CEO Craig Keeger as he attempts to turn things around.

When the Queen Spoke to the Nation - 2022 - This film takes a look at Queen Elizabeth's ever-popular Christmas speeches and some of the other times she addressed her country.

Winterwatch - 2005 to present - It may be dark and cold, but there's still plenty to see out in nature. Broadcasting from the Scottish Highlands, the *Winterwatch* team looks at what's going on with the local wildlife, along with a bit on how all of Britain's wildlife is doing.

The Women of World War One - 2014 - Kate Adie takes a look at the impact women had on the outcome of WWI. Though not on the front lines, women contributed to the war effort in many ways.

PBS MASTERPIECE

Website: http://amazon.com/channels/masterpiece

Description: Only available via Amazon, this PBS channel offers a wide variety of British programmes, particularly period dramas and mysteries. It also offers a number of foreign-language "Walter Presents" shows.

Available On: Roku, Amazon Fire TV, Android devices, iPad, desktop, Chromecast, and most smart TVs.

Cost: $5.99/month

Now Streaming

Agatha and the Curse of Ishtar - 2021 - Agatha Christie enthusiasts will know she famously disappeared for eleven days during 1926. This film picks up in 1928, with Agatha having travelled to Baghdad seeking peace.

Agatha and the Midnight Murders - 2021 - Set in London in 1940, this film sees Agatha Christie dealing with the war and killing off her most famous creation. Helen Baxendale (*Cold Feet*) stars as Ms. Christie.

Agatha and the Truth of Murder - 2018 - This film imagines what might have happened during Agatha Christie's famed disappearance in 1926. With her personal life in upheaval, the film sees her solving a real-life murder.

All Creatures Great and Small - 2020 - This remake of the much-loved classic 1930s-based Yorkshire veterinary series is based on the books by James Herriot. Newcomer Nicholas Ralph plays James Herriot, while Samuel West (*Mr. Selfridge*) plays Siegfried Farnon. Though Dame Diana Rigg played Mrs. Pumphrey in Series 1, her recent death has led producers to put Patricia Hodge (*Miranda*) in the role for Series 2. **Season 3 premieres January 8th.**

Anne of Green Gables - *Canada* - 2016 to 2018 - PBS offers three film adaptations of L.M. Montgomery's *Anne of Green Gables*:

Anne of Green Gables, Anne of Green Gables: The Good Stars, and *Anne of Green Gables: Fire & Ice*.

Annika - 2021 - Based on the BBC Radio 4 drama *Annika Strandhed*, the series stars Nicola Walker (*Unforgotten*) as DI Annika Strandhed. Newly transferred to the Glasgow Marine Homicide Unit, she brings a teenage daughter and a boatload of investigative skills.

Apple Tree Yard – 2017 - This miniseries is based on Louise Doughty's novel by the same name, and it's a suspenseful combination of sex and murder. When a woman gets an intriguing proposition, it excites her – until she realizes it may not be quite what it seemed. Emily Watson and Ben Chaplin star.

A Room with a View - 2007 - Elaine Cassidy (*No Offence*) stars alongside Rafe Spall (*Desperate Romantics*) in this story about a young Englishwoman in 1912 who finds love on a trip to Italy.

Around the World in 80 Days - 2022 - David Tennant (*Doctor Who, Broadchurch*) stars in this adaptation of the classic Jules Verne novel in which the wealthy Phileas Fogg wagers he can circumnavigate the globe in a mere 80 days. **The series has been renewed for a second season.**

Arthur and George - 2015 - Martin Clunes (*Doc Martin*) stars as Sir Arthur Conan Doyle. When he finds himself outraged at an injustice against an Anglo-Indian solicitor, he uses his own fictional detective's methods to get justice for him.

As Time Goes By: Reunion Specials - 2005 - This much-loved British comedy returns for two final episodes in which Jean Hardcastle is very much hoping for grandchildren.

Atlantic Crossing - *Norway* - 2020 - Set in Norway and the US during WWII, this miniseries tells the story of Norway's Crown Princess Martha as she rose to international prominence. Though not British, it does include portrayals of King George VI and Queen Elizabeth.

Baptiste - 2019 to 2021 - This spinoff from the series *The Missing* sees Tchéky Karyo returning as Julien Baptiste, a clever detective who agrees to help the Dutch police look for a missing sex worker in Amsterdam. Tom Hollander (*Rev*) and Jessica Raine (*Call the Midwife*) also appear.

Beecham House - 2019 - Set in 1795, this period drama depicts the lives of a former East India Company soldier who's determined to create a safe home in Delhi for his family. Critics have dubbed it "The Delhi Downton". Tom Bateman (*Vanity Fair*) and Lesley Nicol (*Downton Abbey*) star.

Before We Die - 2022 - Based on a Swedish series of the same name, this series follows Bristol detective Hannah Laing (Lesley Sharp) as she investigates the murder of her lover.

The Boleyns: A Scandalous Family - 2022 - This three-part period drama follows the rise and fall of the Boleyns.

Breathless - 2013 - Set in early 1960s England, this series looks at the lives of hospital staff who perform illegal off-site abortions in their spare time.

Broadchurch – 2013 to 2017 - When an 11-year-old boy is murdered in a quiet coastal community, town secrets are exposed. David Tennant (*Deadwater Fell*) and Olivia Colman (*Rev*) star.

Capital - 2015 - Toby Jones and Rachael Stirling (both of *Detectorists*) star in this drama about residents on a fictional street who receive postcards that read: "We want what you have." As the mystery unfolds, their interweaving stories will also play out.

The Chaperone - 2018 - With a screenplay by Julian Fellowes (*Downton Abbey*), this period drama focuses on Norma Carlisle, a middle-aged woman charged with chaperoning the teenage Louise Brooks, not yet a flapper icon and sex symbol.

The Child in Time - 2018 - Benedict Cumberbatch (*Sherlock*) stars in this film about a man struggling to find purpose after the disappearance of his daughter. It's based on a novel by Ian McEwan.

Churchill's Secret - 2016 - Set during the summer of 1953, this film sees Michael Gambon portraying Winston Churchill as he recovered from a life-threatening stroke.

Cobra - 2020 to present - Robert Carlyle stars as UK Prime Minister Robert Sutherland in this political thriller. To date, each season has followed his actions as massive catastrophes threaten the country. **Season 2 premiered July 10th.**

Collision – 2009 - After a multi-car accident, a group of relative strangers see their secrets unfold around that single event that ties them together. This short series was written by Anthony Horowitz of *Midsomer Murders* fame, and *Shetland* fans will immediately notice Douglas Henshall as DI John Tolin.

The Crimson Field - 2014 to 2015 - At a busy WWI hospital, Kitty tries to escape her past.

Dancing on the Edge – 2013 - In early 1930s London, a black jazz group is coming up in the world. Unfortunately, tragedy strikes before they can fully appreciate their success. This miniseries contrasts British high society and the much uglier underbelly of racism and poverty.

Dark Angel – 2017 - *Downton Abbey*'s Joanne Froggatt plays the Victorian poisoner Mary Ann Cotton, a woman who murdered a number of her husbands and children.

Death Comes to Pemberley – 2014 - Three episodes pay homage to Jane Austen's *Pride and Prejudice*, bringing us into the home of Elizabeth and Darcy after six years of marriage. As they prepare for their annual ball, tragedy brings the festivities to a halt.

Deep Water - 2019 - Anna Friel (*Marcella*) stars in this miniseries about three mothers struggling with challenging moral and ethical problems.

Elizabeth I: The Virgin Queen – 2005 - Anne-Marie Duff stars in this fascinating miniseries about Queen Elizabeth I, the enigmatic and long-reigning queen who never took a husband. Tom Hardy stars as her dear friend and possible lover Robert Dudley, 1st Earl of Leicester, and Emilia Fox takes on the role of Dudley's wife.

Elizabeth is Missing - 2019 - Glenda Jackson stars as a woman trying to solve two mysteries while suffering from dementia. Her only friend has gone missing, and she's not sure what information she can trust.

Endeavour – 2012 to present - In this prequel to Inspector Morse, a young Endeavour works with Sergeant Thursday to develop his investigative skills. Shaun Evans stars as Morse during this 1960s period mystery. **Season 8 premiered June 20th.**

The Escape Artist – 2014 - David Tennant stars in this three-episode series about a junior barrister whose specialty is getting clients out of very tough spots. Unfortunately, this means his hands aren't entirely clean when those clients re-offend. Sophie Okonedo (*Mayday*) stars as his courtroom rival, Maggie Gardner.

Excalibur: Behind the Movie - 2020 - The 1981 film Excalibur is still considered by some to be one of the finest adaptations of the Arthurian legend. It also launched the careers of several well-known Irish and British actors including Ciarán Hinds, Liam Neeson, Sir Patrick Stewart, Helen Mirren, and Gabriel Byrne. This documentary takes a look back at the masterpiece.

Exile – 2011 - John Simm (*Life on Mars*) stars in this mystery-thriller about a man who returns home after his life falls apart – only to find a different kind of trouble there.

Far From the Madding Crowd (1998) - This television movie is an adaptation of Thomas Hardy's novel of the same name, this time starring Paloma Baeza (*A Touch of Frost*) and Nathaniel Parker (*Inspector Lynley Mysteries*). Set against the backdrop of rural southwest England during Victorian times, it follows the life of Bathsheba Everdene and the people she knows in her small farming community.

Flesh & Blood - 2020 - When a widow finds unexpected romance with a retired surgeon, her family's reactions are mixed. A web of lies and secrets brings chaos and eventually, murder. This one's full of crazy relatives, dark secrets, and for good measure, a nosy neighbor played by Imelda Staunton.

The Forsyte Saga – 2002 - This adaptation of John Galsworthy's novel follows the life of an English family over 34 years stretching from Victorian England to World War 1.

Frankie Drake Mysteries – *Canada* - 2018 to present - Set in 1920s Toronto, Frankie Drake is a great series for anyone who loved Miss Fisher's Murder Mysteries. Ms. Drake is a female detective whose Drake Detective Agency takes on the cases police don't want. Along with her trusty partner Trudy, they get into all manner of trouble.

Grantchester – 2014 to present - In the village of Grantchester, a clever vicar assists a local police detective with his investigations. James Norton (*Happy Valley*) stars as vicar Sidney Chambers, and Robson Green (*Wire in the Blood*) plays DI Geordie Keating. Later in the series, Tom Brittany takes over for him in the role of Reverend Will Davenport, a former inner-city chaplain. **Season 7 premiered July 10th.**

The Great Fire - 2015 - This four-part series is a dramatisation of 1666's Great Fire of London. The fire went on for four days, leaving nearly 90% of the city's population homeless.

Great Performances: Macbeth - 2010 - Sir Patrick Stewart stars in this acclaimed adaptation of Shakespeare's "Scottish Play".

Guilt - 2019 - After two Scottish brothers cover up a hit and run accident, their lives begin to implode. Mark Bonnar (*Catastrophe*) and Jamie Sives (*Game of Thrones*) star. **Season 2 premiered in August.**

Halifax: Retribution - *Australia* - 2021 - When a sniper terrorises the city, Commander Tom Saracen calls in a professor of forensic psychiatry, Jane Halifax, to help find the culprit.

Henry and Anne: The Lovers Who Changed History - 2014 - Historian Dr. Suzannah Lipscomb tells the story of the love affair between Henry VIII and Anne Boleyn.

Henry IX: Lost King - 2017 - Many have called Henry Frederick, Prince of Wales the best king England never had. Though bright and promising, he died at the age of 18 from typhoid fever. This documentary looks at the achievements in his short life, along with what might have been.

Home Fires – 2015 to 2017 - In WWII-era Britain, a group of women get by in a small village.

Hotel Portofino - 2022 - Set in the 1920s, this period drama follows the British Ainsworth family as they attempt to operate their upscale hotel along the Italian coastline. Despite only being open for a short time, troubles are already mounting.

Howards End – 2018 - This miniseries is based on the E.M. Forster novel, and it examines class differences in 1900s England through the lens of three families.

Indian Summers - 2015 - This drama dives into live in a social club during the final years of British colonial rule of India.

Inside the Court of Henry VIII - 2015 - This documentary takes a look at why things were so terribly chaotic and brutal inside the court of Henry VIII.

Inspector Lewis - 2006 to 2015 - Inspector Lewis was a lovely parting gift after the departure of Inspector Morse. In Lewis, Kevin Whately returns to play Morse's former sidekick once more – except this time, he's the DI and his sidekick is DS James Hathaway.

Jamaica Inn - 2014 - Jessica Brown Findlay (*Downton Abbey*) stars in this adaptation of Daphne du Maurier's classic novel about a young woman who moves in with a Cornish aunt and uncle, only to quickly discover unsavoury activities in her new home.

Jamestown – 2017 to 2019 - This series goes 400 years back in time to follow a group of English settlers in 1619 Virginia. When it opens, it's a little more than a decade since a group of men settled Virginia, and a group of women is arriving to marry the men who settled the area and paid their way over.

Jekyll & Hyde - 2015 - Set in 1930s London, this variation of the classic story sees Robert Jekyll living in London, a sensitive young man trying to find his way independent of his foster family. Unfortunately, be begins to feel the influence of a powerful darkness that's

outside his control – and he realises his parents had been trying to protect him all along. Young Robert has inherited his grandfather's curse, and he's soon drawn into Hyde's dark and unsavoury world. Tom Bateman stars as Dr. Robert Jekyll.

The Jewel in the Crown - 1984 - This award-winning television serial is set during the final days of the British Raj in India during and after World War II. The series is based on Paul Scott's *Raj Quartet* novels.

Kidnap & Ransom - 2011 - This three-part miniseries follows Trevor Eve (*Shoestring*) as a skilled British hostage negotiator who travels around the world to work on high-profile cases.

Land Girls - 2009 to 2011 - This period drama follows four women in the Women's Land Army during WW2.

Les Misérables – 2018 - Victor Hugo's epic tale of love and poverty in war-torn France returns to the screen in this 2018 adaptation starring Olivia Colman, Dominic West, and Lily Collins. The 6-episode miniseries takes a deeper dive into some characters who have traditionally gotten a bit less screentime (like Fantine), making the progression slower and more grueling – but also much more dramatic.

The Long Song - 2018 - Based on Andrea Levy's 2010 novel about the end of slavery in Jamaica, this miniseries sees Tamara Lawrance playing a slave and Hayley Atwell playing the plantation owner.

Lovejoy - 1986 to 1994 - Ian McShane (*Deadwood*) stars as Lovejoy, the slightly shady antiques dealer and part-time detective. *Downton Abbey* fans will be delighted to see a young Phyllis Logan (aka Mrs. Hughes) in this early role.

Lucy Worsley Investigates - 2022 - Historian Lucy Worsley takes a look at new evidence related to some of the most fascinating bits of British history.

Lucy Worsley's Royal Myths and Secrets - 2020 - This three-part series sees historian Lucy Worsley travelling across Europe in search of places central to royal history.

Lucy Worsley's 12 Days of Tudor Christmas - 2019 - Lucy Worsley takes us on a fun and educational stroll through Tudor Christmas festivities.

Magpie Murders - 2022 - Based on a novel by *Foyle's War* creator Anthony Horowitz, this mystery follows an editor who's given the unfinished manuscript of one of authors, no dead. The mystery that follows will change her life. **Premieres October 16th.**

The Making of a Lady - 2012 - This film follows Emily, an educated but penniless woman who goes into service as a lady's companion.

Man in an Orange Shirt - 2018 - This two-part series tells two separate love stories set 60 years apart. One, a forbidden relationship, takes place during WWII, while the other is modern.

Mansfield Park (2007) - Billie Piper (*Doctor Who*) stars in this television movie adaptation of Jane Austen's third novel. It's about a young woman sent to live with wealthier relatives, who later falls in love with her sensitive cousin.

Margaret: The Rebel Princess - 2019 - A controversial figure in her time, Princess Margaret was a reflection of many of the societal changes going on during her time.

The Mayor of Casterbridge - 2003 - Ciarán Hinds (*Above Suspicion*) and James Purefoy (*Rome*) star in this adaptation of Thomas Hardy's novel of the same name. It tells the story of a drunken farmer who auctions off his family, only to realise the horror of what he's done and change his life.

The Miniaturist – This 2017 BBC miniseries is an adaptation of Jessie Burton's novel by the same name. In 17th century Amsterdam, a woman moves in with her new husband and his sister. Oddly, the husband gives her a mysterious dollhouse to occupy her time.

Miss Scarlet and the Duke - 2020 - When Eliza Scarlet is left destitute after her father's death, she can either get married or take over his detective agency. Because she's living in the 1880s and it's deemed inappropriate for a woman to take part in the trade, she gets a partner - Scotland Yard's Detective Inspector William Wellington, "The Duke". **Season 2 will premiere on October 16th.**

Mr. Selfridge - 2013 to 2016 - Jeremy Piven (*Entourage*) stars as the American Harry Gordon Selfridge, a man who revolutionised British retail.

Mrs. Wilson – 2018 - Mrs. Wilson is fascinating because it's not just a true story, it's a true story about the grandmother of Ruth Wilson (*Luther*), the actress playing the title role. Alison Wilson was widowed in 1963, only to realize her husband had been leading a secret life. Iain Glen (*Jack Taylor*) plays her departed husband, a foreign intelligence officer with more than one "Mrs. Wilson" in his life.

My Mother & Other Strangers – 2017 - This period drama is set in 1940s Northern Ireland, documenting the culture clash that occurred when American servicemen were stationed along the Ards Peninsula.

Nicholas and Alexandra: The Letters - 2019 - Dr. Suzannah Lipscomb presents this two-part docudrama about the love story between Tsar Nicholas II and his wife Alexandra.

Northanger Abbey (2007) - Felicity Jones (*Brideshead Revisited*) stars in this adaptation of Jane Austen's classic parody of Gothic fiction. She plays seventeen-year-old tomboy Catherine Morland, a young woman with a wild imagination and love of Gothic novels.

Pie in the Sky - 1994 to 1997 - When DI Crabbe leaves the police force to open a restaurant, they continue to pull him back in for part-time crime-solving.

Pollyanna - 2003 - Pam Ferris (*Rosemary & Thyme*), Kenneth Cranham, and Tom Ellis (*Miranda*) are among the stars of this television movie based on the Pollyanna novels of American author Eleanor H. Porter. Georgina Terry (*William and Mary*) stars as Pollyanna.

Poldark Revealed - 2016 - This programme goes on set to get a look at what makes Poldark such an enduring favourite.

Press - 2019 - This series follows the rivalry between two major newspapers, taking a hard look at some of the awful things they do to get a scoop. David Suchet (*Poirot*) appears.

Prime Suspect: Tennison – 2017 - Set in the 1970s, this series is a prequel to the Helen Mirren classic, *Prime Suspect*.

Prince Charles at 70 - 2019 - This documentary takes a look at the now King Charles' ongoing charity work and his likely future role as monarch of the United Kingdom.

Prince Philip: The Plot to Make a King - 2016 - This one-episode special tells the story of what went on behind the scenes when Queen Elizabeth II fell in love with Prince Philip. Royal courtiers felt Philip was rough, poorly educated, and unlikely to make a good or faithful husband. Many disapproved of his German roots and ambitious family. The film takes a look at maneuvers for the marriage that took place as early as 1939-40, when the future queen was just 13.

Professor T - 2021 - Ben Miller stars in this British adaptation of the Belgian series of the same name. In it, he plays an eccentric Cambridge criminology professor who consults with the police on challenging cases. In real life, actor Ben Miller pursued a PhD in solid state physics at Cambridge while also working on the beginnings of his career in entertainment.

Queen and Country - 2012 - Trevor McDonald walks us through some of the British monarchy's greatest traditions and institutions.

The Queen at War - 2020 - This documentary takes a look at how Queen Elizabeth II served her country during WWII, and how the war shaped her.

Queen Elizabeth's Secret Agents - 2018 - This docuseries takes a look at the incredible father-and-son team that kept Queen Elizabeth I safe during her reign.

Rebecca – 1997 - Emilia Fox and Charles Dance star as the new Mr. and Mrs. Maxim de Winter in this adaptation of Daphne du Maurier's classic gothic suspense novel. Diana Rigg plays Mrs. Danvers, the housekeeper still loyal to her dead mistress, Rebecca.

Reilly, Ace of Spies – 1983 - In this series, we get a glimpse at the life of Sidney Reilly, the spy who inspired James Bond.

Remember Me – 2014 - Michael Palin (*Monty Python, Great Railway Journeys*), Jodie Comer (*Killing Eve*), and Mark Addy (*The Syndicate*) star in this sublimely creepy three-part mystery about a series of unfortunate events that unfold around an unhappy pensioner who fakes a fall in order to be moved to a care home. The scenery is perfectly bleak and atmospheric, and the cast is outstanding.

Ridley Road - 2022 - Set in 1962, this period drama follows the post-WWII rise of a Nazi-inspired movement in England, along with the Jewish anti-fascist group that opposed them.

The Rivals of Sherlock Holmes - 1971 to 1973 - This vintage British mystery series offers up a variety of detective story adaptations from Sir Arthur Conan Doyle's contemporaries.

Roadkill - 2020 - Hugh Laurie (*House*) and Helen McCrory (*Peaky Blinders*) star in this four-part political thriller about a charismatic politician whose personal life is in shambles thanks to the enemies he's made. Now, he's in a race against time to do the things he wants to do before the problems of his past bring him down. Laurie stars as politician Peter Laurence.

Royal Flying Doctor Service - *Australia* - 2021 - This drama follows the lives of those who work in Australia's Royal Flying Doctor Service.

Royal Paintbox - 2014 - Hosted by the now King Charles, this documentary takes a look at rarely seen art created by British royals from the past and present.

Royal Wives at War - 2016 - This documentary uses dramatised monologues to give us a closer look at the 1936 abdication crisis through the eyes of the two women most deeply involved - Elizabeth the Queen Mother and American Wallis Simpson.

Rumpole of the Bailey – 1978 to 1992 – Leo McKern starred as Horace Rumpole, a defense barrister who often took on underdog clients.

Sanditon - 2019 - Prior to her early death at the age of 41, Jane Austen began a new and different sort of work. It was the story of Sanditon, a fledgling seaside resort town along the southern coast of England. It was never finished. In this miniseries, screenwriter Andrew Davies (*Mr. Selfridge, Pride & Prejudice*) finishes her final masterpiece. Rose Williams (*Curfew*) stars as Charlotte Heywood, and Theo James plays the outrageous Sidney Parker. Anne Reid (*Last Tango in Halifax*) and Kris Marshall (*Death in Paradise*) also appear.

Secrets of Britain - 2014 - This series takes a look at the secrets behind some of Britain's most notable landmarks and institutions. It covers the Tower of London, Selfridges, Scotland Yard, the London Underground, Her Majesty's Secret Service, and Westminster.

Secrets of Britain's Great Cathedrals - 2019 - Though many travel shows visit the great cathedrals, few of them offer as much detail as this eight-part series. It covers York Minster, Canterbury Cathedral, St. Paul's Cathedral, Westminster Abbey, Salisbury Cathedral, Wells Cathedral, Bath Abbey, Gloucester Cathedral, Durham Cathedral, Lincoln Cathedral, Worcester Cathedral, Tewkesbury Abbey, St. David's, Brecon, St. Asaph, Bangor Cathedral, Ely Cathedral, Peterborough Cathedral, and King's College Cambridge.

Secrets of Highclere Castle - 2013 - This hour-long documentary takes a look at the stately home made famous by *Downton Abbey*.

Secrets of Iconic British Estates - 2013 - This lovely British tour series takes us to Hampton Court, Althorp, and Chatsworth.

Secrets of the Six Wives - 2017 - Historian Dr. Lucy Worsley hosts this series about the most dramatic moments in the lives of Henry VIII and his many wives.

The Sinking of the Laconia - 2015 - This miniseries is a dramatic retelling of the 1942 German U-boat attack on the British RMS Laconia and its 2000 passengers.

Spying on the Royals - 2018 - In the late 1930s, King Edward VIII and his American lover were considered a significant security risk to the country. This documentary looks at the controversial espionage operation that kept tabs on the pair.

Suspects - 2014 to 2016 - Three Greater London detectives investigate serious crimes in this gritty - and heavily improvised - series.

Tales from the Royal Bedchamber - 2014 - Historian Dr. Lucy Worsley examines our lengthy fascination with what goes on inside the royal bedchambers.

Three Sovereigns for Sarah - 1986 - Vanessa Redgrave (*Mrs. Dalloway*) stars in this historic drama about the Salem witch trials.

To Walk Invisible: The Brontë Sisters – 2017 - This two-part series takes a look at the incredible Brontë sisters and their unexpected success in light of their male-dominated time period.

The Trick - 2022 - Jason Watkins (*McDonald & Dodds*) stars in this conspiracy thriller based on the 2009 Climategate scandal. It follows a professor and his team as they find themselves involved in the first "fake news" attack.

The Trouble with Maggie Cole - 2020 - Dawn French brings us this new comedy-drama about the dangers of gossip. She plays Maggie Connors, a seaside village busybody who likes to ignore the saying that "those who live in glass houses shouldn't throw stones."

Unforgotten – 2015 to present - Cassie and Sunny use modern technology to get to the bottom of very cold cases. This recent crime drama is based in London and stars Nicola Walker and Sanjeev Bhaskar as Cassie and Sunny.

Us - 2020 - This four-part dramedy is based on English author David Nicholls' novel by the same name, and it sees a man trying to win back his wife's love over the course of a dream holiday in Europe. Tom Hollander (*Rev*) and Saskia Reeves (*Close My Eyes*) star.

Van der Valk - 1972 to 1992 - Based on the novels of Nicolas Freeling, this series features Barry Foster as Piet Van der Valk, a Dutch policeman with an unorthodox approach to his investigations.

Van der Valk - 2020 to present - This reboot of the 1970s series will see Marc Warren (*Beecham House*) as Commissaris Piet Van der Valk. Set in modern Amsterdam, it's a major departure from the original Nick Freeling novels. **Season 2 premieres September 25th.**

Victoria and Albert: The Wedding - 2019 - Historian Lucy Worsley re-stages the wedding of Queen Victoria and Prince Albert, using historic documents, diary entries, and archives to pull together all the necessary details. More than just a re-enactment, she also talks about how the wedding changed history and created new traditions.

Vienna Blood - 2019 - Set in 1900s Vienna, this three-part drama follows brilliant English doctor Max Liebermann as he studies under Sigmund Freud. When Liebermann encounters Austrian detective Oskar Rheinhardt, they forge a partnership to take on some of Vienna's most deadly and disturbing cases.

What the Durrells Did Next - 2019 - Hosted by *The Durrells* star Keeley Hawes, this special takes a look at what happened to the real-life Durrell family after they left Corfu.

What to Do When Someone Dies - 2011 - Anna Friel (*Marcella*) plays schoolteacher Ellie Manning, a woman trying to have a baby with her husband Greg (Marc Warren, *Jonathan Strange & Mr. Norrell*). One night, he doesn't return home from work. Ellie is horrified to learn he has been killed in a terrible car accident, and he wasn't alone – there was a woman in the passenger seat. A tormented Ellie begins to question: who is the mystery woman and was Greg having a secret affair?

Wide Sargasso Sea - 2006 - This prequel to Jane Eyre tells the story of the first Mrs. Rochester and how she ended up in the attic at Thornfield Hall. Rebecca Hall (*Parade's End*) and Rafe Spall (*The Big Short*) star.

The Widower - 2015 - Reece Shearsmith (*Inside No. 9*) and Sheridan Smith (*Gavin & Stacey*) star in this miniseries about Malcolm Webster, a man who worked as a nurse and also happened to be a serial killer.

The Windermere Children - 2020 - This movie tells the true story of child survivors of the Holocaust and their rehabilitation in the Lake District in England.

The Windermere Children: In Their Own Words - 2020 - This documentary talks with some of the children whose new, post-Holocaust lives began along the shore of Lake Windermere in England.

The Windsors: A Royal Family - 2018 - This four-part documentary offers an in-depth look at Britain's current royal family, including interviews with friends, aides, and family members.

Wolf Hall - 2015 - This historical drama charts Thomas Cromwell's rise in the Tudor Court as he moved from a poor blacksmith's son to the closest advisor of Henry VIII. The series is based on Hilary Mantel's award-winning novel of the same name.

The Woman in White – 2018 - This BBC miniseries adaptation of Wilkie Collins' famous book of the same name includes Jessie Buckley, Ben Hardy, and Olivia Vinall. This classic gothic tale begins when a man meets a mysterious woman in white before heading to Limmeridge House to tutor his nieces. He's told its a woman who escaped from an asylum, but already, a mystery has begun to unfold around him...

World on Fire - 2019 - This miniseries shines a light on the lives of ordinary people from Poland, France, Germany, and the United Kingdom during the early years of World War II. The large and talented cast includes Helen Hunt (*Mad About You*), Lesley Manville (*Mum*), and Sean Bean (*Game of Thrones*).

Wuthering Heights - 2009 - Charlotte Riley (*Press*) and Andrew Lincoln (*The Walking Dead*) star in this two-part adaptation of Emily Brontë's classic novel.

BBC SELECT

Website: https://bbcselect.com

Description: BBC Select offers an eclectic variety of non-fiction programming from the BBC's own archives. NPR fans will likely enjoy this channel's mix of political and social documentaries, as well as its history and travel shows.

Available On: Apple TV, Roku TV, and Amazon Prime Video Channels

Cost: $4.99/month

Now Streaming

100 Days to Victory - 2021 - Towards the end of WWI, the Germans were making startling progress against the Allied Forces, leading them to realise they needed an entirely different strategy in order to win.

100 Vaginas - 2019 - This documentary follows Laura Dodsworth's project to photograph 100 vulvas.

1945: The Savage Peace - 2015 - World War II ended in 1945 and brought peace and freedom to millions. For some, however, the suffering was only beginning. This documentary looks at some of the violence carried out against the defeated Germans.

21st Century Mythologies - 2020 - This short documentary takes a look at the myths surrounding a variety of modern phenomena.

The $50 Million Art Swindle - 2019 - Michael Cohen was a high school drop-out who went on to become a successful art dealer, but when he got in financial trouble, he swindled his wealthy clients and went on the run.

9/11: Truth, Lies, and Conspiracies - 2016 - Roughly half of all Americans believe there's something they aren't being told about 9/11. This documentary explores what happened, and why so many people think the full story may never come out.

A Brief History of Graffiti - 2015 - Dr. Richard Clay takes a look at the history of graffiti and why some humans are driven to mark their territory.

Accidental Anarchist - 2017 - At one time, Carne Ross was one of western democracy's biggest supporters. Disillusioned with his work, however, he set off on a quest to find out whether anarchy might actually be the solution to all our problems.

Afghanistan: The British Lion's Last Roar? - 2014 - After 9/11, the British Army entered Afghanistan, confident that they could keep peace and improve the nation. In 2014, they gave up. This series takes a closer look.

Africa & Britain: A Forgotten History - 2016 - Historian David Olusoga takes a look at the enduring relationship between Great Britain and Africa.

Africa with Ade Adepitan - 2019 - Journalist and athlete Ade Adepitan travels the continent of Africa to examine the changes that are underway.

A History of Christianity - 2009 - Historian Diarmaid MacCulloch takes a look at the origins of Christianity and what it means to be a Christian in the modern world.

A Life in Ten Pictures: Elizabeth Taylor - 2021 - Elizabeth Taylor was enormously popular during her lifetime, both for her work and her love life. This short documentary attempts to find her hidden depths using ten photos from defining points in her life.

Amazing Hotels: Life Beyond the Lobby - 2017 - Food critic Giles Coren and chef Monica Galetti take a look behind the scenes at some of the world's most extraordinary hotels. The series includes visits to Marina Bay Sands in Singapore, Giraffe Manor in Kenya, Mashpi Lodge in Ecuador, and Icehotels in Sweden.

American History's Biggest Fibs - 2019 - British historian Lucy Worsley digs deep into America's history to find out the motives behind some of its most enduring legends.

Amish: A Secret Life - 2012 - This groundbreaking documentary sees an Old Order Amish couple who have taken the risk of allowing cameras into their home.

Ancient Worlds - 2010 - Archaeologist Richard Miles takes a look at how religion, power and society made us the humans we are today.

Ancient Treasures with Bettany Hughes - 2021 - Historian Bettany Hughes guides us on this six-part tour of the ancient world's most significant artifacts.

The Anti-Vax Conspiracy - 2021 - A small but not insignificant number of people have been convinced that COVID-19 and vaccines are part of a sinister government plot. This documentary takes a look at how people get like that, and what drives people to spread such lies.

Apples, Pears, & Paint: How to Make a Still Life Painting - 2014 - This hour-long documentary takes a look at the history of still life paintings and why artists have devoted so much time and canvas to the reproduction of very ordinary images.

Archaeology: A Secret History - 2013 - This series sees archaeologist Richard Miles battling heat, ticks, and leeches as he goes out in search of ancient secrets.

Are You Scared Yet, Human? - 2021 - There's no doubt that AI is changing the world, but is it for the better? This documentary considers the future of a world with advanced artificial intelligence.

Armada: The Untold Story - 2015 - When Elizabeth I became queen, she rejected Philip II of Spain. Years later, he would lead an invasion against her, attempting to bring England back into the Catholic fold.

The Art of Architecture - 2019 - This ten-part series travels the globe to look at some of the world's most architecturally interesting buildings.

Art of America - 2011 - Historian Andrew Graham-Dixon walks us through the history of American art, from its Native American beginnings to pop art and other modern movements.

Art of China - 2014 - Historian Andrew Graham-Dixon takes us on a journey through 3000 years of Chinese art.

Art of France - 2017 - Over the course of three episodes, Andrew Graham-Dixon walks us through the rich history of French art.

Art of Gothic - 2014 - Art historian Andrew Graham-Dixon dives into the history of England's Gothic Revival.

Art of Russia - 2009 - Art expert Andrew Graham-Dixon takes a closer look at Russian art and its preoccupation with icons.

Art of Scandinavia - 2016 - Though it's a region where darkness reigns for months on end, art expert Andrew Graham-Dixon discovers surprising creativity, playfulness, and eroticism in Scandinavian art.

Art of Spain - 2008 - Critic and historian Andrew Graham-Dixon goes out on the road to reveal some of Spain's greatest artistic treasures.

The Art Mysteries - 2020 - Art historian Waldemar Januszczak looks for the hidden meaning behind some of the world's most recognizable paintings.

A Royal Guide to... - 2022 - The British royal family is known for its strange traditions. Some babies are christened in holy water from the River Jordan. Little boys wear shorts until they're eight. This series takes a look at the reasons why.

A Slow Odyssey: The Great Wall of China - 2019 - This feature-length, commentary-free video takes you on an aerial journey along the Great Wall of China.

A Tribute to Her Majesty The Queen - 2022 - Featuring interviews with her children and others who've known her, this tribute takes a look back at a long life dedicated to service of crown and country.

A Tribute to HRH The Duke of Edinburgh - 2021 - This hour-long documentary celebrates the life of Prince Philip, the man who stood beside his queen for more than 70 years.

A Very British Murder with Lucy Worsley - 2013 - Historian Lucy Worsley takes a look at the British fascination with murder and mystery, along with some of the famous murders of 19th century Britain.

A Year in Tibet - 2008 - This series takes an up-close look at the lives of people in one of the most remote locations on the planet.

Auschwitz: The Nazis and the Final Solution - 2005 - Using computer graphics, reconstructions, and interviews, this docu-series attempts to offer insight into the full scale of the atrocities that took place at Auschwitz.

Australia on Fire: Climate Emergency - 2020 - Terrifying and deadly wildfires are becoming more and more common. This documentary examines whether they offer a glimpse into our shared future.

Avicii: True Stories - 2018 - Produced before his untimely death April 2018, this feature-length documentary tells the story of a regular Swedish teenager who went on to become one of the world's leading DJs.

Bacchus Uncovered: Ancient God of Ecstasy - 2018 - Historian Bettany Hughes takes a closer look at Bacchus, the god of wine, as well as the history of alcohol and its role in communities.

Barack Obama: Reflections on a Presidency - 2020 - Former American president Barack Obama sits down with historian David Olusoga to talk about his life and politics.

The Battle for Britney - 2021 - This documentary takes a look at the long-lasting constraints placed upon Britney Spears' assets after her mental health issues more than a decade ago.

The BBC at War - 2015 - Presenter Jonathan Dimbleby shows us how the BBC helped out in the fight against Hitler and fascism, and how it's helped to shape the British government over time.

The Beauty of Anatomy - 2014 - Dr. Adam Rutherford takes a look at the close relationship between art and anatomy over the years.

The Bible's Buried Secrets - 2011 - Biblical scholar Francesca Stavrakopoulou takes us on a journey to find historical evidence to support the Old Testament's best-known tales.

Bin Laden: The Road to 9/11 - 2021 - Bin Laden began life as the quiet son of a billionaire before transforming into one of the world's most despised terrorists. This documentary takes a look at how it happened.

The Birth of Empire: The East India Company - 2014 - This documentary takes a look at how the East India Company became the world's first multinational, as well as a massively corrupt imperial power.

The Black American Fight for Freedom - 2021 - This hour-long special takes a look at racial inequality in America.

Blitz Spirit with Lucy Worsley - 2021 - While most people believe Londoners were entirely united in their efforts during The Blitz, Dr. Lucy Worsley takes a look at the more complicated truth.

Body Beautiful: Ancient Greeks, Good Looks, and Glamour - 2015 - Why were the Ancient Greeks so obsessed with the nude form? Classicist Natalie Haynes draws a line between our modern obsession with appearances and the way those thoughts and desires manifested in ancient times.

The Boy Who Tried to Kill Trump - 2017 - In 2016, a young man from a town in the UK attempted to steal a gun and kill Donald Trump. This short documentary takes a look at what changed a young man with no history of violence.

Brazil with Michael Palin - 2012 - In spite of its size and population, Brazil is a destination that eluded Michael Palin for decades. In this series, he visits the country, exploring everything from the cities to the most remote areas.

Bright Lights Brilliant Minds: A Tale of Three Cities - 2014 - Art expert James Fox takes a look at the underbelly of three cities - Paris, Vienna, and New York - at important moments in their cultural histories.

The Brilliant Brontë Sisters - 2013 - Sheila Hancock takes us on a journey through

Yorkshire, looking at these incredible sisters who changed British literature forever.

Britain's Forgotten Slave Owners - 2015 - This two-part series takes a look at who owned slaves in Britain, and the country's unusual decision to compensate slave owners for "loss of property" when slavery was outlawed in 1834.

Britain's Vaccine - 2020 - During the height of the COVID epidemic, the promising Oxford-AstraZeneca vaccine suffered a number of setbacks and safety scares. This documentary takes a look at the mistakes and successes of the unprecedented efforts to develop a vaccine to prevent COVID infections.

Calculating Ada: The Countess of Computing - 2015 - This hour-long documentary takes a look at Lord Byron's daughter Ada, the unlikely computer pioneer of the early 19th century.

Celebs, Brands, and Fake Fans - 2013 - This undercover sting takes a look at some of the less-than-honest things marketers do to promote their clients in the new world of online influence.

Charles and Di: The Truth Behind Their Wedding - 2019 - The now King Charles proposed to Diana after just twelve meetings, and the two would walk down the aisle together just five months later. This documentary takes a look at what was really going on behind the fairy tale.

Children of God - 1994 - Sylvia Padilla and her children spent 18 years in the Children of God cult. After fleeing, she told of horrific sexual and financial abuse. This documentary tries to get to the bottom of what really goes on in the organisation.

China: A New World Order - 2019 - Since Xi Jinping came to power, Communist power has increased and more dissent has been quieted. This series take a look at the causes and implications of these changes.

Churchill's Desert War: The Road to El Alamein - 2012 - This documentary takes a look at the significance of the skirmishes in North Africa during World War II.

Churchill: Winning the War, Losing the Peace - 2015 -

Civilization: Is the West History? - 2011 - Historian Niall Ferguson takes a look at whether the West's power is coming to an end.

Climate Change: Ade on the Frontline - 2021 - Ade Adepitan travels to places hit hard by climate change, examining the impact and looking at things we can do to adapt.

Clothes to Die For - 2014 - This hour-long documentary tells the story of garment workers who were killed in the Rana Plaza building's collapse in Bangladesh.

Confessions of a Serial Killer - 2019 - This documentary takes a look at how Samuel Little got away with murdering as many as 93 women over the course of 40 years.

Confucius - 2015 - This film explores the life and times of Confucius, one of history's most influential men.

Conspiracy Files: George Soros - The Billionaire Global Mastermind? - 2019 - This documentary explores how George Soros became the world's favourite billionaire bogeyman.

Conspiracy Files: Vaccine Wars - 2019 - This documentary takes a look at how one man - the disgraced former doctor Andrew Wakefield - kicked off a dangerous anti-vax movement with his fraudulent data.

The Coronation of Queen Elizabeth II - This documentary uses archival footage and eyewitness interviews to take a closer look at Queen Elizabeth's coronation.

Countdown to War - 2021 - In September of 1939, Hitler invaded Poland. Just three days later, Britain had declared war. This docuseries takes a look at those three pivotal days.

Crime & Punishment - 2019 - This series takes a look at the UK justice system as it deals the pressure of increasing caseloads and strained budgets.

The Crusades - 2012 - Both Muslim and Western nations have been known to twist the truth about the Crusades, but this documentary attempts to find out what really happened.

Cuba with Simon Reeve - 2012 - Journalist and adventurer Simon Reeve heads to Cuba to find out what modern Cuba is really like.

The Cult of Conspiracy: QAnon - 2020 - Donald Trump may be out of the White House, but do his fanatics still pose a threat to democracy? This documentary takes a look at what's behind the QAnon movement.

Damned in the USA - 1992 - This award-winning documentary takes a look at some of the censorship battles that took place in America during the 1980s as conservative groups attempted to restrict the freedoms of their fellow citizens.

Danceworks - 2020 - Dance puts enormous physical and creative strain on those who do it at the highest levels. This docuseries takes a look at the people behind the movement.

The Dark Charisma of Adolf Hitler - 2012 - Why did millions support this hateful man, ultimately destroying their own country by following him? This compelling docuseries takes a look at how regular people can become devoted to a horrible person.

Dark Son: The Hunt for a Serial Killer - 2019 - Criminologist David Wilson leads a modern investigation into the "Jack the Stripper" murders that terrorised 1960s London.

David Bowie: Finding Fame - 2019 - David Bowie might be a legend now, but his career began with plenty of mistakes and false starts. This series takes a look at what finally worked to propel him to stardom.

Death Camp Treblinka - 2022 - During WWII, 900,000 Jewish men and women were murdered at a tiny camp located deep in the woods. It was never liberated, and the only way out was to fight. Survivors tells their stories in this documentary.

The Decade the Rich Won - 2022 - In the years since the global financial crisis of 2008, a tiny percent of the very wealthiest humans have leveraged financial catastrophe and corrupt politicians to carve out an even bigger portion of the pie for themselves. A variety of experts explain and weigh in on where it all went wrong.

Diana: 7 Days That Shook the World - 2017 - This documentary takes a look at the public reaction after Diana's death, along with her death's impact on the royal family.

Diana's Decades - 2021 - This docuseries takes a look at the three decades of Lady Diana's public life.

Divine Women - 2012 - Historian Bettany Hughes takes a look at the complex relationship between women and religion over the course of human history.

Don't Panic: The Truth About Population - 2013 - Swedish statistician Professor Hans Rosling uses data to demonstrate that the population crisis isn't what it's been made out to be, and that human population is on track to stabilise by the end of the century.

Drowning in Plastic - 2018 - Wildlife biologist Liz Bonnin talks with scientists who are trying to get the plastic problem under control before it ruins our planet.

The Duke in His Own Words - 2021 - This hour-long special takes a look back at the life of Prince Philip.

Edward VIII: Britain's Traitor King - 2022 - In 1936, Edward VIII stepped down from the throne, going on to marry an American divorcée and become a suspected Nazi sympathiser. This documentary takes a look at his life and actions.

Elizabeth I & II: The Golden Queens - 2020 - Over the course of two episodes, this series looks at the difference and similarities of two of England's greatest monarchs.

Elizabeth & Philip: Love & Duty - 2017 - Kirsty Young offers a look back at the Queen and Prince Philip's life together.

Elizabeth: Her Passions & Pastimes - 2022 - This film celebrates the interests Queen Elizabeth pursued away from her professional duties.

Elizabeth: The Unseen Queen - 2022 - Queen Elizabeth II is one of the most recognisable women on the planet, but few know much about what she's really like. This documentary uses rare footage and body language experts in an attempt to find out who she really is.

Epidemic: The Great Plague - 2020 - This three-part series examines how lessons from the Bubonic Plague might be applied to the COVID-19 pandemic of 2020.

Eugenics: Science's Greatest Scandal - 2019 - Eugenics suggests that humans could be improved upon through selective breeding. While scientists explored the topic academically, the Nazis actually attempted to put it into practice. This two-part series looks at its history and legacy.

Extraordinary Places to Eat - 2018 - Accomplished London maître d' Fred Sirieix travels to some of the world's finest restaurants in its finest cities.

Extraordinary Women - 2009 - This docuseries takes a look at some of the most notable women of recent history, along with the challenges they faced. The thirteen episodes include Maria Montessori, Dr. Ruth, Audrey Hepburn, Agatha Christie, and Hedy Lamarr.

Extreme Combat: The Dancer and the Fighter - 2020 - Dancer Akram Khan takes a look at the rise of MMA and what draws people to its spectacle.

Fake News: A True History - 2019 -This documentary takes a look at the history and consequences of "alternative facts".

Fashioning a Monarch - 2022 - This tribute sees presenter Fiona Bruce examining how Queen Elizabeth's style reflected her commitment to duty and country.

Fighter Pilot: The Real Top Gun - 2019 - Follow fighter pilot recruits as they compete to fly the Royal Air Force's new F35 Lightning jet.

Fighting for King and Empire: Britain's Caribbean Heroes - 2015 - This documentary highlights the black Caribbean volunteers who joined the fight against Hitler during WWII.

Filthy Cities - 2011 - We may think our cities are filthy now, but this series sees historian Dan Snow taking us through what it would have been like to live in medieval London, revolutionary Paris, and industrial New York.

The Flu That Killed 50 Million - 2018 - This documentary takes a look at the Spanish Flu and the lessons we can learn from it.

Frankenstein & the Vampyre: A Dark & Stormy Night - 2014 - This documentary explores a fateful night in Lake Geneva when Mary Shelley, Lord Byron, and some of their contemporaries gathered to tell ghost stories.

Gandhi - 2009 - Journalist Mishal Husain takes a look at Mahatma Gandhi's complicated legacy and impact on India.

Gauguin: The Full Story - 2003 - Art historian Waldemar Januszczak takes a look at artist Paul Gauguin's life and artistic influence, not shying away from some of the unpleasant accusations made against him.

Generation Porn - 2019 - This documentary considers the effects of widespread porn availability on young minds and relationships.

Genderquake - 2018 - This two-part series puts 11 people of differing gender

identities in a house together in hopes of promoting discussion and understanding.

The Genius of Carl Faberge - 2013 - Originally made for the Russian Tsars as Easter gifts, these expensive eggs have a fascinating history. Cultural commentator Stephen Smith goes on a hunt to uncover their secrets.

Genius of the Ancient World – 2015 - Historian Bettany Hughes travels the world to study the lives and times of great philosophers like Socrates, Confucius, and Buddha.

Genius of the Modern World – 2016 - Historian Bettany Hughes looks at the world that helped shape intellectual greats like Friedrich Nietzsche, Sigmund Freud, and Karl Marx.

The Genius of Roald Dahl - 2012 - Comedian and bestselling author David Walliams delves into Roald Dahl's world, chatting with those who knew him best. He meets Dahl's widow at the family home, and chats with longtime illustrator Quentin Blake as he draws a Dahl villain.

Germany's New Nazis - 2016 - In Germany, right-wing extremism is reaching its highest levels since the Third Reich. This documentary takes a look at what we can learn about the conditions that allow such extremist views to flourish.

Gorbachev: The Man Who Changed the World - 1996 - This documentary takes a look at how the son of a peasant family grew up to become the last leader of the Soviet Union, ushering in a new era of change and collaboration.

Grayson Perry: All Man - 2016 - Dress-wearing artist Grayson Perry takes a look at what really constitutes manhood.

Grayson Perry: Big American Road Trip - 2020 - Artist Grayson Perry travels the US to get a closer look at the increasingly deep lines between people of different races, classes, and political leanings.

Grayson Perry: Rites of Passage - 2018 - Wondering if the West has lost touch with its traditions, British artist Grayson Perry travels the world to see how other cultures celebrate life's milestones.

Grayson Perry's Art Club - 2020 - Throughout the lockdown, artist Grayson Perry offered artistic expression and escapism through his art club.

Grayson Perry: Who Are You? - 2014 - Artist Grayson Perry explores the concept of identity in a world where we're constantly bombarded by our own curated image of ourselves.

Harry Potter: A History of Magic - 2017 - JK Rowling invites us into her private archive to learn more about what inspired the enchanting world she created.

Harry Styles Live in Manchester - 2017 - Former One Direction member Harry Styles performs for a live audience.

The High Art of the Low Countries - 2015 - Andrew Graham-Dixon explores the region that gave us Vermeer, Rembrandt, Mondrian, Magritte, and Van Gogh.

Hiroshima: The Real History - 2015 - This documentary takes a closer look at what we know about the bombing of Hiroshima and the new age it ushered in.

History of Mother Earth: Gaia Uncovered - 2021 - Historian Bettany Hughes takes a closer look at the relationship we have with Mother Earth.

History's Deadliest Tsunami - 2021 - Using eyewitness accounts, this docuseries looks at the horrific 2004 tsunami in Indonesia and Thailand - and whether anything could have been done to mitigate the disaster.

Hokusai: Old Man Crazy to Paint - Katsushika Hokusai may not be a household name, but most people have seen his painting, *The Great Wave off Kanagawa*. This documentary takes a look at the man who inspired Van Gogh and influenced the creation of manga.

Horror in the East - 2000 - This series takes a look at the post-WWI cultural changes that influenced the atrocities committed by Japan during WWII.

Hotel Secrets with Richard E. Grant - 2012 - Oscar-nominated Richard E. Grant gives us unprecedented access to some of the world's most luxurious hotels.

House of Maxwell - 2022 - Ghislaine Maxwell's name may instantly conjure up images of sex and scandal, but she's not the first Maxwell to sully the family name. This documentary takes a look at her father Robert, and how his actions may have contributed to the life she pursued.

House of Saud - 2018 - This documentary takes a closer look at both the wealth and the challenges faced by Saudi Arabia's new Crown Prince Mohammad bin Salman.

How I Created a Cult - 2016 - This series takes a closer look at Andrew Cohen's EnlightenNext cult, including input from former members and even Cohen himself.

How to Go Viral - 2019 - Digital culture expert Richard Clay meets modern meme designers and internet trolls to find out how memes influence us.

The Hunt for Bin Laden - 2012 - America spent many millions of dollars and a number of years on the hunt for Bin Laden. This documentary attempts to explain why he was so difficult to track down.

Hyper Evolution: Rise of the Robots - 2016 - Evolutionary biologist Ben Garrod and electronics engineer Danielle George take a look at whether robots will ultimately be for the good, or whether we may one day find ourselves competing against them.

The Impressionists – 2015 - British art critic Waldemar Januszczak travels around the world investigating the great Impressionists.

The Industrial Revolution - 2013 - Historian Jeremy Black takes a look back at the Industrial Revolution and why it happened in the UK rather than France or the US.

In Louboutin's Shoes - 2015 - For many years, Louboutin shoes were known exclusively among the fashion elite and extremely wealthy. This documentary looks at how the shoe became such a well-known status symbol.

In Search of Frida Kahlo - 2014 - This documentary heads to Mexico City to learn more about artist Frida Kahlo's difficult life and work.

Inside the American Embassy - 2018 - This documentary takes a look at how American diplomats are dealing with the troubles brought about by comments from Donald Trump.

Inside the Billionaire's Wardrobe - 2016 - Reggie Yates traces the path from animal to closet, investigating whether "sustainable killing" can clear a buyer's conscience.

Inside the EU: The Mad World of Brexit - 2018 - This three-part series examines what Brexit is, why it happened, and what it means for the future of the UK.

The Instagram Effect - 2022 - In a relatively short period of time, social media platforms like Instagram have had an enormous impact on things like body image and self-harm in young people. In this documentary, former employees speak out about their concerns.

I Shot My Parents - 2017 - In 2013, 14-year-old Nathon Brooks shot both of his parents while they slept. Incredibly, both survived. This series takes a look at what drove a young boy to do such a thing.

Isis: The Origins of Violence - 2017 - English historian Tom Holland explores the tensions between Islam and the Western world, asking difficult questions about the origins of violent Islamist terrorism.

I Was Once a Beauty Queen - 2012 - Beauty contests were popular on British TV in the 1970s and 80s, but what happened to the women once it was all over?

Japan with Sue Perkins - 2019 - Comedian Sue Perkins travels Japan to immerse herself in some of their strangest cultural offerings.

Jennifer & Joanna: Absolutely Champers - 2017 - The two Absolutely Fabulous stars set off on a road trip to France's Champagne region.

Joanna Lumley in the Kingdom of the Thunder Dragon - 1997 - Joanna Lumley explores Bhutan, a land-locked country in the midst of the Himalayas.

Joanna Lumley in the Land of the Northern Lights - 2008 - *Absolutely Fabulous* star Joanna Lumley takes us on a tour of the Arctic Circle in hopes of catching a glimpse of the Northern Lights.

Joanna Lumley's Britain - 2021 - Joanna Lumley takes us on a trip to some of Britain's loveliest locations, including the Lake District, Scotland, and Wales.

Joanna Lumley's India - 2017 - Joanna Lumley returns to the country of her birth to explore a variety of landscapes and locations.

Joanna Lumley's Japan - 2016 - Actress and activist Joanna Lumley (*Absolutely Fabulous*) explores some of Japan's biggest cities and most remote islands.

Joanna Lumley's Trans-Siberian Adventure - 2015 - Actress Joanna Lumley takes a 6000-mile rail trip from Hong Kong to Moscow via China and Mongolia.

Joanna Lumley's Unseen Adventures - 2020 - Assembled during the pandemic, this series uses previously unseen footage from Joanna Lumley's adventures all over the world.

Joanna Lumley: The Quest for Noah's Ark - 2012 - Joanna Lumley embarks on a trip of discovery to explore truths surrounding the tale of Noah's ark and a great flood.

The Joy of AI - 2018 - Jim Al-Khalili takes a look at the history and future of AI - along with the potentially devastating consequences that could accompany its refinement.

The Joy of Chance - 2012 - Professor David Spiegelhalter explores the way chance works - and how we can make it work for us.

The Joy of Logic - 2013 - Professor Dave Cliff takes a look at the necessity of logic in virtually all fields, as well as the inherently illogical nature of our own brains.

The Joy of Stats - 2010 - Hans Rosling offers insight into how statistics can be used to help us see the world as it really is, but how they can just as easily be used to harm us.

The Joy of Winning - 2018 - Mathematician Dr. Hannah Fry takes a look at how you can apply game theory to your daily life to improve your odds of success.

The Kinky Sex Survey - 2015 - Brits aren't known for their exotic sexual practices (unless you classify "thinking of England" as an exotic practice) - but that doesn't mean all Brits limit their activities to married, heterosexual, lights-off action. This hour-long documentary looks at what Brits are really doing behind closed doors.

Kissinger: Statesman or War Criminal - 2011 - Henry Kissinger was one of the most powerful US diplomats in the late 1900s, but he wasn't without controversy. This documentary takes a look back at his career.

KKK: The Fight for White Supremacy - 2015 -

Kolkata with Sue Perkins - 2015 - *Great British Bake Off* presenter Sue Perkins travels to the Indian city of Kolkata to offer up an interesting look at modern India.

The Last Igloo - 2018 - This feature-length documentary follows one man as he sets off into the wilderness of Greenland to hunt, fish, and build and igloo. Along the way, he laments the fact that this simple, but highly-skilled way of life is dying out.

Leaving Amish Paradise - 2011 - This documentary follows two Amish families as they struggle to adapt to the modern world.

Liberty of London - 2014 - This seven-part series takes a look behind the scenes of the iconic London department store.

Lost Home Movies of Nazi Germany - 2019 - This two-part series uses recently discovered footage of ordinary Germans to see what life was really like in Nazi Germany.

Louis Theroux: A Different Brain - 2016 - Documentarian Louis Theroux takes a look at how patients and families cope with life-changing brain injuries that come with little to no outward physical signs.

Louis Theroux: Altered States - Choosing Death - 2018 - Louis Theroux looks at the growing movement urging governments to allow euthanasia for the terminally ill.

Louis Theroux: Altered States - Love Without Limits - 2018 - Louis Theroux visits Portland, the US capital of polyamory, to learn more about couples who've opened up their relationships.

Louis Theroux: Altered States - Take My Baby - 2018 - In this hour-long documentary, Louis heads to the open adoption state of California, where he talks with women handing over their babies to families paying tens of thousands of dollars.

Louis Theroux: Beware of the Tiger - 2011 - The United States has more captive tigers than the total number of wild tigers in the rest of the world. British filmmaker Louis Theroux visits breeder and collector Joe Exotic at his Oklahoma zoo to investigate why people collect rare and dangerous animals.

Louis Theroux: Drinking to Oblivion - 2016 - Louis Theroux spends time at King's College in London as liver specialists try to help alcoholics who can't seem to help themselves.

Louis Theroux: Extreme Love - Autism - 2012 - British filmmaker Louis Theroux looks at how autistic children perceive the world around them, and the impact it can have on their families.

Louis Theroux: Extreme Love - Dementia - 2012 - Filmmaker Louis Theroux visits Phoenix, dementia capital of America, to see how it affects patients and their loved ones.

Louis Theroux: Jimmy Savile Revisited - 2016 - Prior to the discovery that Jimmy Savile was a paedophile, Louis Theroux interviewed him. Many years later, he reflects on the encounter and how men like Savile are able to get away with such horrific acts for so long.

Louis Theroux: LA Stories - City of Dogs - 2014 - Louis Theroux travels to LA to learn about the city's vast dog population - from weaponised dogs in downtrodden areas to the pampered pooches of Beverly Hills.

Louis Theroux: LA Stories - Edge of Life - 2014 - Louis Theroux visits America to take a look at the country's for-profit healthcare system and how its extremely high costs can impact end-of-life decisions for patients and their families.

Louis Theroux: Law and Disorder in Johannesburg - 2008 - Louis Theroux takes a look at the lengths wealthy South Africans go to in order to stay safe in the often dangerous city of Johannesburg.

Louis Theroux: Law and Disorder in Lagos - 2010 - British filmmaker Louis Theroux spends time with some of Nigeria's paramilitary state groups and youth gangs to help make sense of a city that can at times seem both lawless and orderly.

Louis Theroux: Life on the Edge - 2020 - Louis Theroux looks back on twenty-five years spent connecting with fringe elements of society.

Louis Theroux: Miami Mega Jail - 2011 - No country in the entire world incarcerates more of its people than the US, and it has created a need for mega jails where inmates can await sentencing. Louis Theroux visits one of those facilities to meet men awaiting their day in court.

Louis Theroux: Most Hated Family in America - 2007 - In this documentary, Louis Theroux spends time with Christian extremists from the Westboro Baptist Church hate group.

Louis Theroux: Mothers on the Edge - 2019 - This documentary takes a look at what happens when new mothers experience postpartum psychosis.

Louis Theroux: Selling Sex - 2020 - In the era of online ordering, it's become increasingly easy to market and sell sex. Should it be as easy as hailing an Uber? Louis Theroux examines the issue.

Louis Theroux: Surviving America's Most Hated Family - 2019 - Thirteen years after he first encountered them, Louis Theroux returns to the extremists of the Westboro Baptist Church to see what happens after a hate group loses its patriarch.

Louis Theroux: Talking to Anorexia - 2017 - Louis Theroux visits two of London's biggest adult eating disorder clinics to find out why anorexia is so deadly and difficult to treat.

Louis Theroux: The Night in Question - 2019 - Louis Theroux visits American universities to meet students whose universities have found them guilty of sexual assault under stricter new policies.

Louis Theroux: The Return of America's Most Hated Family - 2011 - A few years after his initial visit with the Westboro Baptist hate group, Louis Theroux returned to the US to accompany the Phelps family as they travelled the country.

Louis Theroux: The Ultra Zionists - 2011 - British documentarian Louis Theroux travels to Israel's West Bank to meet the extreme Jewish nationalists who consider it their obligation to populate its most contested and sensitive areas.

Louis Theroux: Under the Knife - 2007 - Filmmaker Louis Theroux travels to Beverly Hills, meeting some of its plastic surgery-obsessed residents and joining them on consultations as they try to stay young.

Love and Hate Crime - 2018 - Over three episodes, this series looks at how dangerous it can be to be different in the United States.

Mad Dog: Inside the Secret World of Muammar Gaddafi - 2014 - This documentary takes a look at the evil reign of Libyan leader Colonel Gaddafi - from his billion-dollar weekly oil income to the torture and murder he used to silence his opposition.

Magic Numbers - 2018 - Dr. Hannah Fry looks at where mathematics comes from and why it's so important.

The Making of Merkel - 2013 - Andrew Marr takes a look back at Angela Merkel's life and rise to power in Germany.

Manolo: The Boy Who Made Shoes for Lizards - 2017 - This documentary takes a look back at the life and work of famed shoe designer Manolo Blahnik.

The Man Who Shot Beautiful Women - 2013 - Erwin Blumenfeld survived two world wars to become one of the world's most famous fashion photographers, only to die mysteriously and become almost unknown to modern society. This documentary takes a look at why that might have happened.

The Man Who Shot New York - 2019 - This hour-long documentary takes a look back at the life and work of street photographer Harold Feinstein.

The Man Who Shot Tutankhamun - 2017 - Photographer Harry Burton's photos of the Tutankhamun excavation in Egypt ignited a worldwide frenzy for all things Egyptian. This documentary looks at how he was able to do it, even with primitive equipment.

Married to a Psychopath - 2022 - Former police detective Charles Henry takes a look back at his most unforgettable assignment - the case of thief, pathological liar, and killer Malcolm Webster.

Mars Uncovered: Ancient God of War - 2019 - Bettany Hughes takes a look at the relationship between violence and religion throughout history.

Masters of Money - 2012 - Three men have had an enormous impact on modern economics and the way we think about money. This docuseries takes a look at the work of John Maynard Keynes, Friedrich Hayek, and Karl Marx.

Meat: A Threat to Our Planet? - 2019 - As cows spew methane into the atmosphere, pig manure pollutes nearby areas, and vital rainforests are cleared for beef production, there's no denying meat is creating problems for our environment. This documentary looks at why it's so destructive and what we can do about that.

Me, My Selfie, and I - 2019 - Many of us have more images of ourselves in our phones than we have from our entire childhoods. This documentary takes a look at whether selfies are a modern phenomenon, and how they impact our well-being.

Me and My Penis - 2020 - This show marked the first time an erect penis was seen on UK television, and it follows artist and sex activist Ajamu as he explores the relationship between men and one of their most beloved parts.

The Mekong River with Sue Perkins - 2014 - British presenter and comedienne Sue Perkins travels along the Mekong River, telling the story of this important river and the people who rely on it.

Meet the Trumps: From Immigrant to President - 2017 - This documentary looks at the Trump family's immigrant history.

Million Dollar Wedding Planner - 2019 - This documentary follows wedding planner Lelian Chew to learn more about the increasingly lavish weddings thrown by Asia's new billionaire class.

Moon Landing - 2019 - Focusing on the Apollo 11 launch and subsequent moon landing, this series aims to help us understand the excitement of the event.

Mozart in London - 2016 - Mozart composed his first symphony in London, but his achievements there would end in suspicion and accusations of fraud. Historian Lucy Worsley takes a look at what happened.

Mums Make Porn - 2019 - A group of five mums get together to create their own ethical pornographic film.

Murder 24/7: True Crime/Real Time - 2020 - This docu-series follows the team of experts who work non-stop to solve violent and deadly crimes.

The Murder Detectives - 2015 - This three-part documentary follows a real-life murder case from the initial call through the arrest and process of building a case.

Murder in the Badlands - 2022 - Over the course of four decades, four women were brutally murdered in Northern Ireland's Badlands. This true crime documentary takes a look at what happened.

Murdoch - 2013 - This two-part series chronicles the rise of Rupert Murdoch's global media empire.

Mystery of the Missing Princess - 2018 - In 2018, Princess Latifa of Dubai fled to India, hoping to escape her life. Unfortunately, she was captured, and it wasn't long before a video detailing her repression and abuse was released. She'd arranged for it to be released if her escape failed.

My Years with the Queen - 2021 - Lady Pamela Hicks opens up about her life growing up with the British Royal Family.

Nature & Us: A History Through Art - 2021 - Dr. James Fox uses art to examine our attitudes towards nature in different times and societies.

Navalny: The Man Putin Couldn't Kill - 2021 - In August of 2020, Aleksei Navalny was poisoned, suspected of having Novichok applied to his underwear. This documentary looks at whether Putin might have been involved - and why he might want him dead.

Nigellissima - 2012 - Nigella Lawson shows viewers how to bring a bit of Italy into their kitchens, even without access to specialty Italian grocery stores.

Nixon in the Den - 2010 - Historian David Reynolds offers a look at one of America's most controversial 20th century leaders.

North Korea: Voices from the Secret State - 2014 - This hour-long documentary offers uncensored opinions from real North Koreans - including army officers, members of the security service, and a family thinking of escape.

Nuremberg: Nazis on Trial - 2006 - Using largely unpublished trial documents, this three-part documentary offers insight into the people leading Hitler's Nazi party.

Oceans Apart: Art & the Pacific - 2018 - This series takes a look at the art of Australia, New Zealand, and the Polynesian Islands.

One Deadly Weekend in America: A Killing at the Carwash - 2017 - In May 2015, an autistic teenager was murdered for wearing the wrong colour of shoes. Through his story, we get a look at what life is like in LA's gangland.

The Palace & the Press - 2021 - This docuseries takes a look at how the relationship between the press and the British royals has evolved over the years.

The Persians: A History of Iran - Journalist Samira Ahmed looks at the rich and complex history of the world's first great empire.

Philosophy: A Guide to Happiness - 2000 - Can philosophy help us find greater happiness in the modern world? British philosopher Alain de Botton examines the question.

Picturing Elizabeth: Her Life in Images - 2022 - Over the course of her lengthy reign, Queen Elizabeth became the most visually represented person in history. From newspapers and souvenirs to stamps and currency, her face has been almost everywhere.

Pilgrimage with Simon Reeve - 2013 - Historian and adventurer Simon Reeve retraces the steps of our ancestors and looks at why people travelled so far to indicate their faith.

The Plastic Surgery Capital of the World - 2018 - With 60% of Korean women in their 20s having had plastic surgery, it's the plastic surgery capital of the world. This documentary takes a look at the cost of the pressure to be perfect.

Poaching Wars with Tom Hardy - 2013 - Actor and animal lover Tom Hardy takes us on a journey through the underside of the illegal poaching and ivory trading that still occurs in Africa - and the people who risk their lives in hopes of stopping it.

The Pregnant Man - 2008 - Trans man Thomas Beatie and his wife Nancy want to have a family together, but it's Thomas who gets pregnant. This documentary takes a look at the legal and medical issues that arise with their unusual situation.

Prince Andrew & the Epstein Scandal - 2019 - For the first time, Prince Andrew speaks with Newsnight about his long relationship with convicted child sex offenders Jeffrey Epstein and Ghislaine Maxwell.

The Prince and the Epstein Scandal - 2019 - Victims of Jeffrey Epstein tell their stories, with one revealing details about her relationship with the scorned Prince Andrew.

The Princes and the Press - 2021 - This two-part series takes a look at how the British press has interacted with and covered the younger members of the royal family.

Princess Diana: A Life After Death - 2007 - This short documentary takes a look at the media fascination with Princess Diana during the summer of 1997.

Putin: A Russian Spy Story - 2015 - After the chance viewing of a Russian spy drama, young Vladimir Putin was inspired to sign up for the KGB, ultimately going on to become the leader of Russia. This documentary interviews members of his inner circle, along with his opponents and victims.

Putin's Russia - 2018 - British journalist David Dimbleby attempts to gain some insight into Russia's long-time, notoriously secretive leader.

Putin's War in Ukraine - 2022 - War in Europe seemed like a thing of the past until Putin decided to invade Ukraine. This short documentary takes a closer look.

Putin: The New Tsar - 2018 - From early days in the KGB to his more recent years as the leader of Russia, Putin is a man of great brutality and mystery. This series looks at his unusual rise to power.

The Queen Mother - 2019 - The Queen Mother never set out to be queen, but she rose to the task and became a much-loved figure. This two-part series takes a closer look at her life and some of its darker secrets.

The Queen's Palaces - 2011 - Fiona Bruce hosts this three-part docuseries which takes a closer look at Buckingham Palace, Windsor Castle, and Holyrood House.

Queen Victoria & Her Nine Children - 2018 - Queen Victoria loved her husband, but he died young and left her with nine children to raise. This series takes a look at how she handled life without her beloved Albert.

Queen Victoria's Children - 2013 - After Albert's death, Queen Victoria is said to have become a deeply attached and domineering mother. This documentary explores what we know of those relationships.

Racism: A History - 2007 - This three-part BBC series takes a look at the history of racism and what drives it.

Rallying: The Killer Years - 2016 - In the 1980s, rallying was immensely popular and incredibly dangerous. This series takes a look at how increasingly powerful cars led to a series of tragedies that would ultimately bring about greater regulation.

Rat Pack: A Conference of Cool - 1999 - For a few short years, Frank Sinatra and his friends were the epitome of cool. This documentary tells the story of their influence.

Rebel Women: The Great Art Fightback - 2019 - This hour-long documentary takes a look at women who rebelled through their artwork in the 1960s.

Reclaiming Amy - 2021 - In 2011, a singer called Amy Winehouse died of alcohol poisoning at the age of 27. Ten years on, her friends and family look back at her life.

Rembrandt - 2014 - Simon Schama takes a look at Rembrandt's final, scandal-plagued years.

The Rise of the Murdoch Dynasty - 2020 - Rupert Murdoch owns the biggest media operation in the planet, and it's given him unprecedented levels of influence. This three-part documentary looks at how it happened.

Rise of the Nazis - 2019 - This docuseries takes a look at the slow build of Nazism in Germany, and the actions that turned a national of normal people into hateful killers and onlookers.

The Romantic Revolution - 2020 - Historian Simon Schama takes a closer look at the roots of the Romantic movement and its key creators.

The Ronnie Wood Show - 2012 - Rock legend Ronnie Wood has conversations with other icons of the music industry.

Royal Cousins at War - 2014 - At the beginning of the 20th century, three cousins ruled Britain, Russia, and Germany. This documentary takes a look at how their chaotic relationships had a devastating impact on Europe.

Russia 1917: Countdown to Revolution - 2017 - In just a few months, Stalin, Lenin, and Trotsky went from troublemakers to world leaders. This documentary takes a look at how it happened so quickly.

Secret Cities - 2017 - Art historians Janina Ramirez and Alastair Sooke take a look at the hidden cultures within Amsterdam, Barcelona, and St. Petersburg.

Secret Rules of Modern Living: Algorithm - 2015 - Algorithms power everything from search engines to dating apps, and mathematician Marcus du Sautoy attempts to demystify them.

The Secrets of Branding - 2015 - This eight-part series takes a look at what makes some brands so memorable and enduring.

Secrets of Silicon Valley - 2015 - Silicon Valley entrepreneurs set out to change the world, but those changes haven't always

been for the best. This series examines whether we're all heading for a tech-led disaster - or whether technology might genuinely improve the human condition.

Secret of the Missing Princess - 2021 - This series is a follow-up to *Mystery of the Missing Princess*, continuing the story of Princess Latifa of Dubai.

Secrets of Sugar Baby Dating - 2019 - High university tuition and soaring housing costs have led some young women to become "sugar babies". This series meets women whose lives are funded by wealthy older men.

Secrets of the Falklands - 2022 - This true crime documentary sees novelist Marcel Theroux taking a look at the disappearance and possible murder of marine Alan Addis as he explores the Falkland Islands.

Secrets of the Superbrands - 2011 - This series attempts to find out why some brands rise to the top, while others never achieve ubiquity.

Sex Actually with Alice Levine - 2021 - Podcaster Alice Levine travels the UK talking to sexually adventurous Brits.

Sex and the Church - 2015 - Professor Diarmaid MacCulloch looks at how Western attitudes on sex and gender have been shaped by Christian influence.

The Sex Changes That Made History - 2015 - When the "sci-fi surgery" of gender reassignment became available in the 1940s, it was a media sensation. This documentary takes a look back at some of the earliest people to make that choice.

Shock of the Nude - 2020 - Classicist Mary Beard takes a closer look at what drives our obsession with the body in art.

The Silk Road - 2016 - Dr. Sam Willis explores how the West was influenced by the East thanks to this infamous 5000-mile trade route.

Simon Schama's Power of Art - 2006 - This eight-part series sees art historian Simon Schama attempting to illustrate the power of art through in-depth looks at eight iconic masterpieces.

Simon Schama's Shakespeare and Us - 2012 - Historian Simon Schama takes a look at what made Shakespeare's plays so groundbreaking and enduring.

The Six Queens of Henry VIII - 2016 - Historians Dan Jones and Suzannah

Lipscomb take a look at what Henry VIII's marriages tell us about the king and his reign.

Soup Cans and Superstars: How Pop Art Changed the World - 2015 - Art historian Alistair Sooke takes a look at how the works of artists like Andy Warhol and Roy Lichtenstein defined their eras.

The Spy Who Fell to Earth - 2019 - Ashraf "The Angel" Marwan was an Egyptian billionaire who was also an Israeli double agent. This series takes a look at his life and mysterious death.

Stacey Dooley Investigates: Beaten by My Boyfriend - 2015 - Journalist Stacey Dooley goes behind closed doors to talk with young people who are dealing with domestic violence.

Stacey Dooley Investigates: Hate & Pride in Orlando - 2016 - In the aftermath of the 2016 Pulse Bar shootings in Florida, journalist Stacey Dooley visits the area to understand whether this might be the event that convinces America to make a change.

Stalin: Inside the Terror - 2003 - At the end of WWII, Stalin gained a vast empire in the East. This documentary looks at how a once-principled man transformed into an evil and controlling despot.

Starbucks & Nespresso: The Truth About Your Coffee - 2020 - The biggest coffee sellers make strong claims about worker welfare, but this undercover investigation reveals shocking activity that's being supported by the dollar votes of coffee lovers around the world.

Statue Wars - 2021 - In the US and UK, people have been tearing down statues to those whose lives don't reflect modern values. This documentary explores the issue.

Stephen Fry: Out There - 2013 - Stephen Fry travels the world to see what it's like to be gay in different countries and cultures.

Story of Maths - 2008 - This series takes a look at the human history behind the development of mathematics.

The Story of Women and Art - 2014 - This three-part series takes a look at some of the largely overlooked women of art history.

Suffragettes - 2018 - In celebration of 100 years of the female vote in Britain, Lucy Worsley takes a look back at the brave women who helped bring about that change.

The Super Rich & Us - 2015 - Years ago, Britain made efforts to attract billionaires to their shores in hopes that the wealth might trickle down to the rest of society. Today, they have more billionaires than anyone, and the hopes for a trickle-down effect didn't pan out. Journalist Jacques Peretti takes a look at what went wrong.

Surviving the Holocaust - 2015 - Holocaust survivor Freddie Knoller shares his story of being young and Jewish during WWII, including his time in Auschwitz.

Taken: Hunting the Sex Traffickers - 2021 - Filmed over three years, this docuseries follows the inside story of an investigation into a criminal gang that snatched young girls in South America and forced them into prostitution in the UK.

Teenage & Gay - 2015 - Acceptance movements have made it easier than ever for gay teens to come out in the UK, but that doesn't mean it's entirely without risk. This documentary follows five teens as they come out.

Thatcher & Reagan - 2022 - In the early 1980s, Ronald Reagan and Margaret Thatcher had a close relationship. This documentary attempts to better understand their diplomatic relations.

Timewatch: Young Victoria - 2008 - This documentary takes a closer look at Queen Victoria's challenging path to the throne.

Transgender Kids: Who Knows Best? - 2017 - In many countries, parents are now encouraged to fully support their children in any desire to change gender. Is this the right approach? This documentary examines whether kids are truly developed enough to make such life-altering decisions.

Travels in Europe with Ed Balls - 2020 - Former UK politician Ed Balls travels through Europe to examine the rise of right-wing fringe activity.

Treasures of the Indus - 2015 - Historian and writer Sona Datta shares the story of the Indian sub-continent (or rather, a very tiny but fascinating bit of it).

Trump in Tweets - 2020 - This hour-long documentary looks at how Trump used social media to shape policy and feud with enemies.

The Trump Show - 2021 - This four-part series takes a look back at Trump's four years in office.

Trump Takes on the World - 2021 - Over three episodes, this docuseries examines Trump's unusual activities while in office.

TV's Black Renaissance: Reggie Yates in Hollywood - 2019 - Actor Reggie Yates travels to LA to explore some of the majority-black television shows of recent years.

Ugly Beauty - 2009 - Art critic Waldemar Januszczak shows us how to look at modern art in a new way.

Ukraine: Lessons from the Battlefield - 2022 - The BBC's Mark Urban talks with Russians and Ukrainians to understand the ongoing war and how it might reshape history and future conflicts.

Utopia: In Search of the Dream - 2017 - Dreamers have always been drawn to the idea of perfect worlds. This series takes a look at various attempts, along with many expert opinions on the topic.

Venus Uncovered - 2017 - Classicist Bettany Hughes sets out to learn more about Venus, the goddess of love, fertility, and sex.

Vienna: Empire, Dynasty, and Dream - 2016 - From its Roman origins onward, Vienna has been a pivotal city in the history of Europe. This series sees historian Simon Sebag Montefiore sharing that history.

Vincent: The Full Story - 2004 - Art critic and historian Waldemar Januszczak takes a fresh look at van Gogh's life and creative development.

Vincent Van Gogh: Painted with Words - 2010 - Benedict Cumberbatch (*Sherlock*) takes on the role of the iconic Dutch post-impressionist. Though dramatised, the dialogue is sourced from Van Gogh's own words.

War Art with Eddie Redmayne - 2015 - Actor Eddie Redmayne takes us on a journey through the world of art inspired by conflict.

What if Putin Goes Nuclear? - 2022 - Broadcaster Jon Snow explores what might happen if Putin decided to use nuclear force as part of their invasion of Ukraine.

The Wheelchair President - 2015 - This two-part series looks at how a man in a wheelchair created the New Deal, led the US through WW2, and became the first and only president to win four terms.

When Louis Met Jimmy Savile - 2000 - Before Jimmy Savile was known as a predatory sex offender, renowned documentarian Louis Theroux interviewed him at length. This footage sees him trying to find out what Savile was all about.

The Whistleblowers: Inside the UN - 2022 - The UN is meant to be a noble, peacekeeping organisation that embodies the best of humanity. This documentary examines whether there might be systematic efforts to hide abuses and atrocities in the interest of keeping a lily-white public image.

Wild Weather: Our World Under Threat - 2021 - All over the world, bizarre weather events are happening with greater frequency. Is it the result of climate change? And is there anything we can do to change it?

Winston Churchill's War - 2021 - This four-part docuseries takes a look at the great, complex, and flawed man who lead the British public through some of the country's darkest days.

The Women of World War One - 2014 - War reporter Kate Adie takes a look at the impact of the work women did on the homefront during WWII.

The World's First Computer - 2014 - The Antikythera Mechanism was discovered on an ancient shipwreck, and it's thought to be one of the world's first computers. This documentary tells the story of the mysterious object thought to have been used to predict solar eclipses and time the Olympics.

World's Greatest Paintings - 2020 - Journalist Andrew Marr takes a closer look at the stories behind ten of the world's most famous pieces of art.

World's Weirdest Homes - 2014 - This programme takes a look at some of the strangest homes the world has to offer, including a toilet house.

World War Two: 1941 & the Man of Steel - 2011 - Historian David Reynolds original correspondence to examine Stalin's approach to WW2.

Write Around the World - 2021 - Actor Richard E Grant guides us on a trip through France, Italy, and Spain to see where great literary works were inspired.

<u>Zelensky: The Making of a President</u> -
2022 - In just a few short years, Volodymyr
Zelensky has gone from actor to beloved
leader of a nation in crisis. This short
documentary takes a look at his rise to
power.

BBC SELECT

INSIDE OUTSIDE

Website: https://www.inside-outside.tv/

Description: This subscription service offers a selection of the best British home and garden television shows. Though the total amount of programming is relatively low, you may still feel it's worth it to subscribe occasionally.

Available On: Roku, Amazon Fire TV, Apple TV, Apple iPhone & iPad, Android TV, Android phones and tablets, computer (via web browser). You can also subscribe via Amazon Prime Video.

Cost: $4.99/month

Now Streaming

The Autistic Gardener - 2015 to 2017 - This fun series sees a team of autistic gardeners - led by an award-winning autistic gardener - as they remodel garden spaces for a variety of individuals around the UK. Aside from gardening knowledge, you'll also learn a thing or two about the unique skills of people on the autism spectrum.

Beat My Build - 2013 - British house flippers compete to see who can make the most profit off a single project.

Big Dreams Small Spaces - Monty Don joins amateur gardeners to help them realise the big dreams they have for their small gardens.

Damned Designs: Don't Demolish My Home - 2015 - In this series, we see individuals whose building projects have somehow broken local rules that put their project at risk. Whether it's an off-grid retreat they built or a home they imported and assembled without proper planning permissions, they fight to get on the good side of local authorities so they can save their homes.

Gardeners' World - 1968 to present - This long-running series offers support, ideas, and guidance for gardeners all over the UK - and the world.

The Garden Pantry* - 2012 - This New Zealand-based series focuses on edible gardening, with loads of great scenery from around the country. Some episodes also get into food prep and preserving.

Garden Rescue - 2016 to present - Charlie Dimmock and the Rich brothers compete to design garden spaces for people around Great Britain.

Greatest Gardens - 2015 - This series seeks out the best private gardens in Northern Ireland.

Great Interior Design Challenge - 2014 to 2017 - Amateur designers attempt to transform inside spaces.

Hoarders, Get Your House in Order - 2012 - This is another show that takes a look at Brits whose collections and obsessions have gotten a bit out of control. They've crossed the line between healthy collecting and real quality of life issues, and the series is aimed at helping them make changes for the better.

Hoarder SOS - 2016 - This series sees professional organizers helping people living in extreme clutter. With a bit of help, they're able to get a new start on life without all the baggage.

Homes Under the Hammer - This long-running British auction series follows property auctions that frequently require a large amount of refurbishment or development. The series follows properties from auction to refurbishment, though not every project is seen through to completion.

How to Haggle for a House - 2012 - In this series, financial expert George Harrigan-Brown goes face-to-face to negotiate with property vendors to help buyers get better deals. He doesn't reveal the deal until after they've seen the house. Episodes featured include Eastbourne, London, Bath, Edinburgh, and Kendal/Lake District.

Jimmy Doherty's Escape to the Wild - This series follows British families who've given up on the rat race and relocated to remote parts of the world. Locations covered in this series include Indonesia, Uganda, and the Yukon.

Kevin McCloud's Escape to the Wild - 2015 - In this series, Kevin McCloud travels all over the globe to meet people who've moved to surprisingly remote and challenging places. From the Arctic Circle to the jungles of Central America, this is a show about people in search of a simpler kind of life.

Kevin McCloud's Man Made Home - 2012 to 2013 - Kevin McCloud attempts to built an eco-friendly shed in the forest.

Love Your Garden - Alan Titchmarsh and his team travel around the country, educating viewers and helping guests find ways to get more from their gardens.

The Manor Reborn - 2011 - Dame Penelope Keith hosts this four-part series about what it takes to restore a grand historic property.

Monty Don's French Gardens* - 2017 - Presenter Monty Don takes us on a journey to some of France's most exquisite gardens.

Monty Don's Italian Gardens* - 2011 - Gardening expert Monty Don travels through Italy, showing us some of the country's most beautiful gardens.

Operation Homefront - 2013 - This series sees ex-British soldiers putting their skills to work in a variety of community projects around the UK. Among the projects are an Oxfordshire Scout Hut, a Glasgow community centre, and a Southampton Boathouse.

Royal Upstairs Downstairs - This 20-episode series travels in the footsteps of Queen Victoria, visiting and exploring the stately homes she visited during her reign.

The series begins with Chatsworth, moving on to Shugborough, Harewood, Holkham, Brighton, Scone, Walmer, Wimpole, Belvoir, Blair, Burghley, Hatfield, Castle Howard, Stoneleigh, Warwick, Penryhn, Floors Castle, Hughenden, and Waddesdon.

The Secret History of the British Garden - 2015 - Monty Don takes us through the history and evolution of the British garden. The series is made up of four hour-long episodes, each one covering a century of gardening history (17th, 18th, 19th, and 20th).

Secret Removers - 2012 - This series follows individuals as they arrange secret moves for friends and family members.

Superior Interiors with Kelly Hoppen* - 2011 - One of the UK's premiere interior designers turns her attention to some clients who aren't quite as flush with cash.

You Deserve This House - 2012 - This heartwarming series seeks out deserving homeowners in desperate need of renovation. From a retired nurse to a speech therapist to an ex-firefighter, you'll see good people getting some much-needed kindness from their fellow Brits.

*This title was not on their Amazon channel at time of publication (but it was on the Roku channel). The two are not always synced, so be sure to check the listings for any shows you really want before you subscribe - just to make sure it's still there.

PRIME VIDEO

Website: http://amazon.com

Description: As part of their Amazon Prime membership, Amazon offers thousands of shows and movies you can view at no additional cost. It's also possible to purchase a Prime Video membership without the free shipping benefits (at a slightly lower monthly cost).

Available On: Roku, Amazon Fire TV, Android devices, iPad, desktop, Chromecast, and most smart TVs.

Cost: $14.99/month or $139/year for Prime, $8.99/month for just Prime Video

---

Now Streaming

Mysteries & Crime Dramas

Agatha Christie's Ordeal by Innocence – 2018 - When a wealthy woman is murdered, her adopted son is arrested in spite of his claims of innocence. Later, his guilt is thrown into doubt and the family scrambles to figure out who killed her.

Agatha Christie's The ABC Murders - 2018 - John Malkovich stars as Hercule Poirot in this adaptation of Agatha Christie's 1936 novel of the same name. In it, Poirot receives letters signed ABC, warning him of upcoming murders related to the sequential letters of the alphabet.

Amnesia - 2004 - This miniseries tells the story of DS MacKenzie Stone, his tireless search for his wife who disappeared 5 years prior, and an amnesiac who factors into the case.

Dead Lucky - *Australian* - 2018 – When a dangerous armed robber resurfaces in Sydney, two very different detectives are forced to work together to catch him.

A Difficult Woman – *Australia* – 1998 - A woman with a brilliant career and promising relationship sees everything derailed when a close friend is murdered.

As she gets more information, it leads her well out of her comfort zone as she pursues the killer.

Endeavour – 2012 to present - In this prequel to Inspector Morse, a young Endeavour works with Sergeant Thursday to develop his investigative skills. Shaun Evans stars as Morse during this 1960s period mystery.

The Fall - 2013 to 2016 - Gillian Anderson (*The X-Files*) and Jamie Dornan (*50 Shades of Grey*) star in this series about a senior investigator who goes head-to-head with a serial killer who's attacking young professional women in Belfast.

Grantchester – 2014 to present - In the village of Grantchester, a clever vicar assists a local police detective with his investigations. James Norton (*Happy Valley*) stars as vicar Sidney Chambers, and Robson Green (*Wire in the Blood*) plays DI Geordie Keating. Later in the series, Tom Brittany takes over for him as the new vicar.

Holby Blue - 2007 to 2008 - This *Holby City* and *Casualty* spin-off follows the police who work with the doctors and paramedics of the other two shows.

Informer - 2018 - Paddy Considine (*Peaky Blinders*) stars as a counterterrorism officer who convinces a young Pakistani man to become an informant.

Injustice - 2011 - A defense barrister has to deal with the consequences of defending an indefensible crime. *Foyle's War* and *Midsomer Murders* screenwriter Anthony Horowitz created the series, and it features an all-star cast with actors like James Purefoy (*Rome*), Dervla Kirwan (*Ballykissangel*), Charlie Creed-Miles (*The Fifth Element*), and Nathaniel Parker (*The Inspector Lynley Mysteries*).

Inside Men - 2012 - This miniseries tells the story of three employees who plan and execute a major heist.

Low Winter Sun - *United States* - 2013 - Mark Strong stars as DS Frank Agnew, a police officer who kills a fellow officer and believes he's committed the perfect murder. Though it originally aired as a British miniseries, this is the 10-part US version (for which Mark Strong returned).

Mayday - 2013 - When the May Queen disappears just before May Day celebrations, a small town is thrown into chaos.

M.I. High - 2007 to 2014 - Hidden away in an ordinary school, four kids work for for the British government.

The Missing – 2014 to 2017 - James Nesbitt (*Cold Feet*) stars in this drama about the disappearance of a 5-year-old and the manhunt that follows.

Murder Call - *Australia* - 1997 to 2000 - This puzzle-based, moderately retro mystery series follows a couple of homicide detectives in Sydney.

The Night Manager – 2016 - Based on John le Carre's novel focuses on an ex-British soldier recruited to join MI-6 and infiltrate a group of arms dealers.

The Pale Horse - 2020 - This two-part adaptation of Agatha Christie's story by the same name was written and executive produced by Sarah Phelps. Written in 1961, the original story is a creepy tale about what happens after a list of names is found in the shoe of a dead woman.

Picnic at Hanging Rock – *Australia* – 2018 - In the year 1900, three schoolgirls and their governess disappeared. From there, the mystery deepens.

Prey – 2014 to 2015 - Manchester detective Marcus Farrow (played by John Simm) is on the run, accused of a crime and desperate to prove his innocence. All the while, his former friends and colleagues do their best to hunt him down. This series reunites Philip Glenister and John Simm, who also appeared together in *Life on Mars*.

Reacher - *United States* - 2021 to present - Based on the Jack Reacher novels by British author Lee Child, this series follows the activities of an ex-military policeman as he travels around the US.

River - 2015 - Stellan Skarsgård, Nicola Walker, and Lesley Manville star in this series about a brilliant police officer haunted by guilt.

Rose & Maloney - 2002 to 2005 - Sarah Lancashire and Phil Davis star in this series about two investigators at the fictional Criminal Justice Review Agency. Together, they take on claims of miscarriage of justice, deciding whether old cases should be re-opened.

Sherlock Holmes and the Leading Lady – 1991 - Sherlock Holmes pauses his retirement to help track down a stolen prototype for a bomb detonator. This production features Christopher Lee and Morgan Fairchild.

Sherlock Holmes in Colour! - 1946 - Basil Rathbone stars as Sherlock Holmes in this restored colour production.

State of Mind - 2003 - After discovering her husband has been unfaithful, Grace takes her son Adam and moves back home with her mother, a busy GP. Niamh Cusack, Rowena Cooper, and Andrew Lincoln star.

Tin Star – 2017 to 2019 - A former British detective moves to the Canadian Rockies and fights crime near a new oil refinery.

The Tunnel - 2013 to 2018 - This British-French co-production follows two detectives working together to solve the case of a serial killer who left half a French politician and half a British prostitute in the Channel Tunnel at the midpoint between France and the UK.

Unforgotten – 2015 to present - Cassie and Sunny use modern technology to get to the bottom of very cold cases. This recent crime drama is based in London and stars Nicola Walker and Sanjeev Bhaskar.

Whitechapel - 2009 to 2013 - An inspector, a detective sergeant, and a historical homicide expert look at crimes that may have connections to Whitechapel.

White Dragon – 2019 - John Simm stars in this tense mystery about a man who starts to notice highly suspicious things after his wife is killed in a car accident in Hong Kong.

The Widow - 2019 - Kate Beckinsale stars in this drama about a woman who believes herself to be a widow, only to find that her husband did not actually die in a plane crash. While watching a news story on unrest in the Congo, she sees a man who looks like her husband and sets off to figure out what happened.

WPC 56 - 2013 to 2015 - This period crime drama follows Gina Dawson, the first woman police constable in her West Midlands hometown. The first two seasons focus on Gina's struggles to gain acceptance in a male-dominated work environment, while the third season follows her successor at the station.

Young Lions – *Australia* – 2002 - This Australian police drama follows the personal and professional lives of a group of young detective senior constables.

Period Dramas

Anzac Girls - *Australia* - 2014 - Heroic women rise to the occasion during the war.

Britannia - 2018 - This US-UK co-production shows the Roman invasion in 43AD Britannia.

Byron - 2003 - Jonny Lee Miller (*Elementary*) stars in this period drama about the life of Lord Byron.

Casualty 1900s: London Hospital - 2006 to 2009 - This medical period drama was inspired by the *Holby City* spinoff *Casualty*, but is otherwise unrelated. It takes place in the receiving room of the London Hospital in London's East End, and each case is based on the writings and memoirs of real doctors and nurses from the time period.

The Collection - 2016 - Richard Coyle (*Coupling*) and Tom Riley (*Da Vinci's Demons*) star in this period drama about the Paris fashion scene after WWII. The series also includes performances from Frances de la Tour (*Hugo, Professor T*), Sarah Parish (*Bancroft*), and Michael Kitchen (*Foyle's War*).

Doctor Thorne - 2016 - This series, based on Anthony Trollope's 1858 novel of the same name, tells the story of penniless Mary Thorne and her relationship with a wealthy family nearby. Julian Fellowes (*Downton Abbey*) adapted it.

Downton Abbey - 2010 to 2015 - This period drama follows the lives of the Crawley family and their servants during the early 1900s.

The Duchess of Duke Street - 1976 - Gemma Jones (*Bridget Jones's Diary*) starred in this series about a woman who worked her way up from servant to cook to owner of an upper-class hotel on Duke Street in London. The story is loosely based on the real life of Rosa Lewis, who ran the Cavendish Hotel.

The Durrells in Corfu – 2016 to 2019 - This popular British series tells the story of a widow who moves her family out of 1930s England in search of a better life.

The English - 2022 - This British-American co-production is a Western drama about an Englishwoman who arrives in the West in hopes of getting revenge on the man responsible for her son's death. Emily Blunt stars, and British TV fans will likely recognise Rafe Spall, Tom Hughes, Stephen Rea, Toby Jones, and Ciaran Hinds among the cast. **Premieres November 11th.**

The Forsyte Saga – 2002 - This adaptation of John Galsworthy's novel follows the life of an English family over 34 years stretching from Victorian England to World War 1.

Hold the Dream - 1986 - This two-part serial is based on Barbara Taylor Bradford's novel of the same name. The story picks up where *A Woman of Substance* left off, with Paula Fairley now in charge of the Harte chain of department stores. Sadly, *A Woman of Substance* is not currently available on any US-based streaming service, but you could always buy the DVD or read the book if you wanted to get everything in order.

King Lear – 2018 - This Prime Original stars Anthony Hopkins as King Lear.

Merlin - 2009 to 2013 - Colin Morgan (*The Fall*) stars as a young Merlin in his days as a mere servant to Prince Arthur of Camelot. In this version of Camelot, magic is banned and Merlin is forced to hide it.

The Musketeers – 2014 to 2016 - This modern retelling of the classic Dumas novel includes appearances by Peter Capaldi, Tom Burke, and Rupert Everett.

The Nativity - 2010 - Writer Tony Jordan adapts the classic tale of Mary and Joseph and baby Jesus. Peter Capaldi (*Doctor Who*) and Tatiana Maslany (*Orphan Black*) are among the stars.

One Child - 2014 - An adopted young British woman travels to China to meet her birth family.

The Paradise - 2012 to 2013 - In this period drama, a young and ambitious woman heads to the city to make her way working in a department store

Poldark – 2015 to 2019 - Ross Poldark returns home to Cornwall after fighting in the American Revolution, only to find his fortune in ruins and the woman he loves promised to another man. Aidan Turner stars in this adaptation of the classic story.

The Pursuit of Love - 2021 - Based on Nancy Mitford's 1945 novel of the same name, this miniseries is set before WWII and it follows the friendship of two cousins as one opts for a stable life and the other takes a more adventurous path. Lily James, Emily Beecham, Andrew Scott, and Dominic West star.

Small Axe - 2020 - This period drama is set in London's West Indian community between the 1960s and '80s, telling five stories in a six-part anthology format. It starts in 1968 with the story of a small restaurant, The Mangrove, opening in Ladbroke Grove. Over time, it becomes an epicenter of resistance in the community.

Spies of Warsaw - 2013 - David Tennant stars in this story set across three European cities ahead of World War II. The series is based on Alan Furst's spy novel of the same name.

Tales of Para Handy - 1994 to 1995 - This Scottish dramedy is set in the 1930s and follows the crew of a small cargo ship called the *Vital Spark*. David Tennant (*Doctor Who*) makes one of his earliest appearances in the second season.

Tom Jones – 1997 - In Georgian England, Tom Jones finds no shortage of trouble or romance.

Vanity Fair (2018) - This ITV production of Thackeray's classic includes performances by Michael Palin, Olivia Cooke, Tom Bateman, Suranne Jones, and Martin Clunes.

A Very English Scandal – 2018 - Hugh Grant stars as the first British politician to stand trial for conspiracy to murder.

Victoria - 2016 to present - This series stars Jenna Coleman (Doctor Who) as Victoria and Tom Hughes (*The Game*) as Prince Albert, along with Peter Bowles (*To the Manor Born, Executive Stress*) as the Duke of Wellington. Much like *The Crown* is to Queen Elizabeth II, *Victoria* follows Queen Victoria as she progresses through her lengthy reign.

Young Charlie Chaplin - 1989 - Ian McShane and Twiggy are among the stars of this biographical series about film's first great comedian.

Other Dramas

The Aliens – 2016 - After aliens crash-land in the Irish Sea, they're allowed onto British soil but forced to live in a ghetto called Troy. Border guard Lewis helps to maintain the separation, but it gets tough when he learns he's half-alien.

Always Greener – *Australia* – 2001 to 2003 - This dramedy tells the story of two families who joke about swapping places, then actually do it. The series takes place in rural Inverness and suburban Sydney.

The Ambassador - 1998 - Pauline Collins stars as Ambassador Harriet Smith, British ambassador to Ireland. She's a woman under pressure from all angles, and she struggles with guilt about her husband's death from a car bomb meant for her.

Atlantis - 2013 to 2015 - This fantasy-adventure series follows a modern-day submarine pilot who's pulled into a bright light, only to wash up on the shores of Atlantis.

Bed of Roses - *Australia* - 2008 to 2011 - A mother and daughter struggle after the death of their husband and father.

Big Sky – *Australia* – 1997 to 1999 - This soap-y drama follows the employees at Big Sky Aviation as they form friendships and fly high over the Australian landscape.

Bluestone Four Two - 2013 to 2015 - This dark comedy follows the lives of British soldiers working in a bomb disposal detachment in Afghanistan.

Chloe - 2022 - Erin Doherty (*The Crown*) stars as a young woman who's obsessed with the Instagram-perfect life of a woman called Chloe. When Chloe dies suddenly, she needs to know why, so she creates an alter ego and cozies up to her friends.

Counterpart - *United States* - 2017 to 2019 - Olivia Williams and Harry Lloyd are among the numerous Brits in this American sci-fi thriller about an unassuming government worker whose rank is too low to justify telling him what he's really working on. In reality, he's been overseeing a checkpoint between two parallel versions of the world.

Critical - 2015 - This Jed Mercurio-penned drama follows the high-paced action at a major trauma centre.

The Deep - 2010 - James Nesbitt (*Cold Feet*) and Minnie Driver (*Good Will Hunting*) star in this series about oceanographers who become stranded in the Arctic while looking for new forms of life beneath the ice.

The Devil's Hour - 2022 - This Amazon-produced thriller follows Lucy Chambers, a woman who wakes up each night at exactly 3:33am. She's also troubled by a mother who talks to chairs, a quiet and withdrawn young son, and a series of brutal murders that seem to be connected to her. **Premieres October 28th.**

Electric Dreams - 2017 - Adapted from the works of Philip K. Dick, this anthology series was produced for Channel 4 and features adaptations by British and American writers. British cast members include Timothy Spall, Richard Madden, and Holliday Grainger. Essie Davis (*Miss Fisher's Murder Mysteries*) also appears.

The Fades – 2011 - A young man is haunted by dreams he can't explain, and he begins to see spirits around him – some of them malicious.

The Feed - 2019 - In this dystopian science fiction drama, people's minds are connected to something called The Feed, offering instant connectivity. Unfortunately, that makes infiltration especially dangerous.

Flack - 2019 to Present - A PR executive specializes in cleaning up after her selfish clients in London. Anna Paquin stars.

Good Omens – 2019 - David Tennant and Michael Sheen star in this adaptation of Neil Gaiman and Terry Pratchett's novel by the same name. In it, two angels have grown quite fond of the human world, and they plan to do everything in their power to stop it from ending in accordance with the Divine Plan.

Hillary - *New Zealand* - 2016 - Andrew Munro (*Hounds*) stars as Sir Edmund Hillary in this biopic about the life of the famed adventurer and philanthropist.

Home & Away – *Australia* – 1988 to 1989 - This soap opera follows the residents of Summer Bay, a coastal town near Sydney in Australia.

Humans – 2015 to 2018 - In a parallel modern world, everyone has a robotic servant.

Hustle - 2004 to 2012 - This series follows a group of talented con artists who prefer to operate long cons on the greedy and corrupt of London.

The Indian Doctor - 2010 to 2013 - An Indian doctor and his wife move to a small Welsh mining village during the 1960s. They have to adjust to culture shock, and Dr. Sharma must win the trust of the locals as their GP.

The Invisibles - 2008 - A couple of retired master burglars tried living in Spain, but after a bout of homesickness, they returned to England with their wives to live in a Devon fishing village. It's not long before a return to familiar shores sees them taking up the same old bad habits.

Jim Henson's The Storyteller - 1987 to 1988 - This British live-action and puppet series re-told a number of European fairy tales using actors and puppets. Sir John Hurt acted as the old storyteller.

Lord of the Rings: The Rings of Power - 2022 - Set thousands of years before JRR Tolkien's The Hobbit, this epic fantasy sees an ensemble cast facing evil in Middle Earth. **Premiered September 2nd.**

Meadowlands, aka Cape Wrath - 2007 - When a family moves to Meadowlands, it seems like a bright new start. Unfortunately, the past is a hard thing to put behind you.

MI High - 2007 to 2014 - This young adult spy thriller follows teens who've been recruited to work for the fictional MI9 intelligence agency. *Death in Paradise* fans will recognise Danny John-Jules as one of their handlers.

The Outlaws - 2021 to present - This darkly funny drama follows a group of people who've all been assigned to do community payback in Bristol. Though they're from different walks of life, their time together results in interesting changes to each of their lives. Stephen Merchant (*Hello Ladies, The Office*), Eleanor Tomlinson (*Poldark*), and Christopher Walken (*The Deer Hunter*) are among the cast members. **Season 2 is now available.**

Public Enemies – 2012 - Released from prison after a 10-year sentence for murder, a man attempts to adjust to life on the outside. Anna Friel stars alongside Daniel Mays.

QB VII - 1974 - Sir Anthony Hopkins stars as a physician who sues a novelist for implying he was a doctor involved in Nazi war crimes.

Queer as Folk - 1999 to 2000 - This groundbreaking British series follows a group of young gay men in Manchester.

Rake - *Australia* - 2011 to 2018 - Defense lawyer Cleaver Greene makes a career out of hopeless cases, perhaps because his own personal life is troubled enough to help him relate.

The Royals - *United States* - 2015 to 2108 - Though American, this prime-time soap stars Elizabeth Hurley and a largely British cast. It tells the story of a fictional British royal family and the power struggles within their ranks.

The Secret Life of Us – *Australia* – 2001 to 2006 - In an apartment block near Melbourne, residents navigate life's challenges with the help of their friends.

The Secret of Crickley Hall – 2012 – Suranne Jones and Tom Ellis star in this supernatural miniseries about a family that relocates to a grand old estate up north after the disappearance of their young son.

Secret State – 2012 – In a miniseries that will reassure you that the US isn't the only place where government and big business are way too close, Secret State shows a Deputy Prime Minister entangled in an international conspiracy.

The Smoke – 2014 - When a fire fighter is badly injured on the job, he spends nearly a year in recovery. On return, he realises he may not be quite as ready as he thinks.

Teachers - 2001 to 2004 - This dramedy follows the teachers and students in one British school. Andrew Lincoln (*The Walking Dead*) stars, but it's also one of James Corden's earliest appearances. You'll also spot a young Shaun Evans (*Endeavour*) and Mathew Horne (*Gavin & Stacey*) in this series.

Undeniable - 2014 - This two-part thriller follows the story of a murderer brought to justice by the woman who saw him killing her mother many years earlier.

Utopia - 2013 to 2014 - When a group of comic book fans become convinced that a graphic novel has predicted a number of real epidemics, they're determined to find the unpublished sequel. Unfortunately, getting their hands on the manuscript means becoming targets for a secret organisation known only as "The Network".

Wheel of Time - *United States* - 2021 - This epic fantasy stars Rosamund Pike (*Love in a Cold Climate*) as Moiraine, a member of a powerful organisation of women who can use magic. The series is based on the Wheel of Time novels by Robert Jordan, and while it's an American production, much of the cast is British.

Wrecking the Uprising (aka Éirí Amach Amú) - *Ireland* - 2016 - Three historical re-enactors from Dublin get the shock of their lives when they suddenly find themselves in a very realistic scene in 1916. *Partially in Gaelic, with English subtitles as needed.*

Comedies

'Allo 'Allo - 1982 to 1992 - This classic British comedy is set in a French café during WWII.

Almost Royal - 2014 to 2016 - This BBC America faux-reality series follows a couple of extremely minor British royals as they visit the US for the first time.

Back to the Rafters - *Australia* - 2021 - This series is a follow-up to the much-loved Australian family dramedy Packed to the Rafters. It picks up six years later when Dave and Julie have built a new life for themselves in the country.

The Bleak Old Shop of Stuff - 2012 - As proprietor of The Old Shop of Stuff, Jedrington Secret-Past sells all manner of unusual items. Unfortunately, Malifax Skulkingworm wants to make his life miserable. Robert Webb (*Peep Show*), Stephen Fry (*Kingdom*), and Katherine Parkison (*The IT Crowd*) star.

Bottom - 1991 to 1995 - Adrian Edmondson and Rik Mayall (both of *The Young Ones*) star in this quirky sitcom about a couple of largely unpleasant flatmates in Hammersmith, London. They spend much of their time pretending to be aristocrats and trying to get women to go to bed with them.

Bucket - 2017 - When free-spirited Mim tells her daughter she's dying, they go on a road trip together. Miriam Margolyes (*Miss Fisher's Murder Mysteries*) stars alongside

Frog Stone (*No Offence*).

Catastrophe – 2015 to present - This Prime Original tells the story of an unintended pregnancy between an American ad man and a British teacher.

Dead Boss – 2012 - Helen Stephens has been wrongly convicted of killing her boss, but everyone she knows seems to want her in prison.

Desmond's - 1989 to 1994 - Known for being the first predominantly black British workplace comedy, the series followed the Ambrose family and their Peckham-based barbershop.

Fleabag – 2016 to 2019 - Phoebe Waller-Bridge stars as Fleabag, a comically troubled young woman who's experienced a great personal tragedy.

Frank of Ireland - 2021 - A perpetually disgruntled thirtysomething musician lives in Dublin with his mother, spending much of his time thinking about his ex-girlfriend.

Fresh Meat – 2011 to 2016 - Six young friends go off to university.

Fungus the Bogeyman - 2015 - Based on the 1977 Raymond Briggs picture book, this series follows Fungus, a working class bogeyman whose job is to scare humans.

Garth Marenghi's Darkplace - 2004 - This cult classic is offered up as a "lost classic of the 1980s", and it revolves around a fictional horror author and a doctor who battles evil forces beneath a hospital in Romford. Matthew Holness (*Back*) and Richard Ayoade (*The IT Crowd*) wrote and starred in the series.

Getting On - 2009 to 2012 - This dark comedy follows the residents and staff in a geriatric ward.

The House of Cards Trilogy - 1990 to 1995 - This sitcom is Andrew Davies' adaptation of Michael Dobbs' novels about greed, ambition, and British politics. It follows Frances Urquhart, an evil but charismatic man who will stop at nothing in the pursuit of power. An American adaptation was later made under the same name. **Only seasons 2 and 3 remain on Prime.**

Hunderby – 2012 to 2015 - Julia Davis stars in this dark period comedy about a woman who washes ashore after a shipwreck off the English coast.

Hyperdrive - 2006 to 2007 - Nick Frost and Miranda Hart are among the stars of this sci-fi sitcom about the crew of HMS Camden Lock as they attempt to protect Britain's interests throughout the galaxy.

The Inbetweeners – 2008 to 2010 - This raunchy teen comedy focuses on a group of young men who aren't quite as cool as they'd like to be.

The Kennedys – 2015 - Katherine Parkinson (*The IT Crowd*) stars in this comedy about a family moving from a housing estate to a home, eager to move up the social ladder.

King Gary - 2020 - Gary and Terri King are childhood sweethearts living in suburban East London. Though he's a grown man with his own family, Gary is constantly trying to get out of his father's shadow.

Mean Mums - 2019 - When her only son starts school, Jess finds herself thrust into the cutthroat world of other mums.

Moone Boy – 2012 to 2014 - A young boy copes with life in a small Irish town, thanks to his imaginary friend.

Mr. Bean - 1992 to 1995 - Bumbling Mr. Bean rarely speaks and has some very peculiar ways of doing things, but it usually works out for him. Rowan Atkinson

(*Maigret*) stars as the iconic British character. See also: *Mr. Bean: The Animated Series, Mr. Bean in Handy Bean*

Mr. D - Canada - 2012 to 2018 - Gerry Dee stars as Mr. Duncan, an under-qualified teacher who prefers to be called Mr. D. Unfortunately, his thunder is stolen when the school's actual Mr. D, Mr. Dwyer, returns.

Pramface – 2012 to 2013 - In Edinburgh, a young woman sleeps with an even younger man and finds herself pregnant.

People Like Us - 1999 - Chris Langham stars as Roy Mallard, a fictional interviewer who probably shouldn't be allowed out of the house.

The Royle Family - 1998 to 2012 - This sitcom features a scruffy, argumentative, telly-obsessed family in Manchester. Ralf Little (*Death in Paradise*) is among its stars.

Threesome – 2011 - A straight couple and their gay friend live together happily until one sordid night changes their lives forever. Amy Huberman (*Finding Joy*) stars.

Truth Seekers - 2020 - Simon Pegg (*Shaun of the Dead*) and Nick Frost (*Hot Fuzz*) star in this comedy series about internet installers who moonlight as part-time paranormal investigators. Using homemade gadgets to track ghosts, their haunted adventures get increasingly terrifying as they're drawn further into the supernatural world.

Weegies - 2021 - Steve and George are best friends and flatmates, and while they're doing their best to get by in the world, the world is making it pretty clear that's not enough. It all changes after a chance encounter with a new downstairs neighbor, though.

PRIME VIDEO

Documentary & Lifestyle

24 Hours in A&E - 2011 to present - This reality series follows NHS doctors and nurses as they deal with urgent medical emergencies.

Big Dreams, Small Spaces - 2014 - Monty Don joins amateur gardeners to help them realise the big dreams they have for their small gardens.

Britain by Narrowboat - 2020 - Colin and his partner Shaun quit their jobs, sell their home, and start up life aboard a narrowboat.

Britain's Best Drives - 2009 - Richard Wilson (*One Foot in the Grave*) celebrates the 50th anniversary of Britain's first motorway with a trip around the country in six classic cars.

Building Dream Homes - 2014 - This BBC series follows some of the country's top architects as they make housing dreams come true.

Charles I: Downfall of a King - 2019 - Historian Lisa Hilton takes a closer look at King Charles I's downfall and the political climate that led to it.

Clarkson's Farm - 2021 - British TV presenter Jeremy Clarkson bought a 1000-acre farm back in 2008, but the local villager who farmed the land retired in 2019. With a global pandemic and an opening on his land, Clarkson decided to try his hand at farming. **This series has been renewed for a second season.**

Cruising the Cut – 2019 to present - This is another series about a different British man who quit his job to go live on the canals and travel.

Dangerous Roads - 2011 to 2012 - This BBC series takes a look at some of the most challenging and dangerous roads in the world.

Edwardian Farm - 2010 - In this series, the creators of *Victorian Farm* turn their attention to the Edwardian period, looking at the way farming life looked a little more than 100 years ago.

Fake or Fortune - 2011 to present - Journalist Fiona Bruce and art historian Philip Mould team up to investigate the provenance and authenticity of potentially significant works of art.

The Force: Manchester - 2015 - This reality series gives us a look inside the work being done by the Greater Manchester Police.

Gadget Man - 2012 to 2015 - Actors Stephen Fry (Series 1) and Richard Ayoade (Series 2-4) take a look at innovative products designed to make our lives easier. Note that Series 1 is listed entirely separate from Series 2-4, but at time of print, both are available on Prime Video.

Gardeners' World - 1968 to present - This long-running series offers support, ideas, and guidance for gardeners all over the UK - and the world.

Garden Invaders - 2000 - Contestants compete to win garden makeovers.

Gordon Behind Bars - 2012 - Scottish celebrity chef Gordon Ramsay goes behind bars to help set up a prisoner-staffed food business.

The Grand Tour – 2017 to 2019 - Jeremy Clarkson, Richard Hammond, and James May roam around and drive unique, luxurious, and exotic automobiles.

Grand Tours of Scotland's Lochs – 2017 - Historian Paul Murton takes us on an incredibly scenic journey around some of Scotland's most beautiful lochs.

The Great British Benefits Handout – 2016 to 2017 - One of the problems with benefits systems is that they pay out tiny amounts over a long time, making it hard for recipients to get ahead. As a social experiment, this show offers benefits recipients the opportunity to quit benefits and receive a year's worth of payments in one lump sum. It follows as they invest in themselves and their new businesses.

Great British Menu - 2006 to present - Some of Britain's top chefs compete for a chance to help prepare part of a banquet for some highly-esteemed guests.

Great Canal Journeys - 2014 to present - This series follows married actors Timothy West and Prunella Scales as they explore the waterways of Britain and beyond. Sadly, Prunella's struggle with Alzheimer's forced them to quit filming by 2020, and a new episode saw Timothy offering the new hosts, Gyles Brandreth and Sheila Hancock, a crash course in narrowboating.

The Great Escapists - 2021 - Richard Hammond and Tory Belleci are shipwrecked on an island in the Pacific, forced to use their engineering know-how to survive and escape.

Great Interior Design Challenge - 2014 to 2017 - Amateur designers attempt to transform inside spaces.

Ground Force - 2005 - Professional gardeners and landscapers help transform unattractive gardens.

Ground Force Revisited - 2004 - Each episode of this gardening series sees a worthy person getting a garden makeover.

The Home Show - 2008 - Architect George Clarke helps turn current homes into dream homes.

The House that 100k (GBP) Built – 2016 - Homes are expensive in the UK, but this series takes a look at people building homes from scratch – and on a budget.

James Martin: Home Comforts - 2014 to 2016 - British chef James Martin tackles dishes suitable for the typical home cook.

James Martin's United Cakes of America - 2013 - British chef James Martin grabs a classic American convertible and tours the US in search of the country's best desserts.

James May: Oh Cook - 2020 - Non-chef James May gives cooking a try, learning to cook dishes that relatively normal people can replicate.

James May: Our Man in Japan - 2020 - James May embarks on a journey across the island nation of Japan, travelling from the icy north to the balmy south.

James May's Cars of the People - 2014 to 2016 - James May takes a look at different cars and the roles they've played in the lives of ordinary people.

King Arthur's Lost Kingdom - 2019 - Professor Alice Roberts takes us inside a stone palace excavation in Cornwall, the supposed birthplace of King Arthur.

The Moors Murders – 2009 - Back in the mid-1960s, Ian Brady and Myra Hindley abducted, tortured, and murdered children and young teenagers, horrifying the British public. This documentary looks back at archival footage, creates dramatic reconstructions, and talks with some of those involved in the case.

Murdertown - 2018 to 2019 - This series tells the stories of shocking and true murders around the UK. The stories are grisly, but they show a fair bit of scenery around the cities and towns in question, so many will enjoy it on that alone.

My Dream Farm - 2010 - Monty Don follows first-time farmers as they learn to give up city life and make a living from the land.

The Mystery of Agatha Christie with David Suchet - 2014 - David Suchet (*Poirot*) embarks on a journey to learn more about Agatha Christie.

The Nurse – 2013 - This series takes a look at district nurses who travel around the UK, caring for patients at home.

Perfect Weapon - 2008 - Archaeologist and weapons expert Stuart Prior teams up with ex-Royal Marine Monty Halls to take a look at some of the tools men have used to kill one another throughout history.

Portrait Artist of the Year - 2020 - Around the UK, various cities play host to this competition to find the UK and Ireland's most talented portrait artists.

The Private Lives of the Tudors - 2016 - This series takes a very personal look at one of Britain's most celebrated dynasties.

Project Restoration – 2016 - Historical building surveyor Marianne Suhr travels the UK helping out on challenging restoration projects.

Richard Hammond's Crash Course - 2012 - *Top Gear* UK star Richard Hammond seeks out some of the United States' toughest vehicles.

Rick Stein & the Japanese Ambassador - 2006 - When the UK's Japanese Ambassador challenges chef Rick Stein to prepare a banquet for his guests, Rick spends a week visiting local markets and restaurants in hopes of doing the cuisine justice.

Rick Stein's Far Eastern Odyssey - 2009 - Chef Rick Stein explores the cuisine of several Asian countries including Vietnam, Thailand, Cambodia, Malaysia, Bangladesh, and Bali.

Rick Stein's India - 2013 - Chef Rick Stein explores different parts of India to learn more about the nation's wide variety of culinary traditions.

PRIME VIDEO

Rick Stein's Mediterranean Escapes - 2007 - Rick Stein explores the best food in a variety of Mediterranean locations.

Rick Steves' Europe – 2000 to 2019 - Seasons 7 to 10 of this popular series are offered on Amazon. Of interest to Anglophiles will be: 7-8, London, 7-9 Northern England, 9-8 Western England, 9-9 Southeast England, 9-10 Cornwall, 10-1 Heart of England, 10-10 Scotland's Highlands, 10-11 Scotland's Islands, and 10-12 Glasgow.

Rome: Empire Without Limit with Mary Beard - 2016 - Classical scholar Mary Beard offers her insight into the myths and beliefs about what happened during the Roman Empire.

Secret Life of the Hospital Bed - 2016 to 2017 - This medical reality series takes a closer look at patients in different departments at hospitals across the country.

Secrets of the Castle - 2014 - Historians and archaeologists learn how to build a castle using medieval-era techniques and tools. Their building experiment is meant to take 25 years to complete.

A Stitch in Time – 2016 - Amber Butchart takes a look at historical figures through the clothing they wore.

Supersize vs. Superskinny - 2008 to 2014 - Each episode of this show features an overweight person and an underweight person, offering professional help as they swap diets.

Surgeons: At the Edge of Life - 2018 to 2020 - Using behind-the-scenes access at the Queen Elizabeth Hospital Birmingham, this series takes a look at the incredible work being done by some of the UK's finest surgeons.

Time Team - 1994 to 2014 - A group of archaeologists travel around Britain working on different excavation sites.

Total Wipeout - 2011 - This British game show sees guests attempting to complete obstacle courses to win cash prizes.

Travel Man – 2015 to present - Richard Ayoade (*The IT Crowd*) takes 48 hour trips to various destinations, always bringing along a celebrity guest.

Travels by Narrowboat – 2018 to presents - Newer than many of the other narrowboating shows on Amazon, this one follows Kevin as he quits his job and embarks on a new life on the canals.

Tudor Monastery Farm - 2013 - Historians and archaeologists look at how the Tudors farmed 500 years ago. See also: *Tudor Monastery Farm Christmas*

Victorian Farm - 2008 to 2009 - This BBC Two observational series sees historian Ruth Goodman and archaeologists Alex Langlands and Peter Ginn immersing themselves in the lifestyle of a Victorian farmer. They spend a full calendar year living on the Acton Scott Estate in Shropshire, working the land with antique tools and machinery.

Wheeler Dealers - 2003 to present - Car enthusiast Mike Brewer presents this series about efforts to save and repair old vehicles.

William the Conqueror - 2015 - This documentary tells the story of William the Conqueror, a man who became ruler at eight and led his country to victory at the Battle of Hastings.

PRIME VIDEO

NETFLIX

Website: http://netflix.com

Description: One of the biggest and oldest streaming services, Netflix offers a wide variety of content from all over the world - along with quite a bit of their own original content.

Available On: Roku, Fire TV, Apple TV, Apple iPhone & iPad, Chromecast, Fire tablets, select Smart TVs, Android phones and tablets, and computer (via web browser).

Cost: $9.99/month (1 screen), $15.99 HD (2 screens same time), $19.99 UHD (4 screens same time)

Now Streaming
Mysteries & Crime Dramas

Behind Her Eyes - 2021 - This psychological thriller blends supernatural elements into the story of Louise, a single woman whose world changes when she starts having an affair with her boss and becomes friends with his wife.

Black Spot - *France* - 2019 - This supernatural thriller follows a Gendarmerie head who teams up with an eccentric new prosecutor to help address the area's unusually high murder rate.

The Chestnut Man - *Denmark* - 2021 - In a quiet Danish suburb, a woman is found murdered on a playground. Above, her, there's a small man made of chestnuts.

Clickbait - *United States, Australia* - Set in Oakland but filmed primarily in Melbourne, this thriller looks at how the internet can fuel outrage that denies the targets any kind of due process.

Collateral – 2018 - When a pizza delivery man is gunned down in London, DI Kip Glaspie refuses to accept that it's just a random act of violence. Her investigation drags her into a dark underworld she never could have predicted. The series stars John Simm of *Life on Mars*, along with Nicola Walker (*River*), Billie Piper (*Doctor Who*), and Carey Mulligan (*Never Let Me Go*).

Criminal: United Kingdom – 2019 - This three-episode series takes a look at the intense interrogation of three different suspects in London.

Deadwind – *Finland* – 2018 to present - Detective Sofia Karppi investigates a murder with ties to a Helsinki construction firm.

Giri/Haji - 2019 - Japanese detective Kenzo Mori travels to London to figure out whether his brother Yuto, presumed dead, is actually dead. Yuto is believed to have killed the nephew of a Yakuza member, and the search draws Kenzo into the dark and dangerous criminal underworld of London.

Gone for Good - *France* - 2021 - Based on a Harlan Coben novel, this limited series follows a man whose girlfriend disappears ten years after the loss of other people in his life.

I Came By - 2022 - Though technically a movie rather than a TV series, Kelly Macdonald (*Trainspotting*) and Hugh

Bonneville (*Downton Abbey*) make this one worthy of a mention. In it, a graffiti artist targets homes of the wealthy - until a dark discovery puts his loved ones in danger.

The Indian Detective – *Canada* – 2017 - A suspended Canadian police officer returns home to Mumbai and helps out with an investigation.

Kiss Me First – 2018 - Two girls become friends in the virtual world of an online game, and one is pulled into something much darker than she had imagined.

Lucifer - *United States* - 2016 to present - Though American, this Los Angeles-based procedural stars British actor Tom Ellis (*Miranda*). He plays Lucifer, the naughty son of God who's decided he's sick of Hell and wants to spend some time on Earth.

Lupin - *France* - 2021 - Inspired by the classic tales of gentleman thief Arsène Lupin, this modern series follows a Senegalese immigrant named Assane Diop. He's seeking revenge for his father's false imprisonment and suicide, and he draws inspiration from the gentleman thief.

Marcella – 2016 to present - After her divorce, Marcella returns to work as a detective in London. A serial killer she once pursued may have done the same.

Marseille - *France* - 2018 - Gérard Depardieu stars in this French political thriller about conspiracy, corruption, and right-wing nationalists.

The One - 2021 - When a DNA researcher believes she's discovered the way to find the perfect partner, she creates an innovative new matchmaking service. Unfortunately, it doesn't take long for problems to arise.

Paranoid – 2016 - What begins as a cozy British mystery quickly evolves into a massive European conspiracy.

Quicksand - *Sweden* - 2019 - After a school tragedy, a teenager finds herself on trial for murder.

Requiem – 2018 - After her mother commits suicide, a young woman finds evidence that might tie her to an abduction in Wales more than 20 years prior.

Safe – 2018 - Michael C. Hall (*Dexter*) tries on a British accent for his role in this series about a widowed surgeon whose teenage daughter goes missing.

The Serpent - 2021 - This true crime dramatisation is based on the activities of Charles Sobhraj, a French serial killer who preyed upon young tourists in Thailand between 1975 and 2000. Jenna Coleman (*Victoria*) is among the stars.

Stay Close - 2021 - James Nesbitt (*Cold Feet*) stars in this adaptation of Harlan Coben's novel of the same name. When a man disappears on the 17-year anniversary of another man's disappearance, it sets off a series of life-destroying events.

The Stranger - 2020 - Based on the Harlan Coben novel of the same title, this series sees a mysterious stranger tell a man a secret that destroys his otherwise nice life.

Tidelands – *Australia* – 2018 - When an ex-con returns to her hometown, it brings long-hidden truths to the surface.

Traitors – 2019 - Near the end of World War II, a young English woman assists a mysterious American agent as he tries to root out Russian infiltration in the British government.

The Valhalla Murders - *Iceland* - 2019 to 2020 - This Icelandic police procedural is based on a real event in which a state-run institution housed and abused young boys (though in real life, there was no murder).

Wanted – *Australia* – 2016 to 2018 - Two strangers become involuntary partners when they witness a murder and get framed for the crime.

You Don't Know Me - 2022 - Based on Imran Mahmood's 2017 novel of the same name, this crime drama follows a young man accused of murder. With overwhelming evidence against him, he takes time to tell the court a story about a mysterious woman he met.

Young Wallander – 2020 - Though the Kenneth Branagh adaptation of *Wallander* left Netflix this year, Netflix made this new series, an adaptation that imagines Kurt Wallander as a police officer in his early 20s in 2020 Sweden.

Dramas

Alias Grace – *Canada* – 2017 - In 19th-century Canada, a murderess might be deemed not guilty by reason of insanity. This limited series is based on Margaret Atwood's novel.

Anatomy of a Scandal - 2022 - This six-part series is based on Sarah Vaughan's 2018 novel, and each season dramatises a different scandal involving privileged Brits. **Premiered April 15th.**

Anne With An "E" – *Canada* – 2017 to 2019 - Based on Anne of Green Gables, this series follows a spirited young orphan who goes to live with a spinster.

Between – *Canada* – 2016 - When a strange disease kills every town resident over the age of 21, the youthful inhabitants of the town are quarantined.

Black Earth Rising – 2018 - Investigator Kate Ashby is forced to investigate her own past when she takes on war crimes cases.

Black Mirror – 2007 to 2019 - This ominous modern thriller anthology gives us glimpses into some very dark possibilities for the future.

Black Mirror: Bandersnatch – 2018 - In 1984, a programmer adapts a novel into a video game, growing less connected to reality as the project moves along. This is an interactive story with multiple endings.

Bodyguard – 2018 - Keeley Hawes and Richard Madden star in this hit drama about a veteran who helps thwart a terrorist attack and gets assigned to protect a prominent politician.

The Borgias – *Canada* – 2011 to 2013 - This period drama follows the notorious and frequently unethical Borgia family.

Bridgerton - 2020 - Based on Julia Quinn's best-selling romance novels, this period drama follows the romantic efforts of the Bridgerton family in Regency London.

Call the Midwife – 2012 to present - This drama looks into the lives of dedicated midwives in impoverished East London of the 1950s and 60s. **Season 11 premiered September 5th.**

The Crown – 2016 to present - This Netflix original follows some particularly dramatic times in Queen Elizabeth's reign during the last half of the 20th century. Claire Foy, Olivia Colman, and Imelda Staunton portray Queen Elizabeth II. **Season 5 is expected to be the last, and it will premiere in late 2022/early 2023.**

Cursed - 2020 - This short-lived series re-imagines Arthurian legend, telling the story from the perspective of Nimue, a young and gifted woman destined to become the Lady of the Lake.

Dark Matter – *Canada* – Waking up on a spaceship with no memories, a crew must attempt to figure out who they are and how they got there.

Dead Set – 2008 - Housemates in a reality show are clueless as the undead attack the compound.

Diana: The Musical - 2021 - Filmed during the pandemic, this is a taping of the Broadway play *Diana: The Musical* (based on Lady Diana Spencer's life).

Dracula - 2020 - Mark Gatiss and Steven Moffat have paired up for this new take on Dracula. Danish actor Claes Bang has been cast as Count Dracula, but the biggest treat might be Joanna Scanlan (*No Offence*) as Mother Superior. The new series has been described as a tale in which Dracula is "the hero of his own story".

The End of the F*ing World** – 2017 to present - A rebel and a psychopath embark on a teenage road trip.

The English Game – 2020 - This sports-themed period drama was developed by Julian Fellowes (*Downton Abbey*), and it follows the origins of modern football in England. Set in the 1870s, it brings us to a time when football was considered a sport for the wealthy – until two players from opposite ends of the spectrum meet.

Freud - *Austria* - 2020 - In 1886 Vienna, a young Sigmund Freud hasn't yet risen to prominence. When a series of murders happens within Vienna high society, he teams up with a medium and a policeman.

Frontier – *Canada* – 2016 to 2018 - In 18th-century North America, trappers and traders try to gain control in the fur trade.

Get Even - 2020 - At the elite Bannerman Independent School, a group of teenage girls band together to expose bullies and fight for justice. It's all going well until one of their targets is killed and found holding a note pointing the finger at their group.

Glitch – *Australia* – 2015 to 2019 - In a small Australian town, seven local residents return from the dead in perfect condition.

Halston - *United States* - 2021 - Scottish actor Ewan McGregor stars in this miniseries about the life of American fashion designer Roy Halston Frowick.

Heartland – *Canada* – 2007 to present - A young woman deals with the stress of potentially losing the family ranch after the sudden death of her mother.

Heartstopper - 2022 - Based on Alice Oseman's graphic novel and webcomic, this coming-of-age story follows two young boys who discover their friendship might be something more.

The Innocents – 2018 - Two teenage lovers find themselves in a world of trouble when one begins to show unexplainable abilities.

The Irregulars - 2021 - Based on the works of Sir Arthur Conan Doyle, this mystery-adventure series follows the Baker Street Irregulars as they work for Dr. Watson to save London from supernatural enemies.

The Last Kingdom – 2020 - Set in the days of Alfred the Great, this Netflix Original takes us on one man's quest to reclaim his birthright.

Last Tango in Halifax – 2012 to 2020 - Once upon a time, they were in love. Now, decades later, they meet again for a second chance.

The Letter for the King - 2020 - Based on the 1962 Dutch novel *De brief voor de Koning* by Tonke Dragt, this series follows an aspiring knight as he attempts to deliver a secret letter to the king.

Merlin - 2009 to 2013 - Colin Morgan (*The Fall*) stars as a young Merlin in his days as a mere servant to Prince Arthur of Camelot. In this version of Camelot, magic is banned and Merlin is forced to keep his talent hidden away.

Nightflyers - *United States* - 2018 - Though it's an American series, much of the cast for this horror-sci fi series is English or Irish. Based on George R.R. Martin's novella and short story series of the same name, the show is set in 2093, and it sees a group of scientists venturing into space to make contact with alien life forms.

Outlander - 2014 to present - In 1945, an English nurse is mysteriously transported back in time to Scotland in 1743. The massively-popular series is based on the novels of Diana Gabaldon.

Peaky Blinders – 2014 to present - Set in early 20th century Birmingham, this series focuses on gang boss Tommy Shelby and his family. **Season 6 (the final season) premiered on June 10th.**

Persuasion (2022) - This adaptation of Jane Austen's last completed novel offers a very modern, Fleabag-esque re-telling for a new generation.

Pine Gap – *Australia* – 2018 - At a top-secret US and Australian defense facility, the alliance begins to show strain.

Post-Mortem: No One Dies in Skarnes - *Norway* - 2021 - A young woman is declared dead, but she later wakes up with a thirst for blood. At the same time, her family's funeral home could use a bit of extra business...

The Queen's Gambit - *United States* - Though not British, this chess drama features a number of British actors. The series follows a young, orphaned chess prodigy from childhood to adulthood.

The Rain - *Denmark* - 2018 to 2020 - After a virus wipes out most of the world's population, two siblings battle to survive their new reality.

Rebellion – 2016 - During WWI, three Irish women must choose sides in the revolt against English rule.

Reign - *United States* - 2013 to 2017 - Though technically American in origin, this series offers a "creative" retelling of the life of Mary, Queen of Scots and her rise to power.

The Sandman - 2022 - This adaptation of English author Neil Gaiman's graphic novels follows Morpheus, the King of Dreams, as he sets off to recover something stolen from him.

Secret City – *Australia* – 2016 - One student's protest leads to government scandal.

Shadow & Bone - *United States* - 2021 - This young adult fantasy series features a cast of many British actors, including Zoë Wanamaker. Based on the *Grisha* novels by Leigh Bardugo, it invites us into a world where some people have the ability to "perform small science". These people are called Grisha, and abilities can range from things like summoning light to healing.

Shameless (US) - *United States* - 2011 to present - This adaptation of Paul Abbott's British series of the same name features an ensemble cast led by William H. Macy and Emmy Rossum.

Top Boy – 2019 to present - This gritty drama focuses on drug dealers in London public housing. See also: *Top Boy – Summerhouse.*

Travelers – *Canada* – 2016 to 2018 - In the far future, special agents are tasked with traveling back in time to prevent the collapse of society.

Troy: Fall of a City – 2018 - This miniseries is a retelling of the siege of Troy, loosely based on the Iliad.

Van Helsing – *Canada* – 2016 to present - After waking up from a coma, a young woman finds the world ravaged by vampires.

Vikings: Valhalla - 2022 - This sequel to Vikings picks up 100 years later with a new generation of heroes.

Watership Down – 2018 - This modern-day retelling of the British classic features a warren of rabbits on a daring journey to find a new place to call home.

Wentworth – *Australia* – 2013 to present - An innocent woman has to figure out how to survive in prison while awaiting trial for the murder of her husband.

White Lines - 2020 - When a popular Manchester DJ's body turns up twenty years after his disappearance from Ibiza, his sister makes a trip to the island in hopes of finding out what really happened. Her quest leads her through shady nightclubs, super yachts, and a multitude of lies and coverups.

The Witcher - 2019 - Henry Cavill stars in this upcoming series about a solitary monster hunter in a world full of wicked people. The series is based on the book series of the same name by Andrzej Sapkowski. See also: *Making the Witcher* and *Inside the Episodes: The Witcher*.

Wyonna Earp – *Canada* – 2016 to present - A descendant of Wyatt Earp teams up with an immortal Doc Holiday in this supernatural comic-inspired Wild West tale.

Comedies

After Life – 2019 to present - After losing his wife to cancer, a suicidal widower struggles to come to terms with his new life. Stars Ricky Gervais (*The Office*).

Crashing – 2016 - A group of young people live as property guardians in an unused hospital in London. Phoebe Waller-Bridge (*Fleabag*) stars.

Crazyhead – 2016 - 20-somethings work on becoming adults while also battling demons in this comedy.

Cuckoo – 2012 to 2019 - When a British woman brings an American hippie back home as her husband, it sets off turmoil in her polite and proper family.

David Brent: Life on the Road - 2016 - Ricky Gervais returns to the role of David Brent in this spin-off film that sees him attempting to become a rock star.

Derek – 2012 to 2014 - Ricky Gervais stars in this comedy about a good-hearted but slow nursing home care assistant.

Derry Girls – 2018 to present - This Northern Irish sitcom takes place in 1990s Derry, where a group of young women grow up during the Troubles. **The third and final season premieres October 7th.**

The Duchess - 2020 - Canadian comedienne Katherine Ryan stars in this comedy about a chaotic single mum who enjoys offending the people around her. When she's not telling off fellow mums or sending nudes to their husbands, she's trying to decide if she should have another child with her ex or accept a "second-hand crack baby" via adoption.

Feel Good - 2020 - This comedy series follows two young women who fall in love in London. Mae is a Canadian comedian, while George is a typical middle-class English woman who struggles to tell others about their relationship. Mae Martin and Charlotte Richie star as Mae and George, while Lisa Kudrow plays Mae's mother.

NETFLIX

Flowers – 2016 to 2018 - Olivia Colman (*Broadchurch*) and Julian Barratt (*Bloods*) star in this dark comedy about a troubled English family.

Greg Davies: You Magnificent Beast - 2018 - British comedian Greg Davies talks manscaping, bad dates, and family pranks.

Hard Cell - 2022 - Catherine Tate (*Doctor Who*) stars as many of the main characters in this mockumentary about the inmate-led production of a musical.

The IT Crowd – 2006 to 2013 - Banished to the basement, two nerds and their clueless leader service the IT needs of a strange and generic corporation.

Jack Whitehall at Large – 2017 - This hour-long comedy special features the standup work of comedian Jack Whitehall.

Jack Whitehall: Christmas With My Father – 2019 - This Christmas special sees Jack Whitehall NOT travelling with his father – instead, taking the stage in London's West End with a host of celebrity guests.

Jack Whitehall: I'm Only Joking - 2020 - Comedian Jack Whitehall talks about life in hotels, human stupidity, and of course, his father.

Jack Whitehall: Travels with My Father – 2017 to present - A man and his father have little in common, but they come together as they travel around the world.

James Acaster: Repertoire – 2018 - This collection features four performances from quirky comedian James Acaster.

Jimmy Carr: Funny Business - 2016 - British comedian Jimmy Carr delivers a set to the UK's Hammersmith Apollo.

Jimmy Carr: His Dark Material - 2021 - This stand-up special sees some of Jimmy Carr's darkest humour.

Jimmy Carr: The Best of Ultimate Gold Greatest Hits - 2019 - This collection gathers up some of the most outrageous and entertaining jokes from Jimmy Carr's stand-up career.

Kath & Kim – *Australia* – 2002 to 2007 - A quirky mother and daughter pair lead an interesting life in the suburbs of Melbourne. See also: *Da Kath & Kim Code* and *Kath & Kimderella*.

Kim's Convenience – *Canada* – 2016 to present - This sitcom focuses on a Korean family that runs a small convenience store in Toronto.

The Letdown – *Australia* – 2019 - A new mum meets strange friends in a new parent support group.

Lovesick (aka Scrotal Recall) – 2014 to 2018 - After finding out he has an STD, a young man must attempt to contact former lovers.

Man Like Mobeen – 2017 to present - In Small Heath, Birmingham, Mobeen tries to be a good Muslim and make sure his sister grows up on the straight and narrow, despite his past as a drug dealer.

Meet the Adebanjos – 2012 to present - In South London, a Nigerian father tries to teach traditional African values to his modern British family – with entertaining results.

Michael McIntyre: Showman - 2020 - Comedian Michael McIntyre talks about family, tech, accents, and sharks in this hour-long stand-up set.

Monty Python's Almost the Truth – 2009 - Though this is technically a documentary, it made sense to include it here alongside the other Monty Python titles.

Monty Python and the Holy Grail – 1975 - King Arthur and his knights seek the Holy Grail, but they're not well-suited to the task.

Monty Python Before the Flying Circus – 2000 - This documentary takes a look at how six talented men became the groundbreaking comedy troupe, Monty Python.

Monty Python Best Bits – 2014 - This series compiles clips + opinions from prominent comedians, many of whom considered Monty Python to be influential on their careers.

Monty Python Conquers America – 2008 - This documentary takes a look at how Monty Python shaped a number of American comedians.

Monty Python's Flying Circus – 1969 to 1974 - The classic British sketch comedy is now streaming on Netflix.

Monty Python's Life of Brian – 1979 - More Monty Python fun revolving around a man who deals with a particularly nasty case of mistaken identity.

Monty Python Live at Aspen – 1998 - The

men of Monty Python reunite to discuss the making of their iconic show.

Monty Python Live at the Hollywood Bowl – 1982 - Clips and animations feature in this live-to-tape performance of Monty Python's greatest hits.

Monty Python Live (Mostly): One Down, Five to Go – 2014 - Live from London in a sold-out final show, the remaining members of Monty Python reunited to reprise their old roles.

Monty Python's Personal Best – 2005 - Members of the Monty Python troupe select their favorite sketches.

Monty Python: The Meaning of Live – 2014 - After a lengthy hiatus, the Monty Python crew reunited for this live performance.

Offspring - *Australia* - 2010 to 2017 - This dramedy follows a thirtysomething obstetrician and her circle of friends in Melbourne.

Ricky Gervais: Humanity - 2018 - Ricky Gervais performs a standup routine on celebrity, mortality, and the way modern society is offended by everything.

Ricky Gervais: Supernature - 2022 - This controversial new set sees Ricky Gervais taking on everything from the rules of comedy to spoiling cats to "old-fashioned women" ("the ones with wombs").

Rita - *Denmark* - 2017 to present - Danish schoolteacher Rita may be popular with her students, but she struggles with adults.

Russell Howard: Recalibrate - 2017 - Comedian Russell Howard talks about everything from politics to porn in this hour-long set.

Russell Howard: Lubricant - 2021 - This two-part stand-up special sees Russell Howard returning to the stage and talking about lockdown.

Sex Education – 2019 to present - Though technically British, there's something VERY American-feeling about this series. It's a series about a socially awkward teen whose mother is a sex therapist.

Sick Note – 2018 - When an aimless young man is misdiagnosed with cancer, his life starts to get exciting.

Simon Amstell: Set Free – 2019 - If you enjoyed *Grandma's House*, you might like this standup set from comedian Simon Amstell (star and co-writer of the British comedy). He's an introspective comic, and this set dives into love, ego, intimacy, and ayahuasca.

Sisters – *Australia* – 2018 - A young woman suddenly finds out she has two sisters and more than 100 brothers.

Some Assembly Required – *Canada* – 2015 - A teenager takes over control of a toy company.

Still Game – 2002 to 2019 - Scottish comedy about three old men in a Glasgow high-rise.

Trailer Park Boys – *Canada* – 2001 to present - This trailer park comedy follows a group of men in constant pursuit of a big score and an easier life. See also: *The Movie, One Last Shot, Trailer Park Boys: Xmas Special, Trailer Park Boys: Live at the North Pole, The Animated Series, Countdown to Liquor Day, Out of the Park: USA, Out of the Park: Europe, Say Goodnight to the Bad Guys, SwearNet, SwearNet Live, Trailer Park Boys: Drunk, High, & Unemployed: Live in Austin,* and *Live in F**kin Dublin.*

Turn Up Charlie - 2019 - Idris Elba (*Luther*) stars as Charlie, a struggling DJ and confirmed bachelor. When he sees a possible upside for his career, he reluctantly agrees to play nanny to a good friend's dreadful young daughter. Piper Perabo (*Coyote Ugly*) stars as his famous friend Sara.

Wanderlust - 2018 - When a couples therapist spots a former patient of hers whose husband committed suicide during therapy, she gets distracted and ends up in a car accident. The recovery process adds to her marital troubles, forcing her to confront issues she'd been avoiding for a long time.

White Gold – 2017 to 2019 - This period comedy takes place in 1980s Essex, where obnoxious salesman Vincent Swan and his team do whatever it takes to sell double-glazed windows.

The Windsors – 2016 to present - This mockumentary parodies the current British royal family.

Workin' Moms – *Canada* – 2017 to present - When their (remarkably long Canadian) maternity leaves are over, a group of moms return to work.

NETFLIX

Documentary & Lifestyle

21 Again - 2019 - A group of young women disguise their mothers as 21-year-olds and send them out into the wild.

Alien Worlds - 2020 - This docu-series mixes fantasy and science to imagine what life might be like on other planets.

Amazing Interiors – 2018 - This British show travels the world to visit eccentric homeowners and their eccentric homes.

Animals on the Loose - 2021 - This interactive adventure prompts you to make choices so Bear Grylls can bring escaped animals back to their sanctuary home.

Baby Ballroom – 2018 - This series goes deep into the cutthroat world of children's ballroom dancing (which we didn't realise existed).

Bad Boy Billionaires: India - 2020 - This docuseries examines the dizzying success and mind-blowing greed of some of India's most infamous tycoons.

Behind Enemy Lines – 2001 - This series takes a look at some of the changes Winston Churchill instituted after WWII setbacks in 1940. He set out to create a force powered by intelligence, stealth, and cunning more than ruthless brute force, and it paid off.

The Big Family Cooking Showdown – 2017 to present - This unscripted reality show brings us some of Britain's most passionate amateur cooks.

The Big Flower Fight – 2020 - This one is best described as *"Great British Bake Off* meets the RHS Chelsea Flower Show".

Breaking Boundaries: The Science of Our Planet - 2021 - Sir David Attenborough and Johan Rockström take a look at the alarming decrease in our planet's biodiversity.

Caught on Camera – 2015 - This series shows crimes caught on CCTV and cell phones, and how technology is used to solve otherwise unsolvable cases.

Churchill's Secret Agents: The New Recruits - 2018 - This reality series takes 14 modern contestants through the same selection process used for World War II spies.

Cocaine – 2005 - This series takes a look at the cocaine industry and its impact on people of all walks of life.

Conspiracies – 2015 - This series dives into a number of potential coverups and secrets.

Crazy Delicious - 2020 - This food competition show rewards talented home chefs with a golden apple.

Dancing with the Birds - 2019 - Stephen Fry narrates this hour-long documentary about bird courtship rituals.

David Attenborough: A Life On Our Planet - 2020 - Sir David Attenborough takes a look back at his life and reflects on the horrific changes he's seen.

Edge of the Universe – 2008 - Astronomers reveal the latest discoveries about the world beyond Earth's atmosphere.

Elizabeth & Margaret: Love & Loyalty - 2020 - This documentary takes a look at the relationship between Queen Elizabeth and her sister.

The Fix - 2018 - Jimmy Carr and a rotating set of comedians sit down and try to solve major world problems with the help of an actual expert.

Glow Up – 2020 - This series aims to see who can take the sexiest selfie – and the loser gets a makeover.

The Great British Baking Show – 2010 to present - This popular British baking show sees amateurs facing off and trying to avoid the dreaded soggy bottom. **New episodes began airing September 16th.**

The Great British Baking Show: Holidays - 2019 - This series gathers up festive holiday episodes of the popular baking competition.

Greatest Events of WWII in Colour – 2019 - This series also takes a look at WWII footage that's been restored with colour.

History 101 – 2020 - This educational series offers short history lessons for those challenged in the "attention span" department – everything from fast food to plastics to the space race and the rise of China.

NETFLIX

Hitler's Circle of Evil – 2017 - This docuseries takes a look at the power struggles, plots, and betrayals that took place behind the scenes within Nazi leadership.

I Am a Killer – 2020 - This show goes to the US, where capital punishment is legal, and follows the stories of Death Row inmates. **Season 3 premiered August 30th.**

I Am a Killer: Released - 2020 - 30 years after being sentenced to death for a murder, a convict is paroled and begins a new life.

Inside the World's Toughest Prisons – 2016 to present - Journalists put themselves inside – behind bars – in some of the world's roughest prisons. **Season 6 premieres September 28th.**

Interior Design Masters – 2019 - Aspiring interior designers transform a variety of spaces in a competition to win a contract with a fashionable London hotel.

Jimmy Savile: A British Horror Story - 2022 - After his death in 2011, numerous complaints emerged about Jimmy Saville's predatory and inappropriate activities. This two-part docuseries looks at the hundreds of allegations that surfaced, leading police to believe he may have been one of the country's most prolific sex offenders.

Keith Richards: Under the Influence - 2015 - This documentary takes a look at the people and music that influenced Keith Richards.

Lady Boss: The Jackie Collins Story - 2021 - This documentary takes a look at the glamorous life and work of English romance author Jackie Collins.

Life in Color with David Attenborough - 2021 - Sir David Attenborough explores how colour serves a variety of purposes in the animal kingdom.

The Meaning of Monty Python - 2013 - Five Pythons take a look back at their decades of comedic success, along with reflections on process, politics, and change.

Memories of a Murderer: The Nilsen Tapes - If you enjoyed *Des* (starring David Tennant), you may also enjoy comparing the dramatised version to this documentary about the same serial killer, Dennis Nilsen.

Million Pound Menu – 2019 - Young restaurateurs open pop-up restaurants in hopes of attracting and impressing investors.

My Beautiful Broken Brain - 2016 - After having a devastating stroke at just 34, a woman documents her rehabilitation efforts.

Myth & Mogul: John DeLorean - 2021 - John DeLorean worked his way up from engineer to inventor and automotive executive, but his career was marred by high-profile failure and later, charges for cocaine trafficking. This docuseries takes a look at his life.

Myths and Monsters - 2017 - This docuseries investigates interesting legends set within the ancient landscapes of Europe.

Nadiya Bakes - 2021 - This series sees chef Nadiya Hussain return to baking, offering recipes from sweet to savoury.

Nadiya's Time to Eat – 2020 - Nadiya Hussain shows how modern families can make great food with limited time.

Our Planet - 2019 - Sir David Attenborough narrates this docuseries on the impact of climate change on living creatures. *See also: Our Planet - Behind the Scenes*

Paul Hollywood's Big Continental Road Trip - 2017 - Celebrity chef and car enthusiast Paul Hollywood explores the food and car cultures of France, Germany, and Italy.

The Puppet Master - 2022 - Robert Freegard is best known for conning a number of women into giving him sex and money by convincing them he worked for MI5. This docuseries tells the surprising true story of his crimes.

Real Crime: Diamond Geezers - 2008 - This docu-film sees a group of old thieves trying - and nearly succeeding - to steal the world's largest perfect diamond.

Real Crime: Supermarket Heist - 2009 - This documentary follows the search for the Tesco bomber, a Bournemouth man who demanded money from the supermarket chain whilst calling himself "Sally".

The Ripper - 2020 - This limited series follows the 1970s search for the Yorkshire Ripper.

Roman Empire - 2019 - This docu-drama follows the reigns of three of the Roman Empire's best-known and most interesting leaders: Commodus, Julius Caesar, and Caligula. Sean Bean (*Game of Thrones*) is among the narrators.

The Royal House of Windsor – 2017 - This docuseries analyzes the British royal family's ability to hold onto power over the last century of struggles and changes.

Secrets of Great British Castles – 2016 - Documentary-style program highlighting some of the largest and most historically-important castles around Great Britain (including Stirling, York, and Edinburgh, among others).

Serial Killer with Piers Morgan – 2018 - Piers Morgan takes a closer look at three convicted serial killers and their crimes.

Sophie: A Murder in West Cork - *Ireland* - 2021 - This three-part true crime documentary tells the story of Sophie Toscan Du Plantier, a French television and film producer who was killed at her holiday cottage in West Cork, Ireland in 1996.

Sunderland 'Til I Die – 2020 - This docuseries follows the Sunderland Association Football Club through the 2017-2018 season as they try to make a big comeback.

They've Gotta Have Us – 2018 - This series interviews black entertainers to trace the history of black cinema.

The Tinder Swindler - 2022 - One man decided to pose as a wealthy jetsetter to con women. This documentary takes a look at the women who want payback.

Win the Wilderness – 2020 - This reality show pits six couples against each other to see who has the best survival skills. The winning couple gets the deed to a home in the wilds of Alaska.

Witches: A Century of Murder – 2015 - Historian Suzannah Lipscomb takes a look at the British witch hunts of the 17th century.

The World's Most Extraordinary Homes – 2017 to present - Caroline Quentin (*Jonathan Creek*) and architect Piers Taylor travel the world to view extraordinary and unusual homes.

World War II in Colour – 2009 - In this 13-episode series, WWII footage is restored and given new life – in colour.

You vs. Wild - 2019 - British survivalist Bear Grylls teaches us about how to survive in some of the world's harshest environments.

You vs. Wild: Out Cold - 2019 - This interactive survival series is hosted by British adventurer Bear Grylls. After a plane crash leaves him with amnesia, you have to make the decisions to survive the adventure.

Kids & Young Adults

The A List - 2018 - This series blends romance, drama, suspense, and mystery when a group of young women go to a remote camp with a supernatural presence.

Angelina Ballerina - 2002 to 2006 - This animated series follows a young mouse who enjoys dancing ballet. Finty Williams did the voice of Angelina, and her mother - Dame Judi Dench - did the voice of Miss Lilly, her ballet teacher.

Big Tree City - 2022 - A team of animals work together to help keep Big Tree City safe for all.

Booba - 2014 to present - A curious creature called Booba gets into all manner of funny situations with his friends.

Bottersnikes and Gumbles - 2015 to present - Set in and near a junkyard, this animated programme sees the fun-loving Gumbles attempting to steer clear of the smelly Bottersnikes. Unfortunately, Netflix decided to re-dub the series with American accents.

The Bureau of Magical Things - *Australia* - 2020 - A teenager's accidental discovery might make her the only one capable of uniting the human and magical realms.

Creeped Out – 2017 to present - A masked figure known only as "The Curious" collects dark tales in this dramatic young adult anthology series.

Danger Mouse - 2015 to present - These modern episodes see Danger Mouse and hamster Penfold returning for more jet-setting spy adventures.

Danger Mouse: Classic Collection - 1981 to 1992 - This collection of classic episodes features the spy Danger Mouse and his sidekick Penfold as they foil evil plots around the world.

Degrassi : Next Class – *Canada* – 2016 to 2017 - This follow-up to the classic Canadian teen drama features a new generation of teenagers.

Dennis and Gnasher Unleashed - 2017 - This cartoon follows fearless Dennis, his dog Gnasher, and his friends as they seek out fun and adventure around their town.

Fate: The Winx Saga - 2021 - A group of teenagers navigate life, love, and magical powers at a boarding school for kids with special abilities.

Free Rein – 2017 to present - A teenager from LA spends the summer in England and bonds with a mysterious horse. See also: *Free Rein: The 12 Neighs of Christmas* and *Free Rein: Valentine's Day*

H2O: Just Add Water – 2009 - A group of young girls deal with turning into mermaids.

Horrid Henry - 2006 to 2019 - Based on Francesca Simon's *Horrid Henry* book series, this show follows the adventures of a very naughty young boy. See also: *Horrid Henry's Gross Day Out*

The Inbestigators - *Australia* - 2019 to present - This light-hearted kids' series follows a group of children who start a detective agency to solve crimes at school and around the neighbourhood.

The Last Bus - 2022 - After a highly eventful field trip, a group of kids band together to save the world from an army of drones.

Little Baby Bum - 2019 - Animated nursery rhyme friends sing fun songs for the little ones. See also: *Learning Songs by Little Baby Bum* and *Little Baby Bum's Go Buster*.

The Loud House Movie - 2021 - Though we don't typically include movies in here, this animated film would be great for anyone taking kids or grandkids to Scotland in the future. It sees Lincoln Loud heading to Scotland, where he learns a bit about his family history.

Morphle - 2020 - Little Mila goes on fun and educational adventures with her magical morphing pet called Morphle.

The Octonauts - 2010 to present - This cartoon follows an underwater exploring crew of animals who live in an undersea base called the Octopod.

Puffin Rock - *Ireland* - 2016 - On Puffin Rock, puffling Oona, her brother, and her friends learn important life skills.

Robozuna - 2018 to present - A young orphan boy builds a homemade robot to help free his country from an evil empire.

Shaun the Sheep - 2007 to present - This *Wallace & Gromit* spin-off follows the

NETFLIX

adventures of an unusually clever sheep named Shaun. See also: *Shaun the Sheep: Adventures from Mossy Bottom* and *Shaun the Sheep: The Farmer's Llamas*

Sunny Bunnies - 2015 to present - These furry, colourful bunnies seek fun and mischief wherever they go in this children's series.

Thomas & Friends - 1984 to present - This animated series follows the friendly blue tank engine who lives on the Island of Sodor. See also: *Thomas & Friends: Digs & Discoveries: All Tracks Lead to Rome, Thomas & Friends: Steam Team to the Rescue, Thomas & Friends: Royal Engine, Thomas & Friends: Digs & Discoveries: Mines of Mystery, Thomas & Friends: Marvelous Machinery: A New Arrival*, and *Thomas & Friends: Marvelous Machinery: World of Tomorrow*.

Timmy Time - 2009 to 2012 - This claymation series is a spin-off of *Shaun the Sheep*, and follows little Timmy the lamb as he enters nursery school.

The Unlisted - *Australia* - 2019 - This thriller sees a pair of identical twins uncovering a secret conspiracy to track and control kids. Together, they team up with a band of rebels to help stop the plot and take back their world.

The Worst Witch – 2017 to present - This young adult comedy follows a bumbling young witch who accidentally stumbles into witching school.

Zero Chill - 2021 - This teen drama follows the MacBentley family as they move from Canada to England to follow their son's hockey dreams.

HULU

Now Streaming

Mysteries & Dramas

The Accident - 2019 - Sarah Lancashire (*Happy Valley*) stars as a hairdresser named Polly in this series about a small Welsh community torn apart by a terrible accident. The series takes us through the aftermath - families waiting for news, lives changed forever, and the search for someone to blame.

Apple Tree Yard - 2017 – This miniseries is based on Louise Doughty's novel by the same name, and it's a suspenseful combination of sex and murder. When a woman gets an intriguing proposition, it excites her – until she realizes it may not be quite what it seemed. Emily Watson and Ben Chaplin star.

Atlantis – 2013 - A young man washes up on the shores of ancient Atlantis.

Bad Banks - *Germany* - 2018 to 2020 - This financial thriller follows a young mother who thinks her banking career is going well until she realises she's caught up in a much larger scheme.

Baghdad Central - 2020 - This six-part period drama is set in US-occupied Iraq in October 2003. In the aftermath of the invasion, the Iraqi army, police forces, and civil leadership have all been disbanded. To reclaim his identity after losing everything, one Iraqi ex-policeman (played by Waleed Zuaiter of *The Spy*) works as a detective to help solve a murder for the coalition forces. Together with British ex-cop Frank Temple (Bertie Carvel, *Doctor Foster*), he works the case while the Iraqi Police Force is being re-built.

Banished – 2015 - British convicts are sent to Australia to pay for their crimes, and both they and the soldiers have a great deal of adapting to do.

Being Erica – *Canada* – 2009 to 2011 - A young woman participates in a strange form of therapy that involves time travel.

The Bisexual - 2018 - This dramedy follows a London-based American woman who breaks up with her girlfriend and decides to give heterosexual relations a try. American Desiree Akhavan (*Flowers*) plays Leila alongside Irish actor Brian Gleeson (*Peaky Blinders*) and English actress Maxine Peake (*Silk*).

Black Narcissus - 2020 - Based on Rumer Godden's 1939 book, *Black Narcissus* tells the story of Sister Clodagh as she leads the nuns of St. Faith's to set up a brand of their order in the Himalayas. They make their home in the remote palace of Mopu, a former home for concubines known as the "House of Women". As time goes on, Sister Clodagh finds herself increasingly tempted by an arrogant land agent, Mr. Dean. She's not the only one, though. The fragile and unstable Sister Ruth is similarly attracted, and both women find themselves struggling with forbidden feelings and unsatisfied desires. This production includes one of Dame Diana Rigg's final performances.

Black Sails - *United States* - 2014 to 2017 - Though technically American, *Black Sails* features a number of British actors like Toby Stephens (*Jane Eyre*) and Rupert Penry-Jones (*Whitechapel*). The series is described as a prequel to Robert Louis Stevenson's *Treasure Island.*

Bleak House (2005) - This classic BBC Dickens adaptation is based on the legal drama of the same name. The central story surrounds a person who left several versions of his will when he died.

Butterfly – 2018 - When a young boy named Max decides he would prefer to live as a girl named Maxine, his parents have to decide how to handle it.

Cardinal - *Canada* - 2017 to 2020 - Based on the crime novels of author Giles Blunt, this series follows two detectives who work out of the fictional city of Algonquin Bay. The lead, John Cardinal, is a troubled officer who was removed from his squad when it was believed he was too obsessed with the case of a missing girl.

Chance - *United States* - 2016 to 2018 - English actor and comedian Hugh Laurie stars in this drama about a doctor who attempts to help a patient escape an abusive husband by enlisting the aid of a mysterious antique furniture restorer.

City Homicide – *Australia* – 2007 to 2011 - In Melbourne, Australia, a group of homicide detectives work to find justice for victims of murder.

Clique - 2017 to 2019 - When two best friends go off to university in Edinburgh, it seems like everything will be amazing. When one of them is pulled into a clique of popular, powerful women, however, their university lives take a dark turn.

Cold Squad – *Canada* – 1998 to 2005 - This long-running Canadian series follows a team that works on cold cases ranging from 5 to 50 or more years old.

Coronation Street - 1960 to present - Running since 1960, and there are more than 9400 episodes of this daytime drama classic. The show is set in the fictional area of Wetherfield, where residents walk cobbled streets among terraced houses and the ever-present Rovers Return pub.

Daniel Deronda (2002) - This adaptation of George Eliot's final novel focuses on a Victorian man torn between the love of two women.

David Copperfield (1999) - Daniel Radcliffe (*Harry Potter*) stars as young David in this adaptation of the Dickens novel.

Demons - 2009 - Philip Glenister (*Life on Mars*), Zoë Tapper (*Grace*), and Holliday Grainger (*CB Strike*) are among the stars of this series about a young man who turns out to be the great-grandson of Abraham Van Helsing. Fans of Mackenzie Crook (*Detectorists*) will enjoy his performance as the demon Gladiolus Thrip.

The Fades – 2011 - A young man is haunted by dreams he can't explain, and he begins to see spirits around him – some of them malicious.

The Great - *United States* - 2020 - Though this dramedy is an American production, much of the cast is British. It's loosely based on the rise of Catherine the Great.

Hard Sun – 2018 - Two detectives work together to fight crime in a world that may be doomed anyway.

Harlots – 2007 to 2019 - In 18th century London, a brothel owner struggles to raise her daughters. The series was inspired by historian Hallie Rubenhold's book, *The Covent Garden Ladies*.

Harrow - *Australia* - 2018 to present - Welshman Ioan Gruffudd stars as Dr. Daniel Harrow, a forensic pathologist with authority issues. Still, his empathy for the dead makes him brilliant at what he does.

Helstrom - *United States* - 2020 - English actor Tom Austen (*Grantchester*) stars in this Marvel-universe series about Daimon and Satana Hellstrom, children of a powerful serial killer who hunt down the worst elements in society.

Hollyoaks - 1995 to present - This young adult soap opera is set in the fictional village of Hollyoaks, a suburb of Chester.

HULU

As a youth-oriented programme, it frequently covers topics considered taboo.

In the Flesh – 2013 - After the government gets a handle on the recent zombie epidemic, they begin to rehabilitate zombies for re-entry into society. They aren't always warmly received.

Intruders – 2014 - John Simm (*Life on Mars*) stars as an ex-cop whose wife goes missing. The ensuing investigation leads him to Seattle, and a secret society dedicated to chasing immortality by hiding in the bodies of others. Based on Michael Marshall Smith's novel.

Jane Eyre (2006) - This two-part adaptation of the classic Charlotte Bronte novel tells the story of a young woman who falls in love with the dark and brooding Mr. Rochester. Ruth Wilson (*Luther*) stars.

Killing Eve – 2018 to present - A bored but highly competent MI5 officer trades her life behind a desk to pursue an elusive and particularly aggressive female serial killer.

Legends - *United States* - 2014 to 2015 - Brit Sean Bean stars as deep cover operative Martin Odum, a man with an abnormally strong ability to change his identity as needed for the job at hand.

Line of Duty – 2012 to present - This suspenseful British police series is set in the fictional "anti-corruption unit" AC-12, where the police police the police. Yes, we know that sounds a bit odd. Lennie James, Vicky McClure, Martin Compston, and Adrian Dunbar all feature.

Luther – 2010 to 2019 - Idris Elba stars as a brilliant London detective who frequently gets into trouble because of his passion for the job.

Murdoch Mysteries - *Canada* - 2008 to present - Set in the 1890s, Murdoch uses early forensics to solve murders. Yannick Bisson stars as Detective William Murdoch, Helene Joy plays Dr. Julia Ogden, and Thomas Craig and Jonny Harris fill the roles of Inspector Thomas Brackenreid and Constable George Crabtree, respectively.

The Musketeers – 2014 to 2016 - This modern retelling of the classic Dumas novel includes appearances by Peter Capaldi, Tom Burke, and Rupert Everett.

My Mad Fat Diary – 2013 to 2015 - In 1990s Lincolnshire, a young woman grapples with depression and body image issues.

National Treasure - 2016 - Robbie Coltrane (*Cracker*) stars as Paul Finchley, a once-popular comedian accused of raping several young women earlier in his career. The miniseries follows his downward spiral and the impact the accusations have on his family. Julie Walters (*Harry Potter*) plays his wife.

National Treasure: Kiri - 2018 - This four-part miniseries stars Sarah Lancashire as Miriam, a social worker handling the adoption of a young black girl named Kiri. The child is abducted and murdered, and the series follows the chaos that ensues.

New Tricks – 2003 to 2015 - This long-running series focuses on a group of police who come out of retirement to work unsolved cases.

Normal People – *Ireland* – 2020 – This series follows a couple navigating their relationship after secondary school. Though they're from the same small Irish town, their different social classes cause friction.

Oliver Twist (2007) - In this adaptation of the Dickens classic, we see appearances from Morven Christie, Tom Hardy, and Sarah Lancashire, among others. The story focuses on the difficult life of a young orphan after he's sold into an apprenticeship with an undertaker.

Prey – 2014 to 2015 - Manchester detective Marcus Farrow (played by John Simm) is on the run, accused of a crime and desperate to prove his innocence. All the while, his former friends and colleagues do their best to hunt him down. This series reunites Philip Glenister and John Simm, who also appeared together in *Life on Mars*.

Pride & Prejudice (1995) - Colin Firth and Jennifer Ehle star in this adaptation of the classic tale of Elizabeth Bennet and the snobbish but enticing Mr. Darcy.

Primeval – 2008 to 2011 - When strange things start happening around England, a professor and his team are forced to capture a variety of unusual creatures from other time periods. Includes Ben Miller (of *Death in Paradise*).

Rules of the Game - 2022 - When Maya begins her new job as director of human resources at Fly, she finds herself up against an unwelcoming lad culture. A death in the workplace will lead her to start digging into old cases of abuse and misconduct.

HULU

The Secret of Crickley Hall – 2012 - Suranne Jones and Tom Ellis star in this supernatural miniseries about a family that relocates to a grand old estate up north after the disappearance of their young son.

Sense & Sensibility (2008) - When a woman finds herself newly widowed and destitute with three unmarried daughters, she downsizes and attempts to find good husbands for them.

Silk – 2011 to 2014 - This series focuses on the challenges modern-day barristers face in their careers.

The Sister - 2020 - *Luther* creator and screenwriter Neil Cross brings us this four-part story "of murder – and perhaps ghosts – which exposes the quiet terror of a man trying to escape his past." It's inspired by Cross's novel *Burial*, released in 2009. Russell Tovey (*Years and Years*) plays Nathan, a man trying to hide a terrible secret. His world is rocked when Bob (Bertie Carvel, *Doctor Foster*) spears on his doorstep with shocking news. Amrita Acharia (*The Good Karma Hospital)* also appears.

Skins – 2007 to 2013 - This racy classic offers a look into modern teenage life in England.

The Split – 2018 to 2020 - After a 30-year absence, a family of female lawyers has enough trouble dealing with their personal lives...and then their long-absent father returns. **Season 3 is now available.**

Taboo - 2017 - Tom Hardy stars as James Keziah Delaney, an adventurer who has returned to London to rebuild his late father's shipping empire during the War of 1812. Unfortunately, he's not the only one with an interest in his father's empire.

Top of the Lake - 2013 to 2017 - This UK/New Zealand co-production follows the investigation into the disappearance of a drug lord's pregnant 12-year-old daughter. In the second series, the story moves to Sydney as the same detective investigates a body found at Bondi Beach.

Treadstone - *United States* - 2019 - Though American, several actors in this series are British, and parts of the action are set in London. Adapted from Robert Ludlum's *Bourne* world, the series explores the story of a fictional CIA black-ops programme that turns recruits into almost superhuman assassins.

Trust Me - 2017 to 2019 - This medical anthology takes a look at what happens when medical professionals violate our trust. In the first series, nurse Cath Hardacre (Jodie Whittaker) loses her job after whistle blowing, then steals a doctor's identity to make a new life in Edinburgh. In the second series, a Syrian tour veteran is recovering from trauma in hospital when he realises an awful lot of patients are mysteriously dying around him.

Upstairs Downstairs - 2010 to 2012 - This series picks up the *Upstairs Downstairs* saga shortly after the period covered by the original series. Covering 1936 to 1939, it tells the story of the new owners of 165 Eaton Place, ending with the outbreak of World War II. Ed Stoppard (*Home Fires*) and Keeley Hawes (*Bodyguard*) play new owners Sir Hallam Holland and Lady Agnes Holland.

Whitechapel - 2009 to 2013 - An inspector, a detective sergeant, and a historical homicide expert look at crimes that may have connections to the Whitechapel district.

Comedies

Absolutely Fabulous - 1992 to 2012 - In this groundbreaking classic, two wild women do everything but act their age. The series was based on a sketch comedy called "Modern Mother and Daughter" by Dawn French (*Vicar of Dibley*) and Jennifer Saunders (Edina Monsoon in *Absolutely Fabulous*). Joanna Lumley stars alongside Saunders as Patsy Stone, and Julia Sawalha plays Edina's daughter Saffron.

The Aliens – 2016 - After aliens crash-land in the Irish Sea, they're allowed onto British soil but forced to live in a ghetto called Troy. Border guard Lewis helps to maintain the separation, but it becomes a tough position to hold when he learns he's half-alien.

Blackadder - 1983 to 1989 - Rowan Atkinson stars as antihero Edmund Blackadder, accompanied by Sir Tony Robinson as his sidekick Baldrick. Each series of this quirky comedy is set in a different period within British history, and Edmund carries different titles throughout. The "essence" of each character remains largely the same in each series, though.

Brassic - 2019 to present - This working-class comedy follows a young man named Vinnie (Joe Gilgun) and his occasionally criminal friends as they go about their lives in the northern English town of Hawley. It's a lively, rough-around-the-edges comedy about desperate small-town life and the ever-present question of whether there might be something better elsewhere. *Brassic* gets its name from Cockney rhyming slang. It's a shortening of "boracic lint", slang for "skint".

Breeders - 2020 - Martin Freeman (*Sherlock*) and Daisy Haggard (*Black Mirror*) star in this sitcom about modern parenting and the inevitable discovery that you're not quite the person you thought you were before you had kids. Freeman was quoted saying it explores "some of the less-discussed truths and challenges of being a parent."

Call Me Kat - United States - 2021 - Mayim Bialik (*Blossom, The Big Bang Theory*) stars in this American adaptation of the British sitcom *Miranda*.

Dead Boss – 2012 - Helen Stephens has been wrongly convicted of killing her boss, and while she hopes she'll be cleared soon, everyone she knows wants her in prison.

Dirk Gently's Holistic Detective Agency – *United States* - 2016 to 2017 - While this reinterpretation of the famous Douglas Adams detective is technically an American production, it's based on the work of a British author, so we'll include it. In this one, a holistic detective investigates cases involving the supernatural.

Doc Martin - 2004 to present - Martin Clunes (*Men Behaving Badly*) stars in this comedy about a brilliant but grumpy London surgeon who suddenly develops a fear of blood. He leaves his high-flying career and takes a post in a Cornish fishing village where he spent holidays as a child with his Aunt Joan. His bad attitude and lack of social skills makes it a challenge to adapt to his new life.

Dream Corp LLC – 2016 to present - Though this animated series is not strictly British, Brit Stephen Merchant plays a lead role as T.E.R.R.Y., and the series includes guest appearances from Liam Neeson, Toby Kebbell, and Rupert Friend. It's a workplace comedy that takes place in a dilapidated dream therapy centre in a strip mall. Patients come to have their dreams recorded, studied, and occasionally, adjusted. Darren Boyd (*The Salisbury Poisonings*) stars.

Gameface – 2014 to 2019 - A young woman navigates her 30s with the help of her friends, a questionable life coach, and her eternally patient driving instructor.

The Hitchhiker's Guide to the Galaxy - 1981 - Arthur Dent is one of the last surviving members of the human race. Still in his dressing gown, he's dragged through an intergalactic portal and sent on an adventure through the universe. The series is based on Douglas Adams' novel of the same name, and he also wrote the TV adaptation.

Horrible Histories – 2009 to present - While designed for children, this amusing educational program is every bit as entertaining for adults. The sketches cover different parts of history, but always with a dramatic or funny take on the event.

Hunderby – 2012 to 2015 - Julia Davis stars in this dark period comedy about a woman who washes ashore after a shipwreck off the English coast.

In My Skin - 2018 - This coming-of-age series follows 16-year-old Welsh teenager Bethan as she deals with growing up, her mother's mental illness, and her own questions about sexuality.

The Kennedys – 2015 - Katherine Parkinson (*The IT Crowd*) stars in this comedy about a family moving from a housing estate to a home, eager to move up the social ladder.

Ladhood - 2019 to present - This coming-of-age sitcom takes a look at mischief and modern masculinity.

Maxxx – 2020 – Maxx is a has-been boy band star working on a comeback, but between the distractions in his life and his massive ego, he'll have some challenges.

The Mighty Boosh – 2003 to 2007 - Two young musicians work for a madman at a zoo.

Misfits – 2009 to 2013 - A group of young offenders develops superpowers when they're struck by lightning.

Moone Boy – *Ireland* - 2012 to 2014 - A young boy copes with life in a small Irish town, thanks to his imaginary friend.

Mr. Bean - 1992 to 1995 - Bumbling Mr. Bean rarely speaks and has some very peculiar ways of doing things, but it usually works out for him. Rowan Atkinson (*Maigret*) stars as the iconic British character.

The Office - 2001 to 2003 - Before there was Michael Scott in the US, there was David Brent in Slough, England. Written by Ricky Gervais (*After Life*) and Stephen Merchant (*Hello Ladies*), this mockumentary-style programme takes place in the office of the fictional Wernham Hogg paper company.

Offspring - *Australia* - 2010 to 2017 - Set in Melbourne, this series follows thirty-something obstetrician Nina and her circle of friends and family.

The Other Guy - *Australia* - 2017 to 2019 - This Australian sitcom follows a radio host who suddenly finds himself single for the first time in many years after his girlfriend cheats on him.

Packed to the Rafters - *Australia* - 2008 to 2013 - This family dramedy follows the Rafter family as they cope with the challenges of modern work, love, and family life.

Peep Show – 2003 to 2015 - Two dysfunctional and very different friends share a flat in London and attempt (rather poorly) to grow up.

Please Like Me - *Australia* - 2013 to 2016 - This dramedy follows a twentysomething man who's been dumped by his girlfriend, only to realise he might be gay. At the same time, he's dealing with a mentally ill mother who has attempted suicide.

Shameless - 2004 to 2013 - Before he created *No Offence*, Paul Abbott created *Shameless* - the story of a rough-around-the-edges family living in a Manchester housing estate. This one contains some strong language and sexual content, so it's not for everyone.

This Way Up - 2019 - Aisling Bea (*Trollied, Finding Joy*) stars as Aine, a single Irish Catholic woman who has a nervous breakdown while living in London and teaching English as a second language. Sharon Horgan (*Catastophe*) co-produces and co-stars as Shona, her older sister.

Wasted – 2016 - In the fictional West Country village of Neston Berry, young slackers spend their days getting drunk and smoking marijuana at "Stoned Henge", a souvenir shop and tattoo parlour.

Wedding Season - 2022 - This dark comedy follows Katie, a woman who finds herself surrounded by the dead bodies of her new husband and his family on her wedding day. No one's sure who did it, but everyone has a different theory. **Premiered September 8th.**

What We Do in the Shadows - *United States* - 2019 to present - Matt Berry (*The IT Crowd*) stars in this comedy about a group of centuries-old vampires who've been living in New York City for the last couple hundred years. **Season 4 premiered July 12th.**

Whose Line Is It Anyway? – 1988 to 1999 - While the US has since made its own version, this is the original *Whose Line*, the show where four performers create characters, songs, and scenes on the spot based on prompts they receive from the host or audience.

The Wrong Mans – 2013 to 2014 - After a council worker answers a ringing phone at the site of a crash, he and an acquaintance in the same building become entangled in a web of crime and corruption. James Corden (*Gavin & Stacey*) and Mathew Baynton (*Horrible Histories*) star.

Zomboat! - 2019 - This apocalypse comedy sees zombies unleashed in Birmingham, England. Two sisters join up with a couple of guys and flee by narrowboat. For those not familiar with narrowboats and British canals, it's worth noting that canal speed limits are generally 3-4 mph, and the boats themselves can't go much faster unless there's a strong current pushing them along.

Documentary & Lifestyle

Absolutely Ascot - 2018 to present - This reality show follows a group of fame-hungry individuals in the Ascot area.

Britain's Best Home Cook - 2018 to present - This cooking competition series pits amateur chefs against one another to find out who's best.

Celebrity Best Home Cook - 2021 - Ten home cooks create and serve their best dishes to celebrities like Dame Mary Berry and Claudia Winkleman.

Dress to Impress - 2017 to present - This British dating show sees competitors choosing attire for a fashion-conscious singleton, with the winner getting the date.

Escape from the City - *Australia* - 2019 - Similar to the UK's *Escape to the Country*, this series follows Australians as they attempt to build new lives outside the country's crowded, expensive cities.

The Farmer Wants a Wife - *Australia* - 2007 to present - Land-owning Australian farmers bring women back home before deciding who to keep.

Gordon Ramsay's 24 Hours to Hell & Back – 2018 to present - In this series, Gordon Ramsay attempts to help failing restaurants in just 24 hours.

Gordon Ramsay's Road Trip - 2021 to present - Celebrity chef Gordon Ramsay embarks on food-filled trips with friends and colleagues.

Gordon Ramsay's The F Word – 2005 to 2010 - Each episode of this cooking series features Gordon Ramsay preparing a meal for 50 guests at The F Word restaurant. In between, there are segments about cooking, farming, and various challenges with guests.

Gordon Ramsey's Ultimate Home Cooking – 2013 - This series helps people learn to cook simple, healthy, practical meals in their own home kitchens.

The Great House Revival - *Ireland* - 2018 - Host Hugh Wallace presents this series about people transforming derelict Irish properties into beautiful modern homes.

Greta Thunberg: A Year to Change the World - 2021 - Swedish activist Greta Thunberg travels around the world, meeting with climate scientists on the front lines of what's happening to our planet.

Hell's Kitchen – *United States* - 2004 to 2009 - This series pits prospective chefs against one another to win accolades and the approval of Scottish celebrity chef Gordon Ramsay.

Hotel Hell - *United States* - 2012 to 2016 - Scottish celebrity chef Gordon Ramsay goes on a quest to fix some of the worst hotels and inns in America.

Impossible Builds - 2018 - This series takes a look at how pre-engineered kit homes are helping people create dream homes in some of the UK's most difficult locations.

Inside Missguided - 2020 - Nitin Passi is the CEO of Britain's fastest-growing fashion brand, and he's aiming to be the first British Asian billionaire. This docuseries charts his struggles.

Jamie: Keep Cooking and Carry On – 2020 – Jamie Oliver shows recipes, tips, and tricks aimed at the unique times we live in. The recipes are prepared with limited ingredients and substitutions.

Jamie Oliver's Food Revolution - 2010 - Celebrity chef Jamie Oliver talks about ways to fight diabetes, obesity, and heart disease through better nutrition.

Kitchen Nightmares - 2007 to 2014 - Acclaimed British chef Gordon Ramsay hosts this series in which he visits struggling American restaurants and spends a week trying to help them be more successful.

Love Island – 2015 to present - This reality series places singles on an island and eliminates contestants based on audience voting. *Hulu currently offers both the UK and Australian versions.*

Next Level Chef - 2022 - Scottish celebrity chef Gordon Ramsay searches for some of the country's best talent in various restaurant-related disciplines.

The Only Way is Essex – 2010 to present - This reality series follows a group of young and "socially ambitious" individuals living in Essex.

Rock Solid Builds - *Canada* - 2021 to present - A third-generation builder completes ambitious building projects and renovations in Newfoundland (also home to the much-loved detective series *Republic of Doyle*).

Shipwrecked - 2019 - This British competition series sees contestants sent to islands to compete against one another.

Tom Kerridge's American Feast - *United States* - 2019 - British chef Tom Kerridge travels the US to discover some of the country's best and most popular contributions to the world's food scene.

Total Wipeout - 2009 - This British game show sees guests attempting to complete obstacle courses to win cash prizes.

Your Garden Made Perfect - 2021 - Angela Scanlon hosts this series which helps homeowners transform their gardens.

Your Home Made Perfect - 2019 - This series pits architects against one another as they attempt to redesign homes for people around the UK.

HULU

SUNDANCE NOW

Website: http://sundancenow.com

Description: Sundance Now is Acorn TV's cousin, and it has a broader focus. Their offerings include a mix of indie and international titles. All Sundance Now offerings are included with an AMC+ subscription.

Available On: Roku, Amazon Fire TV, Apple TV, Apple iPhone & iPad, Android TV, Android phones and tablets, Google Chromecast, computer (via web browser). You can also subscribe via Amazon Prime Video.

Cost: $6.99/month, $59.99 billed yearly

Now Streaming

Accidental Anarchist - 2017 - At one time, Carne Ross was one of western democracy's biggest supporters. Disillusioned with his work, however, he set off on a quest to find out whether anarchy might be the solution to all our problems.

A Discovery of Witches – 2018 to present – When an Oxford historian and reluctant witch is able to access a book no one else can, it sets off a chain of events involving an eternal feud between witches and vampires. **Season 3 creator series premiered August 11th.**

Alone Across the Arctic - *Canada* - 2019 - Adam Shoalts, often referred to as the "Canadian Indiana Jones", embarks on a 4000-km solo journey across the Canadian Arctic by foot and canoe.

Back - 2017 to present - After the death of his father, 42-year-old Stephen returns home to take over the family pub in Stroud, Gloucestershire. At the same time, Andrew, a former foster child briefly raised by his parents, returns to renew his relationship with the family. What happens next is a serious case of sibling rivalry. The series sees David Mitchell and Robert Webb (both of *Peep Show* fame) together again.

Bad Mothers - *Australia* - 2019 - This juicy Australian drama sees a group of misfit women coming together to help each other out with parenting, work challenges, relationships, and murder.

The Bad Seed - *New Zealand* - 2019 - Successful obstetrician Simon Lampton thinks he's left his dysfunctional past behind him, but when a neighbour and former patient is brutally murdered, everything he's built comes crumbling down.

Bang - 2017 to present - In this bilingual Welsh crime drama, a man comes into possession of a gun and his life is forever changed.

The Beast Must Die - 2021 - Cush Jumbo (*Deadwater Fell*) stars as Frances, a woman who takes matters into her own hands after police drop the investigation into the hit-and-run accident that killed her young son.

Being Human - *Canada* - 2011 to 2014 - This is the North American adaptation of the British series about a set of supernatural roommates trying to keep their secrets and live normal lives.

Blinded - *Sweden* - 2019 - When a young financial journalist has a secret affair with a bank director, it complicates both her personal life and her career. **Season 2 premiered August 18th.**

The Bureau - *France* - 2020 - This French spy series has taken inspiration from the real accounts of former spies, weaving their experiences into new stories inspired by current events. It takes place within the "Bureau of Legends", an agency responsible for training and handling deep cover agents as they complete long-term missions in areas with French interests. Fans of the charming French film *Amélie* may recognise Mathieu Kassovitz as intelligence officer Guillaume Debailly.

Cheat - 2019 - When university lecturer Dr. Leah Dale confronts a student about suspected cheating, the student takes it as a personal attack. A simple academic issue soon spirals out of control, putting both women at risk. Katherine Kelly (*Happy Valley*) and Molly Windsor (*Three Girls*) star in this chilling psychological drama.

Cheyenne & Lola - *France* - 2020 - Recently released from prison, 35-year-old Cheyenne cleans the ferries between the UK and France while she saves money for a better life. Unfortunately, her plans for a life on the straight-and-narrow are upended when she witnesses a murder.

Cleaning Up - 2019 - Sheridan Smith (*Gavin & Stacey*) stars as Sam, a debt-ridden mum trying to get by on a zero-hour contract cleaning job while her husband attempts to gain full custody of their children. While on the job, she overhears information that leads her into the world of insider trading.

Close to Me - 2021 - Jo Harding's life seems wonderful until she falls and loses a year of her memory. As she works to piece things together, she realises her old life may have been a long way from perfect. This psychological thriller is based on Amanda Reynolds' novel of the same name.

Cold Call - 2019 - When a single mum gets caught up in a cold call phone scam, her entire life is turned upside down.

The Commons - *Australia* - 2019 to 2020 - This series sees Joanne Froggatt (*Downton Abbey*) starring as Eadie, a 38-year-old woman who just wants to have a child. Unfortunately, IVF treatments have failed and the world around her is in a chaotic state of global warming, parasitic disease, and increasing gaps between the rich and poor.

Couple Trouble - *Denmark* - 2018 - Anders and Lise are a generally happy thirtysomething couple with a daughter, but after seven years of marriage, the dull routine of marriage and parenthood has begun to get them. This series follows them as they seek counseling to save their relationship.

The Crimson Petal and the White – 2011 – In late 1800s London, a prostitute finds her position greatly improved after becoming the mistress to a powerful man.

The Cry - *Australia* – 2018 – Jenna Coleman stars in this miniseries about a young couple dealing with the abduction of their baby.

Dead Lucky - *Australian* - 2018 – When a dangerous armed robber resurfaces in Sydney, two very different detectives are forced to work together to catch him.

Dead Places - *South Africa* - 2021 - A London-based paranormal investigator returns to South Africa to unravel the mystery of who - or what - killed his sister.

Deadwater Fell - 2019 - David Tennant stars in this dark miniseries about a Scottish family that's murdered one night, tearing apart their otherwise peaceful village and bringing secrets to the surface.

Des - 2020 - David Tennant (*Doctor Who*) stars as Dennis Nilsen, a Scottish serial killer and necrophile arrested in 1983 after murdering at least a dozen young men and boys. He was caught when human remains were discovered to be the cause of a drain blockage near his home.

The Drowning - 2021 - This four-part thriller follows Jodie, a struggling businesswoman who never quite recovered after her four-year-old son drowned ten years earlier. Though assumed dead, his body was never recovered. Now, she's spotted a teenage boy who looks just like she imagines her son would.

Everything: The Real Thing Story - 2021 - This documentary takes a look at The Real Thing, a pioneering all-black group from Liverpool that helped change the musical landscape for people of colour in Britain.

The Fall - 2013 to 2016 - Gillian Anderson (*The X-Files*) and Jamie Dornan (*50 Shades of Grey*) star in this series about a senior investigator who goes head-to-head with a serial killer who's attacking young professional women in Belfast.

Finding Joy - *Ireland* - 2018 to present - A young Irish woman named Joy struggles in the aftermath of a breakup, but not nearly as much as her dog (who becomes incontinent). At the same time, Joy is promoted to a position that takes her out of her comfort zone.

Fingersmith - 2005 – In Victorian England, a young female thief hatches a plan to get close to an heiress and scam her. It doesn't go as planned.

Gold Digger - 2019 - Julia Ormond (*Sabrina*) stars as Julia Day, a wealthy 60-year-old woman who falls in love with a handsome man 26 years her junior. As secrets come to light, no one can be sure what's real and what's merely convenient.

Good Grief - *New Zealand* - 2021 - When their grandfather dies, two sisters inherit a funeral home in a small New Zealand town. They soon find out that helping others with their grief helps them confront the hard truths of their own lives. **Season 2 premiered August 4th.**

The Gulf - *New Zealand* - 2019 - This series follows Detective Jess Savage (Kate Elliott, *Wentworth*) as she investigates crimes in Waiheke Island. After losing her memory in the same car crash that killed her husband, she sets her sights on finding the killer and bringing him or her to justice. Unfortunately, her memory issues and increasing reliance on morphine make the investigation difficult, and she begins to become paranoid that someone is out to get her because of something she knows.

Hollington Drive - 2021 - In an idyllic suburb, a 10-year-old boy goes missing. Anna Maxwell Martin and Rachael Stirling star as two sisters who fight to hold their lives and families together as long-held secrets begin to emerge within the community.

The Hunt for a Killer - *Sweden* - 2021 - This true crime dramatisation is based on the efforts of detectives Pelle Åkesson and Monica Olhed to find the killer of 10-year-old Helén Nilsson.

Idiomatic - *Finland* - 2018 - This modern-day Scandinavian rom-com follows an educated left-wing couple after they move to an apartment owned by Micke's wealthy parents.

Innocent – 2018 – *Innocent* is a "one story per season" anthology series about people who've been released after a wrongful conviction.

Interview with a Murderer - 2016 - Criminologist and professor David Wilson conducts a series of interviews with convicted murderer Bert Spencer. Bert was convicted for the murder of farmer Hubert Wilkes, but he's always been suspected of the brutal killing of a young newspaper delivery boy, Carl Bridgewater.

The Ipcress File - 2022 - This cold war spy thriller is loosely based on both the 1962 Len Deighton novel and the 1965 film, adopting elements of each. In it, an ex-smuggler turned spy finds himself in the middle of an undercover mission involving kidnapped and brainwashed scientists.

Law & Order: UK - 2009 to 2014 - This adaptation of the successful American courtroom drama sees the format carried over to the British legal system. It's one-part law (investigative work) and one-part order (the court proceedings).

Liar – 2017 to 2020 – After a seemingly pleasant date, a schoolteacher accuses a prominent local surgeon of rape. The situation continues to spiral out of control as more information comes to light. The second series takes a different angle, but there's little we can say without it being a spoiler.

The Light in the Hall -2022 - This Welsh thriller follows a journalist and long-grieving mother as each are forced to confront the past in light of the murderer's upcoming parole hearing.

The Little Drummer Girl – 2018 – An English actress is recruited by the Israelis to help infiltrate a Palestinian assassin's terrorist cell.

McMafia – 2018 to present - James Norton (*Grantchester*) stars as the English-raised son of a Russian mafia figure who was exiled from his country. Though his family tried to correct course, a murder draws them back in. A second series is on the way, though we've yet to see a date for it.

Moloch - *France* - 2020 - In an industrial seaside town, people burst into flames for no apparent reason. No one knows if it's suicide, murder, or perhaps even something supernatural. Together, an ambitious young journalist and brilliant psychiatrist will investigate.

Motherland – 2016 to present – Mums take on the challenges of middle-class motherhood, and it's not always pretty. This 30-minute comedy aims to show real motherhood, not the pretty and acceptable public idea of what motherhood should be.

Murder in the Valleys - 2022 - This true crime docuseries tells the story of the June 1999 murder of a three generations of a family in Clydach, South Wales. Despite a conviction, the case would go on to divide the local community for decades to come. **Premieres September 27th.**

The Murders - *Canada* - 2019 - Detective Kate Jameson wants to be a good cop like her father, a decorated officer killed in the line of duty. Sadly, a single mistake results in the death of her partner, and she's left trying anything to make amends.

Murder Trial: The Disappearance of Margaret Fleming - 2020 - Two carers were accused of murdering a 35-year-old woman and claiming benefits in her name for 16 years. This series takes a look at their trial.

The Name of the Rose - 2019 - In 1327, a friar and his apprentice investigate deaths at a nearby abbey. They soon find themselves mixed up in something much bigger than they might have imagined. Rupert Everett (*My Best Friend's Wedding*) and John Turturro (*Barton Fink*) star.

The Nest - 2020 - Sophie Rundle (*Bodyguard*) and Martin Compston (*Line of Duty*) star in this Glasgow-based drama about a couple who would do almost anything to have a child. When they meet a troubled young woman, they make her an irresistible offer.

New Gold Mountain - *Australia* - 2021 - This series follows the events of the Australian gold rush from the perspective of the Chinese miners who came in search of unlikely fortunes.

The Night Caller - *Australia* - 2020 - This four-part true crime drama follows the investigation into a serial killer who terrorised Perth, Australia between 1959 and 1963. In their determination to stop the killings, police arrested two different men, both of whom would be convicted and serve time in spite of their innocence.

One Lane Bridge - *New Zealand* - 2020 - While working a murder investigation, a young Maori detective accidentally awakens a spiritual gift that may harm the case.

The Pact - 2021 - When a young brewery boss turns up dead, four female brewery employees find themselves caught up in a pact of silence. As the investigation deepens, it seems everyone involved in the brewery had some kind of dark secret.

Penance - 2020 - After her son's death in Thailand, a woman begins having lusty thoughts about a young man she met in grief counseling (who just happens to look a lot like her dead son). Julie Graham (*Queens of Mystery*), Neil Morrissey (*Men Behaving Badly*), and Nico Mirallegro (*Hollyoaks*).

Playing for Keeps - *Australia* - 2018 to 2019 - This soapy drama dives into the world of footballer's wives in Australia.

Poisonous Liaisons - *Australia* - 2019 - This true crime series takes a look at poisoners throughout history.

The Real Des - 2020 - If you watched the David Tennant series *Des*, you may also want to watch this documentary about professor David Wilson, a criminologist who spend decades interviewing and corresponding with serial killer Dennis Nilsen (the subject of *Des*).

The Red Shadows - *France* – 2019 – In 1993, a five-year-old girl was kidnapped. 25 years later, her sister uncovers clues that suggest she may still be alive.

The Replacement - 2017 - Morven Christie (*The Bay*) and Vicky McClure (*Line of Duty*) star in this thriller about a woman heading out on maternity leave who begins to believe her replacement is trying to take over her entire life.

The Restaurant - *Sweden* – 2017 to 2018 – At the end of WWII, two strangers cross social classes with a kiss that has lasting repercussions. This series has been called a Swedish *Downton Abbey*.

Restless – 2012 – This two-part TV movie is based on a bestselling spy novel by William Boyd. It focuses on a young woman who finds out her mother was a spy for British intelligence during WWII, and that she's been on the run ever since.

The Returned - *France* - 2013 - In a peaceful French village, people begin returning home. Unfortunately, the people returning have all been dead for years, so nobody was actually expecting them to return home. At the same time, there's a series of gruesome murders that looks suspiciously like those of a serial killer from the past.

River - 2015 - Stellan Skarsgård, Nicola Walker, and Lesley Manville star in this series about a brilliant police officer haunted by guilt.

Riviera – 2017 to present – Riviera is a UK production set in France. When a newlywed's wealthy husband is killed in an explosion, she's stunned to learn what lurked behind the facade of their upper-class lifestyle.

Rose West: Born Evil? - 2021 - This documentary takes a look at the life and possible motivations of English serial killer Rose West. Together with her husband, she was responsible for the deaths of at least nine young women.

Safe House – 2015 to 2017 – Christopher Eccleston (*Doctor Who*) stars in this series about a married couple asked to turn their guest house into a safe house.

Sanctuary - *Sweden* - 2019 - This psychological thriller sees a woman lured to the Alps to visit her twin sister, only to find herself trapped in her sister's life and imprisoned in a sanatorium where no one believes her.

The Secrets She Keeps - *Australia* - 2020 - When two heavily pregnant women from different worlds meet in an upmarket Sydney supermarket, they have no idea their lives are about to come together in a very dramatic way. **Season 2 premiered September 1st.**

Shadow Lines - *Finland* - 2019 - In the 1950s, the Cold War raged in the small nation of Finland. This espionage thriller focuses on a secret intelligence team who sought to maintain Finland's independence at any cost.

Showtrial - 2021 - When a wealthy entrepreneur's daughter is arrested after the disappearance of a fellow working-class student, the trial that follows becomes something of a circus. Can justice truly be served under such conditions?

Slings & Arrows - *Canada* - 2003 to 2006 - This Canadian dark comedy is set at a fictitious Shakespeare festival in Canada as they embark on a production of Hamlet. Paul Gross (*Due South*) stars as washed-up actor Geoffrey Tennant, along with Rachel McAdams (*Wedding Crashers, The Notebook*), Luke Kirby (*The Marvelous Ms. Maisel*), Stephen Ouimette (*Mentors*), and Mark McKinney (*Kids in the Hall, Superstore*), who is also the co-creator/co-writer.

The Split – 2018 to 2020 - After a 30-year absence, a family of female lawyers has enough trouble dealing with their personal lives...and then their long-absent father returns. **Season 3 is now available.**

State of the Union - 2019 - Chris O'Dowd (*The IT Crowd*) and Rosamund Pike (*Pride & Prejudice*) star in this short-form comedy about a couple that visits a pub each week before their marriage counseling session. Season 2 follows a new couple played by Brenda Gleeson and Patricia Clarkson.

Stella Blomkvist - *Icelandic* – 2017 – A young and morally dubious lawyer takes on dangerous murder cases.

Striking Out - *Ireland* - 2017 - Amy Huberman (*Finding Joy*) stars as Tara Rafferty, a successful Dublin lawyer who abandons her safe life after discovering that her fiancé is cheating on her. She cancels the wedding, quits her job, and begins a new and unconventional private practice. Neil Morrissey (*Men Behaving Badly*) and Rory Keenan (*War & Peace*) also star.

The Suspect - *Canada* - 2020 - This true-crime series takes a look at the murder of Richard Oland, the prosecution of his son Dennis, and the fight for a retrial.

The Suspect - 2022 - Based on Michael Robotham's novel of the same name, Aidan Turner (*Poldark*) stars as psychologist turned murder suspect Dr. Joseph O'Loughlin. O'Loughlin became a hero after the live-streamed rescue of a suicidal patient, but he may also be hiding a dark secret. **Premieres November 3rd.**

Ten Percent - 2022 - Based on the hit French series, *Dix pour cent* (*Call My Agent* in the US), this UK adaptation follows a talent agency that's forever scrambling to keep their clients happy.

Thin Ice - *Sweden* - 2020 - When a research vessel disappears off the coast of Greenland, it's hard to be sure whether it's coincidence or something much more sinister.

This is Going to Hurt - 2022 - Ben Whishaw (*London Spy*) stars in this brutally realistic depiction of a junior doctor in a labor and delivery ward. The series is based on the memoirs of Adam Kay.

Three Families - 2021 - Though the Abortion Act of 1967 allowed abortion in the UK, Northern Ireland was denied that new freedom. Set between 2013-2019, this two-part series dramatises the stories of three families profoundly affected by the decision. **Premiered July 14th.**

Too Close - 2021 - Emily Watson stars in this series about a forensic psychiatrist assigned to assess the sanity of a woman accused of the attempted murder of two children. As she gets drawn into the case, she finds herself feeling sympathy and understanding for the woman. Is the woman truly the victim of mental illness, or is she playing games with the doctor?

Total Control - *Australia* - 2019 - Deborah Mailman (*Offspring*) and Rachel Griffiths (*Dead Lucky*) star in this political drama about a charismatic indigenous woman recruited by the prime minister to help further her own agenda.

Trial in the Outback - *Australia* - 2020 - This three-part documentary looks back at the case of Lindy Chamberlain, a woman who claimed a dingo killed her 9-week-old baby. Convicted with very little evidence, she spent the next 30 years of her life trying to prove her innocence.

Trickster - *Canada* - 2021 - Indigenous teen Jared is already struggling to help out his troubled family, but it gets even crazier when he starts seeing things. Soon, he's drawn into a world of spirits and ancient magic.

Upright - *Australia* - 2020 - Comedian Tim Minchin stars in this series about two people trying to get an upright piano from one side of Australia to the other.

We Got This - *Sweden* - 2020 - After career failure and an enormous tax bill, American George English emigrates to Sweden in hopes of solving a murder case to receive a substantial reward. Along with a team of misfits, he attempts to solve what seems to be an unsolvable crime - and finds himself in dangerous territory.

The Wimbledon Kidnapping - 2021 - This true crime documentary searches for the truth of what happened when a woman was mistaken for Rupert Murdoch's wife and kidnapped by the mafia for ransom.

The Wine Show - 2016 to present - Matthew Goode (*A Discovery of Witches*) and Matthew Rhys (*Perry Mason*) star in this series about some of the world's best, most exotic, and most interesting wines. Travelling the world and chatting with prestigious chefs and experts, they offer an educational but also accessible take on the popular beverage.

Wisting - *Norway* - 2019 – Norwegian detective William Wisting discovers a corpse at a Christmas tree farm that may be connected to an American serial killer. He may be living among them. **Season 2 premiered June 30th.**

Witches: A Century of Murder – 2015 - Historian Suzannah Lipscomb takes a look at the British witch hunts of the 17th century.

AMC+

Website: https://www.amcplus.com

Description: AMC+ bundles all content from Sundance Now, Shudder, and IFC Films Unlimited, along with a number of top shows from AMC. We haven't included the Sundance Now titles here since they're in the previous section.

Available On: Roku, Apple TV, Amazon Prime Video Channels, some cable providers

Cost: $8.99/month, $83.88/year.

Now Streaming

Everything on Sundance Now + the titles below...

Almost Royal - 2014 to 2016 - This BBC America faux-reality series follows a couple of extremely minor British royals as they visit the US for the first time.

Antiques Roadshow - 1979 to present - Filmed at a variety of stately homes around the country, this series allows members of the public to bring in cherished items for expert appraisal. *See also: Antiques Roadshow Detectives*

Apple Tree Yard – 2017 - This miniseries is based on Louise Doughty's novel by the same name, and it's a suspenseful combination of sex and murder. When a woman gets an intriguing proposition, it excites her – until she realizes it may not be quite what it seemed. Emily Watson and Ben Chaplin star.

A Wild Year on Earth - 2021 - This series follows some of the world's most interesting seasonal animal behaviour over the course of a year.

Baroness Von Sketch Show - *Canada* - 2016 to present - This all-female comedy takes a look at the absurdity of modern life.

Cold Courage - *Finland* - 2020 - This international crime drama follows a couple of Finnish women who become involved with a secret organisation while living in London.

CripTales - 2020 - This BBC America series sees a variety of differently-abled adults performing dramatic monologues about life-changing moments. Liz Carr (*Silent Witness*) is among them.

Doctor Who: Fury from the Deep - 2021 - Though the original 1968 episode is missing from the BBC archives, this animated special recreates the episode. It follows along as the TARDIS lands off the Dover coast and they end up getting tranquilised in a restricted area.

Doctor Who: The Evil of the Daleks - 2021 - This animated episode recreates the missing 1967 episode in which the Doctor and Jamie are kidnapped and taken to 1866.

Doctor Who: The Faceless Ones - 1967 - This animated special features original audio from the "mostly lost" eighth serial of the fourth season of the original *Doctor Who*. Patrick Troughton is the Doctor.

Doctor Who: The Macra Terror - 2019 - When the TARDIS lands at a human colony where everyone seems happy, it takes a moment before they realise all isn't as it seems.

Gangs of London – 2020 to present – This drama takes a look at the struggles of rival gang families in modern-day London. The series begins after the murder of Finn Wallace, the most powerful criminal in London. Nobody knows who did it or why, and his absence has created a dangerous power vacuum. **Season 2 premieres November 17th.**

The Graham Norton Show - 2021 - Presenter Graham Norton chats with some of the world's biggest celebrities.

Happy Valley - 2014 to present - Sarah Lancashire stars as Catherine Cawood, a Yorkshire-based police officer struggling to raise her grandson after the suicide of her teenage daughter. **After several years, the series will be returning for a third season in 2022 or 2023.**

Interview with the Vampire - *United States* - 2022 - Sam Reid (*Prime Suspect 1973*) stars as Lestat in this gothic drama based on Anne Rice's 1976 novel. Jacob Anderson (*Broadchurch*) will play his lover and protégé Louis de Pointe du Lac. **Premieres October 2nd.**

Killing Eve – 2018 to 2022 - A bored but highly competent MI5 officer trades her life behind a desk to pursue an elusive and particularly aggressive female serial killer.

Kin - *Ireland* - 2021 - A small but close Dublin crime family goes up against a powerful drug cartel.

Low Winter Sun - 2013 - Mark Strong stars as DS Frank Agnew, a police officer who kills a fellow officer and believes he's committed the perfect murder. Though it originally aired as a two-part British miniseries, this is the 10-part American version (for which Mark Strong returned).

Meerkat Manor - 2005 to 2008 - This British series follows a family of meerkats in the Kalahari Desert. Though commercially successful, it's worth mentioning that the producers did not intervene when animals were sick or injured, as it was filmed in conjunction with a research project.

Meerkat Manor: Rise of the Dynasty - 2021 - This series follows three descendants of the legendary meerkat Flower from the original *Meerkat Manor*.

The North Water - 2021 - Jack O'Connell (*This is England*), Stephen Graham (*This is England*), and Colin Farrell (*Ballykissangel*) star in this series about a whaling expedition that turns murderous.

Orphan Black - *Canada* - 2013 to 2017 - A young woman's life is changed when she learns she's been part of a clone experiment, and she has a number of sister clones around North America and Europe.

Planet Earth: Dynasties II - 2022 - This docuseries by Sir David Attenborough follows the lives and activities of different dynasties within the animal kingdom.

Princess Diana: A Life After Death - 2019 - On the 20th anniversary of her death, this documentary looks at Diana's legacy.

The Prisoner - 2009 - This British-American co-production attempted to re-make the classic British series *The Prisoner*, with Sir Ian McKellen playing Number 2 and Jim Caviezel as Number 6.

Queers - 2017 - This series features stories about homosexual men in Britain, told in celebration of the 50th anniversary of The Sexual Offenses Act. The historic act partially decriminalised homosexual activities between men in the UK.

Quiz - 2020 - Matthew Macfadyen (*Pride & Prejudice*) stars as Charles Ingram in this drama based on the real-life story of a man accused of cheating his way to the top prize on *Who Wants To Be A Millionaire?*.

Ragdoll - 2022 - This AMC+ original series is based on Daniel Cole's novel of the same name, and it follows a group of detectives attempting to solve the mystery of a body discovered suspended from the ceiling of a London flat. The most horrifying part is that the body is a sewn-together mix of parts from six different victims.

The Salisbury Poisonings - This factual drama miniseries takes a look at the 2018 Novichok poisonings in Salisbury, England. Mark Addy (*Game of Thrones*), Anne-Marie Duff (*Shameless*), Amber Aga (*Shakespeare & Hathaway*), and Rafe Spall (*Hot Fuzz*) are among the cast members.

Snatches - 2018 - This series features monologues inspired by women who have spoken out or changed the status quo.

Soulmates - *United States* - 2020 to present - This American anthology series is set in a future time when a test is able to determine, with 100% accuracy, who will be your soulmate. Though American, the cast features a large number of British cast members.

Spy City - *United States* - 2020 to present - Shortly before the construction of the Berlin Wall, an English spy is sent over to find a traitor. Dominic Cooper stars.

Tea with the Dames - 2018 - Dames Maggie Smith, Judi Dench, Eileen Atkins, and Joan Plowright come together to share stories of their lives and careers.

That Dirty Black Bag - *United States* - 2022 - Though American, a number of British and Irish actors appear in this gritty western. It follows the duel between a troubled sheriff and a headhunter known for decapitating his bounties and carrying them around in a bag.

Top Gear - 2002 to present - This long-running remake of the classic 1970s series sees Jeremy Clarkson and a variety of other presenters checking out some of the world's finest cars.

The War of the Worlds - 2019 - After a meteor touches down in Surrey, humans face a battle for survival against an alien race. The classic HG Wells tale is told through the lens of Amy and George, two people who are in love and ready to embark on a new (though forbidden) life together.

The Watch - 2021 - This comedy-fantasy police procedural was inspired by Sir Terry Pratchett's *Discworld* series. It's set in the world's principal city of Ankh-Morpork, and Sir Pratchett himself described it as a "Pratchett-style CSI".

Wild Tokyo - 2021 - Though it's one of the most densely populated urban areas on Earth, the people of Tokyo share their city with a surprising number of wild animals.

AMC+

HBO MAX

Website: http://hbomax.com

Description: HBO Max is HBO's standalone streaming platform. They offer a variety of original programming and existing British shows.

Available On: Roku, Fire TV, Apple TV, Apple iPhone & iPad, Chromecast, Android phones and tablets, Amazon, and computer (via web browser).

Cost: $9.99/month or $99.99/year with ads, $14.99/month or $149.99/year without ads.

Now Streaming

Adult Material - 2020 - Hayley Squires stars as Jolene Dollar, a mother of three and proud breadwinner in spite of her unusual career as a famous porn star. Her life is basically good, and she's come to act as a mother figure for other young women in the industry - until she meets 19-year-old Amy. Though she tries to look after Amy like the others, the relationship soon causes all sorts of problems in both her work and home life.

The Alienist - *United States* - 2018 - Though American, this series stars Welshman Luke Evans. It's a period crime drama set in late 1800s New York City, with the first season focusing on finding someone who's killing boy prostitutes. The second season sees some of the characters working as private detectives to find a kidnapped infant.

Avenue 5 - *United States* - 2020 - Hugh Laurie and Josh Gad star in this science fiction comedy about a space cruise ship. They've been thrown off course, and it's estimated that it will take them three years to get back to Earth - but they only have enough supplies for eight weeks. Along with Hugh Laurie, you'll spot a number of popular British actors including Daisy May Cooper (*This Country*) and Matthew Beard

(*Vienna Blood*). **Season 2 premieres October 10th.**

The Baby - 2022 - This horror/comedy follows a thirtysomething woman whose life is upended when she unexpected finds herself with a controlling and violent baby.

Beforeigners - *Norway* - 2019 to present - In modern Norway, people from different time periods suddenly appeared in the present. The series is partially a crime drama, but it also follows the attempts of the new arrivals to integrate into modern life. **Season 2 is now available.**

The Bridge (2020) - 2020 - James MacAvoy narrates this reality series about British people who are thrown into the wild and asked to build an 850-foot bridge with only their hands and limited supplies. **Season 2 premiered June 30th.**

The Casual Vacancy - 2015 - This miniseries is based on JK Rowling's novel of the same name, and it tells the story of a town resident's sudden death and how it impacts the local community.

Catherine the Great - 2019 - Helen Mirren stars as Catherine the Great in this four-part miniseries. The series covers the later portion of her life, from 1764 until her death in 1796. Jason Clarke (*Zero Dark Thirty*), Rory Kinnear (*Penny Dreadful*), Richard Roxburgh (*Rake*), and Paul Ritter (*No Offence*) also appear.

C.B. Strike (aka Strike) - 2017 to present - Based on the *Cormoran Strike* novels written by JK Rowling under the Robert 7 Galbraith pseudonym, this series sees war veteran Cormoran Strike team up with a highly-competent assistant who helps him solve cases and transform his ailing business.

Chernobyl - 2019 - Screenwriter Craig Mazin created this moving five-part historical adaptation of the Chernobyl nuclear disaster. The series includes a number of actors likely to be familiar to British TV fans, including Jared Harris (*The Crown*), Stellan Skarsgård (*Pirates of the Caribbean*), Paul Ritter (*No Offence, Friday Night Dinner*), and Emily Watson (*Miss Potter*).

Chewing Gum - 2015 to 2017 - A young woman from a poor religious family is ready to grow up - and as she sees it, the first step is to have sex.

Doctor Who - 1963 to present - A mysterious Time Lord travels through time and space, exploring and saving the world in equal measure. HBO Max has all the modern Doctor Who episodes, while the classic episodes are over on BritBox.

The Dog House UK - 2019 - This series follows the dedicated animal heroes at Wood Green animal charity in Godmanchester as they help homeless dogs find new humans.

Family Tree – 2013 - This hilarious series follows one man's efforts to track down long-lost members of his family tree.

Five Days - 2007 to 2010 - Each series covers five non-consecutive days in a major police investigation.

Frayed - 2019 - In this period comedy-drama, a wealthy London housewife faces serious chances of circumstance after her husband dies. It's 1988, and she's forced to move herself and her two children back to her hometown of Newcastle in Australia, only to find that no one there likes her. Star Sarah Kendall was also the creator and writer of the six-episode series.

Game of Thrones - 2011 to 2019 - In a mythical world, families fight for control of the Iron Throne. The series is based on the novels of George R.R. Martin, and the show is estimated to have had the largest cast on television.

Gentleman Jack - 2019 to present - The incomparable Sally Wainwright (*Happy Valley, Last Tango in Halifax*) ventures into historical drama, bringing us the story of 19th century English industrialist, landowner, and lesbian Anne Lister. Suranne Jones (*Doctor Foster*) stars as Lister, a Yorkshire woman who was very much ahead of her time. Other cast members include Sophie Rundle as Ann Walker, Timothy West as Jeremy Lister, and Stephanie Cole as Aunt Ann Walker. **Season 2 is now available.**

Getting On (US) - *United States* - 2013 to 2015 - This American adaptation of the the British original is a dark comedy that follows the residents and staff in a geriatric care facility.

Ghosts - 2019 to present - This series focuses on a group of ghosts who have accumulated over the course of centuries in a country house. When a young couple inherits the grand but crumbling pile, they have to learn to co-exist. The series was written and performed by a number of cast members from the BBC children's series *Horrible Histories*. **Season 4 began filming in January 2022.**

The Gilded Age - *United States* - 2022 - Created by Julian Fellowes (*Downton Abbey*), this period drama is set in 1880s New York City, following the lives and conflicts of members of the old rich and the new rich. **Renewed for season 2, date TBD.**

The Girl Before - 2021 - Based on JP Delaney's 2016 novel of the same name, this series follows a young woman who moves into a beautiful minimalist house with many rules. Soon, she finds out that the previous inhabitant died under mysterious circumstances.

The Great Pottery Throwdown - 2015 to present - This competition series follows a group of amateur potters as they compete to see who's best.

Gunpowder - 2017 - Kit Harington (*Game of Thrones*) stars in this three-part period drama about the Gunpowder Plot of 1605.

Harry Potter - 2001 to present - Though not a television series, HBO Max is the streaming home for the series of films about the boy wizard and his training at

HBO MAX

Hogwarts. This includes the recent cast reunion and the *Fantastic Beasts* films that also take place in the *Harry Potter* world.

Harry Potter: Hogwart's Tournament of Houses - 2021 - Harry Potter superfans attempt to answer trivia questions to win the title of House Cup Champion.

Hello Ladies – *United States* - 2013 - While not technically British, this series comes from Stephen Merchant, a British actor and writer who has partnered with Ricky Gervais. It sees him playing an awkward Englishman looking for love in LA.

His Dark Materials - 2019 - Based on the trilogy by Oxford novelist Philip Pullman, this eight-episode fantasy series takes place in an alternate world where each human has an animal companion called a daemon. A young orphan girl living at Jordan College, Oxford, is drawn into a dangerous puzzle when her friend, a fellow orphan, is kidnapped. Among the stars are Lin-Manuel Miranda (*Hamilton*), Ruth Wilson (*Luther*), James McAvoy (*Shameless*), David Suchet (*Poirot*), and Andrew Scott (*Fleabag*). Dafne Keen (*The Refugees*) plays Lyra. **Season 3 expected by the end of 2022, date TBD.**

House of the Dragon - 2022 - This Game of Thrones prequel is set 200 years prior to the original series, and it deals with who will take over the Iron Throne after King Viserys I (played by English actor Paddy Considine). **Premiered on August 21st.**

I Hate Suzie - 2020 - Billie Piper (*Doctor Who*) stars in this eight-part original drama about a young woman whose life is upended when her phone is hacked and a compromising photo of her goes public. Lucy Prebble (*Secret Diary of a Call Girl*) was Piper's co-creator on the series.

I May Destroy You - 2020 - This sexual consent drama consists of twelve half-hour episodes in which Michaela Coel (*Chewing Gum*) plays a care-free Londoner whose existence is turned upside-down after her drink is spiked with a date-rape drug.

Industry - 2020 - Lena Dunham (*Girls*) will direct and executive produce this eight-part series about a group of young people trying to break into the world of high-finance in London around the 2008 market collapse. As a note, this series has some fairly extreme adult content involving sex and drug use. **Season 2 premiered August 9th.**

It's a Sin - 2021 - This Russell T Davies series follows a group of gay men in London during the HIV/AIDS crisis of the 1980s. Olly Alexander stars as Ritchie Tozer, and the cast includes a number of well-known actors including Keeley Hawes, Neil Patrick Harris, and Stephen Fry.

Julia - 2022 - Sarah Lancashire (*Happy Valley*) stars as famed chef Julia Child in this series inspired by her life and work.

Landscapers - 2021 - Olivia Colman stars in this miniseries about a mild-mannered woman and her husband...and the body found in the back garden of their Nottinghamshire home.

Mare of Easttown - *United States* - 2021 - English actress Kate Winslet stars in this American series about a Pennsylvania detective investigating the murder of a teenage mother. She's haunted by another unsolved case, and her town is losing faith in her.

Miss Sherlock - *Japan* - 2018 - This Japanese adaptation of the Sherlock Holmes story sees a young "Miss Sherlock" working alongside the Tokyo police.

The Murders at White House Farm - 2020 - This crime drama series is an adaptation of real-life events that took place in August 1985, when Jeremy Bamber murdered his entire family. Freddie Fox (*Cucumber*) plays Jeremy Bamber, Mark Addy (*Game of Thrones)* plays Stan Jones, a detective convinced of his guilt, and Cressida Bonas (Prince Harry's ex) fills the role of Bamber's sister Sheila.

The Nevers - 2021 - Joss Whedon (*Buffy the Vampire Slayer*) is the creator for this Victorian sci-fi drama about a group of Victorian women with unusual abilities. The cast includes Laura Donnelly, Olivia Williams, Eleanor Tomlinson, and James Norton.

The New Pope - 2020 - Jude Law returns as a comatose Pope Pius XIII in this follow-up to The Young Pope. John Malkovich joins the cast as Pope John Paul III.

The No. 1 Ladies' Detective Agency - 2009 - Based on the novels of Scottish author Alexander McCall Smith, this series follows a young woman in Botswana as she opens her country's first female-owned detective agency.

Our Flag Means Death - 2022 - This period comedy follows along as an aristocrat abandons his easy life to become a "gentleman pirate" on the high seas. **This series has been renewed for a second season, date TBD.**

The Outsider - *United States* - 2020 - Based on the Stephen King novel of the same name, this miniseries includes British stars Paddy Considine (*Peaky Blinders*) and Cynthia Erivo (*Mr. Selfridge*). The series follows the puzzling investigation into the murder of a young boy.

Parade's End - 2013 - Benedict Cumberbatch (*Sherlock*) stars in this series adapted from Ford Madox Ford's tetralogy of novels. It focuses on the lives and relations of three Brits just before and at the outset of World War I.

Pennyworth - *United States* - 2019 to present - Jack Bannon (*Endeavour*) stars as Alfred Pennyworth, a former British SAS soldier who will ultimately become Batman's butler. **Season 3 premieres October 6th.**

Perry Mason - *United States* - 2020 - Welshman Matthew Rhys stars in this prequel to the original *Perry Mason*. It's set in 1932 Los Angeles, when Mason is struggling to get back on track after a divorce and his war trauma.

Pure - 2019 - This quirky sitcom focuses on a young woman who is plagued by constant, irrepressible sexual thoughts. She doesn't know what's wrong with her, but it's intruding on her ability to function normally. As she attempts to get a handle on her problem, she's also embarking on a journey of personal growth and exploration in the city of London. The series is an adaptation of Rose Cartwright's book.

Run (US) - *United States* - 2020 - This comedy-thriller begins with two people who once made a promise that if either ever texted the word "RUN" to the other, they'd drop everything and meet in Grand Central Terminal and travel the country together. While this is an American series, Brit Phoebe Waller-Bridge is both executive producer and a recurring character. One of the leads, Domhnall Gleeson, is Irish.

Sally4Ever - 2018 - A woman decides to leave a boring man to have an affair with a woman instead.

Sarah Jane Adventures - 2007 to 2011 - This children's show is a *Doctor Who* spin-off that follows former companion Sarah Jane Smith, now an investigative journalist.

Singletown - 2019 - This British reality series follows a group of young people who've agreed to pause their current relationships and spend a month going on dates with other people.

The Staircase - 2022 - Colin Firth (*Pride & Prejudice*) stars as Michael Peterson, a man who was investigated for the suspicious death of his wife Kathleen (played by Toni Collette).

Starstruck - 2021 - Jessie is a young woman from New Zealand who's struggling to get by in London, and her life is flipped upside-down when she realises she slept with a famous actor on New Year's Eve.

Stath Lets Flats - 2018 to present - This sitcom follows Stath Charalambos, a wildly incompetent Greek-Cypriot letting agent in London. He only has a job because his father owns the company, and he's constantly in competition with Carole (Katy Wix, *Agatha Raisin*), his more capable co-worker.

The Third Day - 2020 - This drama follows the individual journeys of a man (Jude Law, *Sherlock Holmes*) and woman (Naomie Harris, *Skyfall*) who are drawn to a mysterious island off the British coast.

The Time Traveler's Wife - 2022 - Rose Leslie and Theo James star in this series adaptation of Audrey Niffenegger's novel of the same name. It follows a couple as they proceed through a marriage inconvenienced by the realities of time travel.

Top Gear - 2002 to present - This long-running remake of the classic 1970s seri sees Jeremy Clarkson and a variety of o presenters checking out some of the world's finest cars.

Torchwood - 2006 to 2011 - A secret agency called Torchwood fights off t from aliens and the supernatural. T series is a spin-off of *Doctor Who*.

The Tourist - 2022 - Jamie Dorna stars in this series about a British finds himself in the Australian O with no idea who he is - and a g rough characters pursuing him

The Trial of Christine Keele miniseries is based on the ev surrounding the Profumo a 1960s, when Secretary of S John Profumo was found t sexual relationship with C

19-year-old aspiring model. Sophie Cookson (*Red Joan*), James Norton (*Grantchester*), and Emilia Fox (*Silent Witness*) are among the stars of the upcoming series.

Two Weeks to Live - 2020 - A relatively dark comedy, *Two Weeks to Live* follows Kim, a young misfit whose mother dragged her off to the country for a survivalist lifestyle after her father died. The series picks up as she sets off on her own, but things go pear-shaped quickly when an awkward young man's prank puts all their lives in danger. Believing the end times are near, she sets out to kill the man who murdered her father.

The Undoing - *United States* - 2020 - A successful New York therapist sees her life start falling apart when she publishes her first book. Though American, Hugh Grant is among the stars.

Wellington Paranormal - *New Zealand* - 2018 to present - This mockumentary-style series follows a group of police officers who track and investigate paranormal occurrences in New Zealand.

Years and Years - 2019 - This series follows the Manchester-based Lyons family as they their lives progress through 15 years of politics, technology, and human events. Emma Thompson, Rory Kinnear, and Anne Reid are among the cast.

The Young Pope - 2016 - This series stars Jude Law as the controversial Pope Pius XIII, along with Diane Keaton as his confidante, Sister Mary.

HBO MAX

STARZ

Website: http://starz.com

Description: Starz is a premium cable network owned by Lions Gate Entertainment. They focus on first-run television shows and major motion pictures. They don't offer a lot of British programming, but what's there is usually quite good.

Available On: Roku, Amazon Fire TV, Apple TV, Apple iPhone & iPad, Android TV, Android phones and tablets, computer (via web browser). You can also subscribe via Amazon Prime Video or your cable company.

Cost: $8.99/month

Now Streaming

American Gods - *United States* - 2017 to present - Though it's an American production, American Gods is based on the novel of the same name by British-born author Neil Gaiman, and the series stars Ian McShane (*Lovejoy*). It tells the story of a prisoner who's just days away from release when he gets the news that his wife has been killed in an accident. After his early release, he encounters a strange man, Mr. Wednesday (McShane), who offers him a job that ultimately brings him into a world of magic and old gods.

Becoming Elizabeth - 2022 - German actress Alicia von Rittberg plays Queen Elizabeth I in this upcoming series about the monarch's younger years. Period drama favourite Romola Garai plays Mary I. **Premiered June 12th.**

Black Sails - 2014 to 2017 - This period drama follows the adventures of Captain Flint and his crew in the years before Robert Louis Stevenson's *Treasure Island* was set.

Da Vinci's Demons - 2013 to 2015 - This historical fantasy offers a fictional retelling of Leonardo da Vinci's early life.

The Deceived - 2020 - After falling for her married lecturer at Cambridge, Ophelia's exciting affair is disrupted by a tragic death. She quickly finds herself in a situation where she's out of her depth and unable to trust her own mind.

Dublin Murders - 2019 - Based on the Dublin Murder Squad book series by Tana French, the first season of this British-American-Irish co-production features eight episodes adapted from In the Woods and The Likeness. Killian Scott (*C.B. Strike*) stars as Rob Reilly, and English detective dispatched to investigate the murder of a young girl just outside Dublin. The case forces Reilly to confront his own dark past, and it puts his relationship with partner Cassie Maddox (Sarah Greene, *Penny Dreadful*) to the test.

The Girlfriend Experience - *United States* - 2016 to present - Each season of this anthology series follows a different woman working as a high-end escort. Though American, Brit Anna Friel appears, and one season is set in London.

The Gloaming - *Australia* - 2020 - This supernatural drama follows policewoman Molly McGee as she investigates an unidentified woman's murder and finds herself pulled into a strange mix of occult practices and political corruption.

Howards End – 2018 - This miniseries is based on the E.M. Forster novel, and it examines class differences in 1900s England through the lens of three families.

Little Birds - 2020 - This series is a TV adaptation of Anaïs Nin's erotic short stories.

The Luminaries - *New Zealand* - 2020 - This British-New Zealand co-production is based on Eleanor Catton's Booker Prize-winning novel of the same name, and it follows a young adventurer named Anna Wetherell as she travels from the UK to New Zealand during the 1860s West Coast Gold Rush.

Men in Kilts - 2021 - Sam Heughan and Graham McTavish (both of *Outlander*) host this travel series in which they escort viewers around their native country of Scotland. **Season 2 will premiere sometime in 2022.**

The Missing – 2014 to 2017 - James Nesbitt (*Cold Feet*) stars in this drama about the disappearance of a 5-year-old and the manhunt that follows.

Outlander - 2014 to present - In 1945, an English nurse is mysteriously transported back in time to Scotland in 1743. The massively-popular series is based on the novels of Diana Gabaldon. **Season 6 premiered on March 6th.**

The Pillars of the Earth - 2010 - This miniseries is based on the 1989 Ken Follett novel of the same name, and it follows the construction of a cathedral during the 12th century.

The Serpent Queen - *United States* - 2022 - Based on Leonie Frieda's novel about the life of Catherine de Medici, this period drama stars English actress Samantha Morton as de Medici and Amrita Acharia (*Good Karma Hospital*) as Aabis. Though technically an American production, most of the cast is British or otherwise European. **Premiered September 11th.**

The Spanish Princess - 2019 - This period drama is based on the novels *The Constant Princess* and *The King's Curse* by Philippa Gregory, and it's a sequel to the previous miniseries *The White Queen* and *The White Princess*. The series follows teenage princess Catherine of Aragon as she travels to Englanth lud to meet her husband by proxy.

The White Princess - 2017 - Based on the Philippa Gregory book of the same name, this miniseries tells the story of Elizabeth of York and her marriage to Henry VII. It's the sequel to *The White Queen*.

The White Queen - 2013 - This miniseries is based on Philippa Gregory's historical series, *The Cousins' War*, and it tells the story of the women involved in the conflict for England's throne during the War of Roses.

Who is Ghislaine Maxwell - 2022 - This two-part docuseries takes a look at the British socialite who enabled and assisted wealthy sexual predators, maintaining a close friendship with Queen Elizabeth's son Andrew. **Premiered June 24th.**

World Without End - 2012 - This miniseries is a sequel to *The Pillars of the Earth*, and it's set 150 years later in the same English town of Knightsbridge. This time, they're facing the outbreak of the Black Death and the Hundred Years' War. It's based on the Ken Follett novel of the same name.

PEACOCK

Website: http://peacocktv.com

Description: This NBC-owned subscription service is the major online home of NBCUniversal content. British programming is limited.

Available On: Roku, Amazon Fire TV, Apple TV, Apple iPhone & iPad, Android TV, Android phones and tablets, most recent game consoles, Google Chromecast, computer (via web browser).

Cost: Limited Free Membership, Peacock Premium - $4.99/month or $49.99/year, go ad-free for an extra $5/month to watch without ads.

Now Streaming

The Accused - 2017 - This two-part docuseries takes a look at what happens when you're accused of a serious crime in the UK.

The Alfred Hitchcock Hour - *United States* - 1962 to 1965 - Alfred Hitchcock hosts this classic mystery and thriller anthology series.

Alfred Hitchcock Presents - *United States* - 1955 to 1962 - The English master of suspense hosts this anthology series full of mystery and murder.

The Almighty Johnsons - *New Zealand* - 2011 to 2013 - This fantasy dramedy follows a young man who turns 21 and learns he and his family members are reincarnated Norse gods.

Antiques to the Rescue - 2012 - Auctioneer John Foster helps cash-poor historic homeowners liquidate valuable heirlooms to cover the costs of maintaining their money-hungry homes.

Bear Grylls: Survival School - 2016 - Adventurer Bear Grylls takes a group of kids out to test their outdoor skills and teach them more about survival.

Beaver Falls – 2011 to 2012 - Three British friends decide to have one last crazy summer working in an American summer camp.

The Bletchley Circle - 2012 to 2014 - In 1952, four former Bletchley Park codebreakers from WWII come together to track a killer.

Bloodline Detectives - 2020 to present - This reality series takes a look at how police are solving cold cases with familial DNA and the help of genealogists.

Boy Meets Girl (2009) - After a freak accident, a man and woman find themselves trapped in each other's bodies. Martin Freeman (*Sherlock*) and Rachael Stirling (*Detectorists*) star in this ITV dramedy.

Brave New World - *United States* - 2020 - The dystopian series takes place in a futuristic World State where citizens are genetically modified and the social hierarchy is determined by intelligence. Harry Lloyd stars as Bernard Marx (*Game of Thrones*), and Jessica Brown-Findlay (*Downton Abbey*) plays Lenina Crowne.

Can't Cope, Won't Cope - *Ireland* - 2016 to 2018 - This sitcom follows two young women in Dublin as their lives move in different directions and their friendship begins to dissolve.

The Capture - 2019 - Holliday Grainger (*C.B. Strike*) stars in this series about a detective who uncovers a massive conspiracy while investigating the charges against a British soldier. **Season 2 premieres November 3rd.**

Case Histories - 2011 to 2013 - Based on the Jackson Brodie novels by Kate Atkinson, this Edinburgh-based series features a tough guy PI with a heart of gold.

Casualty 24/7 - 2018 to present - At Barnsley A&E, doctors, nurses, and support staff work around the clock to to treat the sick and injured.

Chancer – 1990 to 1991 - Clive Owen plays Stephen Crane, a schemer who takes advantage of opportunities using manipulation and misdirection. As a young business analyst/con man in London, he's called in to help save a struggling motor company.

Chateau DIY - 2018 to present - This *Escape to the Chateau* spinoff follows a variety of British families who are renovating French chateaux. Dick Strawbridge narrates, and he and his wife offer up advice to others following in their footsteps.

Code 404 - 2020 - When the talented detective John Major (Daniel Mays, *Good Omens*) is killed during a sting operation, he's brought back as part of an experimental project. Understandably, the newly-revived detective is intent on finding his killer.

The Courtship - 2022 - Inspired by shows like *Bridgerton*, this reality series sees men in Regency-era dress attempting to woo a young woman.

Dead Lucky - *Australia* - 2018 – When a dangerous armed robber resurfaces in Sydney, two very different detectives are forced to work together to catch him.

Departure - 2019 - This series follows the mystery of the disappearing passenger flight 716.

Derren Brown: The Experiments - 2011 - English mentalist Derren Brown uses a variety of tricks and suggestive techniques to convince people they have no fear.

Devil's Advocate - 2022 - This short docuseries takes a look at the life of Giovanni Di Stefano, a man who pretended to be a lawyer and went on to defend some of the most well-known criminals in recent history - including Saddam Hussein.

Downton Abbey - 2010 to 2015 - This popular period drama follows the lives of the Crawley family and their servants during the early 1900s. *See also: Downton Abbey, A New Era on Peacock*

East West 101 - *Australia* - 2007 to 2011 - Malik and Crowley are a study in opposites as they investigate major crimes.

Escape to the Chateau - 2016 to 2019 - This British reality series follows Dick Strawbridge and Angela Adoree as they buy and renovate the 19th century Château de la Motte-Husson in Martigné-sur-Mayenne, France.

Escape to the Chateau: Make Do & Mend - 2020 to present - Dick and Angel Strawbridge help families address home design problems and DIY disasters.

The Fall - 2013 to 2016 - Gillian Anderson (*The X-Files*) and Jamie Dornan (*50 Shades of Grey*) star in this series about a senior investigator who goes head-to-head with a serial killer who's attacking young professional women in Belfast.

The Family Farm - 2018 - In this four-part docu-series, three UK families with no farming experience volunteer to spend a summer working on a farm in Wales. High in the Snowdonia mountains, they seek a simpler kind of life.

Five Bedrooms - *Australia* - 2019 - Five people bond at the singles table at a wedding, then get drunk and decide the best thing to do would be to buy a house together.

Gadget Man - 2012 to 2015 - Actors Stephen Fry (Series 1) and Richard Ayoade (Series 2-4) take a look at innovative products designed to make our lives easier.

Garth Marenghi's Darkplace - 2004 - This cult classic is offered up as a "lost classic of the 1980s", and it revolves around a fictional horror author and a doctor who battles evil forces beneath a hospital in Romford. Matthew Holness (*Back*) and Richard Ayoade (*The IT Crowd*) wrote and starred in the series.

Go Girls – *New Zealand* – 2009 to 2013 - Three twentysomething women realize they've made little progress towards their life goals, and vow to achieve their respective goals of being married, rich, and famous within a year.

Hammer House of Horror – 1980 - This classic anthology series tells tales of mystery, suspense, and horror.

Hell's Kitchen – 2004 to 2009 - This series pits prospective chefs against one another, with the winner getting a head chef position.

Hitmen - 2020 - This comedy follows two best friends who have fallen into a career in contract killing. Mel Giedroyc (*Spies of Warsaw*) and Sue Perkins (*The Great British Baking Show*) star.

Hoarder SOS - 2016 - This reality series attempts to help Brits with far too much stuff.

Homefront - 2012 - This dramatic miniseries follows the lives of the wives and girlfriends of soldiers serving in Afghanistan.

Intelligence - 2020 - An NSA agent joins forces with a computer analyst to establish a new cyber crimes department in the UK. American David Schwimmer (*Friends*) stars.

Interview with a Murderer - 2016 - Criminologist and professor David Wilson conducts a series of interviews with convicted murderer Bert Spencer. Bert was convicted for the murder of farmer Hubert Wilkes, but he's always been suspected of the brutal killing of a young newspaper delivery boy, Carl Bridgewater.

The Invisibles - 2008 - A couple of retired master burglars tried living in Spain, but after a bout of homesickness, they returned to England with their wives to live in a Devon fishing village. It's not long before a return to familiar shores sees them taking up the same old bad habits.

Kitchen Nightmares - 2007 to 2014 - Acclaimed British chef Gordon Ramsay hosts this series in which he visits struggling American restaurants and spends a week trying to help them be more successful.

Ladies of London - *United States* - 2014 to present - This American reality series heads to London to spend time in the world of wealthy British socialites and American ex-pats. *Downton Abbey* actress Joanne Froggatt appears in one episode.

Last Light - 2022 - Joanne Froggatt (*Downton Abbey*) stars in this environmental thriller about what it might be like if the world we know began to crumble. **Premiered September 8th.**

Line of Duty - 2012 to present - This series focuses on a group of officers in the ACU (Anti-Corruption Unit), a team that investigates the wrongdoings of its fellow officers. **Peacock has the first four seasons.**

Manhunt: Catch Me if You Can - 2019 - In a specialist tactical unit in Kent, police officers track and capture suspects on the run. This three-part docuseries follows their work.

Mean Mums - 2019 - When her only son starts school, Jess finds herself thrust into the cutthroat world of other mums.

Meet the Family - *Canada* - 2013 to 2015 - This Canadian adaptation of the British series sees young and unsuspecting people meeting what they think are the families of their significant others - except that they're paid actors who intend to make the whole thing as uncomfortable as possible.

More Manners of Downton Abbey - 2016 - Alastair Bruce interviews *Downton Abbey* cast members and looks at the social rules of early 1900s Britain.

Moving On – 2009 to 2016 - This anthology series gives us stories of people preparing to move on to something new in their lives.

Murdered in the Line of Duty - 2016 - A number of British police have been killed in the course of trying to prevent criminal activities. This docuseries takes a look at a few of them.

Murder, She Wrote - United States - 1984 to 1996 - Though it's an American series, star Angela Lansbury was born in London. The classic cozy mystery follows writer Jessica Fletcher - and murder follows her.

Not Going Out - 2006 to present - This long-running British comedy favourite follows a young slacker and the people around him. Lee Mack stars, but the series has featured a number of well-known actors including Miranda Hart, Bobby Ball, Hugh Dennis, and Katy Wix.

Noughts & Crosses - 2020 - Based on the Malorie Blackman novel of the same name, this series is set in an alternate reality where black "Cross" people rule over white "Noughts". Jack Rowan (*Peaky Blinders*) and Masali Baduza (*Trackers*) star as Callum and Sephy, an interracial couple whose romance leads them into danger.

Our Guy in China - 2016 - Racer Guy Martin heads to China to take in the culture and check out some of their motorbike innovations.

Our Guy in India - 2015 - Guy Martin sets off on a 1000-mile journey through India on a motorbike before arriving at Rider Mania.

Our Guy in Russia - 2018 - In Russia, Guy Martin visits Moscow, performs in a Soviet Air Force jet, visits a diamond mine, crosses Siberia, and eventually heads out of Russia and over to Chernobyl.

Police: Suspect No. 1 - 2020 to present - This gripping docuseries follows a Norfolk-based police unit in real time as they attempt to catch criminals.

The Saint - 1962 to 1969 - Roger Moore stars as Simon Templar, a wealthy adventurer who travels the world solving crimes and engaging in all manner of secret agent hijinks. Though the settings are occasionally exotic, nearly every episode was filmed at a studio in Hertfordshire using "blue-screen" technology. The series was based on the Simon Templar novels by Leslie Charteris.

Save Me - 2018 - Lennie James and Suranne Jones star in this series about a man who will do anything to find his missing daughter.

The Search - 2021 - This docuseries follows the efforts of Northern Ireland's Search and Rescue Technicians as they try to find people reported missing.

The Secret Life of the Cruise - 2018 - The world's largest cruise ships are akin to floating cities. This documentary looks at what it takes to make it all work.

The Secret Life of the Hospital - 2018 - This documentary takes a look behind the scenes at British hospitals.

The Secret Life of the Long-Haul Flight - 2017 - Millions of passengers take long-haul flights each year, but few of us know how much is involved in keeping those lengthy voyages going.

Secret State – 2012 – In a miniseries that will reassure you that the US isn't the only place where government and big business are way too close, Secret State shows a Deputy Prime Minister entangled in an international conspiracy.

Seesaw - 1998 - David Suchet (*Poirot*) and Geraldine James (*Back to Life*) star in this series about what happens in the aftermath of a kidnapping when ransom has been paid and the loved one is returned home.

Smother - *Ireland* - 2021 - Dervla Kirwan (*Ballykissangel*) stars in this thriller about a woman whose husband is found dead beneath a cliff after a family party. When she starts to investigates, she learns things she might have been happier not knowing.

Speed with Guy Martin - 2013 to 2016 - Motorcycle racer Guy Martin performs a variety of speed challenges.

Step Dave – *New Zealand* – 2014 to 2015 - A young slacker in New Zealand meets the woman of his dreams, only to realize she's 15 years older than him and comes with major baggage.

Terry Pratchett's Going Postal - 2010 - This adaptation of Pratchett's novel sees con man Moist von Lipwig (Richard Coyle, *Chilling Adventures of Sabrina*) caught by the law and given two choices: suffer a painful death, or take over a derelict post office. Also starring David Suchet (*Poirot*), Charles Dance (*Game of Thrones*), and Claire Foy (*The Crown*).

Travel Man – 2015 to present - Richard Ayoade (*The IT Crowd*) takes 48 hour trips to various destinations, always bringing along a celebrity guest.

Treadstone - *United States* - 2019 - Though American, several actors in this series are British, and parts of the action are set in London. Adapted from Robert Ludlum's *Bourne* world, the series explores the story of a fictional CIA black-ops programme that turns recruits into almost superhuman assassins.

Treasure Detectives - *United States* - 2013 - British fakes and forgeries expert Curtis Dowling helps to uncover the truth about supposed treasures.

Trigger Point - 2022 - Vicky McClure (*Line of Duty*) as Lana Washington, a former military operative who leads a bomb squad for the Metropolitan Police. She and her team have to work fast to uncover terrorist activity in London before things escalate and even more people get hurt. **Premiered July 8th.**

The Undeclared War - 2022 - Set in 2024, this British cyber thriller follows a young GCHQ intern who suddenly finds herself in the middle of large-scale digital warfare after a routine stress test goes wrong. **Premiered June 30th.**

Underground Britain - 2008 - Engineer Rob Bell takes us below the surface to see what goes on beneath the UK.

Vigil - 2021 - Suranne Jones (*Gentleman Jack*), Martin Compston (*Line of Duty*), and Shaun Evans (*Endeavour*) are among the stars of this crime drama set on a nuclear-powered submarine off the coast of Scotland. DCI Amy Silva (Jones) has been sent to investigate a death on board.

The War of the Worlds - 2019 - After a meteor touches down in Surrey, humans face a battle for survival against an alien race. The classic HG Wells tale is told through the lens of Amy and George, two people who are in love and ready to embark on a new (though forbidden) life.

We Are Lady Parts - 2021 - This Channel 4 series follows the adventures of an all-female Muslim punk band in London. **Renewed for season 2, date TBD.**

Westside – *New Zealand* – 2015 to 2017 - This prequel to *Outrageous Fortune* is set between 1974 and 1979, and it recounts stories of crime and passion in Auckland.

Wolfblood - 2013 - Wolfblood teenagers have a number of heightened abilities, but their powers also bring danger and a need for secrecy.

Wonders of Britain - 2015 - Julia Bradbury embarks on a 12,000-mile journey around Great Britain to discover some of its most wonderful sites.

For the Kids

Fifi & the Flowertots - 2006 to 2010 - This British stop-motion children's show follows a group of flower characters on their adventures in the garden.

Legend of the Dragon - 2005 to 2008 - This British-German animated series begins when a previous Golden Dragon has passed on to the afterlife and a couple of 17-year-old twins are next in line for the Golden Dragon power band. When the band chooses brother Ang over his twin sister Ling, they become enemies.

Little Charley Bear - 2011 to 2015 - This 3D/CGI-animated series follows the adventures of a little bear who likes to pretend. The series is narrated by James Corden.

Maisy - 1999 to 2000 - Based on the book series by Lucy Cousins, this animated series follows the lives of Maisy Mouse and her friends. They make noises instead of speaking, and a narrator explains the action and communicates with the characters.

Noddy's Toyland Adventures - 1992 to 2000 - This series follows the adventures of a little wooden doll who lives in Toyland and drives a taxi. He spends much of his time getting in trouble and trying to earn money. The series is based on the *Noddy* stories by Enid Blyton. See also: *Noddy in Toyland* and *Make Way for Noddy*.

Postman Pat - 1981 to 2007 - This stop motion series follows the adventures of postman Patrick Clifton and his cat Jess as they deliver the post around the valley of Greendale. While he does his job honourably, he's often distracted by the problems of people he encounters on his route. See also: *Postman Pat: Special Delivery Service.*

Raa Raa the Noisy Lion - 2011 to 2018 - This stop motion series follows a group of animals as they go on adventures in the Jingly Jangly Jungle.

Roary the Racing Car - 2007 to 2010 - Join in on the adventures of five racing vehicles: Roary, Maxi, Drifter, Cici, and Tin Top. This series is set around the fictional Silver Hatch racing circuit, and most of the action takes place in the pits and workshop.

PEACOCK

EPIX

Website: https://www.epix.com/

Description: Epix is a subsidiary of Metro-Goldwyn-Mayer. Their content is a mix of older motvies, original TV shows, documentaries, and music/comedy specials.

Available On: The EPIX NOW app is available for download on iPhones and iPads, Apple TV, Android phones, tablets and TVs, Roku and Fire TV.

Cost: $5.99/month

Now Streaming

Belgravia - 2020 - *Belgravia*'s story opens on the eve of Napoleon's battle against the Duke of Wellington at Waterloo, taking place at a high society ball attended by a number of people who will go on to die in the conflict. It then picks up decades later when a newly emerging upper class begins to butt heads with the established upper classes. Even then, the events of 25 years prior continue to resonate. Julian Fellowes (*Downton Abbey*) is the creator of this period drama. **Renewed for season 2, date TBD.**

Berlin Station - *United States* - 2016 to 2019 - Though American, this series stars Englishman Richard Armitage and Welshman Rhys Ifans. It follows Daniel Miller (Armitage), a man with a clandestine mission to uncover the source of a CIA leak at a station in Berlin, Germany.

Brittania - 2017 to present - This US-UK co-production shows the Roman invasion in 43AD Britannia.

Condor - *United States* - 2018 to present - Max Irons (son of British acting legend Jeremy Irons) stars in this thriller about a young CIA analyst who happens upon a plan that threatens millions. When his office is massacred, he's forced from the office into the real world.

Deep State - 2018 to present - Mark Strong (*The Imitation Game*) stars as Mark Easton, a former MI6 agent who returns to the field to avenge the death of his son.

Domina - 2021 - This British-Italian co-production takes a look at the politics and power struggles of Ancient Rome from a female perspective. **Renewed for season 2, no date yet.**

Pennyworth - *United States* - 2019 to present - Jack Bannon (*Endeavour*) stars as Alfred Pennyworth, a former British SAS soldier who will ultimately become Batman's butler.

Perpetual Grace, LTD - *United States* - 2019 - Sir Ben Kingsley stars as Pastor Byron Brown in this series about a young grifter who attempts to prey on a pastor who's more dangerous than he initially appears.

War of the Worlds - *United States* - 2019 to present - Not to be confused with the 2019 British production, this adaptation of the H.G. Wells classic is worthy of mention here for a few reasons. Aside from Wells himself being English, stars Gabriel Byrne, Natasha Little, Stephen Campbell Moore, Aaron Heffernan, and Daisy Edgar-Jones all hail from the British Isles. American Elizabeth McGovern (Cora Crawley in *Downton Abbey*) also appears. **Season 3 expected in 2022.**

APPLE TV+

Website: https://www.apple.com/apple-tv-plus

Description: Apple TV+ is Apple's ad-free, monthly subscription service. Though mostly American, it does have some British programming.

Available On: Virtually all Apple devices (TVs, computers, iPads, and iPhones), Roku, PlayStation, Xbox, Fire TV, Android TV, Google TV, any device with a web browser, and most smart TVs.

Cost: $4.99/month

Now Streaming

Bad Sisters - *Ireland* - 2022 - Set in London and Dublin, this dark comedy is based on the Flemish series *Clan*, which tells the story of sisters brought close together by the death of their parents. When their brother-in-law dies, his life insurance company endeavours to prove one or more of the sisters had malicious intent. **Premiered August 19th.**

Becoming You - 2020 - Olivia Colman (*Broadchurch*) narrates this series about how a child's first 2000 days will shape the rest of their lives.

The Earth at Night - 2020 to present - Tom Hiddleston narrates this nature series about the nighttime lives of wild animals.

The Essex Serpent - 2022 - Claire Danes and Tom Hiddleston star in this Victorian-era period drama about a newly-widowed woman who's eager to start fresh after the death of her abusive husband. She heads to a small Essex village and finds herself quickly wrapped up in tales of a mythical sea dragon and a clash with the local vicar.

Long Way Down - 2007 - This docuseries follows Scottish actor Ewan McGregor and English presenter Charley Boorman as they take a motorcycle trip from John o'Groats in Scotland to Cape Town in South Africa.

Long Way Round - 2004 - This docuseries follows Scottish actor Ewan McGregor and English presenter Charley Boorman as they travel from London to New York City on motorcycles. They travel east through Europe and Asia, then take a flight to Alaska and continue by road to New York.

Long Way Up - 2020 - This docuseries picks up more than a decade after *Long Way Round* and *Long Way Down*, following Ewan McGregor and Charley Boorman as they travel from Argentina to Los Angeles.

Shantaram - *United States* - 2022 - Based on Gregory David Roberts' novel of the same name, this period drama follows an Australian bank robber called Lin Ford (English actor Charlie Hunnam, *Sons of Anarchy*) who flees to India. Richard Roxburgh (*Rake*) appears as DS Marty Nightingalem. **Premieres October 14th.**

Slow Horses - 2022 - Gary Oldman stars in this series about a team of British intelligence agents who each find themselves dumped in a department at Slough House after career-ending mistakes. **Season 2 is expected in late 2022.**

Surface - *United States* - 2022 - British actress Gugu Mbatha-Raw (*Bonekickers, Black Mirror*) stars in this psychological thriller about a San Francisco woman who survives a suicide attempt but loses all her recent memories. **Premiered July 29th.**

Suspicion - 2022 - After being identified as suspects in the kidnapping of an American media mogul's son, five people see their lives turned upside down.

The Me You Can't See - *United States* - 2021 - Celebrities Oprah Winfrey and Prince Harry discuss the hardships in their lives and the ways they've suffered, offering advice on mental health.

Ted Lasso - 2020 to present - Jason Sudeikis plays an American college football coach who takes over as head coach of a British football club (aka "soccer" in the US). **Season 3 is expected in late 2022, date TBD.**

Trying - 2020 to present - This sitcom follows a couple, Nikki and Jason, who desperately want to become parents but struggle to conceive a child. They decide they'll adopt, only to face a whole new set of challenges. **Season 3 premiered July 22nd.**

The Year Earth Changed - 2021 - The pandemic-driven lockdowns may have been hard on people, but while the people were inside, nature thrived.

APPLE TV+

TOPIC

Website: http://topic.com

Description: This new service focuses on international programming, and it includes a number of countries often overlooked (including the Middle East and African countries). Their British library is relatively small but there are some good titles.

Available On: Roku, Fire TV, Apple TV, Apple iPhone & iPad, Android phones and tablets, and computer (via web browser). You can also subscribe via Amazon Prime Video.

Cost: $5.99/month, $59.99/year

Now Streaming

The Bridge - *Denmark/Sweden* - 2011 to 2018 - This crime drama begins with the discovery of a dead body along the border between Denmark and Sweden, and the investigation that followed.

Capital - 2015 - When property values soar on a once middle-class London street, residents receive mysterious postcards saying, "We want what you have."

Catching a Killer - 2017 to present - This gritty true crime docuseries documents the work of the Thames Valley Police as they investigate murders.

Chimerica - 2019 - Based on real events, this series follows a photojournalist attempting to uncover the identity of the protester who stood in front of the tanks in Tiananmen Square.

Come Home - 2018 - After nineteen years of marriage, a woman suddenly walks out on her family.

Deceit - 2021 - This miniseries is based on the true story of a 1992 police honeytrap set up as part of the investigation of a London mother's murder.

Down from London - 2019 - This British comedy follows a couple that attempts to ignore their relationship troubles by taking trips away from London.

Enterprice - 2019 - In this BBC Three sitcom, a couple of young entrepreneurs in South London attempt to launch their new delivery service, Speedi-Kazz.

Intruders – 2014 - John Simm (*Life on Mars*) stars as an ex-cop whose wife goes missing. The ensuing investigation leads him to Seattle, where a secret society chases immortality by hiding in the bodies of others.

Miriam's Big American Adventure - 2018 - Miriam Margolyes (*Call the Midwife, Bucket*) sets off on a fun and entertaining road trip around the United States. She begins in Chicago before moving on to an Indiana summer camp and a prison in Ohio. In the final entry, she ponders whether the United States is actually "the Divided States".

The Missing Children - *Ireland* - 2021 - From 1922 to 1998, the Catholic Church in Ireland imprisoned more than 80,000 unwed mothers and stole their babies. At one of the 44 institutions where these human rights abuses occurred, they found nearly 800 baby corpses in the sewers. This docuseries tells the true story of what happened and who tried to cover it up.

Monkman & Seagull's Genius Guide to Britain - 2018 - This fun travel series originally aired on BBC Two in the UK, and it follows a couple of quiz show champions as they visit some of the country's greatest triumphs of science and engineering. If you enjoy great scenery and more insight into the way things work, you'll love this one. One episode is dedicated to each of the four countries of the UK.

Moses Jones - 2009 - After a body is discovered in the Thames, DI Moses Jones investigates possibilities of witchcraft in London's Ugandan exile community. Shaun Parkes (*Line of Duty, Hooten & the Lady*) stars as DI Moses Jones, with Matt Smith (*Doctor Who*) and Dennis Waterman (*New Tricks*) in supporting roles.

Not Safe for Work - 2015 - When budget cuts move Katherine's civil servant job to Northampton, she reluctantly goes along with the relocation.

The Office - 2001 to 2003 - Before there was Michael Scott in the US, there was David Brent in Slough, England. Written by Ricky Gervais (*After Life*) and Stephen Merchant (*Hello Ladies*), this mockumentary-style programme takes place in the office of the fictional Wernham Hogg paper company. Mackenzie Crook (*Detectorists*) and Martin Freeman (*Sherlock*) are also among the stars.

Run - 2013 - Olivia Colman and Lennie James star in this four-part miniseries about four seemingly unconnected people whose lives intersect after a random act of violence.

The Virtues - 2019 - When his personal life falls apart, Joseph travels to Ireland in hopes of making amends with his estranged sister Anna. In doing so, he unearths the horrors of his past while also finding a path to move forward. Stephen Graham (*Snatch*) stars.

Year of the Rabbit - 2019 - Matt Berry (*The IT Crowd*) stars in this period comedy about an eclectic group of Victorian detectives who fight crime whilst mingling with street gangs, spiritualists, politicians, Bulgarian princes, and even the Elephant Man.

SHOTIME

Website: http://showtime.com

Description: Showtime primarily focuses on major motion pictures and original television series, along with some sporting events.

Available On: Roku, Fire TV, Apple TV, Apple iPhone & iPad, Chromecast, Android phones and tablets, and computer (via web browser). You can also subscribe via Amazon Prime Video or Hulu.

Cost: $10.99/month

Now Streaming

The Affair - 2014 to 2019 - A man (Dominic West) and woman (Ruth Wilson) have an affair that leads to a complex series of events.

Back to Life - 2019 to Present - Following an 18-year prison sentence, Miri Matteson (*Daisy Haggard*) returns home to Hythe, Kent, and attempts to rebuild her life.

The Borgias - *Canada/Hungary* - 2011 to 2013 - Though not strictly British, much of the cast of this series is, including Jeremy Irons (*Brideshead Revisited*) and Holliday Grainger (*CB Strike*). It follows the rise of Italy's Borgia family during the Renaissance, along with their struggle to hold onto the power they've gained.

Brotherhood - *United States* - 2006-2008 - Irish-American brothers' lives intertwine as they go their own way.

The End - *Australia* - 2020 - Frances O'Connor (*Mansfield Park*) stars as Dr. Kate Brennan, a palliative care specialist who's passionate about her opposition to euthanasia. Her mother Edie (played by Dame Harriet Walter) believes just as strongly that she has a right to die on her own terms.

Episodes - *United States* - 2011 to 2017 - Two married British TV producers are offered a deal in the US, and then everything goes wrong. Stephen Mangan (*Hang-Ups*) and Tamsin Greig (*Friday Night Dinner*) star.

Guerrilla - 2017 - Set in early 1970s London, Guerrilla tells the story of a politically active couple whose relationship and values are tested when they liberate a political prisoner and form a radical underground cell.

Happyish - *United States* - 2015 - Brit Steve Coogan (*The Trip*) stars as a depressed middle-aged man who contents himself with feeling merely "happy-ish".

Just Another Immigrant - 2018 - British Comedian Romesh Ranganathan uproots his entire family and moves to the US.

The Man Who Fell to Earth - *United States* - 2022 - Based on the 1963 Walter Tevis novel of the same name, this series is a sequel to the 1976 film starring David Bowie. It stars British-born Chiwetel Ejiofor as an alien who arrives on Earth, with fellow Brit Bill Nighy playing the role previously occupied by Bowie.

Patrick Melrose - 2018 - Based on the semi-autobiographical Patrick Melrose novels by Edward St. Aubyn, this miniseries tells the story of an upper class man's addictions and family troubles.

Penny Dreadful - 2014 to 2016 - A group of explorers and adventurers team up to fight supernatural threats in Victorian England.

Penny Dreadful: City of Angels - *United States* - 2020 - Penny Dreadful hops the pond to become an LA-based period drama exploring storylines connected to the devil and deity Santa Muerte. Set in 1938, creator John Logan has created a new set of cases about Los Angeles residents becoming entangled with supernatural forces.

Ripley - 2021 - Andrew Scott (aka *Fleabag*'s hot priest) stars in this period drama about a grifter in 1960s New York. He's hired to fly to Italy to convince a wealthy man's son to return home, but the job drags him into something much more complicated. **Showtime lists this as "coming soon", but they've yet to confirm a date.**

Shameless (US) - *United States* - 2011 to present - This American series is an adaptation of Paul Abbott's British series of the same name and features an ensemble cast led by William H. Macy and Emmy Rossum.

The Tudors - 2007 to 2010 - The Tudors is a drama about Henry VIII and his extensive love life.

We Hunt Together - 2020 - This drama sees two conflicted detectives tracking down a pair of deadly killers. Starring Eve Myles (*Torchwood*). **Season 2 premiered June 24th.**

FREE WITH ADS

This section is devoted to (legal) streaming services that allow you to watch British TV shows for free with ads. These shows are not pirated or uploaded by unauthorised individuals - they're properly licensed and you can rest assured the appropriate people are getting compensated.

All of these services can be watched in a standard web browser, and most also have Roku apps and mobile/tablet apps so you can easily watch them on your TV or mobile device. IMDb TV can be watched through the Amazon Video channel/app.

- **Tubi**: https://tubitv.com/
- **Roku Channel**: https://therokuchannel.roku.com/
- **Freevee**: https://www.amazon.com/adlp/freevee-about
- **Pluto**: https://pluto.tv/
- **Crackle**: https://www.crackle.com/
- **Vudu (free section)**: https://www.vudu.com/

Now Streaming
Mysteries & Crime Dramas

Alex Rider - 2020 - *Midsomer Murders* and *Foyle's War* writer Anthony Horowitz is behind this teenage spy series based on his popular young adult novels. Unbeknownst to Alex, his uncle and reluctant guardian has been training him as a spy. When he's suddenly forced to go on an undercover mission at Point Blanc academy, he begins to realise he has skills he wasn't even aware of. **Freevee**

Amber - *Ireland* - 2014 - This crime drama follows a Dublin family whose teenage daughter disappears after her father drops her off near a friend's house. **Tubi, Pluto**

Apparitions - 2008 - Martin Shaw stars in this supernatural drama about a priest drawn into the world of demons and exorcism. **Freevee, Roku, Tubi, Pluto**

Appropriate Adult – 2011 - A woman finds herself involved in a serial killer case as the "appropriate adult" who helps vulnerable adults facing criminal charges. **Freevee, Roku**

Bedlam – 2011 to 2012 - When a haunted former asylum is turned into a high-end apartment building, it has unexpected consequences for the building's new tenants. **Tubi, Roku**

The Bletchley Circle - 2012 to 2014 - In 1952, four former Bletchley Park codebreakers from WWII come together to track a killer. **Freevee, Pluto**

Blood Ties - *Canada* - 2007 - When a Toronto detective begins losing her eyesight, she becomes a PI and teams up with a 470-year-old vampire (who is also the illegitimate son of Henry VIII). The series is an adaptation of author Tanya Huff's *Blood* novels. **Freevee, Roku, Tubi, Pluto, Vudu**

Blue Murder - 2003 to 2009 - DCI Janine Lewis struggles with the challenge of being a single mom to four kids while leading a team of detectives through homicide investigations. Caroline Quentin (*Jonathan Creek*) stars. **Freevee, Roku, Pluto, Tubi**

The Blue Rose - *New Zealand* - 2013 - This investigative drama sees a group of law firm employees joining together to figure out what happened in the mysterious death of a co-worker. **Freevee, Tubi**

Bonekickers – 2008 - This short-lived drama follows a team of archaeologists at the fictional Wessex University. Hugh Bonneville (*Downton Abbey*) and Julie Graham (*Queens of Mystery*) star. **Freevee**

Bounty Hunters – 2017 to 2019 - Jack Whitehall and Rosie Perez star in this series about a sheltered Brit and a tough Brooklynite who must work together to help save his family's business after a dodgy antiques deal involving looted treasures. **Pluto, Tubi**

Boy Meets Girl (2009) - After a freak accident, a man and woman find themselves trapped in each other's bodies. Martin Freeman (*Sherlock*) and Rachael Stirling (*Detectorists*) star in this ITV dramedy. This is not to be confused with the other *Boy Meets Girl* on BritBox. **Freevee, Roku, Tubi**

The Broker's Man – 1997 to 1998 - A former detective investigates insurance claims while trying to hold his family life together. Features Kevin Whately (*Inspector Morse*) in the lead. **Freevee, Roku, Tubi, Pluto**

Cadfael - 1994 to 1998 - In 12th century Shrewsbury, a monk solves mysteries. Sir Derek Jacobi (*Last Tango in Halifax*) stars. **Freevee, Roku, Tubi, Pluto**

The Case - 2011 - This legal drama tells the story of a man put on trial for the murder of his terminally ill partner after he helped her commit suicide. **Roku, Pluto**

Case Histories - 2011 to 2013 - Based on the *Jackson Brodie* novels by Kate Atkinson, this Edinburgh-based series features a tough guy PI with a heart of gold. **Freevee, Roku, Vudu, Pluto, Tubi**

Case Sensitive - 2011 to 2012 - DS Zailer and DC Waterhouse take different perspectives on the murder of a mother and her 5-year-old daughter. **Tubi**

Chiller – 1995 - Martin Clunes and Nigel Havers star in this horror series about a group of friends who receive prophecies during a seance in the basement of a London cafe. **Freevee, Roku, Tubi**

CI5: The New Professionals - 1999 - Billed as an updated version of the 1970s series *The Professionals*, this *James Bond*-style series follows a group of men at the fictional CI5 (Criminal Intelligence Department 5). **Pluto, Tubi, Roku**

The City & the City – 2018 - David Morrissey stars in this BBC sci-fi/mystery production about an inspector in the Extreme Crime Squad of the fictional European city-state of Beszel. When a student is murdered in Beszel's twin city of Ul Qoman, he investigates. **Freevee**

City Homicide – *Australia* – 2007 to 2011 - In Melbourne, Australia, a group of homicide detectives work to find justice for victims of murder. **Freevee, Pluto**

City of Vice – 2008 - This historical crime drama is set in Georgian London and executed with incredible attention to detail. **Freevee, Tubi, Vudu**

Cold Squad – *Canada* – 1998 to 2005 - This long-running Canadian series follows a team that works on cold cases ranging from 5 to 50 or more years old. **Freevee, Roku, Tubi**

Colonel March of Scotland Yard – 1956 - This vintage detective series offers 26 episodes of classic 1950s British mystery. **Freevee, Roku, Tubi**

Cracker - 1993 to 1996 - Though he's obnoxious and anti-social, Fitz is a brilliant criminal psychologist and police consultant. **Pluto**

Cracker (US) – *United States* - 1997 to 1998 - While this is the US version, we're including it here because it's inspired by the original British show, *Cracker*. It's the story of an unlikeable, anti-social criminal psychologist who proves brilliant in assisting on tough cases. **Roku, Tubi, Pluto, Freevee**

Cuffs – 2015 - In quirky coastal Brighton, police officers are over-stretched and under-resourced, but they do the best they can with what they've got. **Tubi, Freevee**

Doctor Finlay - 1993 to 1996 - After WW2 and before the NHS is created, a doctor returns to his Scottish hometown. **Freevee, Tubi**

Donovan – 2004 - This psychological thriller follows Joe Donovan, a forensics expert turned author who investigates some of the most evil crimes. Some of them hit a little too close to home. **Freevee, Roku**

Durham County – *Canada* – 2007 to 2010 - A man moves his family in hopes of a new start, then a local serial killer throws a wrench in that peaceful new beginning. **Freevee**

Exile – 2011 - John Simm (*Life on Mars*) stars in this mystery-thriller about a man who returns home after his life falls apart – only to find a different kind of trouble there. **Tubi**

Extremely Dangerous - 1999 - Sean Bean stars in this crime drama/thriller about a former intelligence agent who's been convicted of his wife's murder. When a strange clue is sent to him in prison, he escapes and goes on the run to try to clear his name. **Pluto**

The Fall - 2013 to 2016 - Gillian Anderson (*The X-Files*) and Jamie Dornan (*50 Shades of Grey*) star in this series about a senior investigator who goes head-to-head with a serial killer who's attacking young professional women in Belfast. **Tubi, Pluto, Freevee**

The Field of Blood - 2011 to 2013 - Set in early 1980s Glasgow, a young woman skillfully solves murders on a police force full of men. Unfortunately, her dedication to the truth also puts her in danger. The series stars BAFTA winner Jayd Johnson (*River City*) as Paddy Meehan, working alongside Peter Capaldi (*Doctor Who*) and David Morrissey (*The Missing*). **Freevee, Pluto, Tubi**

The Gentle Touch - 1980 - Jill Gascoine stars as Britain's first female police detective. Within hours of her promotion to Detective Inspector, she learns her husband has been gunned down. **Freevee, Roku, Tubi**

The Ghost Squad - 2005 - Similar to *Line of Duty*, this series follows an Internal Affairs division designed to help find and fix corruption within the police. Elaine Cassidy (*No Offence*) stars. **Tubi, Freevee**

Gracepoint - *United States* - 2014 - This American *Broadchurch* adaptation sees David Tennant put on an American accent and return to the central role, this time as Detective Emmett Carver. It tells the story of a coastal California town turned upside-down when a young boy is found dead on the beach. **Tubi, Pluto, Freevee**

Hamish Macbeth - 1995 to 1997 - Hamish Macbeth (Robert Carlyle, *The Full Monty*) is a talented but unambitious Highlands constable who doesn't always follow the rules. The series was filmed in the lovely Highland village of Plockton on the shores of Loch Carron, and it's a great watch for those who enjoy good scenery. **Tubi, Pluto, Freevee**

Hammer House of Horror – 1980 - This classic anthology series tells tales of mystery, suspense, and horror. **Freevee, Roku, Tubi, Pluto**

Heat of the Sun – 1998 - This series was filmed on location in Africa, and set in 1930s high society Kenya. It follows a policeman working within the close-knit community of expats – many of whom harbour dark secrets. **Freevee**

He Kills Coppers - 2008 - This three-part miniseries follows the death of three police officers during the 1966 World Cup celebrations, looking closely at the three men most connected to the unfortunate deaths. **Freevee, Tubi, Roku, Pluto**

Hidden - 2011 - This four-part BBC conspiracy thriller stars Philip Glenister (*Life on Mars*) as Harry Venn, a high street solicitor who's unwittingly drawn into the investigation of his brothers murder 20 years prior. Thekla Reuten (*The American*) and David Suchet (*Poirot*) also appear. **Tubi, Pluto**

Hustle - 2004 to 2012 - Adrian Lester (*Bonekickers*), Robert Vaughn (*The Man from U.N.C.L.E.*), and Robert Glenister (*Paranoid*) star in this series about grifters who live by the motto, "you can't cheat an honest man". The specialise in long cons on the undeserving wealthy. **Tubi, Pluto, Freevee**

Inspector Alleyn Mysteries - 1990 to 1994 - Based on the novels of Dame Ngaio Marsh, this 1930s and 40s period mystery follows the crime-solving adventures of Inspector Alleyn (Simon Williams and Patrick Malahide) and his right-hand man Inspector Fox (William Simons). **Tubi**

The Interceptor - 2015 - Trevor Eve (*Waking the Dead*) and Jo Joyner (*Shakespeare & Hathaway*) are among the stars of this drama about a customs officer recruited to a new law enforcement team formed to track down some of London's worst criminals. **Tubi**

The Jury – 2002 to 2011 - This series follows the men and women brought together to act as jurors in a high-profile case involving a young Sikh student. **Freevee, Roku, Pluto, Tubi**

Kavanagh QC - 1995 to 2001 - John Thaw (*Inspector Morse*) stars as James Kavanagh QC, a barrister with a working-class background and a strong sense of right and wrong. It was one of Thaw's final roles before he died of cancer at the age of 60. It's loaded with actors who went on to well-known roles, including Lesley Manville (*Mum*), Larry Lamb (*Gavin & Stacey*), Barry Jackson (*Midsomer Murders*), Phyllis Logan (*Downton Abbey*), Bill Night (*Love Actually*), and Julian Fellowes (*Downton Abbey*). **Freevee, Roku, Tubi, Pluto**

Kidnap & Ransom - 2011 - This three-part miniseries follows Trevor Eve (*Shoestring*) as a skilled British hostage negotiator who travels around the world to work on high-profile cases. **Pluto, Tubi**

Kiss of Death - 2008 - This two-part series follows the investigation that occurs after human body parts are found on the mudflats along a river. **Freevee**

Law & Order: UK – 2009 to 2014 – This popular procedural is adapted from the American series *Law & Order*. Though set within a different legal system, the basic formula is the same. In the first half of an episode, police investigate a crime. In the second half, prosecutors take the case to court. **Tubi, Freevee**

Leverage - *United States* - 2008 to 2012 - This series follows a group of high-tech criminals who attempt to steal from wealthy people who don't deserve their money. Though it's American, it stars British actress Gina Bellman (*Coupling*). For a British series that's somewhat similar in tone, check out *Hustle*. **Freevee**

Leverage: Redemption - *United States* - 2021 - This Freevee series is a reboot of *Leverage*. On the anniversary of a friend's death, the team gets back together to take down a billionaire making money on the opioid crisis. **Freevee**

Line of Duty – 2012 to present - This suspenseful British police series is set in the fictional "anti-corruption unit" AC-12, where the police police the police. Lennie James, Vicky McClure, Martin Compston, and Adrian Dunbar all feature. **Freevee, Roku, Pluto**

Luther – 2010 to 2019 - Idris Elba stars as a brilliant London detective who frequently gets into trouble because of his passion for the job. **Pluto**

McCallum - 1995 to 1998 - Pathologist McCallum and his team help the dead tell their stories. **Freevee, Tubi, Roku**

Midsomer Murders - 1998 to present - In Midsomer County, the landscapes are beautiful, the villagers all have secrets, and murder is rampant. This British mystery classic features John Nettles as DCI Tom Barnaby through the first 13 seasons, with Neil Dudgeon as DCI John Barnaby for the later seasons. **Freevee, Roku, Tubi, Pluto**

Mom P.I. – *Canada* – 1990 to 1991 - Rosemary Dunsmore stars as Sally Sullivan, a widowed mother who teams up with PI Bernie Fox (Stuart Margolin) to solve mysteries and bring down criminals. **Freevee, Roku**

Moses Jones - 2009 - After a body is discovered in the Thames, DI Moses Jones investigates possibilities of witchcraft in London's Ugandan exile community. Shaun Parkes (*Line of Duty, Hooten & the Lady*) stars as DI Moses Jones, with Matt Smith (*Doctor Who*) and Dennis Waterman (*New Tricks*) in supporting roles. **Tubi, Freevee**

Murder City - 2004 to 2006 - DI Susan Alembic (Amanda Donohoe) and DS Luke Stone (Kris Marshall) are opposites, but they're very effective at working together to solve tough crimes. **Freevee, Roku**

Murder Most Horrid - 1991 - Dawn French (*Vicar of Dibley*) stars as a different character in each episode, with murder being the only common thread throughout. **Freevee**

Murphy's Law – 2003 to 2007 - James Nesbitt stars as DS Tommy Murphy, a maverick cop with a dark personal history. When given a final chance to prove his suitability for duty, he takes on a dangerous undercover assignment. **Tubi, Pluto, Freevee**

No Offence - 2015 to 2018 - This gritty Manchester-based police drama showcases

FREE

the work of some talented serious crimes investigators under the straight-talking DI Viv Deering. **Pluto**

Out of the Blue - 1995 to 1996 - Set in Yorkshire, this procedural follows the personal and professional lives of the detectives at Brazen Gate CID. **Freevee**

Paradox – 2009 - This sci-fi police drama focuses on a group of investigators who seek out evidence for crimes that haven't yet occurred. **Freevee**

Pretty Hard Cases - *Canada* - 2021 - Two tough female cops team up when they realise they're both going after the same dealer. **Freevee**

The Protectors – 1972 to 1974 - Robert Vaughn stars in this 1970s series about a London-based crime-fighting team that strives to protect the innocent and apprehend the guilty. **Freevee, Roku, Vudu, Tubi**

Remember Me – 2014 - Michael Palin (*Monty Python, Great Railway Journeys*), Jodie Comer (*Killing Eve*), and Mark Addy (*The Syndicate*) star in this sublimely creepy mystery about a series of unfortunate events that unfold around an unhappy pensioner who fakes a fall in order to be moved to a care home. **Pluto, Tubi, Roku**

Rush - *Australia* - 2008 to 2011 - This crime drama follows the activities of the Police Tactical Response team in Melbourne (based on the real-life Victoria Police Critical Incident Response Team). **Tubi**

The Ruth Rendell Mysteries - 1994 to 2000 - This collection includes a variety of suspenseful tales adapted from the novels of author Ruth Rendell. **Freevee**

Second Sight – 2001 - Clive Owen (*Chancer*) stars in this series about an ambitious detective who is slowly but surely losing his sight. **Freevee**

Secrets and Lies – *Australia* – 2014 - A regular suburban family guy finds the body of a young child and promptly becomes the leading suspect. **Freevee, Tubi**

See No Evil: The Moors Murders - 2006 - Joanne Froggatt (*Downton Abbey*), Sean Harris (*Prometheus*), and Maxine Peake (*Shameless*) star in this true crime drama about notorious child killers Ian Brady and Myra Hindley. **Freevee**

The Shadow Line - 2011 - DI Jonah Gabriel returns to work after a near fatal return,

quickly finding himself going deep into the dangerous world of drug dealing. The miniseries includes performances from Christopher Eccleston, Tobias Menzies, Lesley Sharp, and Rafe Spall. **Pluto, Tubi, Freevee, Roku**

The Silence – 2010 - While struggling to integrate into the hearing world, a young girl with a new cochlear implant witnesses the murder of a police officer. Douglas Henshall (*Shetland*) is among the stars of this miniseries. **Freevee, Roku, Pluto, Tubi**

Silent Witness - 1996 to present - A team of pathologists investigates crimes based on evidence gleaned from autopsies. **Freevee**

Single-Handed - 2007 to 2010 - *Ireland* - Jack Driscoll is transferred back to his hometown to take over the Garda Sergeant role his father left. **Freevee, Roku, Vudu**

Sirens - 2002 - This two-part miniseries follows DC Jay Pearson (Daniela Nardini) and DI Clive Wilson (Robert Glenister) investigating a serial rapist attacking young women around Islington. **Roku, Freevee**

SS-GB - 2017 - In a parallel world where Germans have occupied England after winning WWII, a British homicide detective works his way through a difficult homicide investigation. **Freevee**

Taboo - 2017 - Tom Hardy stars as James Keziah Delaney, an adventurer who has returned to London to rebuild his late father's shipping empire during the War of 1812. Unfortunately, he's not the only one with an interest in his father's empire. **Crackle**

Thorne - 2010 - This collection of two Thorne movies includes *Scaredy Cat* and *Sleepyhead*. In *Sleepyhead*, DI Thorne (David Morrissey, *Men Behaving Badly*) is in a race against time to find a serial killer who enjoys making unusual attacks on young women. *Scaredy Cat* sees Thorne is working with a new team to tackle a tough double murder case, but it's not long before he's hunting down two different serial killers. **Freevee**

Touching Evil – 1997 to 1999 - Robson Green (*Grantchester*) and Nicola Walker (*River*) star in this series about a police officer with a special ability to detect criminals. **Freevee, Roku**

Trinity – 2009 - Convinced her father's death is somehow linked to prestigious

Trinity College, Charlotte enrolls there to get to the bottom of the mystery. Charles Dance stars as Dr. Edmund Maltravers, and Antonia Bernath plays Charlotte. **Tubi**

Ultimate Force - 2002 to 2007 - Ross Kemp (*EastEnders*) stars in this action series about a Special Air Service team that stops things like anthrax poisonings, assassinations, and bank sieges. **Freevee, Tubi, Pluto**

Ultraviolet - 1998 - Jack Davenport (*Coupling*) stars as DS Michael Colefield, a man whose investigations into the disappearance of a friend lead him into the dark underworld of a paramilitary vampire-hunting organisation. Idris Elba (*Luther*) also appears. **Freevee, Tubi, Crackle, Pluto**

Undeniable - 2014 - This two-part thriller follows the story of a murderer brought to justice by the woman who saw him killing her mother many years earlier. **Tubi**

Underbelly – *Australia* – 2011 to 2013 - Each season of this Australian series focuses on the rise and fall of a different underworld figure. While not all seasons are available on Prime, you can enjoy Series 6, about Leslie Squizzy Taylor, and Series 4, about two Australian crime queens. **Freevee, Roku, Tubi**

Vexed – 2010 to 2012 - A young male and female detective team frustrate each other with their different attitudes and complicated personal lives. **Freevee, Tubi, Crackle, Pluto, Roku**

The Vice – 1999 to 2003 - Inspector Chappel leads the Metropolitan Vice Squad, investigating cases of prostitution and pornography in London. **Freevee**

Vincent - 2005 to 2006 - Vincent is an ex-cop who becomes a private investigator and takes on the tough cases. Ray Winstone (*The Trials of Jimmy Rose*) and Suranne Jones (*Doctor Foster*) star. **Freevee, Roku**

Wolcott – 1981 - Warren Clarke (*Dalziel & Pascoe*) and George Harris (*Casualty*) star in this miniseries about a black policeman promoted to the CID in London's East End. **Freevee, Roku, Tubi**

Wycliffe - 1993 to 1998 - Based on W.J. Burley's novels, this Cornwall-based series features DS Charles Wycliffe, a man who investigates murders with a unique level of determination and accuracy. **Freevee, Roku, Pluto, Tubi**

Dramas

Act of Will - 1989 - Based on the 1986 novel by Barbara Taylor Bradford, this series tells the story of three generations of women. It also features early performances by Elizabeth Hurley and Stuart Milligan (*Jonathan Creek*). **Freevee**

All Saints - *Australia* - 1998 to 2009 - This long-running Australian medical series follows the staff of Ward 17 at the fictional All Saints Western General Hospital. **Tubi, Freevee**

The Ambassador - 1998 - Pauline Collins stars as Ambassador Harriet Smith, British ambassador to Ireland. She's a woman under constant pressure from all angles, and she still struggles with guilt about her husband's death from a car bomb meant for her. **Tubi, Roku**

Anna Karenina - 1977 - Nicola Pagett (*Upstairs Downstairs*) stars as Anna

Karenina in this retelling of Tolstoy's classic tale of family passions in 1870s Russia. **Pluto**

Anzac Girls - *Australia* - 2014 - Heroic women rise to the occasion during the war. **Tubi, Roku**

Archangel - 2006 - Daniel Craig stars as a middle-aged former Oxford historian whose studies in a Moscow Library lead him into the middle of a dark and dramatic plot. This series was produced by the BBC and also includes Gabriel Macht of *Suits* fame. **Pluto, Freevee, Roku, Vudu**

A Thing Called Love - 2004 - After a drunken night out and an episode of infidelity, a Nottingham man decides it's time to settle down and focus on real love. **Freevee**

At Home With the Braithwaites – 2000 to 2003 - With an all-star cast that includes

Amanda Redman, Peter Davison, and Julie Graham, this drama follows the life of Alison Braithwaite and her family. She wins 38 million pounds in the lottery, only to hide it from her family in favour of setting up a secret charity to do good things with the money. **Freevee, Tubi, Roku, Vudu, Pluto**

A Young Doctor's Notebook and Other Stories - 2013 to 2014 - Starring Daniel Radcliffe (of *Harry Potter*), this series is about a young doctor's memories of working in a rural village. **Tubi**

Band of Gold – 1995 to 1997 - Geraldine James stars in this Bradford-based series about desperate streetwalkers trying to make their way through hard times in Northern England. **Freevee**

Being Human – 2008 to 2013 - A vampire, werewolf, and ghost try to coexist as roommates. **Freevee, Tubi, Vudu, Roku, Pluto, Crackle**

The Bench – 2001 to 2002 - This legal drama takes place in a busy magistrates court in Wales. It follows the challenges they face in court, along with the general pressures of working on a high-profile legal team. **Freevee, Tubi**

Blackpool - 2004 - Shortly after Ripley Holden opens his arcade, a man is murdered. The investigation jeopardizes all his big plans. **Pluto, Roku**

The Bleak Old Shop of Stuff - 2012 - As proprietor of The Old Shop of Stuff, Jedrington Secret-Past sells all manner of unusual items. Unfortunately, Malifax Skulkingworm wants to make his life miserable. Robert Webb (*Peep Show*), Stephen Fry (*Kingdom*), and Katherine Parkison (*The IT Crowd*) star. **Pluto**

Bluestone 42 - 2013 to 2015 - This dark comedy follows the lives of British soldiers working in a bomb disposal detachment in Afghanistan. **Pluto**

Body and Soul - 1993 - Kristin Scott Thomas stars as Sister Gabriel, a nun forced to leave the convent when her brother dies and her family needs her help to save their mill. This miniseries is based on Marcell Bernstein's novel. **Freevee, Roku, Tubi**

Bomb Girls - *Canada* - 2012 to 2013 - Set during World War II, BOMB GIRLS tells the remarkable stories of women who risked their lives in a munitions factory to make bombs for the Allied Forces. The series stars Meg Tilly (*The Big Chill*), Jodi Balfour (*Quarry*), Charlotte Hegele (*When Calls the Heart*) and Ali Liebert (*Ten Days in the Valley*). **Freevee, Vudu, Tubi, Crackle**

The Book Group - 2002 to 2003 - When an American woman moves to Glasgow, she starts a book group to make friends. **Freevee, Tubi, Pluto, Roku**

Bramwell – 1995 to 1998 - In 1895, Dr. Eleanor Bramwell does her best to improve public health in Victorian London. **Freevee, Tubi, Roku, Crackle**

Brideshead Revisited - 1981 - Jeremy Irons and Anthony Andrews star in this adaptation of Evelyn Waugh's novel by the same name. *The Telegraph* awarded it the top position in its list of greatest television adaptations of all time. **Roku, Tubi, Vudu, Crackle, Pluto Freevee**

The Brief – 2004 to 2005 - This legal series comes from the creators of *Inspector Morse* and *Kavanagh QC*, and it stars Alan Davies (*Jonathan Creek*) as a criminal lawyer with a penchant for gambling in all areas of his life. **Freevee, Roku, Pluto**

Camomile Lawn – 1991 - Felicity Kendal (*The Good Life*) and Jennifer Ehle (*Pride & Prejudice* '95) star in this series about a family spending the summer of 1939 together, just as World War II begins. **Tubi, Roku, Freevee, Pluto**

Captain Scarlet & the Mysterons – 1967 - This 1960s series followed an unkillable agent in charge of the fight against extraterrestrial terrorists. **Freevee, Tubi**

Care - 2018 - Sheridan Smith (*Gavin & Stacey*) stars as a single mother struggling to raise her two children after a family tragedy. After her husband's departure, she's fully reliant on the childcare her mother Mary (Alison Steadman, also from *Gavin & Stacey*) provides. That all changes when Mary suffers a devastating stroke and develops dementia. **Freevee, Tubi**

Chancer – 1990 to 1991 - Clive Owen plays Stephen Crane, a schemer who takes advantage of opportunities using manipulation and misdirection. As a young business analyst/con man in London, he's called in to help save a struggling motor company. **Freevee, Tubi, Vudu, Roku**

Class - 2016 - This *Doctor Who* spinoff follows the students of Coal Hill Academy, an unlucky bunch forced to contend with all the usual challenges of growing up...along with the possible end of existence. **Tubi**

The Clinic - *Ireland* - 2003 to 2009 - This prime-time medical drama follows the staff of the Clarence Street Clinic in an affluent Dublin neighbourhood. Long-time British TV fans will recognise a number of familiar faces, including Aidan Turner (*Poldark*), Amy Huberman (*Finding Joy*), Lorraine Pilkington (*Monarch of the Glen*), and Chris O'Dowd (*The IT Crowd*). **Tubi**

Clink - 2019 - This drama is set in the fictional BPS Bridewell women's prison, and focuses on the women who live there, and the woman who runs the place. Many have compared it to British prison series *Bad Girls*, and at least one cast member, Alicya Eyo (who plays new Governor Dominique Darby), was also in *Bad Girls*. **Freevee, Tubi**

Cold Feet - 1998 to 2003 - This long-running dramedy follows the lives of six thirtysomething friends living in Manchester, England as they do their best to get their lives sorted. **Freevee, Tubi, Pluto, Roku**

Collision – 2009 - After a multi-car accident, a group of relative strangers see their secrets unfold around that single event that ties them together. This short series was written by Anthony Horowitz of Midsomer Murders fame, and Shetland fans will immediately notice Douglas Henshall as DI John Tolin. **Crackle, Tubi, Roku, Freevee, Pluto**

Crownies – *Australia* – 2011 - Marta Dusseldorp (*A Place to Call Home*) stars in this series about young solicitors who act as primary points of contact for police, witnesses, and victims. **Freevee, Tubi**

Cucumber - 2015 - This series offers a peek inside the lives of gay men in modern Manchester. **Freevee**

Dancing on the Edge – 2013 - In early 1930s London, a black jazz group is coming up in the world. Unfortunately, tragedy strikes before they can fully appreciate their success. This six-episode series features a mixture of British high society and the much uglier underbelly of racism and poverty in London at the time. **Roku, Tubi, Pluto**

Danger Man, aka Secret Agent – 1961 to 1968 - Patrick McGoohan (*The Prisoner*) stars as John Drake, a special operative for NATO specialising in security assignments involving threats to world peace. **Freevee, Roku**

The Darling Buds of May - 1991 to 1993 - Based on the 1958 H.E. Bates novel of the same name, this series is set in rural 1950s Kent and follows the Larkin family as they go about their daily lives. This early 90s dramedy was a breakout role for Welsh actress Catherine Zeta-Jones. **Freevee, Tubi, Roku, Pluto**

The Day of the Triffids - 1981 - Based on John Wyndham's deeply unsettling novel, this miniseries follows along after a comet blinds nearly everyone and an evil plant species begins to take over. **Pluto**

Deep Water - 2019 - Anna Friel (*Marcella*) stars in this miniseries about three mothers struggling with challenging moral and ethical problems. **Pluto, Tubi, Roku**

The Delivery Man – 2015 - Former police officer Matthew begins work as a midwife. He's the first male midwife to hit the unit, and he hopes his new career will give him more satisfaction than his previous work. **Freevee, Roku, Tubi, Pluto**

The Devil's Mistress – 2008 - During the English Civil War, a young woman exploits a country in crisis for her own self-preservation. Also known as *The Devil's Whore*. The follow-up to this series is called *New Worlds*. **Freevee, Tubi, Pluto, Roku**

The Diplomat, aka False Witness - 2009 - When a British diplomat attempts to stop a terrorist trade, he finds himself caught up in a larger plot involving the Scotland Yard and the Russian mafia. **Pluto, Tubi, Roku**

Emmerdale - 1972 to present - Originally known as *Emmerdale Farm*, this series was initially set in a village called Beckindale. In the 90s, the show rebranded and began to focus on the entire village of Emmerdale. Now, storylines are bigger, sexier, and more dramatic than ever. **Freevee, Roku, Vudu, Tubi**

Enemy at the Door – 1978 - This drama focuses on life in the British Channel Islands during the German occupation in WWII. **Freevee, Roku**

Eternal Law - 2012 - In *Eternal Law*, angels live among us and help humans when they're at their most desperate – in this case, the angels are lawyers in the lovely and historic city of York. **Freevee, Tubi**

A Family At War - 1970 - In this classic family saga, we follow the daily life of the

Ashtons, a working-class family in Liverpool during the time of WWII. **Freevee, Tubi**

Flickers – 1980 - During the early days of silent film, a lovable Cockney tries to make his fortune in the industry. **Freevee**

Flood – 2008 - An engineer must rush to save millions of Londoners when floods threaten the city. **Freevee, Tubi, Pluto**

The Fortunes & Misfortunes of Moll Flanders – Daniel Craig stars in this miniseries adaptation of the classic Daniel Defoe novel. **Freevee**

The Fragile Heart - 1996 - Nigel Hawthorne (*Yes Minister*) stars as a brilliant and successful surgeon whose work heading a medical delegation in China forces him into a serious ethical dilemma. **Tubi, Freevee, Pluto**

From There to Here – 2014 - In 1996, England took on Scotland at the European Championship. At the same time, three men are caught up in an IRA explosion at a local pub, changing their lives forever. **Freevee**

Go Girls – *New Zealand* – 2009 to 2013 - Three twentysomething women realize they've made little progress towards their life goals, and vow to achieve their respective goals of being married, rich, and famous within a year. **Freevee, Tubi**

Grafters - 1998 to 1999 - Robson Green (*Grantchester*) and Stephen Tompkinson (*DCI Banks*) star in this series about two brothers who work together as builders and have terribly dysfunctional family lives. **Freevee, Roku, Tubi**

The Grand - 1997 to 1998 - This period drama was written by Russell T Davies (*Doctor Who*) and takes place in 1920s Manchester. It follows the Bannerman family as they re-open The Grand after WWI. **Freevee, Roku, Pluto**

The Great Fire - 2015 - This four-part series is a dramatisation of 1666's Great Fire of London. The fire went on for four days, leaving nearly 90% of the city's population homeless. **Tubi, Roku, Pluto**

The Guilty – 1992 - Michael Kitchen (*Foyle's War*) and Caroline Catz (*Doc Martin*) star in this miniseries in which a young man gets in over his head during a search for his real father. **Freevee**

Hamlet, Prince of Denmark - 1980 - Sir Derek Jacobi stars as Hamlet in this 3.5 hour adaptation of Shakespeare's classic. **Pluto**

Hearts & Bones – 2000 to 2001 - This drama follows a group of 20 and 30-something friends who move to London and transition into proper adult lives. **Freevee, Roku, Vudu, Tubi, Pluto**

Heartbeat - 1992 to 2010 - This Yorkshire-based period crime drama ran for 18 seasons and 372 episodes, focusing on the lives of characters in a small village. Initially, it focused on a central couple, PC Nick Rowan and Dr. Kate Rowan, but as time went on, it branched out to include storylines all over the village. The series is based on the "*Constable*" novels written by Peter N. Walker under the pseudonym Nicholas Rhea. **Freevee, Tubi, Roku**

Homefront - 2012 - This dramatic miniseries follows the lives of the wives and girlfriends of soldiers serving in Afghanistan. **Tubi, Roku, Freevee**

The Hour - 2011 - This period drama takes us behind the scenes during the launch of a new London news programme during the mid-1950s. Ben Whishaw (*Spectre*), Romola Garai (*Emma*), Dominic West (*The Affair*), and Peter Capaldi (*Doctor Who*) are among the cast members. **Pluto, Tubi, Roku**

The House that Dripped Blood - 1971 - This anthology series tells four stories about a haunted home in the UK. Christopher Lee and Peter Cushing are featured. **Tubi, Pluto, Vudu**

The Incredible Journey of Mary Bryant - 2007 - After stealing a woman's picnic, starving Mary Broad is convicted to death. Before realizing that fate, however, she's granted mercy and allowed to live out her life on a penal colony in New South Wales, Australia. **Freevee, Roku, Pluto**

Inside Men - 2012 - This miniseries tells the story of three employees who plan and execute a major heist. **Pluto, Roku**

Island at War – 2004 - This miniseries depicts life under Nazi occupation on St. Gregory Island (a fictionalized version of the Channel Islands – see *The Guernsey Literary and Potato Peel Pie Society* on Netflix for something similar). **Freevee, Roku**

Jackson's Wharf – *New Zealand* – 1999 to 2000 - Set in a fictional coastal town, this series revolves around the rivalry between two brothers: cop Frank and lawyer Ben. **Freevee, Roku, Tubi**

Jane Eyre (1983) - This 1983 miniseries adaptation of Charlotte Brontë's novel sees Zelah Clarke and Timothy Dalton in the leading roles. **Pluto**

Jason and the Argonauts - *United States* - 2000 - Though this was a Turkish-American co-production, you'll likely spot a number of familiar British faces in this adaptation of the classic mythological story of Jason and the Argonauts. Derek Jacobi (*Cadfael, Last Tango in Halifax*) stars alongside Angus Macfadyen (*Braveheart*), Ciarán Hinds (*Above Suspicion*), Adrian Lester (*Hustle*), and Olivia Williams (*Emma*). **Tubi, Pluto, Crackle, Roku**

Jekyll & Hyde - 2015 - Set in 1930s London, this variation of the classic story sees Robert Jekyll living in London, a sensitive young man trying to find his way independent of his foster family. Unfortunately, be begins to feel the influence of a powerful darkness that's outside his control – and he realises his parents had been trying to protect him all along. Young Robert has inherited his grandfather's curse, and he's soon drawn into Hyde's dark and unsavoury world. Tom Bateman stars as Dr. Robert Jekyll. **Tubi, Roku, Pluto**

Jessica – *Australia* – 2003 - In Australia, a young girl is placed in an asylum on false pretenses, and her only hope is a less-than-promising lawyer. **Freevee**

Joe 90 – 1968 - Another marionette-based programme, this one follows the adventures of a pre-teen secret agent who can almost instantly have any skills loaded into his brain. **Freevee, Tubi, Pluto**

K-9 - 2009 - This *Doctor Who* spin-off follows the robot dog companion K-9. **Pluto**

Labyrinth - *Germany/South Africa* - 2012 - This international co-production jumps between modern and medieval France, and includes a cast of mostly British and Irish actors. It follows two women across time in their searches for the Holy Grail. **Freevee, Tubi**

The Last Place on Earth - 1985 - This seven-part serial is based on the book *Scott & Amundsen* by Roland Huntford, and it follows the expeditions of Captain Robert F. Scott and his Norwegian rival Roald Amundsen. **Roku, Tubi, Pluto, Freevee**

Lillie - 1978 - This period drama tells the story of Lillie Langtry, a beautiful woman who managed to woo tons of wealthy men and become a well-known actress. Francesca Annis (*Reckless*) and Peter Egan (*Downton Abbey*) star. **Freevee, Roku**

Lip Service - 2010 to 2012 - This serial drama takes a look at the lives of a group of lesbian women living in Glasgow, Scotland. **Pluto, Tubi, Roku**

Little Dorrit (2008) - Claire Foy and Matthew Macfayden star in this adaptation of Dickens' story of struggle in 1820s London. **Pluto**

Liverpool 1 - 1998 to 1999 - This gritty, Liverpool-based police drama dives into the city's underworld. We follow the vice squad at Bridewell as they fight drug dealers, paeodophiles, pimps, and porn peddlers in this rough-around-the-edges port city. Samantha Womack stars as DC Isobel de Pauli. **Freevee, Tubi, Pluto**

London's Burning - 1988 to 2002 - This series about a London fire brigade began as a TV movie and evolved into a long-running drama series. **Freevee**

Lost in Austen – 2008 - A bored young Pride and Prejudice fan is changed forever when Elizabeth Bennet stumbles into her modern bathroom. This miniseries includes Hugh Bonneville (*Downton Abbey*) as Mr. Bennet, Morven Christie (*Grantchester*) as Jane Bennet, and Jemima Rooper (*Gold Digger*) as lead Amanda Price. **Pluto**

Love/Hate - *Ireland* - 2010 to 2014 - When a young man returns to Dublin after a year away, he wants to stay clean, but circumstances drag him into the world of Irish gangs. **Freevee**

Love Lies Bleeding – 2006 - A self-made millionaire finds himself caught up in a strange and deadly conspiracy after an old friend shows up. **Freevee**

Love My Way - *Australia* - 2004 to 2007 - This Australian drama follows a thirtysomething woman as she attempts to juggle her desires for a rewarding career, a good relationship, and a healthy family life. Claudia Karvan (*Newton's Law*) stars. **Freevee**

Married Single Other - 2010 - Set in Leeds, this series follows a group of young friends trying to figure out their love lives. **Freevee**

McLeod's Daughters - 2002 to 2009 - Two sisters separated as children are reunited when they jointly inherit a ranch in the Australian bush: the independent Claire

McLeod (Lisa Chappell, *Gloss*) and her estranged half-sister, Tess (Bridie Carter, *800 Words*), a stubborn city girl with a drive to change the world. Together, they build an all-female workforce and commit to life at Drovers Run. Nearby, the men of the Ryan family help keep things interesting. **Freevee, Vudu, Roku, Pluto, Tubi, Crackle**

Merlin - 2009 to 2013 - Colin Morgan (*The Fall*) stars as a young Merlin in his days as a mere servant to Prince Arthur of Camelot. In this version of Camelot, magic is banned and Merlin is forced to keep his talent hidden away. **Pluto, Tubi, Roku**

Merlin's Apprentice - *United States/Canada* - 2005 - This miniseries is a follow-up to the 1998 NBC miniseries called *Merlin*, not the longer-running British TV show *Merlin*. The series features British actress Miranda Richardson (*Blackadder*) as The Lady of the Lake, and much of the rest of the cast is from the Commonwealth. **Roku, Tubi, Pluto, Freevee**

MI High - 2007 to 2014 - This young adult spy thriller follows teens who've been recruited to work for the fictional MI9 intelligence agency. *Death in Paradise* fans will recognise Danny John-Jules as one of their handlers. **Pluto**

The Mill - 2013 to 2014 - This period drama is based on the real stories of textile mill workers in 1830s England. Set in Cheshire, it depicts the harsh realities of the Industrial Revolution. **Tubi, Freevee**

Misfits – 2009 to 2013 - A group of young offenders develops superpowers when they're struck by lightning. **Tubi, Freevee, Pluto, Roku**

The Mixer – 1992 - Though technically a French and German production, this series is set in 1930s London. It focuses on a penniless nobleman who robs thieves of their stolen property with the help of his trusty valet. **Freevee**

Mobile – 2007 - Michael Kitchen (*Foyle's War*) appears in this miniseries about a fictional mobile phone conglomerate and a conspiracy tied into a gangland shooting. **Freevee**

Moby Dick – 2011 - This British, Australian, and American co-production tells Herman Melville's story of Captain Ahab and the great white whale, Moby Dick. **Freevee, Roku**

Monarch of the Glen - 2000 to 2005 - Young Archie MacDonald returns home to the Scottish Highlands to take his place as laird and save the family estate. **Tubi, Pluto, Freevee, Roku**

Monroe - 2011 to 2012 - James Nesbitt (*Cold Feet*) stars in this medical drama about a brilliant but quirky neurosurgeon and the talented doctors who work with him. **Freevee**

Mount Royal – *Canada* – 1988 - This drama brings to mind shows like Dallas or Dynasty, but it's set against the cosmopolitan backdrop of 1980s Montreal. **Freevee, Roku**

The Musketeers – 2014 to 2016 - This modern retelling of the classic Dumas novel includes appearances by Peter Capaldi, Tom Burke, and Rupert Everett. **Tubi, Pluto, Roku**

My Uncle Silas – 2001 to 2003 - Based on stories by H.E. Bates, this series follows a boisterous Bedfordshire uncle as he cares for his nephew over the summer in turn-of-the-century England. Stars Sue Johnston and Albert Finney. **Freevee, Roku, Tubi, Pluto**

Neverland – 2011 - In turn-of-the-century London, a couple of pickpockets discover a portal to Neverland. **Freevee**

Neil Gaiman's Neverwhere - 1996 - Based on Neil Gaiman's fantasy novel, this miniseries follows Scotsman Richard Mayhew after he encounters an injured girl named Door on the streets of London. Against his fiancee's wishes, he decides to help the girl, following her into "London Below" and ceasing to exist on the surface. **Pluto**

Nero: The Obscure Face of Power - 2004 - John Simm (*Life on Mars*), Liz Smith (*Lark Rise to Candleford*), and Ian Richardson (*House of Cards*) are among the British actors that appear in this epic British-Italian miniseries about the Roman empire. **Tubi, Roku**

The New Tomorrow - *New Zealand* - 2005 - After a virus kills all the adults, kids are left to take care of themselves. **Freevee, Tubi, Pluto**

The Nightmare Worlds of HG Wells – 2016 - This four-part series dramatizes several of Wells' short stories. **Freevee, Pluto, Tubi**

Northanger Abbey - 1987 - Katharine Schlesinger (*Doctor Who*) stars in this adaptation of Jane Austen's classic parody of Gothic fiction. She plays seventeen-year-old tomboy Catherine Morland, a young woman with a wild imagination and love of Gothic novels. Robert Hardy (*All Creatures Great & Small*) and Peter Firth (*Spooks*) are also among the cast members. **Pluto**

Nothing Trivial – *New Zealand* – 2011 to 2014 - For one group of thirtysomething friends, a weekly trivia night is the only thing that's constant in their lives. **Freevee**

NY-LON - 2004 - This drama follows a transatlantic romance between New York record shop worker Edie (Rashida Jones) and London stock broker Michael (Stephen Moyer). Filming took place in both cities. **Freevee, Tubi, Roku**

The Other Wife - 2012 - This two-part drama tells the story of a woman who finds out about her husband's secret life after he dies in a plane crash. Rupert Everett (*Parade's End*), John Hannah (*McCallum*), Natalia Wörner (*Berlin Station*), and Phyllida Law (*Kingdom*) star. **Tubi**

Our Girl - 2013 to present - This series follows a young woman from East London as she embarks on her career as an army medic. Lacey Turner (*EastEnders*) stars as Molly Dawes, with Michelle Keegan (*Brassic*) entering later as Georgie Lane. **Tubi, Pluto, Freevee, Roku**

Outrageous Fortune – *New Zealand* – 2005 to 2010 - A colourful family of criminals tries to clean up their act. **Freevee, Tubi, Roku**

The Palace – 2008 - A fictional British royal family deals with all manner of upper class problems. **Freevee, Pluto, Roku**

Party Tricks - *Australia* - 2014 - This Australian series follows Kate Ballard (Asher Keddie, *X-Men Origins: Wolverine*), a woman facing her first election for State Premier. Victory seems guaranteed until the opposition brings in a new shock candidate – David McLeod (Rodger Corser, *The Heart Guy*). McLeod is a popular media figure, but more concerning is the fact that she had a secret affair with him years earlier. **Freevee, Tubi**

Peak Practice - 1993 to 2002 - This drama takes place in and around a GP surgery in the fictional town of Cardale in Derbyshire's Peak District (mostly filmed in the real-life village of Crich, also in Derbyshire). The series was popular during its run, lasting for 12 series and 147 episodes. Fair warning, though: it ends on a cliffhanger. Cast members over the years included Kevin Whately (*Lewis*), Amanda Burton (*Silent Witness*), Clive Swift (*Keeping Up Appearances*), and Sarah Parish (*Bancroft*). **Freevee, Tubi, Pluto**

Pinocchio – 2008 - Robbie Kay plays Pinocchio alongside Bob Hoskins as Geppetto. **Freevee, Tubi**

Porterhouse Blue - 1987 - This British comedy classic takes place at the fictional Porterhouse College at Cambridge, where everyone is rich and male and stuck in the past. When the old headmaster dies and a new one comes to power, he attempts to make changes. **Roku, Tubi**

Primeval – 2008 to 2011 - When strange things start happening around England, a professor and his team are forced to capture a variety of unusual creatures from other time periods. Includes Ben Miller (of *Death in Paradise*). **Pluto, Tubi, Crackle**

The Prisoner –1967 - Patrick McGoohan stars in this surprisingly well-aged series about a secret agent who's abducted and taken to a mysterious prison dressed up as an idyllic seaside village. **Freevee, Tubi, Pluto, Roku**

Prisoners' Wives - 2012 to 2013 - In South Yorkshire, four different women struggle to deal with life after men in their lives go to prison. Iain Glen (*Jack Taylor*) fans will be delighted to see him opposite Polly Walker (*Age Before Beauty*). **Tubi, Freevee, Pluto, Freevee**

Proof - *Ireland* - 2004 to 2005 - Orla Brady (*The South Westerlies*) stars alongside Finbar Lynch (*Mind Games*) in this thriller about human smuggling and corrupt European politicians and financiers. **Freevee, Tubi**

QB VII - *United States* - 1974 - Welshman Sir Anthony Hopkins stars in this miniseries about a Polish doctor who escapes from a concentration camp, only to later face accusations of war crimes. **Roku**

Queens: The Virgin & the Martyr - 2017 - This costume drama explores the rivalry between Queens Mary Stuart of Scotland and Elizabeth I of England. **Tubi**

Queer as Folk - 1999 to 2000 - This groundbreaking drama followed the lives and loves of a group of young gay men in Manchester. **Roku, Tubi**

FREE

Robin of Sherwood - 1984 to 1986 - This period adventure has been described by historian Stephen Knight as "the most innovative and influential version of the myth in recent times". Though originally advertised as "family friendly", some conservative groups argued that there was too much violence for children. **Pluto**

Rosamund Pilcher's September - 1996 - In a Highland village, a young woman causes a stir when she returns after once leaving under a cloud of suspicion. **Tubi**

The Royal – 2003 to 2011 - This *Heartbeat* spinoff is set in the 1960s and focuses on an NHS hospital serving the seaside Yorkshire town of Elsinby. **Freevee, Roku**

The Saint - 1962 to 1969 - Roger Moore stars as Simon Templar, a wealthy adventurer who travels the world solving crimes and engaging in all manner of secret agent hijinks. Though the settings are occasionally exotic, nearly every episode was filmed at a studio in Hertfordshire using "blue-screen" technology. The series was based on the Simon Templar novels by Leslie Charteris. **Freevee, Tubi, Roku, Vudu**

Sapphire and Steel – 1979 to 1982 - Interdimensional operatives save the world from evil forces on a regular basis. Stars Joanna Lumley and David McCallum. **Freevee, Tubi**

Sara Dane - *Australia* - 1982 - This miniseries follows a young woman banished from England to Australia for a crime she didn't commit. **Freevee**

Secret Diary of a Call Girl - 2007 to 2011 - Billie Piper (*Doctor Who*) stars as a high-end London call girl. **Tubi, Freevee**

Secret Smile – 2005 - David Tennant stars as a smooth and manipulative spurned lover seeking revenge. **Freevee**

Secret State – 2012 – In a miniseries that will reassure you that the US isn't the only place where government and big business are way too close, Secret State shows a Deputy Prime Minister entangled in an international conspiracy. **Roku, Tubi, Pluto**

Sense and Sensibility (1981) - This seven-part adaptation of Jane Austen's 1811 novel follows the newly widowed and destitute Mrs. Dashwood as she attempts to survive and marry off her three daughters. This adaptation is unique in that it omits the character of Margaret Dashwood. **Pluto**

Shameless - 2004 to 2013 - Before he created *No Offence*, Paul Abbott created *Shameless* - the story of a rough-around-the-edges family living in a Manchester housing estate. It was later adapted into an American series starring William H. Macy. This one contains some strong language and sexual content, so it's not for everyone. **Pluto, Tubi**

Soldier Soldier – 1991 to 1997 - Robson Green and Jerome Flynn star in this military drama about soldiers in the King's Own Fusiliers regiment. **Freevee, Tubi, Roku**

Space: 1999 - 1975 to 1977 - This British-Italian sci-fi series begins when nuclear waste on the far side of the moon explodes, sending both it and its inhabitants out of orbit and into space. At the time it was produced, *Space: 1999* was the most expensive British television series ever produced. Married American actors Martin Landau and Barbara Bain starred. **Vudu, Tubi, Pluto, Freevee, Roku**

Spirited - *Australia* - 2010 to 2011 - This supernatural dramedy stars Claudia Karvan (*Love My Way*) as dentist Suzy, a woman who leaves a loveless marriage and moves into an apartment inhabited by Henry, the ghost of an English rock star from the 1980s. **Freevee**

Stingray – 1964 - This 1960s marionette-based series focused on the missions of the World Aquanaut Security Patrol. **Freevee, Tubi, Pluto**

The Street – 2006 to 2009 - This drama features a number of familiar faces as they go on about their lives in a rough-around-the-edges Northern English town. **Freevee**

Sword of Honour - 2001 - This two-part TV movie sees a young man coming face to face with the realities of British Army life. Daniel Craig stars. **Roku, Tubi, Pluto**

The Syndicate – 2013 - Each season of this series looks at what happens after a group of people wins the lottery. **Freevee**

The Take - 2009 - Shaun Evans (*Endeavour*) and Tom Hardy (*Peaky Blinders*) star in this four-part 2009 miniseries about a man newly released from prison (Hardy) who learns his cousin (Evans) is trying to build a criminal reputation on the back of his reputation. Fun fact: Tom Hardy met Charlotte Riley (*Press*) while filming this series, and the two later married. **Freevee, Roku, Tubi**

A Tale of Two Cities - 1980 - Chris Sarandon and Peter Cushing star in this classic Dickens story of love and sacrifice amidst the French Revolution. **Freevee, Tubi, Roku**

Tales of the Unexpected – 1979 to 1988 - This anthology series features terrifying tales and a variety of well-known Brits, including Roald Dahl and Timothy West (*Great Canal Journeys*). **Freevee**

Teachers - 2001 to 2004 - This dramedy follows the teachers and students in one British school. Andrew Lincoln (*The Walking Dead*) stars, but it's also one of James Corden's earliest appearances. You'll also spot a young Shaun Evans (*Endeavour*) and Mathew Horne (*Gavin & Stacey*). **Tubi, Pluto**

Then There Were Giants - 1994 - John Lithgow, Michael Caine, and Bob Hoskins star in this miniseries about how Roosevelt, Churchill, and Stalin navigated the events of World War II. **Freevee, Tubi**

Thriller – 1973 to 1976 - This long-running 1970s anthology series includes a few supernatural tales, but mostly a lot of suspense and mystery. It also includes a surprising number of American guest stars. **Tubi, Pluto, Freevee**

Thunderbirds – 1966 - This 1960s TV series used marionettes to tell the story of the 21st century Tracy family, who operated a private emergency response service. **Freevee, Roku, Tubi**

The Time of Our Lives - *Australia* - 2013 to 2014 - This drama follows the lives of an extended family in inner-city Melbourne as they build families, pursue careers, and work on their relationships. **Freevee**

To the Ends of the Earth – 2005 - This BBC series is based on William Golding's novels of a sea journey to Australia from England in 1812-13. Benedict Cumberbatch (*Sherlock*) stars. **Freevee, Roku, Vudu, Pluto**

Treasure Island - 2012 - Eddie Izzard stars as Long John Silver in this retelling of the classic Robert Louis Stevenson story. **Pluto**

The Tribe – *New Zealand* – 1999 - In a world where all the adults were killed off by a virus, a group of young people try to stay alive. **Freevee, Tubi, Pluto**

Truckers - 2013 - Stephen Tompkinson (*DCI Banks*) stars in this drama about a group of truck drivers in Nottinghamshire. **Freevee, Tubi, Pluto, Roku**

Two Thousand Acres of Sky - 2001 - Michelle Collins (*EastEnders*) and Paul Kaye (*After Life*) star in this series about two young Londoners who pretend to be married so they can relocate to a Scottish island in need of a young family to keep the local school open. **Freevee**

A Very British Coup - 1988 - When a radical Labour Party politician becomes Prime Minister, he quickly finds he has a lot of enemies. **Tubi, Freevee**

The Village - 2013 to 2014 - Written by Peter Moffat (*Cambridge Spies*), this series is set in a Derbyshire village between 1914 and the mid-1920s. Though originally envisioned as a 42-hour epic televised drama, it lasted just two seasons. It tells the story of life and history through the eyes of Bert Middleton and his fellow villagers. **Roku, Tubi, Pluto**

The War of the Worlds - 2019 - After a meteor touches down in Surrey, humans face a battle for survival against an alien race. The classic HG Wells tale is told through the lens of Amy and George, two people who are in love and ready to embark on a new (though forbidden) life together. **Pluto, Tubi, Plex, Roku**

We'll Meet Again – 1982 - Set in 1943, this series shows us what happens in a small East Anglian town when war-weary Brits play host to American troops. **Freevee**

Where the Heart Is – 1997 to 2004 - Pam Ferris and Sarah Lancashire star in this Yorkshire-based UK drama. It follows a group of dedicated nurses and their community. **Freevee, Roku**

Wild at Heart - 2006 to 2013 - Stephen Tompkinson (*DCI Banks*, *Ballykissangel*) stars in this series about a British veterinarian who takes his family along to South Africa to release an animal back into the wild. When he sees the area and meets pretty game reserve owner Caroline (Hayley Mills), he ultimately decides to stay. **Freevee, Tubi, Pluto, Roku**

The Wild Roses – *Canada* – 2009 - In Alberta, a woman and her daughters own the land an oil firm sits on. **Freevee, Tubi**

William & Mary – 2003 to 2005 - Martin Clunes and Julie Graham star in this dramedy about an odd couple – a woman who welcomes people into the world, and a man who guides them out of it. **Freevee, Roku**

FREE

161

Wired – 2008 - Jodie Whittaker stars alongside Riz Ahmed, Laurence Fox, Charlie Brooks, and Toby Stephens in this suspenseful London-based thriller about a young woman whose high-profile promotion carries unexpected costs. She's quickly pushed into a criminal underworld she had no desire to be a part of. **Freevee, Tubi, Pluto, Roku**

Wonderland – *Australia* – 2014 to 2015 - This relationship drama takes place in a Sydney apartment building where most of the characters live. **Freevee, Tubi**

Young Charlie Chaplin - 1989 - Ian McShane and Twiggy are among the stars of this biographical series about film's first great comedian. **Tubi**

Comedy

50 Ways to Kill Your Mammy - 2014 to 2016 - Irish comedian Baz Ashmawy takes his septuagenarian mother on a thrill-seeking adventure around the world. **Freevee**

8 Out of 10 Cats - 2005 to present - This quirky panel show comes up with unusual questions and then polls the general public to get their take on the issues. **Freevee.**

Ambassadors - 2013 - David Mitchell and Robert Webb (both of *Peep Show*) star in this series about employees at the British embassy in the fictional Asian country of Tazbekistan. **Freevee, Pluto**

Asylum - 2015 - Ben Miller (*Death in Paradise*) plays Daniel Hern, a man stuck in a London embassy with an immature hacker. Both men face extradition if they decide to leave the premises. **Freevee, Tubi, Roku**

At Last the 1948 Show – This sketch series preceded Monty Python's Flying Circus, and included several cast members. **Roku, Tubi**

A Very British Coup - 1988 - When a radical Labour Party politician becomes Prime Minister, he quickly finds he has a lot of enemies. **Freevee, Tubi**

Baroness Von Sketch Show - *Canada* - 2016 to present - This all-female comedy takes a look at the absurdity of our modern lives. **Pluto**

Beaver Falls – 2011 to 2012 - Three British friends decide to have one last crazy summer working in an American summer camp. **Freevee, Tubi**

Big School - 2013 to 2014 - A new French teacher arrives at Greybridge School and gives the long-time Deputy Head of Science second thoughts about resigning. **Pluto, Roku**

Black Books – 2000 to 2004 - Bernard Black runs a bookshop, but he's not particularly good at dealing with customers. **Freevee, Roku, Tubi, Crackle, Pluto**

Blandings – 2013 to 2014 - This fun period comedy follows an eccentric aristocratic family and their crumbling ancestral home. It's based on the writings of PG Wodehouse, and stars Timothy Spall and Jennifer Saunders. **Freevee, Tubi, Pluto**

Bridget & Eamon – 2016 to 2019 - Bridget and Eamon are an Irish couple living with an unknown number of children in the Midlands in the 1980s. **Freevee, Roku, Tubi, Pluto**

Bromwell High - 2005 - This animated comedy follows a group of naughty schoolgirls at an under-funded South London secondary school. **Pluto**

Budgie - 1971 to 1972 - Pop star Adam Faith (*Love Hurts*) starred in this series about a recently released prisoner who always manages to find trouble. The first four episodes were filmed in black and white due to the ITV Colour Strike of late 1970 to early 1971. **Tubi, Roku, Freevee**

Call the Experts - 2020 - Two inexperienced young Londoners go into business offering "any and all services". **Tubi**

Can't Cope, Won't Cope - *Ireland* - 2016 to 2018 - This sitcom follows two young women in Dublin as their lives move in different directions and their friendship begins to dissolve. **Tubi, Roku**

The Colour of Magic - 2009 - This series is based on the *Discworld* series of novels by Terry Pratchett, and features Sean Astin as tourist Twoflower alongside Sir David Jason as wizard Rincewind. When a fire breaks out during Twoflower's holiday, the two flee the city together, beginning an interesting magical journey. **Freevee, Roku, Tubi, Pluto**

Carters Get Rich - 2017 - This British sitcom follows a family after their child develops an app and sells it for £10 million. James van der Beek (*Dawson's Creek*) appears as the wealthy CEO who buys the app and later tries to mentor the young programmer. **Tubi**

Chelmsford 123 - 1988 to 1990 - In AD123, the town of Chelmsford looks a lot different. Jimmy Mulville and Rory McGrath star in this sitcom about the power struggles between the local chieftain and the new Roman governor. **Tubi**

Crims – 2015 - This sitcom follows two young men sent to a young offenders' institution after one got the other involved in a bank robbery without his knowledge. **Freevee, Roku, Tubi**

Doc Martin - 2004 to present - Martin Clunes (*Men Behaving Badly*) stars in this comedy about a brilliant but grumpy London surgeon who suddenly develops a fear of blood. He leaves his high-flying career and takes a post in a Cornish fishing village where he spent holidays as a child with his Aunt Joan. His bad attitude and lack of social skills makes it a challenge to adapt to his new life. **Tubi, Crackle, Vudu, Roku, Pluto**

Doctor at Large - 1971 - Bill Oddie, John Cleese, Graham Clapham, and a number of other British comedy greats were involved in the script for this short-lived series about a group of newly-qualified doctors heading to work. The first six episodes were filmed in black and white due to the ITV Colour Strike of late 1970 to early 1971. **Freevee, Roku, Tubi, Pluto**

Detectorists - 2014 to 2017 - Two quirky friends scan the fields of England with metal detectors, hoping for the big find that will finally let them do the gold dance. **Freevee, Tubi, Pluto, Crackle, Roku**

Drifters – 2013 to 2016 - Meg, Bunny, and Laura share a flat in Leeds and face the ups and downs of post-university life. **Freevee, Roku, Tubi, Pluto, Vudu**

Extras - 2005 to 2007 - Ricky Gervais (*The Office*) stars as an actor reduced to working as an extra, forever making himself look bad as he attempts to get ahead. **Crackle**

Father Ted – 1995 to 1998 - This classic Britcom follows a group of zany priests on the fictional Craggy Island in Ireland. **Freevee, Roku, Tubi, Pluto, Crackle, Vudu**

The Fenn Street Gang – 1971 to 1973 - This spin-off of *Please Sir!* follows the students after they leave school. **Freevee**

French & Saunders - 1987 to 1999 - Dawn French (*Vicar of Dibley*) and Jennifer Saunders (*Absolutely Fabulous*) perform a variety of comedy sketches. **Crackle**

Fresh Meat – 2011 to 2016 - Six young friends go off to university. **Pluto, Roku, Tubi, Crackle**

Friday Night Dinner – 2001 to 2020 - Each Friday night, a Jewish British family meets for dinner. It never goes smoothly (and it always includes a visit from eccentric neighbour Jim). **Roku Channel**

Game On - 1995 to 1998 - Three oddly-matched young adults share a flat in London. **Tubi**

Getting On - 2009 to 2012 - This dark comedy follows the residents and staff in a geriatric ward. **Pluto, Roku**

The Goes Wrong Show - 2019 - This sitcom follows an amateur dramatic society as they perform a variety of short plays in which everything that can go wrong, does go wrong. **Tubi, Roku, Vudu**

Green Wing – 2004 to 2007 - This zany medical comedy features a largely incompetent staff that does very little actual medical work. Among the stars are Tamsin Greig (*Friday Night Dinner*), Mark Heap (*Friday Night Dinner*), Olivia Colman (*Broadchurch*), and Stephen Mangan (*Hang-Ups, Episodes*). **Freevee, Roku, Tubi, Pluto, Crackle**

High & Dry - 2018 - This sitcom follows five people who find themselves trapped together on a remote island after a plane crash. Though four of them want to be rescued, the fifth is not entirely sane. **Tubi**

High Times - 2008 - Set in a Glasgow tower block, this sitcom follows Rab and Jake and their oddball neighbours. **Freevee, Tubi, Pluto**

Him & Her - 2010 to 2013 - This sitcom follows the life of a twenty-something working-class couple. **Pluto**

Horrible Histories – 2009 to present - While designed for children, this amusing educational program is every bit as

FREE

entertaining for adults. The sketches cover different parts of history, but always with a dramatic or funny take on the event. **Freevee**

Kingdom - 2007 to 2009 - Stephen Fry (*QI*) stars as a country solicitor in the small town of Market Shipborough. Working with his trusty secretary Gloria and reasonably capable assistant Lyle, it should be a peaceful life. The only problem? He has a crazy sister and he recently lost his half-brother in mysterious circumstances. Hermione Norris (*Cold Feet*) and Celia Imrie (*Bergerac*) also star. **Pluto, Tubi, Roku**

Laid – *Australia* – 2011 to 2012 - When she realizes all her former lovers are dying in unusual ways, a young woman tries to save the remaining men. **Freevee, Tubi, Roku**

Little Mosque on the Prairie - *Canada* - 2007 to 2012 - When a group of Muslims rent a small Saskatchewan town's Anglican Church to use as a mosque, it becomes clear that everyone will need to make some adjustments. **Freevee, Tubi, Roku**

London Irish – 2013 - This occasionally off-colour comedy focuses on a group of Northern Irish ex-pats in the city of London. The series was written by Lisa McGee, best known as the writer and creator of *Derry Girls*. **Freevee, Tubi, Roku, Pluto**

Love & Marriage - 2013 - Alison Steadman (*Gavin & Stacey*) stars in this series about a woman who's had enough of her own family and moves in with her unconventional sister. **Freevee**

Love Soup - 2006 to 2008 - Tamsin Greig (*Friday Night Dinner*) stars in this sitcom about two people who are perfect for one another, but completely unaware of each other's existence. **Crackle**

Lunch Monkeys – 2009 to 2011 - This comedy focuses on the administrative staff at a British law firm. **Freevee, Tubi, Roku**

Man Stroke Woman – 2005 to 2007 - This British sketch comedy includes appearances by Nick Frost, Daisy Haggard, Nick Burns, and Amanda Abbington. **Pluto, Tubi**

Market Forces – *New Zealand* – 1998 - This satirical comedy revolves around a group of government employees in New Zealand. **Freevee, Roku**

Men Behaving Badly – 1992 to 2014 - Two young male flatmates act like...a couple of young male flatmates. The two explore adult life and love, frequently acting like cads. Stars Martin Clunes (*Doc Martin*), Neil Morrisey (*Line of Duty*), and Caroline Quentin (*Jonathan Creek*). **Freevee, Tubi**

Mind Your Language – 1977 to 1979 - This series follows Jerry Brown, an eager young teacher who takes a job teaching English to students from all over the world. **Freevee**

Mr. Bean - 1992 to 1995 - Bumbling Mr. Bean rarely speaks and has some very peculiar ways of doing things, but it usually works out for him. Rowan Atkinson (*Maigret*) stars as the iconic British character. **Pluto, Tubi, Vudu, Roku**

My Family - 2000 to 2011 - Set in Chiswick, this family sitcom was conceived as a British version of the classic American sitcom. It follows the fictional Harper family, and the central cast includes Robert Lindsay, Zoe Wanamaker, and Kris Marshall. **Pluto**

Not Going Out - 2006 to present - This long-running British comedy favourite follows a young slacker and the people around him. Lee Mack stars, but the series has featured a number of well-known actors including Miranda Hart, Bobby Ball, Hugh Dennis, and Katy Wix. **Pluto**

Only When I Laugh – 1979 to 1982 - A group of patients constantly attempt to one-up each other, driving hospital staff crazy. **Freevee**

Outnumbered - 2007 to 2014 - Hugh Dennis and Claire Skinner star in this sitcom about a couple who are outnumbered by their three children. **Roku, Tubi**

Packed to the Rafters - *Australia* - 2008 to 2013 - This family dramedy follows the Rafter family as they cope with the challenges of modern work, love, and family life. **Tubi, Freevee**

Parents - 2012 - A businesswoman finds out her husband has lost their life savings on the day she loses her job, and they have to go live with her parents. **Freevee, Tubi**

Peep Show – 2003 to 2015 - Two dysfunctional and very different friends share a flat in London and attempt (rather poorly) to grow up. **Freevee, Roku, Tubi, Pluto, Crackle**

Pete vs. Life - 2010 to 2011 - Journalist Pete is a pretty normal guy, except that he's constantly observed and analysed by a

FREE

couple of sports commentators. **Freevee, Roku, Pluto**

Plebs - 2013 to present - Three young men make their way in Ancient Rome. Tom Rosenthal (*Friday Night Dinner*) is among the stars. **Tubi, Freevee, Crackle, Pluto, Roku**

Plus One - 2008 - A man attempts to find a date to an ex's wedding. **Tubi**

Porters - 2017 to present - Simon Porter dreams of being an NHS doctor, but he's just a porter for now. Jo Joyner (*Shakespeare & Hathaway*) and Sanjeev Bhaskar (*Unforgotten*) are among the cast. **Roku**

QI - Stephen Fry stars in this entertaining quiz show where contestants are more amply rewarded for interesting answers. **Tubi** (but enter it as "Q.I." with periods or it won't come up)

Red Dwarf - 1988 to 2020 - In the far future, the last human lives aboard a spaceship with a highly evolved cat-man. **Crackle**

Reggie Perrin - 2009 to 2010 - Martin Clunes stars in this remake of the classic Reginald Perrin stories. **Pluto, Roku**

The Royal Bodyguard - 2011 to 2012 - Follow the exploits of Captain Guy Hubble, a fictional ex-guardsman who now works as a Royal Bodyguard after saving the queen's life on the day of the State Opening of Parliament. Sir David Jason stars. **Tubi, Roku**

Sam's Game - 2001 - This short-lived comedy starred TV presenter Davina McCall as Sam, a single woman living in a London flat over a High Street shop. To help pay the rent, she illegally sublets to Alex (comedian Ed Byrne), an Irishman who seems to find no end of troubles. **Freevee, Tubi, Roku**

Sick of It - 2018 to 2020 - This dark comedy sees Karl Pilkington (An Idiot Abroad) playing a middle-aged taxi driver who discovers a misanthropic inner voice that says all the things he's really thinking. **Roku**

Smack the Pony – 1999 to 2003 - This British sketch comedy features an all-female cast, including Fiona Allen, Doon Mackichan, and Sally Phillips. **Tubi**

Some Girls - 2012 to 2014 - This sitcom follows a group of teenage girls who live in the same South London housing estate. **Roku, Tubi**

Spaced – 1999 to 2001 - To get an affordable flat in North London, two young people pretend to be a couple. Simon Pegg (*Shaun of the Dead*) and Jessica Hynes (*There She Goes*) star. **Freevee, Roku, Tubi**

Spy – 2011 to 2012 - When a man loses his self-esteem and the respect of his loved son, he has to take drastic action to get it back. He applies for a job as a civil servant, but accidentally applies to become a spy. **Tubi, Roku**

Step Dave – *New Zealand* – 2014 to 2015 - A young slacker in New Zealand meets the woman of his dreams, only to realize she's 15 years older than him and comes with major baggage. **Freevee, Roku, Tubi**

Still Standing – *Canada* – 2015 - Comedian Jonny Harris embarks on a road trip around Canada, finding the humor in small and remote towns. **Freevee, Tubi**

Switch – 2012 - In this short-lived supernatural comedy, a group of young witches lives it up in the big city. **Freevee**

Terry Pratchett's Going Postal - 2010 - This adaptation of Pratchett's novel sees con man Moist von Lipwig (Richard Coyle, *Chilling Adventures of Sabrina*) caught by the law and given two choices: suffer a painful death, or take over a derelict post office. Also starring David Suchet (*Poirot*), Charles Dance (*Game of Thrones*), and Claire Foy (*The Crown*). **Freevee, Roku**

Terry Pratchett's Hogfather – 2006 - The Hogfather has gone missing on Hogswatch, and Death must take his place. **Freevee, Tubi, Pluto**

That's My Boy – 1981 to 1986 - Mollie Sugden (*Are You Being Served?*) visits an employment agency and quickly finds herself under the employ of the son she gave up for adoption years earlier. **Freevee**

Threesome - 2011 - A straight couple and their gay friend live together happily until one sordid night changes their lives forever. **Pluto, Roku**

Timewasters - 2017 to 2019 - This sitcom follows a struggling South London jazz band after they find themselves transported to 1920s London. They soon find it's a tough time to be young and black. **Freevee**

Trollied - 2011 to 2018 - Jason Watkins (*McDonald & Dodds*) stars as Gavin Strong, a mild-mannered supermarket manager who is utterly dedicated to his job (even though

FREE

no one around him shares his dedication).
Pluto, Roku

Two's Company – 1975 to 1979 - This sitcom follows the relationship between an American woman and a British gentleman. **Freevee**

Vicious - 2013 to 2016 - Sir Ian McKellen and Sir Derek Jacobi star as an aging gay couple with a hilariously snarky love/hate relationship. The two live together in a Covent Garden flat, entertaining frequent guests, hoping for Freddie's big acting break, and checking to make sure their elderly dog is still alive. **Tubi**

Warren – 2019 - In this offbeat Lancashire-based comedy, Martin Clunes (*Doc Martin*) stars as an impatient and unsuccessful driving instructor who has recently moved in with his partner and her teenage sons. Unfortunately, it wasn't renewed for a second series. **Roku, Freevee, Tubi**

Weirdsister College - 2002 - Set a few years after *The Worst Witch*, Mildred Hubble is now enrolled at the elite Weirdsister College in London. Here, she'll face a whole new set of social and magical challenges. **Freevee, Tubi, Roku**

Westside – *New Zealand* – 2015 to 2017 - This prequel to *Outrageous Fortune* is set between 1974 and 1979, and it recounts stories of crime and passion in Auckland. **Freevee, Roku**

Whites - 2010 - Alan Davies (*Jonathan Creek*) stars as a chef in a posh country hotel. **Tubi, Freevee**

White Van Man - 2011 - Will Mellor (*No Offence*) and Georgia Moffett (*The Bill*) are among the stars of this sitcom about a terribly incompetent handyman and his assistant. **Freevee, Roku, Pluto, Tubi**

Whose Line Is It Anyway? – 1988 to 1999 - While the US has since made its own version, this is the original *Whose Line*, the show where four performers create characters, songs, and scenes on the spot based on prompts they receive from the host or audience. **Roku, Tubi, Pluto**

Would I Lie to You? - 2007 to present - Rob Brydon (*Gavin & Stacey*) hosts this game show in which he and team captains David Mitchell and Lee Mack must figure out whether the celebrity guests are lying to them. **Freevee**

You, Me, & Them - 2013 to 2015 - Anthony Head and Eve Myles star in this sitcom about an age gap romance. **Tubi, Roku**

The Young Person's Guide to Becoming a Rock Star - 1998 - A young Gerard Butler (*P.S. I Love You*) stars in this series about a young Glasgow band trying to get their big break. **Tubi**

Kids & Young Adults

The Adventures of Paddington Bear - 1997 to 2000 - This classic animated series follows the adventures of a Peruvian bear who comes to England as a refugee from an earthquake. The Brown family finds him in Paddington Station and adopts him. **Tubi, Roku**

Atlantis High – *New Zealand* – 2001 - This teen show is set in a school believed to be build atop the Lost City of Atlantis. **Freevee, Vudu, Tubi**

Enid Blyton Adventure Series – *UK/New Zealand* – 1996 - This series sees a group of kids on adventures in New Zealand, and it's based on Enid Blyton's novels. **Freevee, Tubi**

Enid Blyton Secret Series – *UK/New Zealand* – 1997 - This fanciful young adult series is based on author Enid Blyton's much-loved *Secret* novels, and it s a follow-up to the Adventure Series. **Freevee, Tubi**

Gordon the Garden Gnome - 2005 to 2006 - TV gardening presenter Alan Titchmarsh voices the lead role in this animated children's series designed to help kids get interested in gardening. **Tubi, Roku**

Half Moon Investigations – 2009 - This comedy-mystery series for kids was filmed in North Lanarkshire, Scotland, and follows young investigator Fletcher Moon as he goes on stakeouts and undercover operations with his partner, Red Sharkey. **Freevee, Tubi**

The Hive - 2010 to 2014 - This animated British children's series educates kids about early life through the activities of the Bee family. **Tubi, Pluto, Vudu**

In the Night Garden - 2007 to 2009 - This live action preschool series is narrated by Derek Jacobi (*Cadfael*) and follows a group of characters who live in a magical forest. **Tubi, Roku**

Mr. Bean Animated Series - 2002 to 2019 - This animated version of the classic British series as the (rare) voice of Mr. Bean, a childish man who rarely does normal things in the normal way. **Tubi, Pluto, Vudu, Roku**

Mr. Benn - 1971 to 1972 - This vintage animated series follows the daily adventures of Mr. Benn, a British man who lives at 52 Festive Road in London. **Tubi**

Rocket's Island – 2012 to 2015 - Filmed on location on the Isle of Man, this young adult fantasy drama follows foster children who go on magical adventures. **Freevee, Roku, Tubi, Pluto**

Roman Mysteries – 2007 to 2008 - This young adult series follows four kids in Ancient Rome as they go on quests and solve mysteries. **Pluto**

Sarah & Duck - 2013 to 2017 - Narrated by Roger Allam (*Endeavour*), this series follows the adventures of a 7-year-old girl and her duck. **Tubi, Pluto**

Simon's Cat - 2008 to present - This animated web cartoon is based on the work of British animator Simon Tofield, and it follows a hungry cat who will stop at nothing to get more food. **Tubi, Roku, Freevee**

Wibbly Pig - 2009 to 2010 - This British-Canadian co-production is based on a series of children's books by Mick Inkpen, and it walks kids through everyday situations with simple language. **Tubi**

Wizards vs Aliens - 2012 to 2014 - Created by *Doctor Who* screenwriter Russell T. Davies, this series follows a teenage wizard and his bright best friend as they fight against an alien race that has arrived to feast on the magical energy of wizards. **Roku**

Wolfblood - 2012 to 2017 - This British-German young adult series revolves around the lives of "wolfbloods", creatures that look like humans but have the ability to transform into wolves at will - and with the full moon. The series focuses on the challenges of growing up and the added difficulties of occasionally transforming. **Roku, Tubi, Pluto, Freevee**

The Worst Witch (1998) - 1998 to 2001 - This British-Canadian co-production was made by ITV, and it follows a group of young witches at a school for magic. Una Stubbs (*Sherlock*) appears as Miss Bat. **Tubi, Freevee, Roku**

Young Dracula - 2006 to 2014 - Count Dracula is a single father, and he's moved his kids Vlad and Ingrid to modern-day Britain. Now, little Vlad wants nothing more than to be a normal British kid and fit in with his friends. **Freevee, Roku, Tubi, Pluto, Crackle, Vudu**

Yakka Dee - 2007 - Chatterbox Dee encourages kids to learn and say simple words. **Tubi, Pluto**

Nonfiction & Documentary

100% Hotter - 2016 to present - Fashion disasters are stripped clean, then made over to be significantly more attractive. **Pluto**

16 Kids & Counting - 2012 - Though the number of kids has increased in recent years (22 as of 2021), this series follows England's fast-breeding Radford family. See also: *17 Kids & Counting, 18 Kids & Counting, and 19 Kids & Counting.* **Tubi**

999 What's Your Emergency? - 2012 - Take a look at what goes on behind the scenes when you dial 999 (the British equivalent of 911). **Pluto, Tubi, Vudu, Freevee**

Aerial Britain - 2019 - Enjoy aerial scenery from England, Scotland, and Wales. Each episode has a theme - stately homes, work and industry, and spiritual locations. **Tubi**

Air Ambulance ER - 2014 - When terrain and road access make it hard for regular ambulances to reach an area quickly, air ambulance teams step in. **Freevee**

A is for Acid – 2002 - Though technically a movie, this one sees Martin Clunes playing

FREE

John George Haigh, the "Acid Bath Murderer" who killed at least 6 people in 1940s England. Also stars Keeley Hawes. **Freevee, Roku**

The Almost Impossible Game Show - 2015 - Contestants attempt ridiculous challenges - among them, the tiny bike, dizzy hurdle, and "groin croissant". **Tubi, Pluto, Freevee**

A Long Weekend in...With Rory O'Connell - 2019 - Rory O'Connell visits a variety of European cities, with an emphasis on exploring the local food scene in each. **Freevee, Roku Channel**

Animal Park - 2000 to 2018 - Presenters Ben Fogle and Kate Humble go behind the scenes at Longleat Estate and Safari Park in Wiltshire, telling the stories of the people and animals who make the park and home so unique. **Freevee, Pluto**

Animal Rescue School - 2018 - Follow Royal Society for the Prevention of Cruelty to Animals candidates as they progress through the grueling 10-month training process. **Tubi, Roku**

Animal Rescue Squad – 2007 - This series takes us along as professionals work tirelessly to rescue animals from dangerous situations. **Freevee, Roku, Pluto**

Anna's Wild Life – 2011 to 2012 - After buying a wildlife park with no actual experience in caring for wild animals, Anna and Colin are somehow surprised to find it's quite challenging to care for 100+ exotic creatures. **Freevee, Tubi, Pluto, Roku**

Antiques Roadshow - 1979 to present - Filmed at a variety of stately homes around the country, this series allows members of the public to bring in cherished items for expert appraisal. **Freevee, Pluto, Tubi, Crackle**

Art Deco Icons - 2009 - David Heathcote visits four Art Deco icons around Britain – Claridge's, London Transport HQ, Casa Del Rio (an art deco home in Devon), and The Orient Express (as it leaves Victoria Station for Venice). **Tubi, Freevee**

At Your Service – *Ireland* - 2016 - This documentary series takes a look at people who specialise in the lost art of service and hospitality. **Tubi**

Auction - 2010 - This series travels the world, looking at some of the most impressive items up for auction. Episodes feature everything from pop art in New York to the letters of Winston Churchill and a clear-out at Chatsworth. **Roku, Freevee**

The Auction House – 2014 - This series goes behind the scenes at Lots Road Auctions in London, where the hardworking staff does their best to find unusual items for wealthy clients. *Endeavour* fans will recognise Roger Allam's voice doing the narration. **Tubi**

Baby Baby – 1997 - This documentary series follows couples as they bring multiples into the world. **Tubi**

Baby Beauty Queens - 2009 - This series follows three young girls, aged seven through nine, as they enter Britain's very first pre-teen beauty pageant. **Tubi**

Baby Hospital – 2005 - This British reality series takes a look at growing families in a variety of different situations. **Tubi**

The Ballymurphy Precedent - 2018 - In August 1971, 10 apparently innocent Catholics were killed in Northern Ireland by an elite British Parachute Regiment. Officially, the British army claimed (and continues to claim) they were armed terrorists. **Freevee, Tubi**

Banged Up - 2008 - This docuseries follows a unique experiment fronted by British Home Secretary the Rt. Hon David Blunkett. For 10 days, the empty Scarborough Prison is re-opened to take in a group of out of control teenagers. **Freevee**

Battle of Kings: Bannockburn - 2014 - King Robert the Bruce's campaign against King Edward II of England culminated in the Battle of Bannockburn in 1314. This docudrama tells the story. **Freevee**

Bear Grylls: Survival School - 2016 - Adventurer Bear Grylls takes a group of kids out to test their outdoor skills and teach them more about survival. **Freevee, Tubi, Roku**

Bear's Wild Weekends - 2011 - Adventurer Bear Grylls takes celebrity guests outside their comfort zones. **Tubi, Pluto, Freevee**

Ben Earl: Trick Artist - 2013 - British magician Ben Earl shows off his skills in the art of deception. **Pluto, Roku, Tubi**

Best Laid Plans - 2018 - Charlie Luxton and Sophie Morgan team up to help British homeowners taking on particularly ambitious projects. **Freevee, Tubi, Roku**

FREE

Bill's Tasty Weekends - 2010 - Australian restaurateur Bill Granger travels the UK to find quick and delicious recipes. **Pluto**

Booze Britain – 2004 - In this series, the cameras follow hard-drinking Brits in a variety of locations, including Newcastle and Isle of Man. **Tubi**

Boozed Up Brits Abroad – In mainland Europe, British tourists have something of a reputation for being drunk and disorderly. This series follows a number of British tourists as they set out on vacations and stag parties. **Tubi**

Brand New House on a Budget - 2014 - This show features home makeovers on a budget. **Tubi, Roku**

Brick by Brick: Rebuilding Our Past – 2011 - Dan Cruickshank and Charlie Luxton follow along with the reconstruction of historic British buildings. **Tubi, Pluto, Roku**

Bridges that Built London – 2012 - This hour-long special examines London's great bridges. **Freevee**

Britain's Best Bakery - 2012 to 2014 - Experts travel Great Britain in search of the best independent bakeries. **Freevee, Tubi, Pluto**

Britain's Most Historic Towns - Professor Alice Roberts visits some of Britain's most interesting historic towns and cities. **Pluto, Tubi**

British Inland Waterways with John Noakes - 2015 - Presenter John Noakes takes us on a canal boating journey across six British counties. **Freevee, Roku**

British Royal Heritage: The Royal Kingdom - 2004 - This series looks at the historic relationships between the British royals and the ancient kingdoms of Sussex, East Anglia, Wessex, and Kent. **Freevee, Tubi, Roku**

Broadmoor: A History of the Criminally Insane – 2016 - This documentary sees criminology professor David Wilson using interviews and archives to look back at Britain's most dreadful criminals and the asylum that held them. **Tubi**

Brushstrokes: Every Picture Tells a Story – 2013 - British art critic Waldemar Januszczak dives into the stories behind four works from Gauguin, Van Gogh, Cezanne, and Dobson. **Freevee**

Build a New Life in the Country – 2005 to 2010 - This series follows families as they relocate to the countryside and build new lives. **Pluto, Freevee, Tubi**

Build a New Life in the Country Revisits – 2007 - This programme is a follow-up to the last entry on this list, revisiting families who have relocated to the British countryside. **Tubi**

Cars, Cops, & Criminals - 2008 - The Association of Vehicle Crime Intelligence Service fights vehicle-related crimes in Great Britain. **Tubi**

Cash Cab - 2006 - When unsuspecting members of the public are picked up by the cash cab, they get the opportunity to play along and potentially win thousands of pounds. **Tubi**

Castle Builders – 2015 - This series takes a look at what was involved in building the great castles of Europe. **Roku**

Castles and Palaces of Europe - 2013 - Take a closer look at castles in Italy, France, Germany, Portugal, and Southern England. **Freevee, Pluto, Roku**

Catherine's Family Kitchen - 2018 - Chef Catherine Fulvio celebrates traditional Irish cooking. **Tubi, Freevee**

Celebrity Restaurant in Our Living Room - 2010 - This version of *Restaurant in Our Living Room* features celebrities to make things a little more interesting. **Tubi**

Celtic Britain - 2000 - This docuseries takes a look at Celtic history in Scotland, Wales, and elsewhere in the British Isles. **Freevee**

The Celts: Blood, Iron, and Sacrifice with Alice Roberts and Neil Oliver – 2015 - Alice Roberts and Neil Oliver examine the origins of the Celts in this three-part documentary. **Freevee**

Charles I: Downfall of a King - 2019 - Historian Lisa Hilton takes a look at how Charles I lost both the throne and his head. **Freevee**

Charles Dickens: The Man That Asked for More - 2006 - This series offers an in-depth biography of author Charles Dickens. **Tubi, Pluto**

Chef's Protégé - 2014 - This BBC Two series follows three Michelin star chefs as they return to their old schools and choose protégés to train. **Freevee, Tubi**

Children's Hospital - 1993 - The Royal Manchester Children's Hospital opens its

doors to let viewers see the challenging work they do. **Tubi**

Choccywoccydoodah - 2011 - This now-defunct Brighton bakery was once famous for its quirky cakes, attracting a slew of celebrity clients. **Tubi**

Classic Mary Berry - 2018 - In this series, famed British chef Mary Berry travels around England, cooking dishes inspired by the various locales she visits. This includes ethnically-diverse South London, the classic British countryside, and even Port Isaac on the Cornish coast (aka Portwenn from *Doc Martin*). **Freevee, Pluto**

Combat Pilot - 2012 - This BBC series follows a handful of hopeful British pilots as they go through training for the RAF. **Pluto**

Comfort Eating - 2017 - Comedian Nick Helm goes on the road seeking out Britain's best comfort foods in Islington, Camden, Leeds, Brighton, Berlin, St. Albans, Paris, Little Europe, Peckham, Essex, Soho, Wales, Notting Hill, Glasgow, and Borough Market. **Freevee, Tubi, Pluto**

Cook Yourself Thin UK - 2007 - This series focuses on helping Brits lose weight by transforming unhealthy dishes into healthier choices. **Tubi**

The Cops - 2018 - Follow British cops equipped with body cams as they keep peace in Great Britain. **Freevee**

The Crest - 2019 - Two cousins meet for the first time in Ireland to celebrate their shared heritage and love of surfing. **Freevee, Tubi, Vudu, Roku**

Crime Secrets - 2013 - This fascinating series takes a look at the tricks criminals use to separate victims from their money and possessions. **Freevee, Roku, Tubi**

Crimes That Shook Britain - 2008 - This true crime series takes a look at some of the most horrifying crimes committed in Great Britain. **Freevee, Tubi**

Darcey Bussell: Looking for Margot - 2016 - Ballerina Darcey Bussell looks back at the life of Margot Fonteyn. **Tubi**

Dark Ages: An Age of Light - 2012 - Art historian Waldemar Januszczak travels the world to show us art that proves the Dark Ages were a time of great creative achievement. **Roku**

David Jason's Secret Service - 2017 - Sir David Jason hosts this fascinating

docuseries about Britain's history of espionage. **Tubi, Pluto, Roku, Freevee**

David Suchet: In the Footsteps of St. Peter - 2014 - David Suchet (Poirot) hosts this series in which he attempts to learn more about the life of St. Peter. **Tubi**

Dermot Bannon's Incredible Homes - *Ireland* - 2018 - Irish architect Dermot Bannon travels the world to show us a variety of incredible and luxurious homes. **Freevee, Tubi, Roku**

Derren Brown: Hero at 30,000 Feet - 2010 - English mentalist Derren Brown takes a group of average people on an extraordinary journey. **Tubi**

Derren Brown Investigates - 2010 to present - English mentalist Derren Brown takes a look at extraordinary claims around the world. **Pluto, Tubi**

Derren Brown: The Experiments - 2011 - English mentalist Derren Brown uses a variety of tricks and suggestive techniques to convince people they have no fear. **Crackle, Tubi, Pluto**

Derren Brown: The Great Art Robbery - 2013 - English mentalist and illusionist Derren Brown bets a renowned art collector he can steal a valuable painting from under his nose. **Pluto, Tubi**

Design Doctors – *Ireland* – 2018 - This series helps Irish homeowners make their homes more attractive. **Freevee, Tubi**

Designer Darlings – This series follows the Bassi family as they run a business selling expensive clothing to parents who don't mind spending a fortune to keep their kids looking fashionable. **Tubi**

The Detectives –2015 to 2017 - More true crime than mystery, this documentary series follows a special sex crimes unit in the Greater Manchester Police. **Freevee**

The Detectives: Murder on the Streets - 2017 - With unprecedented levels of access, this series takes a look at the activities of Manchester's homicide detectives as they work complex cases over the course of a year. **Pluto, Tubi**

Diana: The New Evidence - 2017 - This documentary takes a look at new evidence in the case of Lady Diana's death. **Freevee, Tubi**

Discovering the World - 2019 - London-based Belgian journalist Pierre Brouwers travels the world, going beyond the typical tourist attractions. Though the British Isles don't factor in too heavily, one episode does visit Scotland. **Tubi**

Distraction - 2003 to 2004 - Comedian Jimmy Carr hosts this game show in which contestants attempt to answer questions while being distracted in a variety of gross, humiliating, or otherwise intense ways. **Pluto**

The Dog Rescuers – 2017 - Alan Davies (*Jonathan Creek, QI*) appears in this series about dog rescues around the UK. **Tubi, Pluto, Roku, Freevee**

Dog School - This series takes a look at what British dogs get up to at day care while their humans are at work. **Tubi, Pluto, Freevee**

Double Your House for Half the Money - 2012 - British families see their homes transformed. **Tubi, Roku**

Drag Queens of London - 2014 - This docuseries follows the fabulous lives of some of London's most talented drag performers. **Pluto**

Drop Zone - 2010 - This British competition show puts contestants through a variety of physical and mental challenges in exotic locations. **Pluto**

Edwardian Farm - 2010 - In this series, the creators of *Victorian Farm* turn their attention to the Edwardian period, looking at the way farming life looked a little more than 100 years ago. **Tubi**

England's Forgotten Queen: The Life and Death of Lady Jane Grey - 2018 - Historian Helen Castor guides us through this documentary series about Lady Jane Grey, the young woman who served as first reigning queen of England. Though she had a reputation as one of the most learned young women of her time, her reign would last just nine days and end in tragedy. **Freevee**

Escape to the Country – 2002 to present - Each episode follows a different set of homebuyers looking to leave crowded areas and find new homes in the British countryside. **Freevee, Roku**

Extreme A&E – 2012 - This graphic series follows top paramedics as they deal with major emergencies around the world - including an episode in London. **Tubi**

Fake or Fortune? - 2011 to present - Philip Mould and Fiona Bruce present this series in which they attempt to authenticate works of art. **Tubi, Roku**

The Farmer's Country Showdown - 2016 - This celebration of rural Britain shows off farming families and the events that show off their hard work. **Tubi**

Farm Fixer – *Ireland* – 2012 - This show visits struggling small farms around Ireland and attempts to help them improve their situations. **Freevee**

Fat Love - 2015 - This series explores the world of feederism and the love of big women. It follows a British man as he ventures to America, citing a lack of sufficiently obese women back home. **Tubi**

Fat Men Can't Hunt - 2008 - Four overweight British men and women are taken to the African desert to try out the hunter-gatherer diet. **Tubi**

Fifth Gear - 2002 to present - This series talks cars, offering reviews, close-up looks, and industry information. **Pluto**

Fill Your House for Free - 2013 - Kirstie Allsopp and her team help people outfit their homes with freecycled goods. **Pluto**

First Homes – This series focuses on first-time homebuyers around the UK, with locations including Glasgow, Chester, and Northampton. **Tubi**

The French Collection - 2016 to present - British bargain hunters visit the antique markets of France in search of deals. **Tubi**

The F Word - 2005 to 2010 - This reality series sees Gordon Ramsay preparing a three-course meal at the F Word Restaurant while interacting with guests and celebrities. **Tubi, Roku, Freevee, Crackle**

Gadget Man - 2012 to 2015 - Richard Ayoade (*The IT Crowd*) takes a look at innovative products designed to make our lives easier. **Pluto, Roku**

Gangs of Britain - 2013 - Martin and Gary Kemp visit a number of cities around Great Britain to investigate their histories with organised crime. **Freevee, Tubi, Pluto, Roku**

Gangsters: Faces of the Underworld - 2009 - This true-crime series takes a look at some of the world's most notorious gangsters. **Pluto, Tubi**

George III: The Genius of the Mad King - 2017 - This documentary takes a look at the newly-unlocked personal papers and documents of King George III. **Freevee, Tubi, Pluto**

George Clarke's Old House New Home - 2016 to present - George Clarke visits historic homes around the UK, helping their owners find ways to adapt them to the needs of modern life. **Pluto**

Getting the Builders In – 2017 - In this series, teams of builders pitch to win a variety of construction and renovation jobs. **Freevee, Roku, Tubi, Pluto**

Glorious Gardens from Above – 2014 - Horticulturist Christine Walkden explores some of Britain's loveliest gardens from a hot air balloon. **Tubi**

Gordon Behind Bars, aka Ramsay Behind Bars - 2012 - Gordon Ramsay goes behind bars to help a group of prisoners start a bakery. **Roku, Tubi, Pluto**

Gordon's Great Escape - 2011 - Gordon Ramsay takes on the challenge of South East Asian cooking. **Tubi, Pluto, Freevee**

Grand Designs – 1999 to present - Kevin McCloud follows people as they attempt to build their dream homes. **Freevee, Tubi**

Grand Tours of the Scottish Islands – 2013 to 2016 - Paul Murton guides us around some of Scotland's most beautiful islands. **Freevee**

Great British Ghosts - 2011 - Presenter Michaela Strachan (*Springwatch*) visits a variety of haunted locations around the UK. **Freevee, Roku**

Great British Menu - 2006 to present - Some of Britain's top chefs compete for a chance to help prepare part of a banquet for some highly-esteemed guests. **Tubi, Pluto, Roku**

Great British Railway Journeys - 2010 to present - Former MP Michael Portillo guides us on journeys around Great Britain's railway system. **Roku**

Great British Waste Menu - 2010 - This series follows some of Britain's top chefs as they look at food waste and create a banquet from discarded food. **Pluto**

Greatest Gardens - 2015 - This series seeks out the best private gardens in Northern Ireland. **Freevee, Tubi**

The Great Gardens of England – 2007 - Alan Titchmarsh takes us on a tour of some of the finest gardens in England. **Freevee**

Grow, Cook, Eat - *Ireland* - 2019 to present - This Irish series is designed for people who don't know much about gardening, but want to try growing something they can eat. **Freevee, Tubi, Roku, Pluto**

Growing Old Disgracefully - 2014 - This series takes a look at British OAPs (old age pensioners) living it up in their later years. **Tubi**

Guy Martin: Industrial Wonders - 2011 - Guy Martin celebrates the best of the Industrial Revolution by getting involved with six large restoration projects. **Pluto**

Guy Martin: Spitfire Restoration - 2014 - Guy Martin helps restore one of the world's most iconic planes. **Pluto**

Guy Martin's Wall of Death - 2016 - British racer Guy Martin takes on his most extreme world record attempt, defying gravity on the largest Wall of Death ever made. **Pluto**

Guy Martin vs. The Robot Car - 2017 - British racer and mechanic Guy Martin takes a closer look at the world of autonomous vehicles. **Pluto, Roku**

Hairy Biker's Asian Adventure - 2014 - The Hairy Bikers embark on a road trip to visit the birthplaces of some of our favourite Asian foods. **Roku**

Hairy Biker's Best of British - 2011 to 2013 - The Hairy Bikers set off to prove that British food is a lot better than its reputation. **Freevee, Pluto**

Hairy Bikers' Chicken & Egg - 2016 - The Hairy Bikers explore some of the world's most-loved recipes involving chicken and eggs. **Crackle, Roku**

The Hairy Bakers: Christmas Special - 2008 - The Hairy Bikers prepare festive Christmas recipes for families who won't be able to spend the holiday together. **Freevee**

Hairy Bikers' Cook Off - 2010 - The Hairy Bikers set off in search of Britain's best family of cooks. **Freevee, Pluto**

Hairy Bikers' Mississippi Adventure - 2012 - The Hairy Bikers take a trip along the Mississippi River in search of good food. **Freevee**

Harry's Arctic Heroes - 2011 - Britain's former working royal Harry takes a team of wounded soldiers to Antarctica. **Pluto**

Helicopter ER - 2016 to present - This series follows the doctors and paramedics of the Yorkshire Air Ambulance. **Tubi, Pluto**

Helicopter Search & Rescue – *Ireland* – 2016 - Watch real-life rescues by some of Ireland's most important rescue services – the Irish Coast Guard, the RNLI, Mountain Rescue Teams, Cork Fire Brigade, and the Irish Naval Services. **Freevee**

Hell's Kitchen – 2004 to 2009 - This series pits prospective chefs against one another, with the winner getting a head chef position. **Pluto, Vudu, Tubi, Crackle, Roku, Freevee**

Henry and Anne: The Lovers Who Changed History - 2014 - Historian Dr. Suzannah Lipscomb tells the story of the love affair between Henry VIII and Anne Boleyn. **Pluto**

Historic Hauntings (aka Castle Ghosts of England) - 1995 - Robert Hardy (*All Creatures Great & Small*) narrates this set of spooky stories about British ghosts. **Freevee, Tubi, Pluto, Roku**

History Cold Case - 2010 to 2011 - Professor Sue Black and her team use modern forensic techniques to examine the remains of the past. **Freevee, Tubi, Pluto**

The History of Britain - 2020 - Sir Tony Robinson offers a look back at some of the most important places and moments in Britain's history. **Tubi, Pluto**

The Hollies: Look Through Any Window - 2011 - This documentary takes a look back at one of the most successful British bands of the 1960s and 70s. **Freevee, Vudu, Tubi, Roku, Pluto**

Home of Fabulous Cakes - 2013 - In this brief series, Leicestershire baker Fiona Cairns shares some of her top cake baking secrets. Royal fans may remember Ms. Cairns as the creator the Duke and Duchess of Cambridge's wedding cake. **Freevee, Tubi, Pluto**

Homes by Design - *Canada* - 2007 - This show takes a look at extraordinary homes around North America and Europe, including some properties in England and Scotland. **Tubi**

Honey, I Bought the House - 2014 to 2017 - Sally Lindsay (*Mount Pleasant*) hosts this series that forces couples to race against time to find the perfect home. **Freevee, Tubi, Pluto, Roku**

The Hotel - 2011 - This hilarious docu-series follows overconfident hotelier Mark Jenkins as he attempts to work in a variety of hotel settings. Hugh Bonneville (*Downtown Abbey*) narrates series two through four. **Tubi**

The House that 100k (GBP) Built – 2016 - Homes are expensive in the UK, but this series takes a look at people building homes from scratch – and on a budget. **Tubi**

The House that 100k Built: Tricks of the Trade – 2015 - This series takes a look at some of the low-cost building and renovation methods used to create really amazing spaces on a budget. **Freevee, Tubi**

How the Victorians Built Britain - 2018 - This docuseries takes a look at the many elements of modern Britain that were put in place by the Victorians. **Tubi, Pluto**

Husbands from Hell - 2019 - Marrying a British man isn't all charming accents and afternoon teas. This series takes a look at some of the worst husbands in the nation. **Tubi**

Idris Elba: King of Speed - 2013 - Idris Elba explores the world's greatest raceways, contemplating the question of why we're so obsessed with speed. In his quest, he travels from London to America to Finland. **Freevee, Tubi, Pluto**

The Impressionists – 2015 - British art critic Waldemar Januszczak travels around the world investigating the great Impressionists. **Freevee**

Inside the Ambulance – 2016 to 2018 - In this series, an ambulance is rigged with cameras to offer a new perspective on the lives of paramedics in the West Midlands region of the UK. **Freevee, Tubi**

Inside the Billionaire's Wardrobe - 2016 - Reggie Yates traces the path from animal to closet, investigating whether "sustainable killing" can clear a buyer's conscience. **Freevee**

Inside the Tower of London: Crimes, Conspiracies, Confessions – 2017 - This four-part series goes into the gruesome history of the Tower of London. **Freevee, Tubi**

Interview with a Murderer - 2016 - Criminologist and professor David Wilson conducts a series of interviews with convicted murderer Bert Spencer. Bert was convicted for the murder of farmer Hubert Wilkes, but he's always been suspected of the brutal killing of a young newspaper delivery boy, Carl Bridgewater. **Freevee**

Inventions that Built Our World - 2017 - This documentary looks at a variety of inventions that shaped history. **Tubi**

The Irish Pub – 2013 - This documentary explores the history and culture of pubs in Ireland. **Freevee, Tubi, Pluto, Roku**

Iron Men - 2017 - This football documentary follows West Ham United as they bid farewell to Boleyn Ground after 112 years. **Tubi, Crackle**

The Island with Bear Grylls - 2014 - Adventurer Bear Grylls puts 13 British men and women on an island to see if they can survive for 6 weeks. **Tubi, Pluto, Freevee**

It Came From Connemara - 2017 - In the mid-1990s, legendary Hollywood producer Roger Corman decided to open a production studio in Ireland. In the following years, he would make numerous feature films using an Irish crew (and a fair bit of funding from the Irish government). This documentary looks at Corman's work in Ireland. **Freevee**

James & Thom's Pizza Pilgrimage – 2017 - James and Thom travel around Italy to learn about pizza, and even sell a bit of it on the street in London. **Tubi**

James Martin: Home Comforts - 2014 to 2016 - British chef James Martin tackles dishes suitable for the typical home cook. **Tubi, Pluto, Roku**

James Martin Home Comforts at Christmas - 2015 - British chef James Martin offers tips for a low-stress Christmas celebration. **Tubi**

James Martin's Mediterranean – 2011 - James Martin shows off what might be the best job in the world as he sails around the Mediterranean and eats...a lot. **Tubi**

James Martin's United Cakes of America – 2012 - British chef James Martin travels the United States in search of cake. **Tubi, Roku, Freevee**

James May's Man Lab – 2010 to 2013 - James May sets out to teach modern men a few useful skills. **Tubi, Roku, Freevee**

James May's Toy Stories – 2009 to 2014 - James May sets out on a mission to get kids away from screens and back to classic toys. **Tubi, Roku, Freevee**

FREE

Jennifer & Joanna: Absolutely Champers - 2017 - The two Absolutely Fabulous stars set off on a road trip to France's Champagne region. **Freevee, Crackle**

The Joy of Techs - 2017 - A technophobe and a technophile join forces to test some of the world's top gadgets. Rather than simply grabbing an iPhone and reviewing it, they put the products into taxing real world situations. They attempt to destroy indestructible gadgets, navigate the French Alps, survive off the grid, and romance women, among other things. **Freevee, Crackle**

Julius Caesar with Mary Beard - 2018 - Historian Mary Beard reveals new insights on Julius Caesar and how he rose to power. **Freevee**

Kate: The Making of a Modern Queen - 2018 - This documentary looks at how Kate Middleton rose from her well-above-average-but-not-noble circumstances to become a much-loved member of the British royal family. **Freevee, Tubi**

Keys to the Castle - 2014 - After four decades in their beloved Scottish castle, a couple prepares to downsize. **Freevee, Tubi**

Kids on the Edge – 2015 - This three-part series takes a look at families involved with the Tavistock Gender Identity Development Service, the NHS's gender identity clinic for children with gender dysphoria. **Tubi**

Killer Roads - 2011 - The UK has a number of dangerous roads that host more than their fair share of devastating accidents. **Tubi**

Kitchen Nightmares - 2007 to 2014 - Acclaimed British chef Gordon Ramsay hosts this series in which he visits struggling American restaurants and spends a week trying to help them be more successful. **Freevee, Vudu, Tubi, Pluto, Crackle, Roku**

Ladette to Lady – 2008 - This series follows a group of young women as they attend a finishing school to teach them proper etiquette, deportment, and elocution. **Tubi**

Landscape Artist of the Year -   Freevee

The Last Days of Anne Boleyn - 2013 - This documentary takes a look at who Anne Boleyn really was, and why her life had to end in such a tragic, violent way. **Freevee**

Laura McKenzie's Traveler - *United States* - 2002 - Though not a British series, this one features three episodes set in the British Isles - London, Dublin, and Edinburgh. **Tubi, Pluto, Vudu**

Legends of King Arthur – 2001 - This series takes a look at the enduring appeal of Arthurian legend. **Freevee, Roku, Tubi, Pluto**

The Life & Crimes of William Palmer – 1998 - Based on a true story, this miniseries tells the story of Victorian doctor and murderer William Palmer. **Freevee**

Life on Marbs - 2015 - This British reality series follows a group of young people who live and party in Marbella, Spain. **Tubi**

Lily Allen: From Riches to Rags - 2011 - This documentary series follows early-2000s pop singer Lily Allen as she and her sister launch a fashion line in London. **Freevee, Tubi**

Living in the Shadow of World War II - 2017 - World War II affected more than just the people on the battlefield. Back home, the war cast a shadow over nearly every aspect of day-to-day life. This series takes a look at the ways the war affected people on the homefront. **Freevee, Tubi, Pluto, Roku**

Living the Tradition: An Enchanting Journey into Old Irish Airs - 2017 - This documentary takes the viewer on a journey into the world of traditional Irish music. **Freevee**

Location, Location, Location - 2000 to present - This popular, long-running British house-hunting show has hosts Kirstie Allsopp and Phil Spencer helping guests find the right house in the right location. **Tubi, Pluto**

Lord Montagu - 2015 - *Upstairs, Downstairs* and *Downton Abbey* fans will enjoy this documentary on one of 20th century England's most controversial aristocrats. **Tubi, Freevee, Vudu, Pluto**

Love London - 2015 - A London taxi driver and a young Londoner travel the city to learn its secrets. **Freevee, Pluto, Roku**

Made Over By - 2016 - This series sees experts transforming the looks of some of the UK's most fashion-challenged residents. **Tubi**

Make Me Perfect - 2006 - This series uses major cosmetic intervention (including surgery) to help people feel better about their appearances and get over past traumas. **Tubi**

Make My Home Bigger – 2015 - Jonnie Irwin follows along as people seek to enlarge their homes. **Tubi, Freevee**

Man & Beast with Martin Clunes – 2012 - Animal lover and actor Martin Clunes sets out to explore the relationship between man and beast. **Freevee**

Manet & the Birth of Impressionism - 2009 - British art critic Waldemar Januszczak takes a look at the difficult artist who is often cited as the father of Impressionism, despite the fact that he intentionally distanced himself from the movement. **Freevee**

The Man Who Cracked the Nazi Code - 2018 - This documentary celebrates the awkward but brilliant man, Alan Turing, whose work helped to make the D-Day landings possible. **Freevee, Pluto, Tubi, Roku**

The Man Who Killed Richard III – 2015 - This documentary attempts to prove that King Richard III was killed by Welshman Sir Rhys ap Thomas of Carew Castle in Pembrokeshire. Richard III's death paved the way for the Tudor monarchy, thus giving Britain its current queen. Many believe we owe ap Thomas a debt of gratitude for that reason, and though a strong case can be made, it's impossible to be 100% certain he was the one who committed the act of regicide. **Freevee, Tubi, Pluto, Roku**

The Many Lovers of Miss Jane Austen - 2011 - Historian Amanda Vickery examines the enduring appeal of Jane Austen's books. **Freevee, Tubi**

Married to a Celebrity – 2017 - This series takes a look at the worst things about being married to a celebrity. **Tubi**

Martin Clunes: A Man and His Dogs - 2010 - Martin Clunes takes a closer look at how and why we've decided to share our lives and homes with dogs. **Freevee, Roku**

Martin Clunes & a Lion Called Mugie – 2014 - Martin Clunes travels to Kenya to meet an orphaned lion cub brought to the Kora National Reserve. **Freevee**

Martin Clunes: Heavy Horsepower – 2010 - *Doc Martin* star Martin Clunes investigates man's relationship with horses. **Freevee, Roku**

FREE

175

Martin Clunes: Last Lemur Standing – 2012 - Martin Clunes travels to the Indian Ocean to find out about the challenges facing lemurs. **Freevee, Roku**

Mary Berry's Absolute Favourites - 2014 to 2015 - Britain's favourite home cook shares some of her absolute favourite recipes from a lifetime of cooking. **Tubi, Pluto**

Mary Berry's Foolproof Cooking – 2015 - Mary Berry offers tips and demonstrations for simple, foolproof recipes anyone can attempt. **Tubi, Pluto**

Masterpiece - 2018 - Alan Titchmarsh stars in this series about antiques enthusiasts attempting to separate trash from treasure. **Tubi**

Meerkat Manor - 2005 to 2008 - This British series follows a family of meerkats in the Kalahari Desert. Though commercially successful, it's worth mentioning that the producers did not intervene when animals were sick or injured, as it was filmed in conjunction with a research project. If you can't watch that sort of thing, skip this series. **Freevee**

Meet the Romans - 2012 - British historian Mary Beard takes us along on a deep dive into what life was like during the Roman Empire. **Freevee, Pluto**

Michael McIntyre: Chat Show - 2014 - Comedian Michael McIntyre takes the interviewer's seat in his own chat show. **Pluto**

Michael McIntyre's Comedy Roadshow - 2009 to 2011 - This series follows Michael McIntyre as he performs in some of the UK and Ireland's most prestigious venues. **Pluto**

Missing Persons Unit - *Australia* - 2006 to 2009 - This series uses footage captured over months of investigative work to show what happens when someone goes missing. **Freevee, Tubi, Pluto**

Modern Irish Food: Kevin Dundon – *Ireland* - 2013 - While there's just one episode of this one, it's great if you want to learn how to tackle oven baked lobster with mustard cream sauce, seared fillet beef and blue cheese salad, apple tart, or potato pie. **Tubi**

Most Haunted - 2002 to present - Yvette Fielding leads this paranormal investigation series that primarily focuses on the UK and Ireland. **Freevee, Tubi, Pluto, Roku**

Mummy's Little Murderer - 2013 - This true crime documentary tells the story of Elliot Turner, a boy whose mother helped him cover it up when he murdered his girlfriend. **Freevee**

Murder Maps - 2015 to present - Host Nicholas Day guides us through a number of shocking murder cases, focusing on the clever police work and early forensics that brought killers to justice. Freevee

My Flat Pack Home – 2010 to 2012 - This British series takes a look at unusual prefab homes and the people who buy them. **Tubi**

My Greatest Dishes - 2019 to present - Professional chefs share the secrets of the best and most important dishes in their lives. **Pluto, Freevee**

My Kitchen Rules UK, aka MKR + UK - 2017 - This British cookery show looks for the UK's top home cooks. **Pluto, Tubi**

My Life on a Plate – 2014 - A variety of notable Brits like Mary Berry and Nigel Havers take a look back at their lives and the foods that accompanied them. **Tubi**

My Pet Shame - 2010 - Joanna Page of *Gavin & Stacey* presents this series about Britain's most embarrassing pet problems. **Tubi**

The Naked Truth - 2019 - Each episode of this series looks at real people and their body issues. **Tubi**

New Scotland Yard Files - 2020 - This reality series talks with real Scotland Yard detectives to hear how they caught killers. **Tubi, Freevee**

Nick Knowles: Original Home Restoration – 2014 - This series follows families as they renovate their historic homes. **Tubi**

Nigel Slater Eating Together – 2014 - Nigel Slater explores modern British home cooking with basics like noodles, soup, custard, and hotpots. **Tubi, Pluto**

Noise Squad - 2011 - This docuseries follows officers who handle everything from loud parties and barking dogs to excessive construction noise. **Tubi**

No Ordinary Party – 2011 - This series takes a look at incredible and extreme parties in the UK – including a puppy party, a naturist party, and a fetish party in Edinburgh. **Tubi**

Older Than Ireland – *Ireland* - 2015 - This series interviews 30 Irish centenarians to build a living history of modern-day Ireland. **Freevee, Tubi, Pluto**

One Born Every Minute - 2010 to 2018 - This popular documentary series highlights the drama of one of the most ordinary things people do – giving birth. Focusing on the human stories behind each situation, you'll see both the highs and lows of a maternity hospital. **Freevee, Tubi**

One Born Every Minute UK: What Happened Next? – 2011 - This series follows up with families from *One Born Every Minute*, seeing how life is going for them after the birth of their children. **Tubi**

One Night Stand with Anne Sibonney - *Canada* - 2014 - This Canadian food and travel series includes an episode in Glasgow. **Freevee**

The Only Way is Essex - 2010 to present - Proof that British TV isn't all thoughtful dramas and intelligent mysteries, this reality series follows a group of wild young people living in Essex. **Pluto, Tubi**

On the Whisky Trail: The History of Scotland's Famous Drink - 2003 - Learn more about the history of whisky and how it's made. **Tubi**

Overcoming Depression: Mind Over Marathon - 2017 - Nick Knowles hosts this two-part series on depression and efforts to raise awareness. **Tubi**

Oxford Street Revealed - 2017 - This series takes a closer look at one of the UK's most famous streets. **Tubi**

Oz & James's Big Wine Adventure - 2007 - Wine expert Oz Clarke takes a wine-tasting trip to France with James May. **Tubi**

Party Wright Around the World - 2014 - Actor Mark Wright leaves the UK to throw wild parties around the world. **Tubi**

Pawnbrokers - 2010 - Take a look inside Uncles, a crazy British pawn shop that's been in business for three generations. **Freevee**

Penelope Keith's Hidden Villages - 2014 to 2016 - Penelope Keith takes us on a tour of the UK's loveliest villages and quirkiest characters. Sometimes called *Britain's Hidden Villages*. **Freevee, Roku, Tubi**

Personal Services Required – 2007 - Two well-off families seek someone to manage their households. **Tubi**

Phil Spencer's Stately Homes - 2016 to present - Property expert Phil Spencer takes us on a tour of some of Britain's finest homes, offering insight into their beauty, history, and cost to maintain. **Pluto**

Posh Neighbours at War – 2016 - This series takes a look at the multi-million pound disputes between London neighbours as they complete noisy building projects in cramped quarters. **Freevee**

Queen Victoria's Letters: A Monarch Unveiled – 2014 - This series takes a look at Queen Victoria through her correspondence and writings. **Freevee, Tubi, Roku**

Quizeum - 2018 - Griff Rhys Jones stars in this quiz show set at some of the most remarkable museums in Britain. **Tubi**

Rachel Allen: All Things Sweet - *Ireland* - 2017 - Irish celebrity chef conquers the perfect desserts for a variety of everyday occasions. **Pluto, Freevee**

Rachel Allen: Easy Meals - *Ireland* - 2011 - Irish chef Rachel Allen focuses on meals anyone can replicate in their homes. **Pluto, Freevee**

Rachel Allen Home Cooking - *Ireland* - Irish chef Rachel Allen goes into the home kitchens of well-known chefs to see how they operate when they're at home. **Tubi**

Rachel Allen's Cake Diaries - *Ireland* - 2012 - Chef Rachel Allen offers tips for cakes of all types. **Pluto, Freevee**

Rachel Allen's Dinner Parties - *Ireland* - 2010 - Irish chef Rachel Allen shows viewers how to throw the perfect dinner party. **Tubi**

Rachel Allen's Everyday Kitchen - 2013 - Rachel Allen conquers simple but delicious meals that are perfect for normal daily life. **Freevee**

Rachel Khoo's Cosmopolitan Cook - 2014 - Rachel Khoo takes us on a culinary tour of some of Europe's most exciting cities. **Pluto, Freevee**

Rachel Khoo's Kitchen Notebook: Melbourne - British chef Rachel Khoo immerses herself in the food culture of Melbourne, Australia. **Pluto, Freevee**

Ramsay's Best Restaurant - 2010 - Gordon Ramsay hosts this reality series which pits some of England's best restaurants against each other. **Tubi, Pluto, Freevee**

The Real Middle Earth - 2007 - Sir Ian Holm narrates this look at the buildings and places that helped shape J.R.R. Tolkien's Middle Earth. **Freevee, Tubi, Pluto**

Remarkable Places to Eat - 2018 - Top chefs in England walk us through some of the best dining experiences in the world, visiting Venice, Edinburgh, Paris, and San Sebastian. **Tubi, Freevee**

Renaissance Unchained – 2015 - British art critic Waldemar Januszczak explores the history of the Renaissance throughout Europe. **Freevee, Pluto**

Restoration Home – 2010 - Actress Caroline Quentin (*Jonathan Creek, Blue Murder*) hosts this series about restoring neglected historic homes around Britain. **Freevee, Tubi, Pluto**

Restoration Man – 2014 - Architect George Clarke helps people all over the UK as they take on ambitious renovations and transformations of unique and historic spaces. **Freevee, Tubi**

Restoration Man Best Builds – 2014 - George Clarke looks at a number of his favourite dramatic building transformations, including old churches, industrial conversions, and towers – including one in the Outer Hebrides islands of Scotland. **Tubi, Freevee**

Retail Therapy – 2011 - This series follows Brits who need serious help as they embark on a shopping excursion. **Tubi**

Richard Wilson On the Road - 2014 - Richard Wilson (*One Foot in the Grave*) takes a trip around Britain with only his antique Shell travel guides to help him. **Pluto, Tubi**

Rick Stein's Long Weekends - 2016 - BBC presenter Rick Stein seeks out the best culinary experiences in a variety of European cities. **Freevee**

Rick Stein's Road to Mexico - 2017 - Inspired by a road trip he did back in the 70s, British chef Rick Stein travels between San Francisco, California and Oaxaca, Mexico. **Freevee, Pluto**

Rick Stein's Secret France - 2019 - Chef Rick Stein travels France in search of the nation's hidden culinary gems. **Freevee**

Rick Stein's Taste of Shanghai - 2016 - Shanghai is one of the largest cities in the world, and much of its cuisine can be unfamiliar to those not raised in China.

Chef Rick Stein takes on some of the best and most unusual dishes the city has to offer. **Freevee**

Rick Stein Tastes the Blues - 2011 - Fascinated by blues music and the dishes featured in its lyrics, chef Rick Stain heads to the Mississippi Delta to learn more. **Freevee**

Rococo Before Bedtime – 2014 - British art historian Waldemar Januszczak examines the history and grandeur of the Rococo period. **Freevee**

Roman Britain: From the Air - 2014 - Christine Bleakley and Dr. Michael Scott check out remnants of Roman Britain that can be seen more clearly from the air than the ground. **Freevee, Tubi**

Rome: The World's First Superpower - 2014 - Larry Lamb (*Gavin & Stacey*) travels to Rome, Pompeii, Sicily, France, and Tunisia to talk to experts and examine the thousand-year story of the Roman Empire. **Freevee, Pluto**

Room to Improve – 2013 to 2019 - Irish architect Dermot Bannan travels Ireland helping people create their dream homes. **Freevee, Tubi**

Ross Kemp: Back on the Frontline - 2011 - Actor Ross Kemp returns to Afghanistan in 2011 to find out how things have changed since 2001 and 9/11. **Freevee, Pluto**

Ross Kemp in Afghanistan - 2007 - Ross Kemp joins his father's old regiment and heads to Afghanistan to serve on the front line. **Pluto**

Ross Kemp: Middle East - 2010 - Ross Kemp offers insight into the conflict in the Middle East. **Pluto**

Ross Kemp: Return to Afghanistan - 2009 - Ross Kemp and his team visit Britain's frontline in Helman province, Afghanistan, offering a view of what it's really like to fight the Taliban. **Freevee, Pluto**

Royal Britain: An Aerial History of the Monarchy - 2013 - Learn a bit of history while getting aerial views of the places the British royals have called home. **Freevee, Tubi**

Rubens: An Extra Large Story - 2015 - British host Waldemar Januszczak takes a look at the world of Sir Peter Paul Rubens. **Freevee**

Rugged Wales - 2014 - Iolo Williams (*Winterwatch*) takes us on an interesting tour of Wales and its landscape. **Pluto**

Salvage Hunters - 2011 to present - Salvage hunter Drew Pritchard criss-crosses the UK in search of incredible finds at sales and antique markets. **Pluto, Crackle**

Saving Poundstretcher - 2017 - This series follows life at Poundstretcher (a UK budget chain) as a new CEO comes in to turn the business around. **Tubi**

Scarlet Woman: The True Story of Mary Magdalene - 2017 - British art historian Waldemar Januszczak takes a look at how faith and art come together in portrayals of Mary Magdalene. **Freevee, Tubi, Pluto**

Scotch: A Golden Dream - 2019 - Jim McEwan takes us on a journey through Scotland to learn more about Scottish whisky. **Tubi, Pluto**

Scotch! The Story of Whisky – 2015 - This short series takes a look at the history and science of the Scottish whisky industry. **Tubi, Roku, Freevee**

Scottish Myths and Legends - 2007 - From the Loch Ness monster to the shape-shifting kelpies, this programme takes a look at the legends of Scotland. **Tubi, Roku**

Secret Dealers - 2010 - Antique dealers go into private homes and bid on items they would like to own, allowing homeowners to choose between sentimental attachment and financial gain. **Pluto, Tubi**

Secret Eaters - 2012 to 2014 - Anna Richardson and her team help overweight people find the problems in their eating habits. **Tubi**

Secret Gardens of England - 2005 - Alan Titchmarsh visits eight lesser-known gardens of England, including Hestercombe House, Brook Cottage, and the Kensington Roof Garden. **Freevee**

The Secret History of the British Garden - 2015 - Gardening expert Monty Don takes a look at the stories behind four of Britain's most famous gardens, digging deep for the details that tell us how British gardens have changed in the last 400 years. **Pluto**

Secret Life of the Holiday Resort - 2017 - If you enjoyed *Benidorm*, you may also enjoy this reality series about what goes on behind the scenes at a Spanish all-inclusive resort that caters to British families. **Tubi**

Secret Nature - 2004 - This series opens up Oxford Scientific Films' archives to take a look at some of the most difficult animals to capture on film. **Freevee, Pluto**

Secrets of the Irish Landscape - *Ireland* - 2018 - Presenter Derek Mooney travels around Ireland and Europe to piece together the history of Ireland's landscape and how it came to be. **Freevee, Tubi**

Secrets of the Stones – 2018 - This two-part series dives into the history and archaeology of Ireland. **Tubi**

Shoreline Detectives - 2017 to 2019 - Dr. Tori Herridge and her team of historians and archaeologists explore seabeds and sand banks to find remnants of Britain's history. **Freevee, Tubi**

Small Animal Hospital - 2014 - This series follows the action at the Small Animal Hospital at the University of Glasgow. **Tubi**

Smart Travels with Rudy Maxa – 2002 to 2006 - Although not exclusively about Great Britain, this series includes episodes in London, the London countryside, Dublin, Ireland's West Coast, Bath, South Wales, Edinburgh, and St. Andrews (not to mention a lot of other lovely cities around the world). **Freevee, Tubi, Vudu**

Snog Marry Avoid? - 2008 - This reality series offers help to women who've gone overboard with things like fake tanner and hair extensions. **Tubi, Freevee**

Snowdonia 1890 - 2010 - Two families live as though they were 19th century farmers on Mount Snowdonia in Wales. **Freevee, Tubi**

Snow Leopards of Leafy London - 2013 - Not far from the city centre, The Cat Survival Trust cares for the largest group of snow leopards outside of Asia. **Tubi, Roku**

Speed with Guy Martin - 2013 to 2016 - Motorcycle racer Guy Martin performs a variety of speed challenges. **Pluto, Tubi**

Spendaholics – 2005 - This show follows a variety of Brits with major spending problems and the debt to match. **Tubi**

The Story of London - 2014 - Six episodes walk us through different sites in London. **Freevee, Pluto, Roku, Tubi**

The Story of Tea - 2007 - Though it's a single-episode documentary, we thought this one worthy of inclusion. It's a great look at the history and appeal of tea. **Vudu, Tubi**

FREE

179

Street Hospital – 2013 - This series follows paramedics as they deal with some of the wildest emergencies the UK has to offer – stag parties gone wrong, births in nightclub basements, and so, so many drunks. **Roku, Tubi**

Streetmate - 2017 - Scarlett Moffatt hits the streets to help singles find matches based on first impressions. **Tubi**

Supersized Hospital – 2010 - This two-part series takes a look at the opening of the New South Glasgow Hospital, the largest medical campus in Western Europe. **Freevee, Tubi**

Supersize vs. Superskinny - 2008 to 2014 - Each episode of this show features an overweight person and an underweight person, offering professional help as they swap diets. **Tubi**

Super Sleuths: Midsomer Murders - 2006 - With interviews from investigative writers, fellow members of the cast and crew, crime writers, and criminologists, this documentary takes a look at how Inspector Barnaby solves crimes on *Midsomer Murders*. **Pluto**

Surgery School - 2010 - Follow the lives of 10 junior doctors setting out as surgical trainees. **Freevee**

This is Personal: The Hunt for the Yorkshire Ripper – 2000 - This short series is a dramatisation of the investigation into the Yorkshire Ripper murders of the 1970s, and the effect it had on the man who led the enquiry. **Freevee**

Time Team - 1994 to 2014 - A group of archaeologists travel around Britain working on different excavation sites. **Freevee, Tubi**

To Build or Not to Build - 2013 - This series follows people who've decided to build their own homes, watching as they learn the necessary skills and battle with their local councils to get the proper permissions. **Tubi**

Tony Robinson's Gods and Monsters – 2011 - Tony Robinson explores the dark corners of Britain's history, including witches, human sacrifice, demons, and sprites. **Tubi**

Total Wipeout - 2009 - This British game show sees guests attempting to complete obstacle courses to win cash prizes. **Tubi, Pluto, Freevee**

Toughest Place to be a... - 2011 to 2013 - This docuseries challenges working or retired professionals to complete their own familiar jobs in more difficult developing world locations. **Pluto**

Tower Block Kids – 2017 - In an attempt to house their poor, the UK built more than 4000 bleak tower blocks. This is the two-part story of kids growing up in those buildings. **Tubi**

Trauma Rescue Squad - 2017 - Britain's toughest medics are ready to go when the worst disasters strike. **Tubi**

Treasure Houses of Britain – 2011 - This series travels around Britain, exploring the history and architecture of some of the island's greatest estates. **Freevee**

The Trial: A Murder in the Family - 2017 - This unique series creates a fictional case in which a university lecturer has been accused of murdering his wife. The legal professionals are real, and the jury consists of members of the public (as opposed to actors). **Freevee**

Trouble in Poundland – 2017 - The modern economy challenges businesses of all types, and this series looks at what Poundland is doing to survive. **Tubi**

Truckers: Eddie Stobart - 2010 to 2014 - Excerpted from *Eddie Stobert: Trucks & Trailers*, this observational series explores the world of Eddie Stobart's UK-based logistics company as they tackle tough and interesting journeys. **Pluto**

Trucking Hell - 2018 to present - This reality series follows men and women who work in the business of cleaning up when big things go wrong. The series includes jack-knifed lorries, broken-down HGVs (heavy goods vehicles), and more. **Tubi, Freevee**

Tudor Feast - 2007 - This documentary sees historians and archaeologists weighing in on what it would be like to host a lavish Christmas dinner suitable for Queen Elizabeth I. **Tubi**

Tudor Monastery Farm - 2013 - Historians and archaeologists look at how the Tudors farmed 500 years ago. **Tubi**

Unreal Estate - *Australia* - 2015 - This series takes a look at some of the most incredible and over-the-top homes in Australia, along with the extravagant folks who live in them. **Tubi, Freevee**

FREE

Valentine Warner's Coast to Coast - 2011 - Valentine Warner takes a trip around the UK to help transform the way we think about fish. **Pluto**

Very British Problems – 2015 to 2016 - This hilarious program interviews celebrities about the cultural quirks of being British. **Freevee, Tubi, Pluto, Roku**

Victorian Farm - 2009 - On the Acton Scott Estate in rural Shropshire, things continue as they might have been more than 100 years ago. *See also: Victorian Farm Christmas Special.* **Tubi**

Walks with My Dog - 2017 - British celebrities like John Nettles and Robert Lindsay explore the countryside with their dogs. **Pluto, Tubi, Freevee, Roku**

Wedding SOS - 2008 - A top British wedding planner helps couples whose weddings seem doomed. **Tubi, Pluto, Freevee, Roku**

Welcome to Mayfair - 2015 - This series takes a look at the people who live in London's Mayfair neighbourhood. **Pluto, Freevee**

What Happens in Sunny Beach - 2013 - This series follows young Brits as they holiday at the seaside resort of Sunny Beach in Bulgaria. **Tubi**

What the Neighbours Did – This show follows Brits as they renovate spaces in their homes. **Tubi**

Whisky: The Islay Edition - 2010 - This special takes a look at what goes on at Islay, the Scottish capital of whisky. **Freevee, Tubi**

Wild Animal Rescue - 2016 - This series follows animal rescue missions to some of the wildest places on the planet. **Tubi, Freevee, Pluto**

William & Kate: A Royal Love Story - 2010 - This documentary follows the courtship and engagement of Will and Kate. **Tubi**

Windsor Castle: After the Fire – 2006 - This one-hour program goes into the aftermath of the fire at Windsor Castle. **Freevee, Tubi, Pluto**

Young, Free, & Single - 2015 - Attractive British singles are paired up in hopes of finding real connections. **Tubi**

Young, Rich, and Househunting – 2010 - This house hunting show focuses exclusively on young buyers at the upper end of the British home market. These lucky buyers are largely financed by relatives. **Tubi**

The Yorkshire Vet - 2015 to present - This engaging series follows the staff of Skeldale Veterinary Centre as they work with the animals. **Tubi, Roku, Pluto, Freevee**

RENEWALS & CANCELLATIONS

This list is based on the best information available at print time (late Feb. 2021). Last-minute changes can always occur, and that's doubly true since the pandemic has had an impact on budgets and availability of cast and crew. The number after the show name represents the season that would/will be next in line.

Shows Not Expected to Return

After Life (4)
No Offence (4)
Scarborough (2)
Wild Bill (2)
Warren (2)
Age Before Beauty (2)
Giri/Haji (2)
Turn Up Charlie (2)
Harlots (4)

Hard Sun (2)
Mum (4)
Still Game (10)
Cold Feet* (10)
Don't Forget the Driver (2)
Friday Night Dinner (7)
Victoria (5)
Lucifer (7)
The Duchess (2)

White Lines (2)
A Discovery of Witches (4)
The Irregulars (2)
Killing Eve (5)
The Crown (6)
Derry Girls (4)
Gentleman Jack (3)
McMafia (2)

Returning for Another Season

Shetland (8)
Vienna Blood (3)
Death in Paradise (12)
Call the Midwife (13)
I Hate Suzie (2)
Life on Mars (3)
Miss Scarlet and the Duke (3)
Grantchester (8)
Balthazar (5)
Sanditon (3)
Dalgliesh (2)
Sister Boniface Mysteries (2)
Brassic (5)
The Great (3)
Whitstable Pearl (2)
The Bay (4)
His Dark Materials (3)
Bridgerton (3)
Gangs of London (2)
All Creatures Great & Small (4)

Ackley Bridge (5)
Ted Lasso (3)
The Capture (2)
Grace (3)
CB Strike (5)
Happy Valley (3)
Trying (3)
Good Omens (2)
Detectorists (Special)
Inside No. 9 (8&9)
The Nevers (1.5)
Doctor Who (14)
Endeavour (9)
Ghosts (4)
Midsomer Murders (23)
The Larkins (2)
Sex Education (4)
Bloodlands (2)
Unforgotten (5)
Around the World in 80 Days (2)

We Are Lady Parts (2)
Vera (12)
Hope Street (2)
Time (2)
World on Fire (2)
Breeders (4)
Crime (2)
Annika (2)
The Curse (2)
Heartstopper (2)
The Cleaner (2)
Guilt (3)
Bad Education (4)

Not Yet Announced

Dead Still (2)
Ms. Fisher's Modern Murder
Mysteries (3)
Black Mirror (6)
Finding Joy (3)
McDonald & Dodds (4)
Flack (3)
Agatha Raisin (5)
Manhunt (3)
Two Doors Down (6)
Queens of Mystery (3)

Shakespeare & Hathaway (5)
Industry (3)
Outlander (8)
We Hunt Together (3)
The Outlaws (3)
London Kills (3)
Good Karma Hospital (5)
Silent Witness (26)
Alex Rider (4)
Cobra (4)
Code 404 (4)

Pennyworth (4)
Bloods (3)
Signora Volpe (2)
Back (3)

*They've ended the current run, but it may return when they hit the next phase of life.

MOVIE NIGHT

While this streaming guide primarily covers television, there are loads of British movies across different streaming services. The main reason we don't issue a guide just for movies is that there are quite a lot of them, and they tend to rotate between services much faster than TV shows.

This "Movie Night" section was a new feature in the spring 2021 edition of the guide, and we hope you find it useful.

Each quarter, we feature 20-30 British films, often (but not always) with some kind of connecting theme. This time around, we're looking at spooky, scary, or generally creepy films for the Halloween season. They're also great for Christmas if you enjoy the British tradition of ghost stories at Christmas.

Mindful that everyone has different preferences and services, we've tried to offer a variety of options across different services and different levels of spookiness.

When we mention "streaming rental or purchase", we mean that you can use outlets like Amazon, Google, or Apple to purchase the rights to stream the film (usually about the same cost as an old-fashioned movie rental, but nobody expects you to rewind).

Creepy & Supernatural Films

Amulet - 2020 - When a homeless ex-soldier is invited to stay with a young woman and her dying mother, begins to suspect their decaying London home is housing something unnatural. Romola Garai (*The Hour*) and Imelda Staunton (*Harry Potter*) are among the stars of this 2020 British supernatural thriller. It's also worth noting that Garai wrote and directed. **Hulu or streaming rental.**

Dead of Night - 1945 - Given that horror films were banned from production in Britain during WWII, this is one of the few produced in the 1940s. It follows an architect who arrives at a country cottage in Kent, only to realise he's seen the other guests in a recurring dream. Despite his unease, they encourage him to stay and they all tell frightening supernatural stories. **Fandor or BFI Player Classics (both available direct or via Amazon Prime).**

Men - 2022 - Rory Kinnear and Jessie Buckley star in this suspenseful film about a woman who decides to holiday alone at an old manor house after the suicide of her husband. Unfortunately, the creepy village is full of frighteningly similar men, and her arrival seems to have awakened something in the forest. **Available for streaming rental or purchase.**

The Rocking Horse Winner - 1949 - Based on DH Lawrence's short story, this film tales the eerie tale of a young boy who learns to pick horse racing winners by riding his own rocking horse. **Criterion or streaming rental.**

The Witches - 1990 - Produced by Jim Henson and starring Anjelica Huston, not everyone remembers the British contributions to this dark fantasy. It follows a young boy who moves to England after the death of his parents, onto to stumble upon a witches convention in Bournemouth. The film includes performances by Rowan Atkinson (Mr. Bean), Brenda Blethyn (Vera), Bill Paterson (Fleabag, Outlander), and Jane Horrocks (Absolutely Fabulous, Trollied). Michael Palin (Monty Python) also has an uncredited role as a witch. **Amazon rental or purchase.**

Blithe Spirit - 2020 - This modern adaptation of Noël Coward's 1941 play is a fun option for those who prefer milder ghost stories, and it includes a dazzling performance by Judi Dench as Madam Arcati. Other stars include Dan Stevens (*Downton Abbey*), Emilia Fox (*Silent Witness*), and Aimee-Ffion Edwards (*Detectorists*). **Showtime or streaming rental.**

The Banishing - 2020 - Jessica Brown Findlay (*Downton Abbey*) stars in this Yorkshire-based haunted house mystery. When a young family moves into a manor house, it's not long before they realise the building has some dark secrets. The film is set in the 1930s and it was filmed around Skipton, North Yorkshire. **AMC+ or Shudder.**

The Little Stranger - 2018 - Set in 1948 England, this movie focuses on a country doctor as he's drawn into the mystery of what's haunting the inhabitants of a decaying country estate. *Luther* fans are sure to notice Ruth Wilson as Caroline Ayres. **Available for streaming rental.**

In Fabric - 2018 - This unusual ghost story is set around a department store during the busy winter sales season, and it follows the path of destruction connected to one red dress. Hayley Squires (*Call the Midwife*), Julian Barratt (*The Mighty Boosh*), and Marianne Jean-Baptiste (*Broadchurch*) all appear. **Showtime or streaming rental.**

A View from a Hill - 2005 - As a continuation of the tradition of telling ghost stories at Christmas, BBC One created the series *A Ghost Story for Christmas*. During the 1970s, they would produce one ghostly movie for Christmas - a tradition they've revived sporadically since 2005. In this one, an archaeologist has a chilling experience after borrowing a pair of binoculars belonging to an outcast historian. **Tubi or BritBox.**

A Warning to the Curious - 1972 - One of the original *A Ghost Story for Christmas* films, this one stars Peter Vaughan (*Chancer*) and Clive Swift (*Keeping Up Appearances*), telling the tale of an archaeologist who searches the coast for a fabled crown that supposedly protects Great Britain from invaders. It's based on the M.R. James story of the same name. **BritBox.**

Harry Price: Ghost Hunter - 2015 - Rafe Spall stars as real-life British ghost hunter Harry Price in this relatively tame ghost story. He's approached on behalf of an MP whose wife's behaviour leads him to believe their home is haunted. Price moves in to investigate, researching the home's history and trying to get to the bottom of the problem. Fans of the recent series *Ghosts* may recognise the Goodwin home as "Button House" from the sitcom. **Peacock, Tubi, Roku, Pluto, or Freevee.**

Altar (aka **The Haunting of Radcliffe House**) - 2015 - A family moves into a beautiful Victorian home with the goal of renovating it, but what they don't realize is that the previous owner murdered his wife - and they may not be entirely alone on the property. **Tubi, Roku, Pluto, or streaming rental.**

The Haunted Hotel - 2021 - This film offers eight tales of ghostly encounters over a number of decades at a fading English hotel. **Amazon Prime Video.**

The House That Dripped Blood - 1971 - This creepy classic anthology film includes stars Peter Cushing, Christopher Lee, and Ingrid Pitt. It sees a Scotland Yard Inspector investigating a haunted mansion while trying to find a missing film star. As the history of the house unfolds, we get four stories of terror and mystery involving previous tenants. **Tubi, Pluto, Shout Factory, Fandor, or streaming rental.**

The Canterville Ghost - 1996 - Sir Patrick Stewart stars as the ghostly Sir Simon de Canterville in this kid-friendly film about a family that moves to England, only to find themselves living in a haunted old castle. Fans of *As Time Goes By* will also notice Joan Sims (who played Madge Hardcastle) playing Mrs. Umney. For a more modern take, you can seek out the 2021 BBC edition (available for streaming rental or purchase only) with Anthony Head (*Ted Lasso*) and Caroline Catz (*Doc Martin*). **Tubi, Pluto, Up Faith Family, Freevee, Roku Channel, or streaming rental.**

Spooky House - 2002 - Though technically American, this family-friendly spook-fest stars Sir Ben Kingsley (*Hugo*) as The Great Zamboni, an illusionist whose wife disappeared after a trick gone wrong. Years later, he's living alone with his pet jaguar, scaring off potential visitors by cultivating a reputation as the local scary fellow. The film was the first unanimous winner at the Chicago International Children's Film Festival. **Amazon Prime Video, Tubi, Roku Channel, or streaming rental.**

Boys from County Hell - 2021 - In the fictional small town of Six Mile Hill in Northern Ireland, a group of construction workers are making way for an unpopular bypass when then accidentally awaken an ancient Irish vampire known as Abhartach. The vampire comes from a real local legend. **AMC+, Shudder, or streaming rental.**

The Turn of the Screw - 1999 - Based on the horror story by Henry James, this film follows a governess who looks after two children at a remote estate and becomes convinced the home is haunted. The 1999 adaptation features Colin Firth and Pam Ferris. **BritBox.**

If that's not to your liking, there's also a 1974 American version starring Lynn Redgrave, or a 2009 adaptation starring Michelle Dockery

(*Downton Abbey*) and Nicola Walker (*Unforgotten*) you can rent or purchase through outlets like Amazon or Google Play. Netflix recently made an American adaptation called *The Haunting of Bly Manor*, too.

Shepherd - 2021 - Tom Hughes (*Victoria*) and Greta Scacchi (*Darby & Joan*) star in this creepy film about a grieving widower who takes a position as shepherd on a remote Scottish island. He's soon doubly tormented by guilt over his wife's death and something much more sinister. **Streaming rental or purchase.**

The Woman in Black - 2012 - Daniel Radcliffe (*Harry Potter*) stars as Arthur Kipps, a widowed lawyer who's been sent to a remote village to deal with the affairs of a recently deceased local eccentric. He soon realises the house is haunted. **Streaming rental.**

The Awakening - 2012 - This supernatural drama stars Rebecca Hall (daughter of Sir Peter Hall) as a ghost hunter investigating the haunting of a Cumbria boys' school shortly after WWI. Imelda Staunton (*Flesh & Blood*) and Dominic West (*John Carter*) also star. **Tubi or streaming rental.**

Nails - 2017 - This British-Irish co-production stars Shauna Macdonald (*Spooks/MI-5*) as a track coach left paralysed after a hit-and-run accident. When she wakes up in the hospital, she's haunted by a ghost who enters her room at night. *QI* fans will recognise comedian Ross Noble in the role of Trevor. **Tubi, Vudu, Peacock, Freevee, or streaming rental.**

The Prestige - 2006 - This period thriller set in Edwardian London was written by Christopher Nolan and follows two rival magicians at the end of the 19th century. Hugh Jackman, Christian Bale, and David Bowie all star. **60 Minutes All Access or streaming rental.**

The Wicker Man - 1973 - This British horror classic has been referred to as "the Citizen Kane of horror movies", and it focuses on a police sergeant sent to an isolated island to investigate the disappearance of a young girl. He's horrified to find that locals claim no knowledge of the girl, and they've abandoned Christianity for Celtic pagan rituals. The movie was filmed around Scotland (including Plockton, which also served as the location for *Hamish Macbeth*), and it had a very small budget due to the production company's precarious financial situation. **MovieSphere, BFI Player Classics, or streaming rental.**

28 Days Later - 2002 - Cillian Murphy (*Peaky Blinders*) and Christopher Eccleston (*Doctor Who*) are among the stars of this post-apocalyptic British horror film. It takes place in London after a deadly virus has been unleashed upon the world, infecting animals and humans and turning them into homicidal maniacs. **HBO Max or streaming rental.**

An American Werewolf in London - 1981 - This classic British-American horror-comedy includes Brits John Woodvine (*The Crown*) and Jenny Agutter (*Call the Midwife*) among the central cast members. It sees two American backpackers trekking across the moors of Yorkshire when they encounter a mysterious and vicious creature. **Amazon Prime Video.**

Ghost Stories - 2017 - Andy Nyman (*Unforgotten*) and Martin Freeman (*Sherlock*) star in this film about a skeptic who devotes his life to uncovering phony psychics and other supernatural con artists. It's all going well until he encounters several cases he can't explain, each of them with connections to his own life. **AMC+, IFC Films Unlimited, or streaming rental.**

Crooked House - 2008 - Not to be confused with the Agatha Christie mystery of the same name (adapted most recently in 2017), this feature-length supernatural anthology was originally broadcast in three 30-minute episodes on BBC Four. Mark Gatiss (*Sherlock, Doctor Who*) wrote and starred. Each of the stories concern the ghostly secrets of the fictional Geap Manor, a demolished Tudor mansion. **Amazon Prime Video.**

CREEPY BRITISH TV

Because a book filled with 2400+ British TV shows (and a few hundred non-British shows) can be a bit intimidating, we often like to include themed show lists to help you explore different topics, regions, and types of shows.

This time, we're focusing on the creepy, spooky, and supernatural.

British TV Shows for Dark & Stormy Nights

Penny Dreadful - This British-American horror series is set in Victorian London and features a number of ghastly, ghoulish characters from 19th century British and Irish fiction. Dracula, Van Helsing, Frankenstein, and Dr. Jekyll all appear. There's also *Penny Dreadful: City of Angels*. It's set in LA so it's not British - but it's a similar type of series. **Showtime.**

The Worst Witch - Mildred Hubble is a just a normal little girl living with her single mother - until a young witch flies into her balcony and changes everything. Suddenly, she's competing for a place at witching school and fending off typical adolescent mean girls who also happen to have magical powers. **Netflix.**

A Discovery of Witches - An academic and reluctant witch finds a mysterious manuscript in Oxford and realizes she can't deny what she is any longer. **Sundance Now or AMC+.**

Spooked: Scotland, aka Haunted Scotland - Presenter Gail Porter leads paranormal investigations into some of Scotland's most haunted locations - including the Edinburgh vaults, Glencoe, Comlongon Castle, Castle Menzies, Dundee's Verdant Works, Culross, Stirling's Old Town Jail, the Tron Theatre in Glasgow, Bannockburn House, and Brodick Castle on the Isle of Arran. **Discovery+.**

The Secret of Crickley Hall - After their young son goes missing, a couple escapes to Crickley Hall in an effort to rebuild their lives.

Though it seems perfect at first, it doesn't take long before strange things begin to happen. Stars Tom Ellis (*Miranda, Lucifer*) and Suranne Jones (*Doctor Foster, Scott & Bailey*). **BritBox, Hulu.**

The Woman in White - After a young man encounters a ghostly woman in white on the side of a darkened road, his life is changed forever. This miniseries is based on the classic mystery novel by Wilkie Collins. **PBS Masterpiece.**

Tony Robinson's Gods & Monsters - Britain's history is full of witch hunts, exorcisms, and human sacrifices. Tony Robinson (*Blackadder*) takes a look at Britain's supernatural past. **Tubi.**

Remember Me - Michael Palin (*Monty Python, Great Railway Journeys*), Jodie Comer (*Killing Eve*), and Mark Addy (*The Syndicate*) star in this sublimely creepy three-part mystery about a series of unfortunate events that unfold around an unhappy pensioner who fakes a fall in order to be moved to a care home. **Tubi, Roku Channel, Pluto, or streaming rental.**

Poirot: Hallowe'en Party - This *Poirot* episode takes place during a village Hallowe'en party, a young girl claims to have seen a murder years earlier...and then she turns up dead in the apple bobbing bucket. You'll find it in season 12, episode 2. **BritBox.**

Great British Ghosts - Presenter Michaela Strachan (*Springwatch*) visits a variety of haunted locations around the UK. Locations include The Mermaid Inn, Michelham Priory in Hailsham, The New Inn in Gloucester, Woodchester Mansion, Prestbury Village, The Red Lion in Colchester, London's Viaduct Tavern, and The Ostrich Inn in Slough. **Freevee, Roku**

Ghosts - This fun and ghostly sitcom sees a young couple, Mike and Alison, moving into a dilapidated country house, only to find it's inhabited by several generations of surly ghosts. It might not be such a problem except that an accident leaves Alison able to see and hear the ghosts. Unfortunately, a sizable mortgage taken out to fund repairs prevents them from moving, so they all have to learn to co-exist. **HBO Max.**

Marley's Ghosts - Sarah Alexander (*Coupling, Jonathan Creek*) stars in this series about a recently widowed woman who can talk to the dead. John Hannah (*Rebus*) and Jo Joyner (*Shakespeare & Hathaway*) also appear. **Streaming purchase or rental.**

The Sister - Bertie Carvel and Russell Tovey star in this paranormal miniseries about a man whose married life is disrupted when a man who was present at his darkest hour shows up on his doorstep. **Hulu.**

Afterlife - Before *The Walking Dead*, Andrew Lincoln starred alongside Lesley Sharp (*Scott & Bailey, Paranoid*) in this British series about a university lecturer who is skeptical about the paranormal until a medium changes his mind. **Streaming rental or purchase.**

The Fades - A teenage boy is haunted by unexplained dreams, then he begins to see dead people haunting the earth. Look out for Tom Ellis (*Miranda, Lucifer*) in the role of Mark. **Hulu, Crackle, Prime Video.**

Chiller - This ghostly anthology series features big name British actors in a variety of self-contained tales. Features Martin Clunes, Nigel Havers, Phyllis Logan, John Simm, and Sophie Ward, among others. **Tubi, Roku Channel, Freevee.**

Randall & Hopkirk (Deceased) - Made once in the 1960s and again in the early 2000s, this series follows two detective partners, one of which is deceased. Only the original 1960s version is available to stream. **Streaming rental or purchase.**

Bedlam - An upscale, newly converted apartment building has a dark and violent past that refuses to stay in the past. **BritBox, Crackle, Roku Channel.**

The Living and the Dead - Psychologist Nathan Appleby inherits a lovely home in a beautiful Somerset valley, but he soon learns it might be haunted. **Streaming rental or purchase.**

Mayday - Mayday is a quaint English village with a strong pagan tradition. Mayday festivities are central to the community, and the May Queen is the highlight of that day - until she disappears. **Freevee.**

Jonathan Creek - Jonathan Creek is a brilliant behind-the-scenes creator of magic tricks who discovers he also has a talent for solving murders. Over the years, he partners with several different co-investigators as he tackles seemingly unsolvable crimes. **BritBox.**

Thriller - Thriller is an anthology show that aired at two separate times during two different decades. The 1960s Thriller featured Boris Karloff as storyteller, and while he was British, the show was filmed in the United States and most of the actors were American. The 1970s version was a British creation, often set around the London commuter belt. Each episode offered a unique and self-contained story, all some variety of thriller (and many with supernatural elements). **Freevee, Pluto.**

Hammer House of Horror - This vintage British anthology series features tales of witches, murders, secret societies, and other generally creepy topics. It's a fun series if you're not too bothered by heaving bosoms. **Peacock, AMC+, Shudder, Pluto, Roku Channel, Freevee, Tubi**.

Tales of the Unexpected - This vintage British anthology series focuses on murder, intrigue, mystery, adventure, and unusual happenings. Timothy West appears in one. **Freevee.**

Magic of Houdini - Alan Davies (of *Jonathan Creek* fame) visits New York and explores the history of famed illusionist Harry Houdini. **Pluto.**

Apparitions - Martin Shaw stars in this series about a priest who's drawn into the darker side of good and evil. **Pluto, Roku Channel, Freevee, Tubi.**

Midwinter of the Spirit - Country Vicar Merrily Watkins consults on a murder investigation and gets on-the-job training in exorcism. **BritBox.**

Intruders - John Simm (*Grace*) stars in this paranormal thriller about a secret society that seeks immortality by taking over the bodies of other people. **Hulu.**

Only on DVD

Looking for more ideas? The shows below are only available via DVD, many of them only in UK-encoded formats. On Amazon, they're often marked as "Playback Region 2".

What does that mean for you? Mainly, it means they won't play on most American DVD players (though some computer DVD drives seem to work). If you want to get into the world of non-US DVDs, you can go to a site like Amazon or eBay and specifically seek out a "region-free" or "all region" DVD player. You can usually find one for $30-50, though there are fancier ones around, too.

A great many shows - especially the older ones - are never released in any format in the US, so they're also great for the British TV fan who's seen everything on the streaming services.

Lizzie Dripping - Back in the early 1970s, the BBC produced this curious show about a young country village girl and her possibly imaginary witch friend.

Beasts - This supernatural anthology series was created in the 1970s and features six self-contained episodes of beastly horror - rats, witches, wolves, and...ghost dolphins terrorize the characters.

Marchlands - Jodie Whittaker (Doctor Who, Broadchurch) stars in this miniseries set in three separate points in time at one haunted house.

Lightfields - Lightfields is a miniseries follow-up to Marchlands, this time starring Dakota Blue Richards (Endeavor, The Golden Compass) and Michael Byrne (Honest, Coronation Street), along with Kris Marshall (Death in Paradise). In the series, a tragic death in 1944 leaves a presence that affects all those who eventually live in the home.

Lightfields - Lightfields is a miniseries follow-up to Marchlands, this time starring Dakota Blue Richards (Endeavor, The Golden Compass) and Michael Byrne (Honest, Coronation Street), along with Kris Marshall (Death in Paradise). In the series, a tragic death in 1944 leaves a presence that affects all those who eventually live in the home.

The Enfield Haunting - Set in 1970s, this miniseries takes you through the very strange events unfolding in an ordinary house in Enfield, North London.

The Ghosts of Motley Hall - This 1970s children's series is about a deserted mansion populated by 5 argumentative ghosts.

The Clifton House Mystery - When a family moves into an old home in Bristol, they discover a secret room with a skeleton. Peter Sallis (Wallace & Gromit, Last of the Summer Wine) appears as a ghost hunter hired to get rid of the spirits in this fun 1970s children's show.

Nobody's House - Two children move into an old Victorian house with their parents, and only they can see its ghostly inhabitant.

Moondial - While staying with an aunt, moonlight falls on a sundial and a little girl is transported back in time. There, she finds two children at the mercy of evil forces.

Robin Redbreast - Another one from the golden age of British TV thrillers, this series follows a young woman who temporarily moves to a remote English villages and becomes pregnant by a handsome gamekeeper. The villagers are a bit strange, and she soon comes to believe they're stopping her from moving home to London.

Children of the Stones - A researcher and his son move to a sleepy English village surrounded by ancient stones, only to realize that all is not as it seems in the town. It's a children's show, but creepy and mature enough for adults to enjoy.

Supernatural - In order to gain entry into a secret society, prospective members must tell a sufficiently frightening story or face death.

Ghostwatch - Back in 1992, this fake documentary saw a TV crew attempting to prove the existence of ghosts in a London home. Unfortunately, a lot of people believed it was real and one child is said to have committed suicide after viewing it. The British Medical Journal reported on PTSD cases in children who watched it. The BBC apologised and never aired it again - but if you look around a bit, you can still find the DVD release available for purchase.

REMEMBERING THE QUEEN

In the days immediately after Queen Elizabeth II's passing, we received numerous emails and private messages asking for viewing recommendations - shows about Queen Elizabeth's life, family, and history. To that end, we've put together this two-part guide in tribute to her many years of devoted service.

In the first section, we look at shows about Queen Elizabeth and her reign - and in the second, we offer suggestions related to her family, recent British history, and the unique array of properties they own.

In addition to what's featured here, you can find coverage of the state funeral, family vigil, and other related events on BritBox.

Tributes & Documentaries About Queen Elizabeth II

The Coronation of Queen Elizabeth II - 2012 - This is where it all began, with Queen Elizabeth's sudden coronation in 1953 after the death of her father. In this 2012 documentary, we get an insider's look at what went on that day. **BritBox.**

A Queen is Crowned - 1953 - Narrated by Sir Laurence Olivier, this feature-length documentary is the only full-length technicolor coverage of the beginning of Queen Elizabeth's historic reign. **BritBox.**

A Tribute to Her Majesty The Queen - 2022 - Featuring interviews with her children and others who've known her, this tribute takes a look back at a long life dedicated to service of crown and country. **BritBox, BBC Select.**

Cameraman to the Queen - 2015 - For nearly 20 years, Peter Wilkinson has enjoyed a high level of royal access as he captured both state events and personal moments. This short documentary is a tribute to the effort, discretion, and loyalty involved in his work. **BritBox, True Royalty.**

Age of Elizabeth - 2022 - This hour-long documentary takes a look back on Queen Elizabeth II's lifetime of public service. **BritBox.**

Elizabeth: The Unseen Queen - 2022 - Though her face is known around the world, few know much about who Queen Elizabeth II really was. With the help of rare footage and body language experts, this documentary attempts to learn more about what she was really like. **BBC Select.**

Fashioning a Monarch - 2022 - This tribute sees presenter Fiona Bruce examining how Queen Elizabeth's style reflected her commitment to duty and country. **BritBox.**

The Queen's Speeches - 2022 - Over a lifetime of service to her country, the Queen has given a great many speeches. This hour-long documentary takes a look back at some of her most iconic public speaking moments. **Streaming rental or purchase.**

Elizabeth: A Portrait in Parts - 2022 - Acclaimed director Roger Mitchell offers a look back at Queen Elizabeth's reign and personal life. **Showtime.**

Her Majesty The Queen's Platinum Jubilee Celebration - 2022 - An all-star cast helps celebrate Queen Elizabeth II's 70 years of service. **BritBox.**

Queen Elizabeth: The Unlikely Queen - 2021 - Queen Elizabeth II wasn't born to lead her country, but she certainly rose to the challenge and delivered on her promise to serve for all her days. **True Royalty.**

The Making of a Queen - 2012 - After her father died, Queen Elizabeth II was unexpectedly thrust into a role for which she hadn't had long to prepare. This documentary looks at how she transformed from young mother and princess to the monarch a nation grew to love. **True Royalty.**

The Queen at War - 2020 - This documentary takes a look at how Queen Elizabeth II served her country during WWII, and how the war shaped her. **PBS Masterpiece, PBS Living.**

The Queen at 90 - 2016 - *Downton Abbey* star Elizabeth McGovern narrates this celebration of Queen Elizabeth's life and reign on her 90th birthday. **Streaming rental or purchase.**

When the Queen Spoke to the Nation - 2022 - This film takes a look at Queen Elizabeth's ever-popular Christmas speeches and some of the other times she addressed her country. **BritBox.**

Gentlemen, The Queen - 1953 - This vintage film provides an up-close look at the early years of Queen Elizabeth II's life, including King George VI's coronation, her first broadcast, the war years, and her engagement. **True Royalty, BritBox.**

Picturing Elizabeth: Her Life in Images - 2022 - Over the course of her lengthy reign, Queen Elizabeth became the most visually represented person in history. From newspapers and souvenirs to stamps and currency, her face has been almost everywhere. **BritBox.**

Elizabeth at 90: A Family Tribute - 2016 - In this feature-length documentary, members of the royal family watch and comment on previously unseen footage of the monarch's life. **Streaming rental or purchase.**

Queen Elizabeth: A Lifetime of Service - 2009 - No monarch in history has completed more foreign visits than Queen Elizabeth II. This hour-long documentary takes a look back at her diplomatic work. **Streaming rental or purchase.**

Elizabeth - 2022 - This nine-part series walks us through every decade of Queen Elizabeth's time on the throne, and it includes interviews with some of those who've known her. **Streaming rental or purchase.**

Queen Elizabeth II: Her Glorious Reign - 2022 - This feature-length documentary takes a look back at how Queen Elizabeth's commitment to duty has transformed her into a figure of strength and dignity throughout the world. **Streaming rental or purchase.**

Elizabeth & Philip: Love, Marriage, & Country - 2021 - For more than 70 years, Queen Elizabeth and Prince Philip maintained a commitment to each other and their country. This documentary looks back on their lives together. **True Royalty.**

Elizabeth: Passions & Pastimes - 2022 - This film celebrates the interests Queen Elizabeth pursued away from her professional duties. **BritBox, BBC Select.**

Queen Elizabeth: Reign Supreme - 1997 - This brief documentary offers a look at Queen Elizabeth's years on the throne - from the perspective of the late 1990s. **True Royalty.**

Days of Majesty - 1993 - This feature-length film celebrates the first 40 years of Queen Elizabeth's reign. **BritBox.**

Our Platinum Queen: 70 Years on the Throne - 2022 - No British monarch has served her people as long as Queen Elizabeth, and this feature-length documentary looks back at her reign from the period just before her Platinum Jubilee. **Streaming rental or purchase.**

The Queen Unseen - 2022 - This brief programme features a variety of photos and footage that haven't been made public in the past. **True Royalty.**

My Years with the Queen - 2021 - Lady Pamela Hicks opens up about her life growing up with the British Royal Family. **BBC Select.**

The Story of Queen Elizabeth II - 2002 - Though a bit older, this programme focuses on Queen Elizabeth's life and reign up to the early twenty-first century. **Freevee.**

Elizabeth I & II: The Golden Queens - 2020 - Though separated by hundreds of years, Queen Elizabeth I and Queen Elizabeth II had a great deal in common. This two-part documentary takes a look at the qualities and circumstances that unite them. **BBC Select.**

The Majestic Life of Queen Elizabeth II - 2012 - Following along from the death of her father through the marriage of Prince William and Catherine, this documentary offers a look at the first 60 years of Queen Elizabeth II's reign. **Amazon Prime Video.**

A Tribute to Her Majesty the Queen - 2022 - This feature-length documentary takes a look back at Queen Elizabeth's life in the aftermath of her death. **BBC Select.**

Queen Elizabeth II: Above All Else - 2022 - Over the course of an hour, this documentary takes a look at the ways in which the world has changed over Queen Elizabeth's reign, and how she has dealt with the challenges she's faced. **Streaming rental or purchase.**

The Royal Beat | Queen Elizabeth: A Tribute - 2022 - This hour-long programme offers a tribute to Queen Elizabeth II in the aftermath of her passing. **True Royalty.**

Other Documentaries About Queen Elizabeth's Family & History

Though not specifically about Queen Elizabeth, these programmes feature a variety of other modern royal topics - her family members, the history surrounding her reign, and the properties where she spent much of her life.

The Queen's Palaces - 2011 - Fiona Bruce hosts this three-part docuseries which takes a closer look at Buckingham Palace, Windsor Castle, and Holyrood House. **BBC Select.**

A Tribute to HRH the Duke of Edinburgh - 2021 - Made shortly after his death in 2021, this hour-long documentary takes a look back at the man who stood beside the Queen throughout her reign. **BBC Select.**

Princess Anne at 70 - 2020 - Hardworking and diligent, Princess Anne has been serving her country in the background for most of her life. In this documentary, she talks about what it means to be a part of "The Firm". **True Royalty.**

Zara and Anne: Like Mother, Like Daughter - 2021 - Like her mother, Queen Elizabeth's daughter Princess Anne has lived a quiet and dignified life of service to her country. This documentary takes a closer look at the much-admired Princess Anne and her daughter. **True Royalty.**

Lucy Worsley's Royal Palace Secrets - 2020 - Respected historian Lucy Worsley offers us a closer look at three of Britain's great royal palaces: the Tower of London, Hampton Court, and Kensington Palace. **PBS Living,**

Inside the Tower of London - 2021 - From Queen Elizabeth I's time in prison to Queen Elizabeth II's 93rd birthday, this docuseries takes a look at the rich history of the Tower of London. **Paramount+.**

Secrets of Royal Travel - 2019 - Nigel Havers offers a peek at the stylish ways the British royal family has travelled over the years. **True Royalty, PBS Living.**

Crown & Country - 1998 - The Queen's son Prince Edward takes us on a tour of some of the most famous landmarks of British history. Over the course of several seasons, he visits places like Hampton Court, Buckingham Palace, the New Forest, Greenwich, and Brighton Pavilion. **Streaming rental or purchase.**

Churchill & the Queen - 2022 - Though Churchill was a skilled strategist and statesman, he's best remembered for the rousing speeches that gave hope to a nation. This documentary looks back at his famous speeches and relationship with Queen Elizabeth II. **Streaming rental or purchase.**

Secrets of the Royal Gardens - 2022 - Over the course of four episodes, enjoy an unusual level of access to a variety of impressive royal gardens. **True Royalty.**

Secrets of Iconic British Estates - 2013 - This docuseries takes us on a tour of some of Britain's most spectacular stately homes, including Althorp, Chatsworth, and Hampton Court. **PBS Masterpiece, PBS Living.**

Prince Edward & Sophie Rhys-Jones - 1999 - Prince Edward married Sophie Rhys-Jones, a commoner who would go on to become one of Queen Elizabeth's closest friends. This programme takes a look at the couple's romance. **True Royalty.**

Kensington Palace: Behind Closed Doors - 2020 - This two-part series offers a behind-the-scenes look at a palace that has been one of the primary homes of royal family members for centuries. **True Royalty.**

The Royal Family Collection - 2015 - In celebration of Queen Elizabeth's 90th birthday, this series of episodes looks back at Queen Elizabeth's life, along with some of the most important moments in her reign and the properties she called home over her years as monarch. Features BBC presenter Fiona Bruce. **Streaming rental or purchase.**

A Royal Guide To... - 2022 - The British royal family is known for following a number of strange traditions. Some royal babies are christened in holy water from the River Jordan. Little boys wear shorts until they're eight. This series takes a look at the reasons behind the rules. **BBC Select.**

The Jubilee Pudding - 2022 - When Queen Elizabeth II celebrated her Platinum Jubilee, a contest was held to determine what would serve as the official pudding of the event. This short documentary takes a look at the lemon Swiss roll and amaretti trifle that ultimately won. **True Royalty.**

Prince Philip: The Plot to Make a King - 2016 - This one-episode special tells the story of what went on behind the scenes when Queen Elizabeth II fell in love with Prince Philip. Royal courtiers felt Philip was rough, poorly educated, and unlikely to make a good or faithful husband. Many disapproved of his German roots and ambitious family. The film takes a look at moves towards the marriage beginning in 1939-40, when the future queen was just 13. **PBS Masterpiece, PBS Documentaries.**

The Windsors at War: Royals on the Front Line - 2018 - This brief programme takes a look at how the Windsors contributed to the war effort during WWII. **True Royalty.**

The Windsors: A Royal Family - 2018 - This four-part series takes a look at four generations of Britain's current royal family. **PBS Masterpiece.**

Royal Paintbox - 2014 - Hosted by Prince Charles himself, this documentary takes a look at rarely seen art created by British royals from the past and present. **PBS Masterpiece.**

The Earthshot Prize: Repairing Our Planet - 2021 - Along with the Queen's close friend Sir David Attenborough, Prince William helps to seek out those who've come up with solutions for the world's environmental woes. **Discovery+.**

Inside Balmoral - 2017 - More than just a royal home in Scotland, Balmoral is said to be one of the Queen's favourite places in the entire world - and now, sadly, we know it to be the place she chose to spend her last days. This three-part docuseries looks back at how Balmoral helped to shape Queen Elizabeth's life. **True Royalty.**

The Queen's Castle: Four Season - 2016 - This documentary follows along through a year in the life of the world's oldest inhabited castle. **True Royalty.**

The Queen & Charles: Mother & Son - 2020 - This short documentary takes a look at some of the most important moments in the shared lives of Queen Elizabeth II and her son, now King Charles III. **True Royalty.**

A Very Royal Christmas: Secrets of Sandringham - 2021 - Each year, Queen Elizabeth and her family would converge upon Sandringham Estate to celebrate the Christmas holiday. This documentary takes a look at what Christmas there is like. **True Royalty.**

Prince Charles at 70 - 2019 - This documentary takes a look at Prince Charles' ongoing charity work and his future role (now present) as monarch of the United Kingdom. **PBS Masterpiece.**

Charles: Fifty Years a Prince - 2019 - The now King Charles was fortunate to enjoy more than 70 years with his mother in his life - as well as decades to prepare for the job that would eventually come to define his life. This short documentary follows along as he completes one of his annual tours of Wales. **True Royalty.**

Prince Charles: The Making of a King - 2022 - King Charles spent more time as heir to the British throne than anyone in history, and unlike his mother, he knew he was destined to be king from birth. This documentary takes a look back at how that destiny shaped his life. **Streaming rental or purchase.**

Queen and Country - 2012 - Trevor McDonald walks us through some of the British monarchy's greatest traditions and institutions. **PBS Masterpiece.**

A Century of the Queen Mother: 100 Years in 100 Minutes - 2000 - This documentary takes a look at Queen Elizabeth's mother's long and interesting life. **Amazon Prime Video.**

FOOTLOOSE TRAVEL VIDEOS

If you watched and enjoyed Rick Steves or Samantha Brown, you'll definitely want to check out the *Footloose* travel videos from Dave and Debra Rixon. Like the others, David and Debra make travel videos about various European destinations – but unlike the others, their videos are delightfully in-depth. Instead of a 20-30 minute overview, they typically offer 1.5-2.5 hours of scenery and commentary.

Amazon's Prime Video recently removed almost all small/independent filmmakers from the free Prime Video catalogue, so we put together this guide to help you find all their titles. Be sure to keep an eye on their YouTube Channel, too, as they've been adding some of their videos over there.

To watch shows on Vimeo, you can use your tablet/phone/computer, but you can also use the Vimeo app on the Roku and similar streaming devices.

Available for Purchase or Rental on Amazon

Footloose in the Cotswolds, Part 2 – UK filmmakers Debra and David Rixon visit Cheltenham, Painswick, Tetbury, and the City of Bath.

Footloose in London: All the Best Sights of our Capital – UK filmmakers Debra and David Rixon offer budget-minded tips for visiting London and viewing its best sites.

Footloose in Oxford & York - Filmed in between lockdowns in 2020, this video takes us on a tour of the Roman city of York, the famed university city of Oxford, and some of the surrounding areas.

Footloose in Austria: Hallstatt & Salzburg – In this video, David and Debra visit Hallstatt in the Salzkammergut region of Austria, taking scenic walks in the mountains, meeting locals, and then heading into the historic city of Salzburg.

Footloose in the Austrian Tyrol – This four-part tour kicks off with scenes from Kitzbühel during the AlpenRallye classic car event, followed by a steam train journey from Mayrhofen to Pertisau, a modern rail journey through the Inn Valley, and a trip to Innsbruck and the Stubai Valley.

Footloose in Switzerland – This two-part tour of Switzerland includes a trip to the Bernese Oberland, full of meadow walks and waterfalls, along with a visit to Lucerne, the beautiful city on the lake.

Footloose in Bavaria – This feature-length video tour takes you through some of Germany's best preserved medieval towns and castles, including Schloss Neuschwanstein, the castle that inspired Walt Disney.

Footloose in Italy: Cinque Terre & Venice – In this video, Dave and Debra take a late summer trip to Italy, following the coastal path of the Cinque Terre before heading to the city of Venice.

Footloose in Italy IV – Follow Debra and David as they visit Rimini and San Marino on the Adriatic, followed by a trip to Tuscany where they take in Florence, Pisa, and Lucca before arriving at Siena. They end the video at Rome, taking in some of the area's best attractions and walking trails.

Footloose in Italy V – The fifth Footloose video in Italy focuses on the southern portion of the country, including Alberobello, cave dwellings in Matera, resorts like Tropea and Scilla, and then a visit to Sicily. They wrap it up with Taormina and a trip to Mount Etna.

Footloose in Spain – David and Debra visit the Alpujarras region of Andalucia in

Southern Spain, then move on to the more glamorous, urban city of Barcelona.

Footloose in Europe: City Breaks – This one is actually a collection of shorter travel videos, each one set in a different European cities. Season 1 visits Rome, Amsterdam, Lucerne, Barcelona, Salzburg, Venice, Regensburg, and Dublin, while season 2 visits Budapest, Prague, Dubrovnik, Tallinn, and Krakow.

Footloose in the Italian Lakes – Debra and David enjoy the incredible scenery of the four major lakes in northern Italy: Lugano, Maggiore, Garda, and Como. There's one section for each lake, and their travels include boat rides, walking trails, gardens, castles, and museums.

Footloose in Italy III – This lengthy tour of Italy sees David and Debra visiting Naples, the volcanic island of Ischia, Pompeii, Vesuvius, and Sorrento before heading to the Amalfi Coast and the Isle of Capri. No longer available through Prime Video, this one is purchase or rental only.

Footloose in Holland – In this first part of this video, we see the cost of the Netherlands and its many resorts and nature reserves. In the second part, Debra and David take us into Amsterdam, visiting popular sites like the Coster diamond factory and the Anne Frank House.

Footloose in Poland – This video finds Debra and David exploring the Tatra mountains, visiting the resort city of Zakopane, and then heading on to Krakow.

Footloose in Rocamadour - This film sees David and Debra walking the Lot/Dordogne region, and it includes some of the prettiest villages in the country before they arrive at Rocamadour.

Keukenhof Gardens & the Dutch Flower Parade – This video offers an hour-long tour of some of the most beautiful gardens in the world, along with a stop by the annual Dutch Flower Parade.

Footloose on Madeira – This feature-length video sees Debra and David visiting the tiny Portuguese island of Madeira. Over the course of five sections, they visit the capital, take a number of walks around the stunning scenery, and then visit the island's famous flower festival.

Footloose in England: Along the Ridgeway – This two-hour walking film takes you along southern England's oldest green road. The 85-mile walk includes stone circles, hill forts, villages, and more.

Footloose in the Cotswolds, Part 1 – UK filmmakers Debra and David Rixon visit Stow, Chipping Camden, Broadway, along with the gardens of Kiftsgate and Hidcote.

A Classic Tour of Scotland: Footloose Special – UK filmmakers Debra and David Rixon travel Scotland in an Airstream trailer, stopping off to visit locations like the Isle of Skye, Glasgow, Stirling Castle, Edinburgh, and Inverness.

Footloose in Ireland – This nearly two-hour programme sees David and Debra visiting Dublin and walking the Dingle Way.

Footloose in Northumberland - David and Debra grab their 1969 Airstream and head up to visit the dramatic coast of England's northernmost county, Northumberland - *Vera* territory! They'll take in the incredible scenery and visit popular sites like Alnwick Castle, Bamburgh Castle, and Hadrian's Wall.

Available for Purchase or Rental on Vimeo

Footloose in London: Undiscovered and Unusual – This episode takes a look at some of London's less conventional attractions.

Footloose in Scotland: The West Highland Way – This two-hour programme follows David and Debra as they walk the 95-mile West Highland Way from Glasgow to Fort William.

Footloose in England: Tales from the Thames – This video follows the River Thames from its modest source in the Cotswolds all the way to Windsor, stopping off at a variety of pubs, villages, and towns along the way.

INDEX

To save space, we've abbreviated some service names. Amazon Prime Video = AMZ, BBC Select = BBC, PBS Masterpiece = PBS, HBO Max = HBO, Sundance Now = Sundance, Inside Outside = IO, and Apple TV+ = Apple.

The Alienist - HBO
The Aliens - Hulu, AMZ
Alien Worlds - Netflix
A Life in Ten Pictures: Elizabeth Taylor - BBC
The A List - Netflix
All Aboard! - BritBox
All Creatures Great and Small (Classic) - BritBox
All Creatures Great and Small - PBS
All Saints - Tubi, Freevee
All's Well That Ends Well (1981) - BritBox
The Almighty Johnsons - Peacock
The Almost Impossible Game Show - Tubi, Pluto, Freevee
Almost Royal - AMC, AMZ
Alone Across the Arctic - Sundance
A Long Weekend in...With Rory O'Connell - Freevee, Roku Channel
Always Greener - AMZ
Amazing Hotels: Life Beyond the Lobby - BBC
Amazing Interiors - Netflix
The Ambassador - Tubi, Roku, AMZ
Ambassadors - Freevee, Pluto
Amber - Tubi, Pluto, Acorn
American Gods - Starz
American History's Biggest Fibs - BBC
A Midsummer Night's Dream (1981) - BritBox
A Midsummer Night's Dream (2016) - BritBox
Amish: A Secret Life - BBC
Amnesia - AMZ
A Model Daughter: The Killing of Caroline Byrne - Acorn
A Mother's Son - BritBox
An Adventure in Space & Time - BritBox
Anatomy of a Scandal - Netflix
Ancient Rome: The Rise and Fall of an Empire - BritBox
Ancient Treasures with Bettany Hughes - BBC
Ancient Worlds - BBC
And Then There Were None - Acorn
Angelina Ballerina - Netflix
A Nightingale Falling - Acorn
Animal Park - Freevee, Pluto

Animal Rescue School - Tubi, Roku
Animal Rescue Squad - Freevee, Roku, Pluto
Animals on the Loose - Netflix
An Inspector Calls - BritBox
Anna's Wild Life - Freevee, Tubi, Pluto, Roku
Anna Karenina - Pluto
Anna of the Five Towns - BritBox
Anne - Acorn
Anne of Green Gables - PBS
Anne With An "E" - Netflix
Annika - PBS
The Anti-Vax Conspiracy - BBC
Antiques Roadshow - Freevee, Pluto, Tubi, Crackle, AMC, BritBox
Antiques to the Rescue - Peacock
Antony and Cleopatra (1981) - BritBox
Anzac Girls - Tubi, Roku, AMZ
A Place to Call Home - Acorn
Apparitions - Freevee, Roku, Tubi, Pluto
Apples, Pears, & Paint: How to Make a Still Life Painting - BBC
Apple Tree Yard - AMC, Hulu, PBS
Appropriate Adult - Freevee, Roku
A Queen is Crowned - BritBox
Archaeology: A Secret History - BBC
Archangel - Pluto, Freevee, Roku, Vudu
Are You Being Served? - BritBox
Are You Being Served? Again! - BritBox
Are You Scared Yet, Human? - BBC
Aristocrats - BritBox
The Aristocrats - BritBox
Armada: The Untold Story - BBC
Armadillo - BritBox
A Room with a View - PBS
Around the World in 80 Days - PBS
Around the World in 80 Faiths - BritBox
A Royal Guide to... - BBC
A Royal Scandal - BritBox

Art Deco Icons - Tubi, Freevee
Arthur and George - PBS
The Art Mysteries - BBC
Art of America - BBC
The Art of Architecture - BBC
Art of China - BBC
Art of France - BBC
Art of Gothic - BBC
Art of Russia - BBC
Art of Scandinavia - BBC
Art of Spain - BBC
A Slow Odyssey: The Great Wall of China - BBC
As Time Goes By - BritBox
As Time Goes By: Reunion Specials - PBS
A Stitch in Time - Acorn, AMZ
A Suitable Boy - Acorn
Asylum - Freevee, Tubi, Roku
As You Like It (1978) - BritBox
A Tale of Two Cities (1980) - Freevee, Tubi, Roku, BritBox
A Tale of Two Sisters - Acorn
A Taste of Italy - Acorn
A Thing Called Love - Freevee
At Home With the Braithwaites - Freevee, Tubi, Roku, Vudu, Pluto
Atlantic Crossing - PBS
Atlantis - Hulu, AMZ
Atlantis High - Freevee, Vudu, Tubi
At Last the 1948 Show - Roku, Tubi, BritBox
A Touch of Frost - BritBox
A Tribute to Her Majesty The Queen - BBC, BritBox
A Tribute to HRH The Duke of Edinburgh - BBC
The Attaché - Acorn
At Your Service - Tubi
Auction - Roku, Freevee
The Auction House - Tubi
Auschwitz: The Nazis and the Final Solution - BBC
Australia on Fire: Climate Emergency - BBC
The Autistic Gardener - IO
Autumnwatch - BritBox
Avenue 5 - HBO
A Very British Coup - Freevee, Tubi
A Very British Murder with Lucy Worsley - BBC, BritBox
A Very English Scandal - AMZ
Avicii: True Stories - BBC
A Wild Year on Earth - AMC

A Woman of Substance - Acorn
A Year in Tibet - BBC
A Young Doctor's Notebook and Other Stories - Tubi
B&B - Acorn
The Baby - HBO
Baby Baby - Tubi
Baby Ballroom - Netflix
Baby Beauty Queens - Tubi
Baby Hospital - Tubi
Bacchus Uncovered: Ancient God of Ecstasy - BBC
Back - Sundance
Back to Life - Showtime
Back to the Rafters - AMZ
Bad Banks - Hulu
Bad Boy Billionaires: India - Netflix
Bad Mothers - Sundance
The Bad Seed - Sundance
Bad Sisters - Apple
Baghdad Central - Hulu
Ballykissangel - BritBox
The Ballymurphy Precedent - Freevee, Tubi
Balthazar - Acorn
Bancroft - BritBox
Band of Gold - Freevee
Bang - Acorn, Sundance
Banged Up - Freevee
Banished - BritBox, Hulu
Baptiste - PBS
Barack Obama: Reflections on a Presidency - BBC
The Barking Murders - BritBox
The Baron - BritBox
Baroness Von Sketch Show - AMC, Pluto
The Battle for Britney - BBC
Battle of Kings: Bannockburn - Freevee
The Bay - BritBox
The BBC at War - BritBox, BBC
BBC's Lost Sitcoms - BritBox
Bean: The Movie - BritBox
Bear Grylls: Survival School - Freevee, Tubi, Roku, Peacock
Bear's Wild Weekends - Tubi, Pluto, Freevee
The Beast Must Die - Acorn, Sundance
The Beatles & India - BritBox
Beat My Build - IO
The Beautiful Lie - Acorn
The Beauty of Anatomy - BBC
Beaver Falls - Freevee, Tubi, Peacock

Becoming Elizabeth - Starz
Becoming You - Apple
Bedlam - Tubi, Roku, BritBox
Bed of Roses - AMZ
Beecham House - PBS
Beechgrove Garden - BritBox
Beforeigners - HBO
Before We Die - PBS
Behind Enemy Lines - Netflix
Behind Her Eyes - Netflix
Being Erica - Hulu
Being Human - Freevee, Tubi, Vudu, Roku, Pluto, Crackle, Sundance
Being Poirot - Acorn
Belgravia - Epix
Belonging - Acorn
The Bench - Freevee, Tubi
Ben Earl: Trick Artist - Pluto, Roku, Tubi
Benidorm - BritBox
Bergerac - BritBox
Berlin Station - Epix
Best in Paradise - BritBox
Best Laid Plans - Freevee, Tubi, Roku
Between - Netflix
The Bible's Buried Secrets - BBC
The Big Bread Experiment - Acorn
Big Dreams Small Spaces - IO, AMZ
The Big Family Cooking Showdown - Netflix
The Big Flower Fight - Netflix
Big School - Pluto, Roku
Big Sky - AMZ
Big Tree City - Netflix
The Bill - BritBox
Billionaire Boy - BritBox
Bill's Tasty Weekends - Pluto
Bin Laden: The Road to 9/11 - BBC
Birds of a Feather - Acorn
The Birth of Empire: The East India Company - BBC
The Bisexual - Hulu
Blackadder - BritBox, Hulu
The Black American Fight for Freedom - BBC
Black Books - Freevee, Roku, Tubi, Crackle, Pluto
Black Earth Rising - Netflix
Black Mirror - Netflix
Black Mirror: Bandersnatch - Netflix

Black Narcissus - Hulu
Blackpool - Pluto, Roku
Black Sails - Hulu, Starz
Black Spot - Netflix
The Blake Mysteries: Ghost Stories - BritBox
Blake's 7 - BritBox
Blandings - Freevee, Tubi, Pluto, BritBox
Bleak House (1985) - BritBox
Bleak House (2005) - BritBox, Hulu
The Bleak Old Shop of Stuff - AMZ, Pluto
Bleak Old Shop of Stuff - BritBox
The Bletchley Circle - Freevee, Pluto, Peacock
The Bletchley Circle: San Francisco - BritBox
Blinded - Sundance
Blinded: Those Who Kill - Acorn
Bliss - BritBox
Blitz Spirit with Lucy Worsley - BBC
Blood - Acorn
Bloodlands - Acorn
Bloodline Detectives - Peacock
Bloodlines - Acorn
Blood Ties - Freevee, Roku, Tubi, Pluto, Vudu
The Blue Boy - BritBox
Blue Murder - Freevee, Roku, Pluto, Tubi, BritBox
The Blue Rose - Freevee, Tubi, Acorn
Bluestone 42 - Pluto, AMZ
Bodily Harm - Acorn
Body and Soul - Freevee, Roku, Tubi
Body Beautiful: Ancient Greeks, Good Looks, and Glamour - BBC
The Body Farm - BritBox
Bodyguard - Netflix
The Boleyns: A Scandalous Family - PBS
Bollywood: The World's Biggest Film Industry - Acorn
Bomb Girls - Freevee, Vudu, Tubi, Crackle
Bone Detectives - Acorn
Bonekickers - Freevee
Booba - Netflix
The Book Group - Freevee, Tubi, Pluto, Roku

Boon - BritBox
Booze Britain - Tubi
Boozed Up Brits Abroad - Tubi
The Borgias - Showtime, Netflix
Bottersnikes and Gumbles - Netflix
Bottom - AMZ
Bounty Hunters - Pluto, Tubi
Boy Meets Girl (2009) - Freevee, Roku, Tubi, Peacock
Boy Meets Girl (2015) - BritBox
The Boy Who Tried to Kill Trump - BBC
The Boy with the Topknot - Acorn
Bramwell - Freevee, Tubi, Roku, Crackle, BritBox
Brand New House on a Budget - Tubi, Roku
Brassic - Hulu
Brave New World - Peacock
Brazil with Michael Palin - BBC
Breaking Boundaries: The Science of Our Planet - Netflix
Breathless - PBS
Breeders - Hulu
Brick by Brick: Rebuilding Our Past - Tubi, Pluto, Roku
Brideshead Revisited (Remastered) - BritBox
Brideshead Revisited - Roku, Tubi, Vudu, Crackle, Pluto, Freevee
The Bridge (2011) - Topic
The Bridge (2020) - HBO
Bridgerton - Netflix
Bridges that Built London - Freevee
Bridget & Eamon - Freevee, Roku, Tubi, Pluto
The Brief - Freevee, Roku, Pluto
Brief Encounters - Acorn
Bright Lights Brilliant Minds: A Tale of Three Cities - BBC
The Brilliant Brontë Sisters - BBC
Britain by Narrowboat - AMZ
Britain's Best Bakery - Freevee, Tubi, Pluto
Britain's Best Drives - AMZ
Britain's Best Home Cook - Hulu
Britain's Biggest Adventures with Bear Grylls - BritBox

Britain's Bloodiest Dynasty - Acorn
Britain's Bloody Crown - Acorn
Britain's Forgotten Slave Owners - BBC
Britain's Most Historic Towns - Pluto, Tubi
Britain's Secret Treasures - BritBox
Britain's Tudor Treasure - BritBox
Britain's Vaccine - BBC
Britannia - AMZ
British Inland Waterways with John Noakes - Freevee, Roku
British Royal Heritage: The Royal Kingdom - Freevee, Tubi, Roku
Brittania - Epix
Broadchurch - PBS
Broadmoor: A History of the Criminally Insane - Tubi
Broken - BritBox
The Brokenwood Mysteries - Acorn
The Broker's Man - Freevee, Roku, Tubi, Pluto, Acorn
Bromwell High - Pluto
Brotherhood - Showtime
Brushstrokes: Every Picture Tells a Story - Freevee
The Buccaneers - BritBox
Bucket - AMZ
Budgie - Tubi, Roku, Freevee
Build a New Life in the Country - Pluto, Freevee, Tubi
Build a New Life in the Country Revisits - Tubi
Building Dream Homes - AMZ
The Bureau - Sundance
The Bureau of Magical Things - Netflix
Butterfly - Hulu
Butterfly Breath (aka Pili Pala) - Acorn
Byron - AMZ
Bäckström - Acorn
C.B. Strike (aka Strike) - HBO
Cadfael - Freevee, Roku, Tubi, Pluto, BritBox
The Cafe - BritBox
Calculating Ada: The Countess of Computing - BBC
Caligula with Mary Beard - Acorn
Call Me Kat - Hulu
Call the Experts - Tubi

Call the Midwife - Netflix
Cameraman to the Queen - BritBox
Camomile Lawn - Tubi, Roku, Freevee, Pluto
Campion - BritBox
Candice Renoir - Acorn
Can't Cope, Won't Cope - Tubi, Roku, Peacock
Capital - Acorn, PBS, Topic
Captain Scarlet & the Mysterons - Freevee, Tubi
The Capture - Peacock
Cardinal - Hulu
Care - Freevee, Tubi, Acorn
Caroline Quentin's National Parks - BritBox
Carols from King's 2022 - BritBox
Cars, Cops, & Criminals - Tubi
Carters Get Rich - Tubi
The Case - Roku, Pluto, Acorn
Case Histories - Freevee, Roku, Vudu, Pluto, Tubi, Peacock
Case Sensitive - Tubi
Cash Cab - Tubi
Castle Builders - Roku
Castles and Palaces of Europe - Freevee, Pluto, Roku
Casualty - BritBox
Casualty 24/7 - Peacock
Casualty 1900s: London Hospital - AMZ, BritBox
The Casual Vacancy - HBO
Catastrophe - AMZ
Catching a Killer - Topic
Catherine Cookson's The Cinder Path - BritBox
Catherine Cookson's The Dwelling Place - BritBox
Catherine Cookson's The Gambling Man - BritBox
Catherine Cookson's The Girl - BritBox
Catherine Cookson's The Glass Virgin - BritBox
Catherine Cookson's The Man Who Cried - BritBox
Catherine Cookson's The Moth - BritBox
Catherine Cookson's The Rag Nymph - BritBox
Catherine Cookson's The Tide of Life - BritBox
Catherine Cookson's The Wingless Bird - BritBox
Catherine the Great - HBO

Catherine's Family Kitchen - Tubi, Freevee
Cat Hospital - Acorn
Caught on Camera - Netflix
The Cazalets - BritBox
Celebrity Best Home Cook - Hulu
Celebrity Restaurant in Our Living Room - Tubi
Celebs, Brands, and Fake Fans - BBC
Celtic Britain - Freevee
The Celts: Blood, Iron, and Sacrifice - Freevee
The Champions - BritBox
Chance - Hulu
Chancer - Freevee, Tubi, Vudu, Roku, Peacock
The Chaperone - PBS
Charles & Diana: Wedding of the Century - BritBox
Charles: The Monarch & the Man - BritBox
Charles and Di: The Truth Behind Their Wedding - BBC
Charles Dickens: The Man That Asked for More - Tubi, Pluto
Charles I: Downfall of a King - Freevee
Charles II: The Power and the Passion - BritBox
Chateau DIY - Peacock
Cheat - Sundance
Chef! - BritBox
Chef's Protégé - Freevee, Tubi
Chelmsford 123 - Tubi
The Chelsea Detective - Acorn
Chernobyl - HBO
The Chestnut Man - Netflix
Chewing Gum - HBO
Cheyenne & Lola - Sundance
The Child in Time - PBS
Children of God - BBC
Children's Hospital - Tubi
Chiller - Freevee, Roku, Tubi
Chimerica - Topic
China: A New World Order - BBC
Chloe - AMZ
Choccywoccydoodah - Tubi
Christopher and His Kind - BritBox
Churchill: The Darkest Hour - BritBox
Churchill: Winning the War, Losing the Peace - BBC
The Churchills - Acorn

Churchill's Desert War: The Road to El Alamein - BBC
Churchill's Secret - PBS
Churchill's Secret Agents: The New Recruits - Netflix
CI5: The New Professionals - Pluto, Tubi, Roku
The Circuit - Acorn
The City & The City - BritBox, Freevee
City Homicide - Freevee, Pluto, Hulu
City of Vice - Freevee, Tubi, Vudu
Civilisation - BritBox
Civilization: Is the West History? - BBC
Civil War - Acorn
Clarkson's Farm - AMZ
Clash of the Santas - BritBox
Class - Tubi
Classic Doctor Who Comic Con Panel - BritBox
Classic Mary Berry - Freevee, Pluto
Clean Break - Acorn
The Cleaner - BritBox
Cleaning Up - Sundance
Click and Collect - BritBox
Clickbait - Netflix
Climate Change: Ade on the Frontline - BBC
The Clinic - Tubi
Clink - Freevee, Tubi
Clique - Hulu
Close to Me - Sundance
Close to the Enemy - Acorn
Clothes to Die For - BBC
Coalition - BritBox
Coast - BritBox
Cobra - PBS
Cocaine - Netflix
Code 404 - Peacock
Code Blue: Murder - BritBox
Code of a Killer - Acorn
Cold Blood - BritBox
Cold Call - Acorn, Sundance
Cold Courage - AMC
Cold Feet - Freevee, Tubi, Pluto, Roku, BritBox
Cold Feet: The New Years - BritBox
Cold Squad - Freevee, Roku, Tubi, Hulu
Collateral - Netflix
The Collection - AMZ
Collision - Crackle, Tubi, Roku,

Freevee, Pluto, PBS
Colonel March of Scotland Yard - Freevee, Roku, Tubi
The Colour of Magic - Freevee, Roku, Tubi, Pluto
Combat Pilot - Pluto
The Comedy of Errors (1983) - BritBox
Come Home - Topic
Comfort Eating - Freevee, Tubi, Pluto
Coming Home - Acorn
The Commander - Acorn
The Commons - Sundance
Condor - Epix
Confessions of a Serial Killer - BBC
Confucius - BBC
Conspiracies - Netflix
Conspiracy Files: George Soros - The Billionaire Global Mastermind? - BBC
Conspiracy Files: Vaccine Wars - BBC
The Constant Gardener - BritBox
Conviction: The Case of Stephen Lawrence - Acorn
The Cook, the Thief, His Wife, & Her Lover - BritBox
Cook Yourself Thin UK - Tubi
The Cops - Freevee
The Coronation of Queen Elizabeth II - BBC
Coronation Street - BritBox, Hulu
The Coroner - BritBox
Countdown to War - BBC
Counterpart - AMZ
Countryfile - BritBox
Couple Trouble - Sundance
The Courtship - Peacock
Cracker (US) - Roku, Tubi, Pluto, Freevee
Cracker - BritBox, Pluto
Craig Ferguson: I'm Here to Help - BritBox
Cranford - BritBox
Crashing - Netflix
Crazy Delicious - Netflix
Crazyhead - Netflix
Creeped Out - Netflix
The Crest - Freevee, Tubi, Vudu, Roku
Crime & Punishment - BBC
Crime - BritBox
Crime Secrets - Freevee, Roku,

Tubi
Crimes That Shook Britain - Freevee, Tubi
Crime Story - BritBox
Criminal: United Kingdom - Netflix
Crims - Freevee, Roku, Tubi
The Crimson Field - PBS
The Crimson Petal & the White - Acorn, Sundance
CripTales - AMC
Critical - AMZ
The Crown - Netflix
Crownies - Freevee, Tubi, Acorn
Cruise of the Gods - BritBox
Cruising the Cut - AMZ
The Crusades - BBC
The Cry - Acorn, Sundance
Cuba with Simon Reeve - BBC
Cuckoo - Netflix
Cucumber - Freevee
Cuffs - Tubi, Freevee, Acorn
The Cult of Conspiracy: QAnon - BBC
Cursed - Netflix
Cymbeline (1982) - BritBox
Dad's Army - BritBox
Daleks' Invasion Earth 2150 A.D. - BritBox
Dalgliesh - Acorn
Dalziel & Pascoe - BritBox
Damned - BritBox
Damned Designs: Don't Demolish My Home - IO
Damned in the USA - BBC
Danceworks - BBC
Dancing on the Edge - Roku, Tubi, Pluto, PBS
Dancing with the Birds - Netflix
Dandelion Dead - BritBox
Danger Man, aka Secret Agent - Freevee, Roku
Danger Mouse - Netflix
Danger Mouse: Classic Collection - Netflix
Dangerous Roads - AMZ
Danger UXB - Acorn
Daniel Deronda (2002) - BritBox, Hulu
Darby & Joan - Acorn
Darcey Bussell: Looking for Margot - Tubi
Dark Ages: An Age of Light - Roku
Dark Angel - PBS
The Dark Charisma of Adolf

Hitler - BBC
Dark Heart - BritBox
Dark Matter - Netflix
Darkness: Those Who Kill - Acorn
Dark Son: The Hunt for a Serial Killer - BBC
The Darling Buds of May - Freevee, Tubi, Roku, Pluto, BritBox
David Attenborough: A Life On Our Planet - Netflix
David Bowie: Finding Fame - BBC
David Brent: Life on the Road - Netflix
David Copperfield (1986) - BritBox
David Copperfield (1999) - BritBox, Hulu
David Jason's Secret Service - Tubi, Pluto, Roku, Freevee
David Suchet: In the Footsteps of St Peter - Tubi
David Suchet on the Orient Express - BritBox
Da Vinci's Demons - Starz
The Day of the Triffids - Pluto
Days of Majesty - BritBox
DCI Banks - BritBox
Dead Boss - AMZ, Hulu
Dead Good Job - BritBox
Dead Lucky - Acorn, AMZ, Peacock, Sundance
Dead Set - Netflix
Dead Still - Acorn
Deadwater Fell - Acorn, Sundance
Death Camp Treblinka - BBC
Death Comes to Pemberley - PBS
Death in Paradise - BritBox
Death on the Tyne - BritBox
The Decade the Rich Won - BBC
Deceit - Topic
The Deceived - Starz
Decline and Fall - Acorn
The Deep - AMZ
Deep State - Epix
Deep Water - Pluto, Tubi, Roku, PBS
Degrassi : Next Class - Netflix
Delicious - Acorn
The Delivery Man Freevee, Roku, Tubi, Pluto
Demons - Hulu

Dennis and Gnasher Unleashed - Netflix
Departure - Peacock
Derek - Netflix
Dermot Bannon's Incredible Homes - Freevee, Tubi, Roku
Derren Brown: Hero at 30,000 Feet - Tubi
Derren Brown: The Experiments - Crackle, Tubi, Pluto, Peacock
Derren Brown: The Great Art Robbery - Pluto, Tubi
Derren Brown Investigates - Pluto, Tubi
Derry Girls - Netflix
Des - Sundance
Design Doctors - Freevee, Tubi
Designer Darlings - Tubi
Desmond's - AMZ
Desperate Romantics - BritBox
The Detectives - Freevee
The Detectives: Murder on the Streets - Pluto, Tubi
Detectorists - Freevee, Tubi, Pluto, Crackle, Roku, Acorn
The Devil's Mistress - Freevee, Tubi, Pluto, Roku
Devil's Advocate - Peacock
The Devil's Hour - AMZ
Dial M for Middlesbrough - BritBox
Diana: 7 Days That Shook the World - BBC
Diana: The Interview that Shook the World - BritBox
Diana: The Musical - Netflix
Diana: The New Evidence - Freevee, Tubi
Diana's Decades - BBC
Dickensian - BritBox
Digging for Britain - Acorn
The Diplomat, aka False Witness - Pluto, Tubi, Roku
Dirk Gently's Holistic Detective Agency - Hulu
Dirk Gently - BritBox
Discovering Britain - Acorn
Discovering Hamlet - Acorn
Discovering the World - Tubi
Distraction - Pluto
Divine Women - BBC
Doc Martin - Tubi, Crackle, Vudu, Roku, Pluto, Hulu, Acorn
Doctor at Large - Freevee, Roku, Tubi, Pluto

The Doctor Blake Mysteries - BritBox
Doctor Finlay - Freevee, Tubi
Doctor Foster - BritBox
Doctors - BritBox
Doctor Thorne - AMZ
Doctor Who (Classic) - BritBox
Doctor Who - HBO
Doctor Who: Fury from the Deep - AMC
Doctor Who: The Doctors Revisited - BritBox
Doctor Who: The Evil of the Daleks - AMC
Doctor Who: The Faceless Ones - AMC
Doctor Who: The Macra Terror - AMC
Doctor Who Specials - BritBox
Doctor Zhivago - BritBox
The Dog House UK - HBO
The Dog Rescuers - Tubi, Pluto, Roku, Freevee
Dog School - Tubi, Pluto, Freevee
Dombey and Son (1983) - BritBox
Domina - Epix
Dominion Creek - Acorn
Do Not Adjust Your Set - BritBox
Donovan - Freevee, Roku
Don't Forget the Driver - BritBox
Don't Panic: The Truth About Population - BBC
Double Your House for Half the Money - Tubi, Roku
Down from London - Topic
Downton Abbey - BritBox, Peacock, AMZ
Downton Abbey Extras - BritBox
Dr. Who and the Daleks - BritBox
Dracula - Netflix
Drag Queens of London - Pluto
Dream Corp LLC - Hulu
Dress to Impress - Hulu
Drifters - Freevee, Roku, Tubi, Pluto, Vudu
Drop Zone - Pluto
Drovers' Gold - BritBox
The Drowning - Acorn, Sundance
Drowning in Plastic - BBC
Dublin Murders - Starz

The Duchess - Netflix
The Duchess of Duke Street - AMZ, BritBox
The Duke in His Own Words - BBC
Dunkirk - BritBox
Durham County - Freevee
The Durrells in Corfu - AMZ
The Earth at Night - Apple
EastEnders - BritBox
East of Everything - Acorn
East West 101 - Acorn, Peacock
Eddie Izzard: Definite Article - BritBox
Eddie Izzard: Glorious - BritBox
Edge of Heaven - BritBox
Edge of the Universe - Netflix
The Edible Garden - BritBox
Edwardian Farm - Tubi, AMZ
Edward VIII: Britain's Traitor King - BBC
Electric Dreams - AMZ
Eleventh Hour - BritBox
Elizabeth & Margaret: Love & Loyalty - Netflix
Elizabeth & Philip: Love & Duty - BBC
Elizabeth: Passions & Pastimes - BritBox
Elizabeth: The Unseen Queen - BBC
Elizabeth I & Her Enemies - Acorn
Elizabeth I & II: The Golden Queens - BBC
Elizabeth I: The Virgin Queen - PBS
Elizabeth is Missing - PBS
Elizabeth R - BritBox
Emma (1972) - BritBox
Emma (2009) - BritBox
Emmerdale - Freevee, Roku, Vudu, Tubi, BritBox
The End - Showtime
Endeavour - AMZ, PBS
The End of the F***ing World - Netflix
Enemy at the Door - Freevee, Roku
England's Forgotten Tudor Queen: The Life & Death of Lady Jane Grey - Acorn, Freevee
The English - AMZ
The English Game - Netflix
Enid Blyton Adventure Series - Freevee, Tubi

Enid Blyton Secret Series - Freevee, Tubi
Enterprice - Topic
Epidemic: The Great Plague - BBC
Episodes - Showtime
The Escape Artist - PBS
Escape from the City - Hulu
Escape to the Chateau - Peacock
Escape to the Chateau: Make Do & Mend - Peacock
Escape to the Country - Freevee, Roku, BritBox
The Essex Serpent - Apple
Eternal Law - Freevee, Tubi
Eugenics: Science's Greatest Scandal - BBC
Everything: The Real Thing Story - Sundance
Excalibur: Behind the Movie - PBS
Exile - PBS, Tubi
Extraordinary Places to Eat - BBC
Extraordinary Women - BBC
Extras - BritBox, Crackle
Extreme A&E - Tubi
Extreme Combat: The Dancer and the Fighter - BBC
Extremely Dangerous - Pluto
The Fades - Hulu, AMZ
Fake News: A True History - BBC
Fake or Fortune? - Tubi, Roku, AMZ
The Fall - Tubi, Pluto, AMZ, BritBox, Peacock, Sundance
Fallen Angel - Acorn
Family Business - Acorn
The Family Farm - Peacock
Family Tree - HBO
Fanny by Gaslight - BritBox
Far From the Madding Crowd (1998) - PBS
The Farmer Wants a Wife - Hulu
The Farmer's Country Showdown - Tubi
Farm Fixer - Freevee, Acorn
Fashioning a Monarch - BritBox
Fate: The Winx Saga - Netflix
Father and Son - BritBox
Father Brown (Classic) - BritBox
Father Brown - BritBox

Father Ted - Freevee, Roku, Tubi, Pluto, Crackle, Vudu
Fat Love - Tubi
Fat Men Can't Hunt - Tubi
Fawlty Towers - BritBox
The Feed - AMZ
Feel Good - Netflix
The Fenn Street Gang - Freevee
The Field of Blood - Freevee, Pluto, Tubi, Acorn
Fields of Gold - BritBox
Fifi & the Flowertots - Peacock
Fifth Gear - Pluto
Fighter Pilot: The Real Top Gun - BBC
Fighting for King and Empire: Britain's Caribbean Heroes - BBC
Fill Your House for Free - Pluto
Filthy Cities - BBC
Finding Alice - Acorn
Finding Joy - Acorn, Sundance
Fingersmith - Acorn, Sundance
First Homes - Tubi
Five Bedrooms - Peacock
Five by Five - BritBox
Five Days - HBO
The Fix - Netflix
Flack - AMZ
Flame Trees of Thika - Acorn
Fleabag - AMZ
Flesh & Blood - PBS
Flickers - Freevee
Flood - Freevee, Tubi, Pluto
Florence Nightingale - BritBox
Flowers - Netflix
The Flu That Killed 50 Million - BBC
The Force: Manchester - AMZ
The Forsyte Saga - AMZ, PBS
The Fortunes & Misfortunes of Moll Flanders - Freevee
Four Seasons - Acorn
Foyle's War - Acorn
The Fragile Heart - Tubi, Freevee, Pluto
Frankenstein & the Vampyre: A Dark & Stormy Night - BBC
Frankie - BritBox
Frankie Drake Mysteries - PBS
Frank of Ireland - AMZ
Frayed - HBO
Free Rein - Netflix
French & Saunders - Crackle
The French Collection - Tubi
Fresh Meat - Pluto, Roku, Tubi,

Crackle, AMZ
Freud - Netflix
Friday Night Dinner - Roku Channel
From Darkness - BritBox
From There to Here - Freevee
Frontier - Netflix
Fungus the Bogeyman - AMZ
Funny is Funny: A Conversation with Normal Lear - BritBox
The F Word - Tubi, Roku, Freevee, Crackle
Gadget Man - Pluto, Roku, Peacock, AMZ
Gameface - Hulu
Game of Thrones - HBO
Game On - Tubi
Gandhi - BBC
Gangs of Britain - Freevee, Tubi, Pluto, Roku
Gangs of London - AMC
Gangsters: Faces of the Underworld - Pluto, Tubi
Gardeners' World - AMZ, IO, BritBox
Garden Invaders - AMZ
The Garden Pantry - IO
Garden Rescue - IO
Garth Marenghi's Darkplace - AMZ, Peacock
Gauguin: The Full Story - BBC
Gavin & Stacey - BritBox
Genderquake - BBC
Generation Porn - BBC
The Genius of Carl Faberge - BBC
The Genius of Roald Dahl - BBC
Genius of the Ancient World - Acorn, BBC
Genius of the Modern World - BBC, Acorn
Gentleman Jack - HBO
Gentlemen, The Queen - BritBox
The Gentle Touch - Freevee, Roku, Tubi
George Clarke's Old House New Home - Pluto
George Gently - Acorn
George III: The Genius of the Mad King - Freevee, Tubi, Pluto
Germany's New Nazis - BBC
Get Even - Netflix
Getting On (US) - HBO

Getting On - Pluto, Roku, AMZ
Getting the Builders In - Freevee, Roku, Tubi, Pluto
Ghosts - HBO
The Ghost Squad - Tubi, Freevee
Gideon's Daughter - BritBox
The Gilded Age - HBO
The Gil Mayo Mysteries (aka Mayo) - BritBox
Gine Yashere: Skinny B*tch - BritBox
Giri/Haji - Netflix
The Girl Before - HBO
The Girlfriend Experience - Starz
Glitch - Netflix
The Gloaming - Starz
Glorious Gardens from Above - Tubi
Glow Up - Netflix
The Gods of Wheat Street - Acorn
The Goes Wrong Show - Tubi, Roku, Vudu
Go Girls- Freevee, Tubi, Peacock
Gold Digger - Acorn, Sundance
Golden Years - Acorn
Gone for Good - Netflix
Good Cop - BritBox
Good Grief - Sundance
The Good Karma Hospital - Acorn
Good Morning Britain - BritBox
Good Neighbors (aka The Good Life) - BritBox
Good Omens - AMZ
Gorbachev: The Man Who Changed the World - BBC
Gordon Behind Bars, aka Ramsay Behind Bars - Roku, Tubi, Pluto, AMZ
Gordon Ramsay's 24 Hours to Hell & Back - Hulu
Gordon Ramsay's The F Word - Hulu
Gordon Ramsay's Road Trip - Hulu
Gordon Ramsey's Ultimate Home Cooking - Hulu
Gordon the Garden Gnome - Tubi, Roku
Gordon's Great Escape - Tubi, Pluto, Freevee
Grace - BritBox
Gracepoint - Tubi, Pluto,

Freevee,

Grafters - Freevee, Roku, Tubi

The Graham Norton Show - AMC

The Grand - Freevee, Roku, Pluto

Grand Designs - Freevee, Tubi, BritBox

The Grand Tour - AMZ

Grand Tours of Scotland's Lochs - AMZ

Grand Tours of Scotland - Acorn

Grand Tours of the Scottish Islands - Freevee

Grantchester - AMZ, PBS

Grayson Perry: All Man - BBC

Grayson Perry: Big American Road Trip - BBC

Grayson Perry: Rites of Passage - BBC

Grayson Perry: Who Are You? - BBC

Grayson Perry's Art Club - BBC

The Great - Hulu

The Great British Baking Show - Netflix

The Great British Baking Show: Holidays - Netflix

The Great British Benefits Handout - AMZ

The Great British Countryside - BritBox

Great British Ghosts - Freevee, Roku

Great British Menu - Tubi, Pluto, Roku, AMZ

Great British Railway Journeys - Roku

Great British Waste Menu - Pluto

Great Canal Journeys - AMZ

The Great Chelsea Garden Challenge - BritBox

Great Escape: The Untold Story - BritBox

The Great Escapists - AMZ

Greatest Events of WWII in Colour - Netflix

Greatest Gardens - Freevee, Tubi, IO

Great Expectations (1981) - BritBox

Great Expectations (1999) - BritBox

Great Expectations (2011) - BritBox

The Great Fire - Tubi, Roku, Pluto, PBS

The Great Gardens of England - Freevee

The Great House Revival - Hulu

Great Interior Design Challenge - AMZ, IO

Great Performances: Macbeth - PBS

The Great Pottery Throwdown - HBO

Green Wing - Freevee, Roku, Tubi, Pluto, Crackle

Greg Davies: You Magnificent Beast - Netflix

Greta Thunberg: A Year to Change the World - Hulu

Ground Force - AMZ

Ground Force Revisited - AMZ

Grow, Cook, Eat - Freevee, Tubi, Roku, Pluto

Growing Old Disgracefully - Tubi

Growing Up Gracefully - Acorn

Guerrilla - Showtime

Guilt - PBS

The Guilty - Freevee

The Gulf - Acorn, Sundance

Gunpowder - HBO

Guy Martin: Industrial Wonders - Pluto

Guy Martin: Spitfire Restoration - Pluto

Guy Martin vs The Robot Car - Pluto, Roku

Guy Martin's Wall of Death - Pluto

H2O: Just Add Water - Netflix

The Hairy Bakers: Christmas Special - Freevee

Hairy Bikers' Bakeation - BritBox

Hairy Bikers' Chicken & Egg - Crackle, Roku

Hairy Bikers' Christmas Party - BritBox

Hairy Bikers' Cook Off - Freevee, Pluto

Hairy Bikers' Everyday Gourmets - BritBox

Hairy Bikers' Mississippi Adventure - Freevee

Hairy Biker's Asian Adventure - Roku

Hairy Biker's Best of British - Freevee, Pluto

Half Moon Investigations -

Freevee, Tubi

Halifax: Retribution - PBS

Halston - Netflix

Hamish Macbeth - Tubi, Pluto, Freevee, Acorn

Hamlet, Prince of Denmark (1980) - BritBox

Hamlet Prince of Denmark - Pluto

Hammer House of Horror - Freevee, Roku, Tubi, Pluto, Peacock

Happyish - Showtime

Happy Valley - AMC

Hard Cell - Netflix

Hard Sun - Hulu

Hard Times - BritBox

Harlots - Hulu

Harrow - Hulu

Harry - Acorn

Harry Potter - HBO

Harry Potter: A History of Magic - BBC

Harry Potter: Hogwart's Tournament of Houses - HBO

Harry Styles Live in Manchester - BBC

Harry Wild - Acorn

Harry's Arctic Heroes - Pluto

Heading Home - BritBox

Heartbeat - Freevee, Tubi, Roku, BritBox

The Heart Guy (aka Doctor Doctor) - Acorn

Heartland - Netflix

Hearts & Bones - Freevee, Roku, Vudu, Tubi, Pluto

Hearts of Gold - BritBox

Heartstopper - Netflix

Heat of the Sun - Freevee

The Heist at Hatton Garden - BritBox

He Kills Coppers - Freevee, Tubi, Roku, Pluto

The Helen West Casebook - Acorn

Helicopter ER - Tubi, Pluto

Helicopter Search & Rescue - Freevee

Hell's Kitchen - Pluto, Vudu, Tubi, Crackle, Roku, Freevee, Peacock, Hulu

Hello Ladies - HBO

Help - Acorn

Helstrom - Hulu

Henry and Anne: The Lovers

Who Changed History - Pluto, PBS

Henry IV: Parts 1 and 2 (1979) - BritBox

Henry IX - Acorn

Henry IX: Lost King - PBS

Henry V (1979) - BritBox

Henry VI: Parts 1-3 (1983) - BritBox

Henry VIII (1979) - BritBox

Her Majesty The Queen's Platinum Jubilee Celebration - BritBox

Hetty Wainthropp Investigates - BritBox

Hidden (2011) - Tubi, Pluto

Hidden (2018) - Acorn

Hidden: World's Best Monster Mystery - Loch Ness - BritBox

Hidden Assets - Acorn

High & Dry - Tubi

The High Art of the Low Countries - BBC

High Times - Freevee, Tubi, Pluto

Highwaymen, Pirates, & Rogues - Acorn

Hillary - AMZ

Him & Her - Pluto

Him - BritBox

Hinterland - Acorn

Hiroshima: The Real History - BBC

His Dark Materials - HBO

Historic Hauntings aka Castle Ghosts of England - Freevee, Tubi, Pluto, Roku

History 101 - Netflix

History Cold Case - Freevee, Tubi, Pluto

The History of Britain - Tubi, Pluto

History of Mother Earth: Gaia Uncovered - BBC

History's Deadliest Tsunami - BBC

The Hitchhiker's Guide to the Galaxy - BritBox, Hulu

Hitler's Circle of Evil - Netflix

Hitmen - Peacock

The Hive - Tubi, Pluto, Vudu

Hoarders, Get Your House in Order - IO

Hoarder SOS - Peacock, IO

Hokusai: Old Man Crazy to Paint - BBC

Holby Blue - AMZ

Hold the Dream - AMZ

Hold the Sunset - BritBox

The Hollies: Look Through Any Window - Freevee, Vudu, Tubi, Roku, Pluto

Hollington Drive - Sundance

Hollyoaks - Hulu

Home & Away - AMZ

Home Away from Home - BritBox

Home Fires - PBS

Homefront - Tubi, Roku, Freevee, BritBox, Peacock

Home of Fabulous Cakes - Freevee, Tubi, Pluto

Homes by Design - Tubi

The Home Show - AMZ

Homes Under the Hammer - IO

Honey, I Bought the House - Freevee, Tubi, Pluto, Roku

Honour - BritBox

Hope Street - BritBox

Horrible Histories - Freevee, Hulu

Horrid Henry - Netflix

Horror in the East - BBC

The Hotel - Tubi

Hotel Hell - Hulu

Hotel Portofino - PBS

Hotel Secrets with Richard E. Grant - BBC

Hound of the Baskervilles - BritBox

The Hour - Pluto, Tubi, Roku, Acorn

The House of Cards Trilogy - BritBox, AMZ

The House of Eliott - BritBox

House of Maxwell - BBC

House of Saud - BBC

House of the Dragon - HBO

The House that 100k Built: Tricks of the Trade - Freevee, Tubi

The House that 100k GBP Built - Tubi, AMZ

The House that Dripped Blood - Tubi, Pluto, Vudu

Howards End - Starz, PBS

How I Created a Cult - BBC

How the Victorians Built Britain - Tubi, Pluto

How to Go Viral - BBC

How to Haggle for a House - IO

How to Murder Your Wife - Acorn

Humans - AMZ

Hunderby - AMZ, Hulu

The Hunt for a Killer - Sundance

The Hunt for Bin Laden - BBC

Husbands from Hell - Tubi

Hustle - AMZ

Hustle - Tubi, Pluto, Freevee

Hyperdrive - AMZ

Hyper Evolution: Rise of the Robots - BBC

I, Claudius - Acorn

I Am a Killer - Netflix

I Am a Killer: Released - Netflix

I Came By - Netflix

The Ice House - BritBox

Idiomatic - Sundance

Idris Elba: King of Speed - Freevee, Tubi, Pluto

I Hate Suzie - HBO

I May Destroy You - HBO

Impossible Builds - Hulu

The Impressionists - Freevee, BBC

The Inbestigators - Netflix

The Inbetweeners - AMZ

The Incredible Journey of Mary Bryant - Freevee, Roku, Pluto

In Deep - Acorn

The Indian Detective - Netflix

The Indian Doctor - Acorn, AMZ

Indian Summers - PBS

The Industrial Revolution - BBC

Industry - HBO

Informer - AMZ

Injustice - AMZ

In Louboutin's Shoes - BBC

In My Skin - Hulu

Innocent - Sundance

The Innocents - Netflix

In Plain Sight - BritBox

In Search of Frida Kahlo - BBC

Insert Name Here - BritBox

Inside Claridge's - BritBox

Inside Men - Pluto, Roku, AMZ

Inside Missguided - Hulu

Inside No. 9 - BritBox

Inside the Ambulance - Freevee, Tubi

Inside the American Embassy - BBC

Inside the Bank of England - Acorn

Inside the Billionaire's Wardrobe - Freevee, BBC

Inside the Court of Henry VIII - PBS

Inside the EU: The Mad World of Brexit - BBC

Inside the Ritz Hotel - Acorn

Inside the Tower of London: Crimes, Conspiracies, Confessions - Freevee, Tubi

Inside the World's Toughest Prisons - Netflix

Inspector Alleyn Mysteries - Tubi

Inspector Lewis - PBS

The Inspector Lynley Mysteries - BritBox

Inspector Morse - BritBox

The Instagram Effect - BBC

The Instant Gardener - BritBox

Intelligence - Peacock

The Interceptor - Tubi

Interior Design Masters - Netflix

Interview with a Murderer - Freevee, Peacock, Sundance

Interview with the Vampire - AMC

In the Dark - BritBox

In the Flesh - Hulu

In the Footsteps of Killers - BritBox

In the Night Garden - Tubi, Roku

Intruder - BritBox

Intruders - Hulu

Intruders - Topic

Inventions that Built Our World - Tubi

The Invisibles - Acorn, AMZ, Peacock

The Ipcress File (1965) - BritBox

The Ipcress File (2022) - Sundance

The Irish Pub - Freevee, Tubi, Pluto, Roku

The Irish R.M. - Acorn

Iron Men - Tubi, Crackle

The Irregulars - Netflix

I Shot My Parents - BBC

Isis: The Origins of Violence - BBC

Island at War - Freevee, Roku

The Island with Bear Grylls - Tubi, Pluto, Freevee

Isolation Stories - BritBox

It Came From Connemara - Freevee

The IT Crowd - Netflix

It Takes a Worried Man - Acorn

It's a Sin - HBO

I Was Once a Beauty Queen - BBC

Jack Irish - Acorn

Jackson's Wharf - Freevee, Roku, Tubi

Jack Taylor - Acorn

Jack Whitehall: Christmas With My Father - Netflix

Jack Whitehall: I'm Only Joking - Netflix

Jack Whitehall: Travels with My Father - Netflix

Jack Whitehall at Large - Netflix

Jamaica Inn - PBS

James & Thom's Pizza Pilgrimage - Tubi

James Acaster: Repertoire - Netflix

James Martin's Mediterranean - Tubi

James Martin's United Cakes of America - Tubi, Roku, Freevee

James Martin: Home Comforts - Tubi, Pluto, Roku, AMZ

James Martin Home Comforts at Christmas - Tubi

James Martin's United Cakes of America - AMZ

James May's Man Lab - Tubi, Roku, Freevee

James May's Toy Stories - Tubi, Roku, Freevee

James May: Oh Cook - AMZ

James May: Our Man in Japan - AMZ

James May's Cars of the People - AMZ

Jamestown - PBS

Jamie: Keep Cooking and Carry On - Hulu

Jamie Oliver's Food Revolution - Hulu

Jane Eyre (1983) - BritBox, Pluto

Jane Eyre (2006) - Hulu, BritBox

Janet King - Acorn

Japan with Sue Perkins - BBC

Jason and the Argonauts - Tubi, Pluto, Crackle, Roku

Jekyll & Hyde - Tubi, Roku, Pluto, PBS, BritBox

Jennifer & Joanna: Absolutely Champers - Freevee, Crackle, BBC

Jericho - Acorn

Jericho of Scotland Yard - Acorn

Jessica - Freevee

The Jewel in the Crown - PBS

Jim Henson's The Storyteller - AMZ

Jimmy Carr: Funny Business - Netflix

Jimmy Carr: His Dark Material - Netflix

Jimmy Carr: The Best of Ultimate Gold Greatest Hits - Netflix

Jimmy Doherty's Escape to the Wild - IO

Jimmy Savile: A British Horror Story - Netflix

Joanna Lumley: The Quest for Noah's Ark - BBC

Joanna Lumley in the Kingdom of the Thunder Dragon - BBC

Joanna Lumley in the Land of the Northern Lights - Acorn, BBC

Joanna Lumley's Britain - BBC

Joanna Lumley's India - BBC

Joanna Lumley's Japan - BBC

Joanna Lumley's Trans-Siberian Adventure - BBC

Joanna Lumley's Unseen Adventures - BBC

The Job Lot - BritBox

Joe 90 - Freevee, Tubi, Pluto

John Bishop: Live: Supersonic - BritBox

Jonathan Creek - BritBox

The Joy of AI - BBC

The Joy of Chance - BBC

The Joy of Logic - BBC

The Joy of Stats - BBC

The Joy of Techs - Freevee, Crackle

The Joy of Winning - BBC

Julia - HBO

Julius Caesar (1979) - BritBox

Julius Caesar with Mary Beard - Freevee

The Jury - Freevee, Roku, Pluto, Tubi, BritBox

Just Another Immigrant - Showtime

Just William - Acorn

K9 & Company: A Girl's Best Friend - BritBox, Pluto

Kat & Alfie: Redwater - BritBox
Kate & Koji - BritBox
Kate: The Making of a Modern Queen - Freevee, Tubi
Kath & Kim - Netflix
Kavanagh QC - Freevee, Roku, Tubi, Pluto, BritBox
Keeping Faith - Acorn
Keeping Up Appearances - BritBox
Keith Richards: Under the Influence - Netflix
The Kennedys - AMZ, Hulu
Kevin McCloud's Escape to the Wild - IO
Kevin McCloud's Man Made Home - IO
Keys to the Castle - Freevee, Tubi
Kidnap & Ransom - Pluto, Tubi, Acorn, PBS
Kids on the Edge - Tubi
Killed By My Debt - BritBox
Killer Net - Acorn
Killer Roads - Tubi
Killing Eve - AMC, Hulu
Kim's Convenience - Netflix
Kin - AMC
King Arthur's Lost Kingdom - AMZ
Kingdom - Pluto, Tubi, Roku, Acorn
King Gary - AMZ
King Lear (1982) - BritBox
King Lear (2018) - AMZ
The Kinky Sex Survey - BBC
Kirstie's Vintage Home - BritBox
Kissinger: Statesman or War Criminal - BBC
Kiss Me First - Netflix
Kiss of Death - Freevee
Kitchen Nightmares - Freevee, Vudu, Tubi, Pluto, Crackle, Roku, Hulu, Peacock
KKK: The Fight for White Supremacy - BBC
Kolkata with Sue Perkins - BBC
The Labours of Erica - Acorn
Labyrinth - Freevee, Tubi
Ladette to Lady - Tubi
Ladhood - Hulu
Ladies of Letters - Acorn
Ladies of London - Peacock
Lady Boss: The Jackie Collins Story - Netflix
Lady Chatterley - Acorn

The Lady Vanishes - BritBox
Lady Windermere's Fan - BritBox
Laid - Freevee, Tubi, Roku
Land Girls - Acorn, PBS
Landscape Artist of the Year - Freevee
Landscapers - HBO
The Larkins - Acorn
Lark Rise to Candleford - BritBox
The Last Bus - Netflix
The Last Days of Anne Boleyn - Freevee
The Last Detective - BritBox
The Last Igloo - BBC
The Last Kingdom - Netflix
Last Light - Peacock
Last Night of the Proms - BritBox
Last of the Summer Wine - BritBox
The Last Place on Earth - Roku, Tubi, Pluto, Freevee
Last Tango in Halifax - Netflix
Laura McKenzie's Traveler - Tubi, Pluto, Vudu
Law & Order: UK - Tubi, Freevee, Acorn, Sundance
Lawless - Acorn
The League of Gentlemen - BritBox
Leaving Amish Paradise - BBC
Legend of the Dragon - Peacock
Legends - Hulu
Legends of King Arthur - Freevee, Roku, Tubi, Pluto
Lennon's Last Weekend - BritBox
Les Misérables - PBS
The Letdown - Netflix
The Letter for the King - Netflix
The Level - Acorn
Leverage - Freevee
Leverage: Redemption - Freevee
Liar - Sundance
Liberty of London - BBC
Licence to Thrill: Paul Hollywood Meets Aston Martin - BritBox
The Life & Crimes of William Palmer - Freevee
The Life and Death of King John (1984) - BritBox
Life in a Cottage Garden -

BritBox
Life in Color with David Attenborough - Netflix
Life in Squares - BritBox
Life Isn't All Ha Ha Hee Hee - Acorn
Life of Crime - BritBox
The Life of Verdi - Acorn
Life on Marbs - Tubi
Life on Mars - BritBox
The Light in the Hall - Sundance
The Lights Before Christmas - BritBox
Like Father Like Son - Acorn
Lillie - Freevee, Roku
Lily Allen: From Riches to Rags - Freevee, Tubi
Line of Duty - Freevee, Roku, Pluto, Acorn, BritBox, Hulu, Peacock
Lip Service - Pluto, Tubi, Roku
Little Baby Bum - Netflix
Little Birds - Starz
Little Boy Blue - BritBox
Little Charley Bear - Peacock
Little Dorrit (2008) - BritBox, Pluto
The Little Drummer Girl - Sundance
Little Mosque on the Prairie - Freevee, Tubi, Roku
Little Women - BritBox
Live at the Apollo - BritBox
Live from the BBC - BritBox
Liverpool 1 - Freevee, Tubi, Pluto, Acorn
Living in the Shadow of World War II - Freevee, Tubi, Pluto, Roku
Living the Dream - BritBox
Living the Tradition: An Enchanting Journey into Old Irish Airs - Freevee
Location, Location, Location - Tubi, Pluto
Loch Ness - Acorn
London Irish - Freevee, Tubi, Roku, Pluto
London Kills - Acorn
London Road - BritBox
London's Burning- Freevee
The Long Call - BritBox
The Long Song - PBS
Long Way Down - Apple
Long Way Round - Apple
Long Way Up - Apple

Looking for Victoria - BritBox
Lord Montagu - Tubi, Freevee, Vudu, Pluto
Lorna Doone - BritBox
Lost Home Movies of Nazi Germany - BBC
Lost in Austen - Pluto
The Loud House Movie - Netflix
Louis Theroux: A Different Brain - BBC
Louis Theroux: Altered States - Choosing Death - BBC
Louis Theroux: Altered States - Love Without Limits - BBC
Louis Theroux: Altered States - Take My Baby - BBC
Louis Theroux: Beware of the Tiger - BBC
Louis Theroux: Drinking to Oblivion - BBC
Louis Theroux: Extreme Love - Autism - BBC
Louis Theroux: Extreme Love - Dementia - BBC
Louis Theroux: Jimmy Savile Revisited - BBC
Louis Theroux: LA Stories - City of Dogs - BBC
Louis Theroux: LA Stories - Edge of Life - BBC
Louis Theroux: Law and Disorder in Johannesburg - BBC
Louis Theroux: Law and Disorder in Lagos - BBC
Louis Theroux: Life on the Edge - BBC
Louis Theroux: Miami Mega Jail - BBC
Louis Theroux: Most Hated Family in America - BBC
Louis Theroux: Mothers on the Edge - BBC
Louis Theroux: Selling Sex - BBC
Louis Theroux: Surviving America's Most Hated Family - BBC
Louis Theroux: Talking to Anorexia - BBC
Louis Theroux: The Night in Question - BBC
Louis Theroux: The Return of America's Most Hated Family - BBC
Louis Theroux: The Ultra

Zionists - BBC
Louis Theroux: Under the Knife - BBC
Love & Marriage - Freevee, Acorn
Love, Lies, & Records - Acorn
Love/Hate - Freevee
Love and Hate Crime - BBC
Love in a Cold Climate - BritBox
Love Island - Hulu
Lovejoy - Acorn, PBS
Love Lies Bleeding - Freevee
Love London - Freevee, Pluto, Roku
Love My Way - Freevee, Acorn
Lovesick (aka Scrotal Recall) - Netflix
Love Soup - Crackle
Love Your Garden - IO
Love's Labour's Lost (1985) - BritBox
Low Winter Sun - AMC, AMZ
Lucan - BritBox
Lucifer - Netflix
Lucy Worsley Investigates - PBS
Lucy Worsley's 12 Days of Tudor Christmas - PBS
Lucy Worsley's Royal Myths and Secrets - PBS
The Luminaries - Starz
Lunch Monkeys - Freevee, Tubi, Roku
Lupin - Netflix
Luther - Hulu, Pluto
M.I. High - AMZ
Macbeth (1983) - BritBox
Macbeth (2018) - BritBox
The Madame Blanc Mysteries - Acorn
Madame Bovary (1975) - BritBox
Madame Bovary (2000) - BritBox
Mad Dog: Inside the Secret World of Muammar Gaddafi - BBC
Made Over By - Tubi
Magic Numbers - BBC
Magpie Murders - PBS
Maigret (1992) - BritBox
Maigret (2016) - BritBox
Maisy - Peacock
Make Me Perfect - Tubi
Make My Home Bigger - Tubi, Freevee

The Making of a Lady - PBS
The Making of Merkel - BBC
The Mallorca Files - BritBox
Man & Beast with Martin Clunes - Freevee
Manet & the Birth of Impressionism - Freevee
Manhunt - Acorn
Manhunt: Catch Me if You Can - Peacock
Man in an Orange Shirt - PBS
Man Like Mobeen - Netflix
Manolo: The Boy Who Made Shoes for Lizards - BBC
The Manor Reborn - IO
Mansfield Park (1983) - BritBox
Mansfield Park (2007) - PBS
Man Stroke Woman - Pluto, Tubi
The Man Who Cracked the Nazi Code - Freevee, Pluto, Tubi, Roku
The Man Who Fell to Earth - Showtime
The Man Who Killed Richard III - Freevee, Tubi, Pluto, Roku
The Man Who Lost His Head - Acorn
The Man Who Shot Beautiful Women - BBC
The Man Who Shot New York - BBC
The Man Who Shot Tutankhamun - BBC
The Many Lovers of Miss Jane Austen - Freevee, Tubi
Mapp and Lucia (1985) - BritBox
Mapp and Lucia (2014) - BritBox
Marcella - Netflix
Marco's Great British Feast - BritBox
Mare of Easttown - HBO
Margaret: The Rebel Princess - PBS
Market Forces - Freevee, Roku
Married Single Other - Freevee
Married to a Celebrity - Tubi
Married to a Psychopath - BBC
Marseille - Netflix
Mars Uncovered: Ancient God of War - BBC
Martin Chuzzlewit (1994) - BritBox
Martin Clunes & a Lion Called Mugie - Freevee

Martin Clunes: A Man and His Dogs - Freevee, Roku

Martin Clunes: Heavy Horsepower - Freevee, Roku

Martin Clunes: Islands of America - Acorn

Martin Clunes: Islands of Australia - Acorn

Martin Clunes: Islands of the Pacific - Acorn

Martin Clunes: Last Lemur Standing - Freevee, Roku

Marvellous - Acorn

Mary Berry's Foolproof Cooking - Tubi, Pluto

Mary Berry: Love to Cook - Acorn

Mary Berry's Absolute - Favourites Tubi, Pluto

Mary Berry's Country House Secrets - Acorn

Masterpiece - Tubi

Masters of Money - BBC

Maxxx - Hulu

Mayday - Acorn, AMZ

The Mayor of Casterbridge - Acorn, PBS

McCallum - Freevee, Tubi, Roku

McDonald & Dodds - BritBox

McLeod's Daughters - Freevee, Vudu, Roku, Pluto, Tubi, Crackle

McMafia - Sundance

Me, My Selfie, and I - BBC

Meadowlands, aka Cape Wrath - AMZ

Me and My Penis - BBC

The Meaning of Monty Python - Netflix

Mean Mums - AMZ, Peacock

Measure for Measure (1979) - BritBox

Meat: A Threat to Our Planet? - BBC

Meerkat Manor - Freevee, AMC

Meerkat Manor: Rise of the Dynasty - AMC

Meet the Adebanjos - Netflix

Meet the Family - Peacock

Meet the Romans - Freevee, Pluto

Meet the Trumps: From Immigrant to President - BBC

The Mekong River with Sue Perkins - BBC

Memories of a Murderer: The Nilsen Tapes - Netflix

Men Behaving Badly - Freevee, Tubi

Men in Kilts - Starz

The Merchant of Venice (1980) - BritBox

Merlin - Pluto, Tubi, Roku, Netflix, AMZ

Merlin's Apprentice - Roku, Tubi, Pluto, Freevee

The Merry Wives of Windsor (1982) - BritBox

The Me You Can't See - Apple

MI-5 (aka Spooks) - BritBox

Michael McIntyre: Chat Show - Pluto

Michael McIntyre: Showman - Netflix

Michael McIntyre's Comedy Roadshow - Pluto

Middlemarch (1994) - BritBox

Midsomer Murders - Freevee, Roku, Tubi, Pluto, Acorn, BritBox

Midsomer Murders: 20th Anniversary Special - Acorn, BritBox

Midsomer Murders: Neil Dudgeon's Top 10 - Acorn

Midsomer Murders Favourites - BritBox

Midwinter of the Spirit - BritBox

The Mighty Boosh - Hulu

MI High - AMZ, Pluto

The Mill - Tubi, Freevee

Million Dollar Wedding Planner - BBC

Million Pound Menu - Netflix

Mind Games - Acorn

Mind Your Language - Freevee

The Miniaturist - PBS

Miranda - BritBox

Miriam's Big American Adventure - Topic

Misfits - Tubi, Freevee, Pluto, Roku, Hulu

Miss Austen Regrets - BritBox

Miss Fisher & The Crypt of Tears - Acorn

Miss Fisher's Murder Mysteries - Acorn

Missing (2006) - Acorn

Missing (2009) - Acorn

The Missing - AMZ, Starz

The Missing Children - Topic

Missing Persons Unit - Freevee, Tubi, Pluto

Miss Marple - BritBox

Miss Scarlet and the Duke - PBS

Miss Sherlock - HBO

The Mixer- Freevee

Mo - BritBox

Mobile - Freevee

Moby Dick - Freevee, Roku

Mock the Week - BritBox

Modern Irish Food: Kevin Dundon - Tubi

Moloch - Sundance

Mom PI - Freevee, Roku

Monarch of the Glen - Tubi, Pluto, Roku

The Monarchy - BritBox

Monday, Monday - Acorn

Monkman & Seagull's Genius Guide to Britain - Topic

Monroe - Freevee

Monty Don's Adriatic Gardens - Acorn

Monty Don's French Gardens - IO

Monty Don's Italian Gardens - IO

Monty Don's Japanese Gardens - Acorn

Monty Don's Paradise Gardens - Acorn

Monty Python's Almost the Truth - Netflix

Monty Python's Flying Circus - Netflix

Monty Python's Life of Brian - Netflix

Monty Python's Personal Best - Netflix

Monty Python: The Meaning of Live - Netflix

Monty Python and the Holy Grail - Netflix

Monty Python Before the Flying Circus - Netflix

Monty Python Best Bits - Netflix

Monty Python Conquers America - Netflix

Monty Python Live (Mostly): One Down, Five to Go - Netflix

Monty Python Live at Aspen - Netflix

Monty Python Live at the Hollywood Bowl - Netflix

Monty Python's Meaning of Life - BritBox

Moone Boy - BritBox, AMZ, Hulu

Moon Landing - BBC

The Moonstone (1972) - BritBox

The Moonstone (2016) - BritBox

The Moorside - BritBox

The Moors Murders - AMZ

More Manners of Downton Abbey - Peacock

Morphle - Netflix

Moses Jones - Tubi, Freevee, Topic

Most Haunted - Freevee, Tubi, Pluto, Roku

Motherland - Sundance

Mother's Day - BritBox

Mount Pleasant - Acorn

Mount Royal - Freevee, Roku

Moving On - BritBox, Peacock

Mozart in London - BBC

Mr. and Mrs. Murder - Acorn

Mr. Bean's Holiday - BritBox

Mr. D - AMZ

Mr. Palfrey of Westminster - Acorn

Mr. Selfridge - PBS

Mr. Stink - BritBox

Mr Bean - Pluto, Tubi, Vudu, Roku, AMZ, BritBox, Hulu

Mr Bean Animated Series - Tubi, Pluto, Vudu, Roku

Mr Benn - Tubi

The Mrs. Bradley Mysteries - BritBox

Mrs. Brown - BritBox

Mrs. Brown's Boys - BritBox

Mrs. Wilson - PBS

Ms. Fisher's Modern Murder Mysteries - Acorn

Much Ado About Nothing (1984) - BritBox

Mum - BritBox

Mummy's Little Murderer - Freevee

Mums Make Porn - BBC

Murder, Mystery, & My Family: Case Closed - BritBox

Murder, Mystery, and My Family - BritBox

Murder, She Wrote - Peacock

Murder, They Hope - BritBox

Murder 24/7: True Crime/Real Time - BBC

Murder Call - AMZ

Murder Case - BritBox

Murder City - Freevee, Roku

The Murder Detectives - BBC

Murdered by My Boyfriend - BritBox

Murdered by My Father - BritBox

Murdered for Being Different - BritBox

Murdered in the Line of Duty - Peacock

Murder in Provence - BritBox

Murder in Suburbia - BritBox

Murder in the Badlands - BBC

Murder in the Valleys - Sundance

Murder Investigation Team - Acorn

Murderland - Acorn

Murder Maps - Acorn, Freevee

Murder Most Horrid - Freevee

Murder on the Blackpool Express - BritBox

The Murders - Sundance

The Murders at White House Farm - HBO

Murdertown - AMZ

Murder Trial: The Disappearance of Margaret Fleming - Sundance

Murdoch - BBC

Murdoch Mysteries - Acorn, Hulu

Murdoch Mysteries: The Movies - Acorn

Murphy's Law - Tubi, Pluto, Freevee, Acorn

Muse of Fire: A Shakespearean Road Movie - Acorn

The Museum (aka Yr Amgueddfa) - BritBox

The Musketeers - Tubi, Pluto, Roku, AMZ, Hulu

My Beautiful Broken Brain - Netflix

My Boy Jack - BritBox

My Dream Farm - AMZ

My Family - Pluto

My Family and Other Animals - BritBox

My Family Secrets Revealed - BritBox

My Flat Pack Home - Tubi

My Greatest Dishes - Pluto, Freevee

My Kitchen Rules UK, aka MKR

+ UK - Pluto, Tubi

My Life is Murder - Acorn

My Life on a Plate - Tubi

My Mad Fat Diary - Hulu

My Mother & Other Strangers - PBS

My Pet Shame - Tubi

The Mystery of Agatha Christie with David Suchet - AMZ

The Mystery of a Hansom Cab - Acorn

The Mystery of Mary Magdalene - BritBox

Mystery of the Missing Princess - BBC

Mystery Road - Acorn

Mystery Road: Origin - Acorn

Myth & Mogul: John DeLorean - Netflix

Myths and Monsters - Netflix

My Uncle Silas - Freevee, Roku, Tubi, Pluto

My Welsh Sheepdog - Acorn

My Years with the Queen - BBC

Nadiya's Time to Eat - Netflix

Nadiya Bakes - Netflix

The Naked Truth - Tubi

The Name of the Rose - Sundance

National Treasure - Hulu

National Treasure: Kiri - Hulu

The Nativity - AMZ

Nature & Us: A History Through Art - BBC

Navalny: The Man Putin Couldn't Kill - BBC

Neil Gaiman's Neverwhere - Pluto

Nero: The Obscure Face of Power - Tubi, Roku

The Nest - Acorn, Sundance

Neverland - Freevee

The Nevers - HBO

New Blood - BritBox

New Gold Mountain - Sundance

The New Pope - HBO

New Scotland Yard Files - Tubi, Freevee

The New Statesman - BritBox

The New Tomorrow - Freevee, Tubi, Pluto

Newton's Law - Acorn

New Tricks - BritBox, Hulu

New Worlds - Acorn

Next Level Chef - Hulu

Nicholas and Alexandra: The

Letters - PBS
Nick Knowles: Original Home Restoration - Tubi
Nigellissima - BritBox, BBC
Nigel Slater Eating Together - Tubi, Pluto
The Night Caller - Sundance
Nightflyers - Netflix
The Night Manager - AMZ
The Nightmare Worlds of HG Wells - Freevee, Pluto, Tubi
Nixon in the Den - BBC
The No. 1 Ladies' Detective Agency - HBO
Noddy's Toyland Adventures - Peacock
Noise Squad - Tubi
No Offence - Acorn, Pluto
No Ordinary Party - Tubi
Normal People - Hulu
The Norman Conquests - Acorn
North & South - BritBox
Northanger Abbey (1987) - BritBox, Pluto
Northanger Abbey (2007) - PBS
Northern Lights - BritBox
North Korea: Voices from the Secret State - BBC
The North Water - AMC
Not Going Out - Peacock, Pluto
Nothing Trivial - Acorn, Freevee
Not Safe for Work - Topic, BritBox
Not the Nine O'Clock News - BritBox
Noughts & Crosses - Peacock
Nuremberg: Nazis on Trial - BBC
The Nurse - AMZ
NW - BritBox
NY-LON - Freevee, Tubi, Roku
Oceans Apart: Art & the Pacific - BBC
The Octonauts - Netflix
The Office - BritBox, Hulu, Topic
Offspring - Netflix, Hulu
Off the Beaten Track - Acorn
The Oldenheim 12 - Acorn
Older Than Ireland - Freevee, Tubi, Pluto
Oliver Twist (1985) - BritBox
Oliver Twist (2007) - BritBox, Hulu
The One - Netflix

One Born Every Minute - Freevee, Tubi
One Born Every Minute UK: What Happened Next? - Tubi
One Child - AMZ
One Deadly Weekend in America: A Killing at the Carwash - BBC
One Foot in the Grave - BritBox
One Lane Bridge - Acorn, Sundance
One Night - BritBox
One Night Stand with Anne Sibonney - Freevee
Only Foals & Horses - Acorn
Only Fools and Horses - BritBox
The Only Way is Essex - Pluto, Tubi, Hulu
Only When I Laugh - Freevee
On the Whisky Trail: The History of Scotland's Famous Drink - Tubi
Open All Hours - BritBox
Operation Homefront - IO
Ordinary Lies - BritBox
Orphan Black - AMC
Othello (1981) - BritBox
The Other Boleyn - BritBox
The Other Guy - Hulu
The Other One - Acorn
The Other Wife - Tubi
Our Cops in the North - BritBox
Our Flag Means Death - HBO
Our Friends in the North - BritBox
Our Girl - Tubi, Pluto, Freevee, Roku, BritBox
Our Guy in China - Peacock
Our Guy in India - Peacock
Our Guy in Russia - Peacock
Our Mutual Friend - BritBox
Our Planet - Netflix
Outlander - Netflix, Starz
The Outlaws - AMZ
Outlier - Acorn
Outnumbered - Roku, Tubi
Out of the Blue - Freevee
Outrageous Fortune - Freevee, Tubi, Roku
The Outsider - HBO
Overcoming Depression: Mind Over Marathon - Tubi
Oxford Street Revealed - Tubi
Oz & James's Big Wine

Adventure - Tubi
Packed to the Rafters - Tubi, Freevee, Hulu
The Pact - Sundance
The Palace & the Press - BBC
The Palace - Freevee, Pluto, Roku
The Pale Horse - AMZ
Parade's End - HBO
The Paradise (2020) - Acorn
The Paradise - AMZ, BritBox
Paradox - Freevee
Paranoid - Netflix
Parents - Freevee, Tubi, Acorn
Party Tricks - Freevee, Tubi, Acorn
Party Wright Around the World - Tubi
The Passing Bells - BritBox
Patrick Melrose - Showtime
Paul Hollywood's Big Continental Road Trip - Netflix
Paul O'Grady: For the Love of Dogs - BritBox
Pawnbrokers - Freevee
Peak Practice - Freevee, Tubi, Pluto
Peaky Blinders - Netflix
Peep Show - Freevee, Roku, Tubi, Pluto, Crackle, Hulu
The Pembrokeshire Murders - BritBox
Penance - Sundance
Penelope Keith's Hidden Coastal Villages - Acorn
Penelope Keith's Hidden Villages - Freevee, Roku, Tubi
Penny Dreadful - Showtime
Penny Dreadful: City of Angels - Showtime
Pennyworth - Epix, HBO
People Like Us - AMZ
Perfect Weapon - AMZ
Pericles, Prince of Tyre (1984) - BritBox
Perpetual Grace, LTD - Epix
Perry Mason - HBO
The Persians: A History of Iran - BBC
Personal Services Required - Tubi
Persuasion (2007) - BritBox
Persuasion (2022) - Netflix
Pete vs Life - Freevee, Roku, Pluto
Philosophy: A Guide to

Happiness - BBC
Phil Spencer's Stately Homes - Pluto
The Pickwick Papers - BritBox
Picnic at Hanging Rock - AMZ
Picturing Elizabeth: Her Life in Images - BritBox
Pie in the Sky - Acorn, PBS
Pilgrimage with Simon Reeve - BBC
The Pillars of the Earth - Starz
Pine Gap - Netflix
Pinocchio - Freevee, Tubi
Pitching In - Acorn
Place of Execution - Acorn
Planet Earth: Dynasties II - AMC
The Plastic Surgery Capital of the World - BBC
Play for Today - BritBox
Playing for Keeps - Sundance
Please Like Me - Hulu
Plebs - Tubi, Freevee, Crackle, Pluto, Roku
Plus One - Tubi
Poaching Wars with Tom Hardy - BBC
Pointless - BritBox
Poirot: Super Sleuths - Acorn
Poisonous Liaisons - Sundance
The Poison Tree - Acorn
Poldark (Classic) - Acorn
Poldark - AMZ
Poldark Revealed - PBS
Police: Suspect No. 1 - Peacock
Pollyanna - PBS
Porridge (1974) - BritBox
Porridge (2016) - BritBox
Porterhouse Blue - Roku, Tubi
Porters - Roku
Portrait Artist of the Year - AMZ
Posh Neighbours at War - Freevee
Post-Mortem: No One Dies in Skarnes - Netflix
Postman Pat - Peacock
Pramface - AMZ
The Pregnant Man - BBC
Press - PBS
Pretty Hard Cases - Freevee
Prey - AMZ, Hulu
Pride & Prejudice (1980) - BritBox
Pride & Prejudice (1995) - BritBox, Hulu
Pride & Prejudice (2005) -

BritBox
Pride & Prejudice: Having a Ball - Acorn
Prime Minister's Questions - BritBox
The Prime of Miss Jean Brodie - Acorn
Prime Suspect - BritBox
Prime Suspect: Tennison - PBS
Primeval - Pluto, Tubi, Crackle, Hulu
Prince Andrew & the Epstein Scandal - BBC
The Prince and the Epstein Scandal - BBC
Prince Charles: Inside the Duchy of Cornwall - Acorn
Prince Charles at 70 - PBS
Prince Philip: The Plot to Make a King - PBS
The Princes and the Press - BBC
Princess Diana: A Life After Death - AMC, BBC
The Prisoner (2009) - AMC
The Prisoner - Freevee, Tubi, Pluto, Roku
Prisoners' Wives - Tubi, Freevee, Pluto, Freevee, Acorn
The Private Lives of the Tudors - AMZ
Professor T - PBS
Project Restoration - AMZ
Proof - Freevee, Tubi, Acorn
The Protectors - Freevee, Roku, Vudu, Tubi
Psychoville - BritBox
Public Enemies - AMZ, Acorn
Puffin Rock - Netflix
The Puppet Master - Netflix
Puppy Love - BritBox
Pure - HBO
The Pursuit of Love - AMZ
Putin: A Russian Spy Story - BBC
Putin: The New Tsar - BBC
Putin's Russia - BBC
Putin's War in Ukraine - BBC
QB VII - AMZ, Roku
QI - BritBox, Tubi
Queen and Country - PBS
The Queen at War - PBS
Queen Elizabeth's Secret Agents - PBS
The Queen Mother - BBC
Queens: The Virgin & the

Martyr - Tubi
Queens of Mystery - Acorn
Queen Victoria & Her Nine Children - BBC
Queen Victoria's Letters: A Monarch Unveiled - Freevee, Tubi, Roku
Queen Victoria's Children - BBC
The Queen's Gambit - Netflix
The Queen's Palaces - BBC
Queer as Folk - Roku, Tubi, AMZ
Queers - AMC
Question Time - BritBox
Quicksand - Netflix
Quirke - BritBox
Quiz - AMC
Quizeum - Tubi
Raa Raa the Noisy Lion - Peacock
Rachel Allen: All Things Sweet - Pluto, Freevee
Rachel Allen: Easy Meals - Pluto, Freevee
Rachel Allen Home Cooking - Tubi
Rachel Allen's Cake Diaries - Pluto, Freevee
Rachel Allen's Dinner Parties - Tubi
Rachel Allen's Everyday Kitchen - Freevee
Rachel Khoo's Cosmopolitan Cook - Pluto, Freevee
Rachel Khoo's Kitchen Notebook: London - BritBox
Rachel Khoo's Kitchen Notebook: Melbourne - Pluto, Freevee
Rachel's Coastal Cooking - BritBox
Racism: A History - BBC
Ragdoll - AMC
The Rain - Netflix
Rake - AMZ
Rallying: The Killer Years - BBC
Ramsay's Best Restaurant - Tubi, Pluto, Freevee
Rat Pack: A Conference of Cool - BBC
Reacher - AMZ
Real Crime: Diamond Geezers - Netflix
Real Crime: Supermarket Heist - Netflix
The Real Des - Sundance

The Real Manhunter - Acorn
The Real Middle Earth - Freevee, Tubi, Pluto
The Real Prince Philip - Acorn
Rebecca - PBS
Rebecka Martinsson - Acorn
The Rebel - Acorn
Rebellion - Netflix
Rebel Women: The Great Art Fightback - BBC
Rebus - Acorn, BritBox
Recipes for Love & Murder - Acorn
Reclaiming Amy - BBC
Red Dwarf - BritBox, Crackle
Redemption - BritBox
The Red Shadows - Sundance
Reel Britannia - BritBox
Reg - BritBox
Reggie Perrin - Pluto, Roku, Acorn
Reign - Netflix
Reilly, Ace of Spies - PBS
Remarkable Places to Eat - Tubi, Freevee
Rembrandt - BBC
Remember Me - Pluto, Tubi, Roku, PBS
Renaissance Unchained - Freevee, Pluto
The Replacement - Sundance
Republic of Doyle - Acorn
Requiem - Netflix
Resort to Murder - Acorn
The Responder - BritBox
The Restaurant - Sundance
Restless - Acorn, Sundance
Restoration Home - Freevee, Tubi, Pluto
Restoration Man - Freevee, Tubi
Restoration Man Best Builds - Tubi, Freevee
Retail Therapy - Tubi
The Returned - Sundance
Rev. - BritBox
Reyka - BritBox
The RHS Chelsea Flower Show - BritBox
Richard Hammond's Crash Course - AMZ
Richard II (1979) - BritBox
Richard Wilson On the Road - Pluto, Tubi
Rick Stein & the Japanese Ambassador - AMZ
Rick Stein Tastes the Blues -

Freevee
Rick Stein's Far Eastern Odyssey - AMZ
Rick Stein's India - AMZ
Rick Stein's Long Weekends - Freevee
Rick Stein's Mediterranean Escapes - AMZ
Rick Stein's Road to Mexico - Freevee, Pluto
Rick Stein's Secret France - Freevee
Rick Stein's Taste of Shanghai - Freevee
Rick Steves' Europe - AMZ
Ricky Gervais: Humanity - Netflix
Ricky Gervais: Supernature - Netflix
Ridley Road - PBS
Ripley - Showtime
The Ripper - Netflix
Ripping Yarns - BritBox
The Rise of the Murdoch Dynasty - BBC
Rise of the Nazis - BBC
Rising Damp - BritBox
Rita - Netflix
The Rivals of Sherlock Holmes - PBS
River - AMZ, BritBox, Sundance
Riviera - Sundance
Roadkill - PBS
Roary the Racing Car - Peacock
Robin of Sherwood - Pluto, BritBox
Robozuna - Netflix
Rocket's Island - Freevee, Roku, Tubi, Pluto
Rock Solid Builds - Hulu
Rococo Before Bedtime - Freevee
Roman Britain: From the Air - Freevee, Tubi
Roman Empire - Netflix
Roman Mysteries - Pluto
The Romantic Revolution - BBC
Rome: Empire Without Limit - Acorn, AMZ
Rome: The World's First Superpower - Freevee, Pluto
Romeo and Juliet (1978) - BritBox
The Ronnie Wood Show - BBC
Room to Improve - Freevee, Tubi
Rosamund Pilcher's

September - Tubi
Rose & Maloney - AMZ
Rosemary & Thyme - BritBox
Rose West: Born Evil? - Sundance
Ross Kemp: Back on the Frontline - Freevee, Pluto
Ross Kemp: Middle East - Pluto
Ross Kemp: Return to Afghanistan - Freevee, Pluto
Ross Kemp in Afghanistan - Pluto
Rowan Atkinson Presents: Canned Laughter - BritBox
The Royal - Freevee, Roku, BritBox
The Royal Bodyguard - Tubi, Roku
Royal Britain: An Aerial History of the Monarchy - Freevee, Tubi
Royal Celebration - BritBox
Royal Cousins at War - BBC
Royal Flying Doctor Service - PBS
The Royal House of Windsor - Netflix
Royal Paintbox - PBS
The Royals - AMZ
The Royal Today - BritBox
Royal Upstairs Downstairs - IO
Royal Wives at War - PBS
The Royle Family - AMZ
RPU: Road Policing Unit - BritBox
Rubens: An Extra Large Story - Freevee
Rugged Wales - Pluto
Rules of the Game - Hulu
Rumpole of the Bailey - PBS
Run (US) - HBO
Run - Acorn, Topic
Rush - Tubi
Russell Brand: Messiah Complex - BritBox
Russell Howard: Lubricant - Netflix
Russell Howard: Recalibrate - Netflix
Russia 1917: Countdown to Revolution - BBC
The Ruth Rendell Mysteries - Freevee
The Ruth Rendell Mysteries: Next Chapters (aka Ruth Rendell Mysteries) - BritBox
Réunions - Acorn

Safe - Netflix
Safe House - Sundance
The Saint - Freevee, Tubi, Roku, Vudu, Peacock
The Salisbury Poisonings - AMC
Sally4Ever - HBO
Sally Lockhart Mysteries - BritBox
Salvage Hunters - Pluto, Crackle
Sam's Game - Freevee, Tubi, Roku
Sanctuary - Sundance
The Sandbaggers - BritBox
Sanditon - PBS
The Sandman - Netflix
Sando - Acorn
Sapphire and Steel - Freevee, Tubi
Sara Dane - Freevee
Sarah & Duck - Tubi, Pluto
Sarah Jane Adventures - HBO
Save Me - Peacock
Saving Britain's Worst Zoo - Acorn
Saving Poundstretcher - Tubi
The Savoy - Acorn
The Scapegoat - Acorn
Scarborough - BritBox
The Scarlet Pimpernel - Acorn
Scarlet Woman: The True Story of Mary Magdalene - Freevee, Tubi, Pluto
Scotch! The Story of Whisky - Tubi, Roku, Freevee, Acorn
Scotch: A Golden Dream - Tubi, Pluto
Scott & Bailey - BritBox
Scottish Myths and Legends - Tubi, Roku
Screw - BritBox
Seachange - Acorn
Seachange: Paradise Reclaimed - Acorn
The Search - Peacock
Second Sight - Freevee
The Secret - Acorn
Secret Cities - BBC
Secret City - Netflix
Secret Daughter - Acorn
Secret Dealers - Pluto, Tubi
Secret Diary of a Call Girl - Tubi, Freevee
Secret Eaters - Tubi
Secret Gardens of England - Freevee

The Secret History of the British Garden - Acorn, IO, Pluto
The Secret Life of the Cruise - Peacock
Secret Life of the Holiday Resort - Tubi
The Secret Life of the Hospital - Peacock
Secret Life of the Hospital Bed - AMZ
The Secret Life of the Long-Haul Flight - Peacock
The Secret Life of Us - AMZ
Secret Nature - Freevee, Pluto
The Secret of Crickley Hall - AMZ, BritBox, Hulu
Secret of the Missing Princess - BBC
Secret Removers - IO
Secret Rules of Modern Living: Algorithm - BBC
Secrets and Lies - Freevee, Tubi
Secrets from the Sky - BritBox
Secret Smile - Freevee
The Secrets of Branding - BBC
Secrets of Britain - PBS
Secrets of Britain's Great Cathedrals - PBS
Secrets of Great British Castles - Netflix
Secrets of Highclere Castle - PBS
Secrets of Iconic British Estates - PBS
Secrets of Silicon Valley - BBC
Secrets of Sugar Baby Dating - BBC
Secrets of the Castle - AMZ
Secrets of the Falklands - BBC
Secrets of the Irish Landscape - Freevee, Tubi
Secrets of the Six Wives - PBS
Secrets of the Stones - Tubi
Secrets of the Superbrands - BBC
The Secrets She Keeps - Sundance
Secret State - Roku, Tubi, Pluto, AMZ, Peacock
The Secret Story of Stuff: Materials of the Modern Age - Acorn
See No Evil: The Moors Murders - Freevee
Seesaw - Peacock

Sense and Sensibility (1981) - BritBox, Pluto
Sense and Sensibility (2008) - BritBox, Hulu
Serial Killer with Piers Morgan - Netflix
The Serpent - Netflix
The Serpent Queen - Starz
Servants - BritBox
Seven Wonders of the Commonwealth - BritBox
Sex Actually with Alice Levine - BBC
Sex and the Church - BBC
The Sex Changes That Made History - BBC
Sex Education - Netflix
Shadow & Bone - Netflix
The Shadow Line - Pluto, Tubi, Freevee, Roku
Shadow Lines - Sundance
Shakespeare & Hathaway - BritBox
Shakespeare: The Legacy - Acorn
Shakespeare in Italy - BritBox
Shameless (US) - Netflix, Showtime
Shameless - Pluto, Tubi, Hulu
Shantaram - Apple
The Shard: Hotel in the Clouds - BritBox
Sharpe - BritBox
Shaun the Sheep - Netflix
She-Wolves: England's Early Queens - Acorn
The Shell Seekers - Acorn
The Shelter: Animal SOS - Acorn
Sherlock Holmes - BritBox
Sherlock Holmes and the Leading Lady - AMZ
Sherlock Holmes in Colour! - AMZ
Sherwood - BritBox
Shetland - BritBox
Shipwrecked - Hulu
Shock & Awe: The Story of Electricity - Acorn
Shock of the Nude - BBC
Shoreline Detectives - Freevee, Tubi
Showtrial - Sundance
Sick Note - Netflix
Sick of It - Roku
Signora Volpe - Acorn
The Silence (2006) - Acorn

The Silence (2010) - Freevee, Roku, Pluto, Tubi, Acorn

Silent Witness - BritBox, Freevee

Silk - BritBox, Hulu

The Silk Road - BBC

Simon Amstell: Set Free - Netflix

Simon Schama's Power of Art - BBC

Simon Schama's Shakespeare and Us - BBC

Simon's Cat - Tubi, Roku, Freevee

The Simple Heist - Acorn

Single-Handed - Freevee, Roku, Vudu, Acorn

Single Father - BritBox

Singletown - HBO

The Sinking of the Laconia - PBS

Sirens - Roku, Freevee

The Sister - Hulu

Sister Boniface Mysteries - BritBox

Sisters - Netflix

The Six Queens of Henry VIII - BBC, BritBox

Skins - Hulu

Slings & Arrows - Acorn, Sundance

Slow Horses - Apple

Smack the Pony - Tubi

Small Animal Hospital - Tubi

Small Axe - AMZ

Small Claims - Acorn

The Small Hand: A Ghost Story - BritBox

Small Island - BritBox

Smart Travels with Rudy Maxa - Freevee, Tubi, Vudu

The Smoke - AMZ

Smother - Peacock

Snatches - AMC

Snog Marry Avoid? - Tubi, Freevee

Snowdonia 1890 - Freevee, Tubi

Snow Leopards of Leafy London - Tubi, Roku

Soldier Soldier - Freevee, Tubi, Roku

Some Assembly Required - Netflix

Some Girls - Roku, Tubi

The Sommerdahl Murders - Acorn

Sophie: A Murder in West Cork - Netflix

Soulmates - AMC

The Sounds - Acorn

Soup Cans and Superstars: How Pop Art Changed the World - BBC

The South Westerlies - Acorn

Space: 1999 - Vudu, Tubi, Pluto, Freevee, Roku

Spaced - Freevee, Roku, Tubi

The Spanish Princess - Starz

Speed with Guy Martin - Pluto, Tubi, Peacock

Spendaholics - Tubi

Spies of Warsaw - AMZ

Spirited - Freevee

The Split - Hulu, Sundance

Springwatch - BritBox

Spy - Tubi, Roku

Spy City - AMC

Spying on the Royals - PBS

The Spy Who Fell to Earth - BBC

SS-GB - Freevee

Stacey Dooley Investigates: Beaten by My Boyfriend - BBC

Stacey Dooley Investigates: Hate & Pride in Orlando - BBC

The Staircase - HBO

Stalin: Inside the Terror - BBC

The Stalker's Apprentice - Acorn

Stand Up for Live Comedy - BritBox

The Stand Up Sketch Show - BritBox

Starbucks & Nespresso: The Truth About Your Coffee - BBC

Starstruck - HBO

State of Mind - AMZ

State of the Union - Sundance

Stath Lets Flats - HBO

Statue Wars - BBC

Stay Close - Netflix

Stealing Van Gogh - Acorn

Stella Blomkvist - Sundance

Step Dave - Freevee, Roku, Tubi, Peacock

Stephen Fry: Out There - BBC

Steve Coogan's Stand Up Down Under - BritBox

Sticks and Stones - BritBox

Still Game - Netflix

Still Life: A Three Pines Mystery - Acorn

Still Open All Hours - BritBox

Still Standing - Freevee, Tubi

Stingray - Freevee, Tubi, Pluto

Stonemouth - BritBox

The Story of London - Freevee, Pluto, Roku, Tubi

The Story of Luxury - BritBox

Story of Maths - BBC

The Story of Tea - Vudu, Tubi

The Story of Women and Art - BBC

Straight Forward - Acorn

The Straits - Acorn

The Strange Calls - Acorn

The Stranger - Netflix

The Street - BritBox, Freevee

Street Hospital - Roku, Tubi

Streetmate - Tubi

Striking Out - Acorn, Sundance

Suffragettes - BBC

Suffragettes Swingin' Christmas - BritBox

Sunderland 'Til I Die - Netflix

Sunny Bunnies - Netflix

Superior Interiors with Kelly Hoppen - IO

The Super Rich & Us - BBC

Supersized Hospital - Freevee, Tubi

Supersize vs Superskinny - Tubi, AMZ

Super Sleuths: Midsomer Murders - Pluto

Supply and Demand - Acorn

Surface - Apple

Surgeons: At the Edge of Life - AMZ

Surgery School - Freevee

Surviving the Holocaust - BBC

The Suspect (2020) - Sundance

The Suspect (2022) - Sundance

Suspect - BritBox

Suspects - Acorn, PBS

Suspicion - Apple

The Suspicions of Mr. Whicher: Beyond the Pale - BritBox

The Suspicions of Mr. Whicher: The Murder at Road Hill House - BritBox

The Suspicions of Mr. Whicher: The Murder in Angel Lane - BritBox

The Suspicions of Mr. Whicher: The Ties That Bind - BritBox

Swallowed by the Sea: Ancient

Egypt's Greatest Lost City - Acorn
Switch - Freevee
Sword of Honour - Roku, Tubi, Pluto
The Syndicate - Freevee
The Syndicate: All or Nothing - Acorn
The Syndicate: Double or Nothing - BritBox
Taboo - Crackle, Hulu
Taggart - BritBox
The Take - Freevee, Roku, Tubi
Taken: Hunting the Sex Traffickers - BBC
Taken Down - Acorn
Tales from the Royal Bedchamber - PBS
Tales of Irish Castles - Acorn
Tales of Para Handy - AMZ
Tales of the Unexpected - Freevee
The Taming of the Shrew (1980) - BritBox
Teachers - Tubi, Pluto, AMZ
Tea with the Dames - AMC
Ted Lasso - Apple
Teenage & Gay - BBC
The Tempest (1980) - BritBox
The Tenant of Wildfell Hall - BritBox
Ten Percent - Acorn, Sundance
Terry Pratchett's Hogfather - Freevee, Tubi, Pluto
Terry Pratchett's Going Postal - Freevee, Roku, Peacock
Terry Pratchett's The Colour of Magic - Acorn
Tess of the D'Urbervilles (2008) - BritBox
That's My Boy - Freevee
Thatcher & Reagan - BBC
That Day We Sang - BritBox
That Dirty Black Bag - AMC
Then There Were Giants - Freevee, Tubi
Therese Raquin - Acorn
There She Goes - BritBox
They've Gotta Have Us - Netflix
The Thick of It - BritBox
The Thief, His Wife, and the Canoe - BritBox
The Thin Blue Line - BritBox
Thin Ice - Sundance
The Third Day - HBO
This Farming Life - BritBox
This is Going to Hurt - Sundance
This is Joan Collins - BritBox
This is Personal: The Hunt for the Yorkshire Ripper - Freevee
This Way Up - Hulu
Thomas & Friends - Netflix
Thorne - Acorn, Freevee, BritBox
Three Families - Sundance
Three Girls - BritBox
Threesome - Pluto, Roku, AMZ
Three Sovereigns for Sarah - PBS
Thriller - Tubi, Pluto, Freevee
Thunderbirds - Freevee, Roku, Tubi
Tidelands - Netflix
Time - BritBox
The Time of Our Lives - Acorn, Freevee
Time Team - Freevee, Tubi, AMZ
The Time Traveler's Wife - HBO
Timewasters - Freevee
Timewatch: Young Victoria - BBC
Timmy Time - Netflix
Timon of Athens (1981) - BritBox
Tina & Bobby - BritBox
The Tinder Swindler - Netflix
Tin Star - AMZ
Tipping the Velvet - BritBox
Titus Andronicus (1985) - BritBox
To Build or Not to Build - Tubi
Tom Jones - AMZ
Tom Kerridge's American Feast - Hulu
Tony Robinson's Gods and Monsters - Tubi
Too Close - Sundance
Top Boy - Netflix
Top Gear - AMC, HBO
Top of the Lake - Hulu
Torchwood - HBO
Total Control - Sundance
Total Wipeout - Tubi, Pluto, Freevee, AMZ, Hulu
To the Ends of the Earth - Freevee, Roku, Vudu, Pluto
To the Manor Born - BritBox
Touching Evil - Freevee, Roku
Toughest Place to be a... - Pluto
The Tourist - HBO
To Walk Invisible: The Brontë Sisters - PBS
The Tower - BritBox
Tower Block Kids - Tubi
Traces - BritBox
The Tragedy of Coriolanus (1984) - BritBox
The Tragedy of Richard III (1983) - BritBox
Trailer Park Boys - Netflix
Traitors - Netflix
Transgender Kids: Who Knows Best? - BBC
Trauma - BritBox
Trauma Rescue Squad - Tubi
Travelers - Netflix
Travel Man - Peacock, AMZ
Travels by Narrowboat - AMZ
Travels in Europe with Ed Balls - BBC
Treadstone - Peacock, Hulu
Treasure Detectives - Peacock
Treasure Houses of Britain - Freevee
Treasure Island - Pluto
Treasures of the Indus - BBC
Trial & Retribution - Acorn
The Trial: A Murder in the Family - Freevee
Trial in the Outback - Sundance
The Trial of Christine Keeler - HBO
The Tribe - Freevee, Tubi, Pluto
The Trick - PBS
Trickster - Sundance
Trigger Point - Peacock
Trinity - Tubi
Trivia - Acorn
Troilus and Cressida (1981) - BritBox
Trollied - Pluto, Roku
Trouble in Poundland - Tubi
The Trouble with Maggie Cole - PBS
Troy: Fall of a City - Netflix
Truckers - Freevee, Tubi, Pluto, Roku
Truckers: Eddie Stobart - Pluto
Trucking Hell - Tubi, Freevee
Trump in Tweets - BBC
The Trump Show - BBC
Trump Takes on the World - BBC
Trust - Acorn
Trust Me - Hulu
Truth Seekers - AMZ

The Truth Will Out - Acorn
Trying - Apple
Tudor Feast - Tubi
Tudor Monastery Farm - AMZ, Tubi
The Tudors - Showtime 2
The Tunnel - AMZ
Turning Green - Acorn
The Turn of the Screw - BritBox
Turn Up Charlie - Netflix
Tutankhamun - BritBox
TV's Black Renaissance: Reggie Yates in Hollywood - BBC
Twelfth Night (1980) - BritBox
Twenty Twelve - BritBox
Two's Company - Freevee
The Two Gentlemen of Verona (1983) - BritBox
Two Thousand Acres of Sky - Freevee
Two Weeks to Live - HBO
Ugly Beauty - BBC
Ukraine: Lessons from the Battlefield - BBC
Ultimate Force - Freevee, Tubi, Pluto
Ultraviolet - Freevee, Tubi, Crackle, Pluto
The Undeclared War - Peacock
Undeniable - AMZ, Tubi
Underbelly - Freevee, Roku, Tubi
Underground Britain - Peacock
Under the Vines - Acorn
The Undoing - HBO
Unfinished Portrait: The Life of Agatha Christie - BritBox
Unforgiven - BritBox
Unforgotten - AMZ, PBS
The Unlisted - Netflix
Unreal Estate - Tubi, Freevee
Upper Middle Bogan - Acorn
Upright - Sundance
The Up Series - BritBox
Upstairs Downstairs (Classic) - BritBox
Upstairs Downstairs - BritBox, Hulu
Upstart Crow - BritBox
Up the Women - BritBox
Us - PBS
Utopia - AMZ
Utopia: In Search of the Dream - BBC
Valentine Warner's Coast to Coast - Pluto
The Valhalla Murders - Netflix

Van der Valk (1972) - PBS
Van der Valk (2020) - PBS
Van Helsing - Netflix
Vanity Fair (1987) - BritBox
Vanity Fair (1998) - BritBox
Vanity Fair (2018) - AMZ
VE Day: Minute by Minute - Acorn
Venus Uncovered - BBC
Vera - BritBox
Vera Postmortem - BritBox
Very British Problems - Freevee, Tubi, Pluto, Roku
Very Small Business - Acorn
Vexed - Freevee, Tubi, Crackle, Pluto, Roku, Acorn
The Vicar of Dibley - BritBox
The Vice - BritBox, Freevee
Vicious - Tubi
The Victim - BritBox
Victoria - AMZ
Victoria and Albert: The Wedding - PBS
Victorian Farm - Acorn, AMZ, Tubi
Victoria Wood's A Nice Cup of Tea - Acorn
Vidago Palace - Acorn
Vienna: Empire, Dynasty, and Dream - BBC
Vienna Blood - PBS
Vigil - Peacock
Vikings: Valhalla - Netflix
The Village - Roku, Tubi, Pluto
Vincent - Freevee, Roku
Vincent: The Full Story - BBC
Vincent Van Gogh: Painted with Words - BBC, BritBox
Virgin Atlantic: Up in the Air - BritBox
The Virtues - Topic
W1A - BritBox
Wainwright Walks - Acorn
Wainwright Walks: Coast to Coast - Acorn
Waiting for God - BritBox
Waking the Dead - BritBox
Walking Through History - Acorn
Walking Tudor England - Acorn
Walks with My Dog - Pluto, Tubi, Freevee, Roku
Wallander - BritBox
Wanderlust - Netflix
Wanted - Netflix
War & Peace - Acorn
War Art with Eddie Redmayne

- BBC
War of the Worlds - Epix
The War of the Worlds - Pluto, Tubi, Plex, Roku, Peacock, AMC
Warren - Roku, Freevee, Tubi
Wartime Farm - Acorn
Wasted - Hulu
The Watch - AMC
Watership Down - Netflix
The Way Back - Acorn
We'll Meet Again - Freevee
We Are Lady Parts - Peacock
Wedding Season - Hulu
Wedding SOS - Tubi, Pluto, Freevee, Roku
Weegies - AMZ
We Got This - Sundance
We Hunt Together - Showtime
Weirdsister College - Freevee, Tubi, Roku
Welcome to Mayfair - Pluto, Freevee
Wellington Paranormal - HBO
Wentworth - Netflix
Westside - Freevee, Roku, Peacock
What Happens in Sunny Beach - Tubi
What if Putin Goes Nuclear? - BBC
What Remains - BritBox
What the Durrells Did Next - PBS
What the Neighbours Did - Tubi
What to Do When Someone Dies - Acorn, PBS
What We Do in the Shadows - Hulu
The Wheelchair President - BBC
Wheeler Dealers - AMZ
Wheel of Time - AMZ
When Louis Met Jimmy Savile - BBC
When the Queen Spoke to the Nation - BritBox
Where the Heart Is - Freevee, Roku
Whisky: The Islay Edition - Freevee, Tubi
The Whistleblowers: Inside the UN - BBC
Whitechapel - AMZ, Hulu
White Dragon - AMZ
White Gold - Netflix

White Heat - BritBox
White Lines - Netflix
The White Princess - Starz
The White Queen - Starz
Whites - Tubi, Freevee, BritBox
White Van Man - Freevee, Roku, Pluto, Tubi
Whitstable Pearl - Acorn
Who is Ghislaine Maxwell - Starz
Whose Line Is It Anyway? - Roku, Tubi, Pluto, Hulu
Wibbly Pig - Tubi
Wide Sargasso Sea - PBS
The Widow - AMZ
The Widower - PBS
Wild Animal Rescue - Tubi, Freevee, Pluto
Wild at Heart - Freevee, Tubi, Pluto, Roku, Acorn
Wild Bill - BritBox
The Wild Roses - Freevee, Tubi
Wild Tokyo - AMC
Wild Weather: Our World Under Threat - BBC
William & Kate: A Royal Love Story - Tubi
William & Mary - Freevee, Roku
William the Conqueror - AMZ
The Wimbledon Kidnapping - Sundance
The Windermere Children - PBS
The Windermere Children: In Their Own Words - PBS
Windsor Castle: After the Fire - Freevee, Tubi, Pluto
The Windsors - Netflix
The Windsors: A Royal Family - PBS
The Wine Show - Acorn, Sundance
Winston Churchill's War - BBC
Winter - Acorn
Winterwatch - BritBox
The Winter's Tale (1981) - BritBox
Win the Wilderness - Netflix
The Wipers Times - Acorn
Wired - Freevee, Tubi, Pluto, Roku
Wire in the Blood - Acorn
Wisting - Acorn, Sundance
The Witcher - Netflix
Witches: A Century of Murder - Netflix, Sundance
Without Motive - BritBox

The Witnesses - Acorn
Wizards vs Aliens - Roku
Wolcott - Freevee, Roku, Tubi
Wolfblood - Roku, Tubi, Pluto, Freevee, Peacock
Wolf Hall - PBS
The Woman in White - BritBox, PBS
Women in Love - BritBox
The Women of World War One - BritBox, BBC
Wonderland - Freevee, Tubi
Wonders of Britain - Peacock
Workin' Moms - Netflix
The World's Most Extraordinary Homes - Netflix
World on Fire - PBS
World War II in Colour - Netflix
World War Two: 1941 & the Man of Steel - BBC
World Without End - Starz
The World's First Computer - BBC
World's Greatest Paintings - BBC
World's Weirdest Homes - BBC
Worst Week of My Life - Acorn
The Worst Witch (1998) - Tubi, Freevee, Roku
The Worst Witch - Netflix
Would I Lie to You? - BritBox, Freevee
WPC 56 - AMZ
Wreckers - Acorn
Wrecking the Uprising (aka Éirí Amach Amú)
Write Around the World - BBC
The Wrong Mans - Hulu
Wuthering Heights (1978) - BritBox
Wuthering Heights (2009) - PBS
Wycliffe - Freevee, Roku, Pluto, Tubi, BritBox
Wyonna Earp - Netflix
Yakka Dee - Tubi, Pluto
The Year Earth Changed - Apple
Year of the Rabbit - BritBox, Topic
Years and Years - HBO
Yes, Minister - BritBox
Yes, Prime Minister - BritBox
Y Golau (aka The Light in the Hall) - Sundance
The Yorkshire Vet - Tubi, Roku,

Pluto, Freevee, Acorn
You, Me, & Them - Tubi, Roku, Acorn
You Deserve This House - IO
You Don't Know Me - Netflix
Young, Free, & Single - Tubi
Young, Rich, and Househunting - Tubi
Young Charlie Chaplin - AMZ, Tubi
Young Dracula - Freevee, Roku, Tubi, Pluto, Crackle, Vudu
Young Hyacinth - BritBox
Young Lions - AMZ
The Young Person's Guide to Becoming a Rock Star - Tubi
The Young Pope - HBO
Young Wallander - Netflix
Your Garden Made Perfect - Hulu
Your Home Made Perfect - Hulu
You vs. Wild - Netflix
You vs. Wild: Out Cold - Netflix
Zelensky: The Making of a President - BBC
Zen - BritBox
Zero Chill - Netflix
Zomboat! - Hulu

COMMON QUESTIONS

Why am I seeing ads on Amazon?

There are two reasons you may see ads on Amazon:

- You're watching a "free with Prime Video" show. If a show has the "Prime" banner that tells you it's free with membership, it will frequently show ads for other Amazon shows.
- You're watching a show on Freevee. It's a free-with-ads service that's part of Amazon's video offerings, and it plays all sorts of different ads (not just Amazon show ads).

Sometimes, a show may be on both Freevee *and* a subscription service you use. For example, Midsomer Murders is on both Acorn TV and Freevee. It's very easy to accidentally watch the Freevee version and get loads of ads.

Though it varies by device, you can usually fix this by going to your computer, visiting Amazon, and adding the show to your watchlist - making sure you're on the page that mentions your subscription.

If you're on a Roku or similar device, you'll often see two options for viewing, and you can select the subscription rather than Freevee.

The Amazon system is a bit wild, so in some cases there's an entirely separate show page for the Freevee version and the subscription version - and not in others. If you continue to have trouble with it, contact Amazon's support for help.

In some cases, you may find it beneficial to take your subscription direct to the company in question - but of course, some people find that shows stream more smoothly through Amazon, and others just like having all the billing in one central location.

How do I watch these channels on my TV? I don't have a smart TV and I don't want to watch on my laptop or tablet.

There are a lot of different ways you can do this, but we'll focus on the simplest. For around $30 (base model), you can buy a device called a Roku. They sell them at Walmart, Target, Best Buy, Amazon, and even some pharmacies and convenience stores. It's our top recommendation because they're easy to use and the remote control has big print and few buttons.

A Roku plugs into your television and you can connect it to your internet wirelessly. Then, you can add channels like Acorn TV, BritBox, or Tubi. Some are free (like Tubi), while others require you to set up a monthly subscription with the company in question (like Acorn or BritBox).

You also have the option of subscribing to Amazon's Prime Video service - and then subscribing to your other channels through the Amazon app so all the billing goes through one place.

You only pay for the Roku device one time. There's no monthly cost associated with having a Roku, and if you were so inclined, you could buy one and only use the free channels.

Nearly all channels offer free trials (usually either 7 or 30 days), and the vast majority allow you to log in online and cancel your account without calling anyone on the phone and waiting on hold.

Some cable companies do offer Acorn TV or BritBox, but we generally don't recommend it if you're able to subscribe another way. We see a lot of reader complaints about poor service or inability to cancel without lengthy phone calls to customer service.

Why is BritBox (or Acorn TV, Sundance Now, etc.) charging me for — show?

This is another area that causes a lot of misunderstanding and frustration. Amazon offers a giant video marketplace, and there are different types of access within the system.

- **Freevee Shows** - Shows in this "section" are free to all with ads.
- **Prime Video** - If you're an Amazon Prime member (or purely a Prime Video member), you get access to a larger set of programmes which are included in the price of membership. Sometimes, only the older seasons of a show are included in this membership.
- **Channel Subscriptions** - Dozens of channels make their programming available through Amazon's platform. That includes Acorn TV, BritBox, Sundance Now, and many of the others in this guide. You pay for these channels on top of the basic Amazon Prime or Prime Video fee. An Acorn TV or BritBox subscription won't give you access to all British TV shows on Amazon - only those offered by Acorn TV or BritBox.
- **Rentals & Purchases** - Some shows are not included in any of the plans above (or you may choose to buy/rent them instead of subscribing to a channel). It's a bit like when we all went to the local video store for things not offered on our cable packages. If you really wanted to see it, you could pay a bit extra to get it right away…or wait and hope it showed up on one of your channels eventually.

Where are the rest of the episodes of Season --- of --- show?

If you only see the first couple episodes of a season, don't panic. Many streaming services "drip" episodes - especially if the show is brand new and they're airing it alongside the UK Release dates.

Other times, they do it because they want to give people an incentive to stay subscribed for a longer period of time.

If you don't like it (some people have trouble remembering all the details), there's a very easy solution. Just use Wikipedia.org or IMDB.com to verify how many episodes are in the season, then you can calculate the ideal time to start watching so you don't forget anything in between episodes.

How can I request a show?

Many streaming services take requests under consideration, but they all have different methods for submitting your wishes. We keep a list of the different links and methods at: IHeartBritishTV.com/requests